Generic Goals and Practices

GG1   Achieve Specific Goals
- GP 1.1   Perform Specific Practices

GG2   Institutionalize a Managed Process
- GP2.1   Establish an Organizational Policy
- GP 2.2   Plan the Process
- GP 2.3   Provide Resources
- GP 2.4   Assign Responsibility
- GP 2.5   Train People
- GP 2.6   Control Work Products
- GP 2.7   Identify and Involve Relevant Stakeholders
- GP 2.8   Monitor and Control the Process
- GP 2.9   Objectively Evaluate Adherence
- GP 2.10   Review Status with Higher Level Management

GG3   Institutionalize a Defined Process
- GP 3.1   Establish a Defined Process
- GP 3.2   Collect Process Related Experiences

W9-BYI-522

CMMI® for Development

Third Edition

The SEI Series in Software Engineering

Software Engineering Institute | **Carnegie Mellon**

♦ Addison-Wesley

Visit **informit.com/sei** for a complete list of available products.

The **SEI Series in Software Engineering** represents is a collaborative undertaking of the Carnegie Mellon Software Engineering Institute (SEI) and Addison-Wesley to develop and publish books on software engineering and related topics. The common goal of the SEI and Addison-Wesley is to provide the most current information on these topics in a form that is easily usable by practitioners and students.

Books in the series describe frameworks, tools, methods, and technologies designed to help organizations, teams, and individuals improve their technical or management capabilities. Some books describe processes and practices for developing higher-quality software, acquiring programs for complex systems, or delivering services more effectively. Other books focus on software and system architecture and product-line development. Still others, from the SEI's CERT Program, describe technologies and practices needed to manage software and network security risk. These and all books in the series address critical problems in software engineering for which practical solutions are available.

CMMI® for Development
Guidelines for Process Integration and Product Improvement

Third Edition

Mary Beth Chrissis
Mike Konrad
Sandy Shrum

✦✦Addison-Wesley

Upper Saddle River, NJ • Boston• Indianapolis • San Francisco
New York • Toronto • Montreal • London • Munich • Paris • Madrid
Capetown • Sydney • Tokyo • Singapore • Mexico City

Software Engineering Institute | Carnegie Mellon

The SEI Series in Software Engineering

Many of the designations used by manufacturers and sellers to distinguish their products are claimed as trademarks. Where those designations appear in this book, and the publisher was aware of a trademark claim, the designations have been printed with initial capital letters or in all capitals.

CMM, CMMI, Capability Maturity Model, Capability Maturity Modeling, Carnegie Mellon, CERT, and CERT Coordination Center are registered in the U.S. Patent and Trademark Office by Carnegie Mellon University.

ATAM; Architecture Tradeoff Analysis Method; CMM Integration; COTS Usage-Risk Evaluation; CURE; EPIC; Evolutionary Process for Integrating COTS Based Systems; Framework for Software Product Line Practice; IDEAL; Interim Profile; OAR; OCTAVE; Operationally Critical Threat, Asset, and Vulnerability Evaluation; Options Analysis for Reengineering; Personal Software Process; PLTP; Product Line Technical Probe; PSP; SCAMPI; SCAMPI Lead Appraiser; SCAMPI Lead Assessor; SCE; SEI; SEPG; Team Software Process; and TSP are service marks of Carnegie Mellon University.

Special permission to reproduce portions of CMMI for Development (CMU/SEI-2010-TR-035), © 2010 by Carnegie Mellon University, has been granted by the Software Engineering Institute.

The authors and publisher have taken care in the preparation of this book, but make no expressed or implied warranty of any kind and assume no responsibility for errors or omissions. No liability is assumed for incidental or consequential damages in connection with or arising out of the use of the information or programs contained herein.

The publisher offers excellent discounts on this book when ordered in quantity for bulk purchases or special sales, which may include electronic versions and/or custom covers and content particular to your business, training goals, marketing focus, and branding interests. For more information, please contact:

> U.S. Corporate and Government Sales
> (800) 382-3419
> corpsales@pearsontechgroup.com

For sales outside the United States, please contact:

> International Sales
> international@pearsoned.com

Visit us on the Web: informit.com/aw

Library of Congress Cataloging-in-Publication Data

Chrissis, Mary Beth.
   CMMI for development : guidelines for process integration and product
improvement / Mary Beth Chrissis, Mike Konrad, Sandy Shrum.—3rd ed.
       p.   cm.
   Includes bibliographical references and index.
   ISBN 978-0-321-71150-2 (hardcover : alk. paper)
  1. Capability maturity model (Computer software) 2. Software
engineering. 3. Production engineering. 4. Manufacturing processes.
I. Konrad, Mike. II. Shrum, Sandy. III. Title.
   QA76.758.C518 2011
   005.1—dc22

                              2010049515

ISBN-13:   978-0-321-71150-2
ISBN-10:   0-321-71150-5

Text printed in the United States on recycled paper at Courier in Westford, Massachusetts.
Third Printing May 2014

This book is dedicated to Watts Humphrey (1927–2011), in appreciation for all he accomplished as a leader, visionary, and teacher. You only needed to be in a room with Watts Humphrey a short time to realize what a special person he was. Watts' leadership, vision, and insights helped many over his lifetime. He was a student of learning and he shared that quest for learning with everyone with whom he came into contact. He had a vision that he shared with the world and the world became a better place. CMMI would not have been possible without Watts Humphrey. May he continue to inspire us for years to come.

CONTENTS

PERSPECTIVES

PREFACE

CMMI (Capability Maturity Model Integration) models are collections of best practices that help organizations to improve their processes. These models are developed by product teams with members from industry, government, and the Software Engineering Institute (SEI).

This model, called CMMI for Development (CMMI-DEV), provides a comprehensive integrated set of guidelines for developing products and services.

Purpose

The CMMI-DEV model provides guidance for applying CMMI best practices in a development organization. Best practices in the model focus on activities for developing quality products and services to meet the needs of customers and end users.

The CMMI-DEV V1.3 model is a collection of development best practices from government and industry that is generated from the CMMI V1.3 Architecture and Framework.[1] CMMI-DEV is based on the CMMI Model Foundation or CMF (i.e., model components common

---

1. The CMMI Framework is the basic structure that organizes CMMI components and combines them into CMMI constellations and models.

to all CMMI models and constellations[2]) and incorporates work by development organizations to adapt CMMI for use in the development of products and services.

Model Acknowledgments

Many talented people were involved in the development of the V1.3 CMMI Product Suite. Three primary groups were the CMMI Steering Group, Product Team, and Configuration Control Board (CCB).

The Steering Group guided and approved the plans of the Product Team, provided consultation on significant CMMI project issues, and ensured involvement from a variety of interested communities.

The Steering Group oversaw the development of the Development constellation, recognizing the importance of providing best practices to development organizations.

The Product Team wrote, reviewed, revised, discussed, and agreed on the structure and technical content of the CMMI Product Suite, including the framework, models, training, and appraisal materials. Development activities were based on multiple inputs. These inputs included an A-Specification and guidance specific to each release provided by the Steering Group, source models, change requests received from the user community, and input received from pilots and other stakeholders.

The CCB is the official mechanism for controlling changes to CMMI models, appraisal related documents, and *Introduction to CMMI* training. As such, this group ensures integrity over the life of the product suite by reviewing all proposed changes to the baseline and approving only those changes that satisfy identified issues and meet criteria for the upcoming release.

Members of the groups involved in developing CMMI-DEV V1.3 are listed in Appendix C.

Audience

The audience for CMMI-DEV includes anyone interested in process improvement in a development environment. Whether you are familiar with the concept of Capability Maturity Models or are seeking information to begin improving your development processes, CMMI-DEV

---

2. A constellation is a collection of CMMI components that are used to construct models, training materials, and appraisal related documents for an area of interest (e.g., development, acquisition, services).

will be useful to you. This model is also intended for organizations that want to use a reference model for an appraisal of their development related processes.[3]

Organization of this Document

This document is organized into three main parts:

- Part One: About CMMI for Development
- Part Two: Generic Goals and Generic Practices, and the Process Areas
- Part Three: The Appendices and Glossary

Part One: About CMMI for Development, consists of five chapters:

- Chapter 1, Introduction, offers a broad view of CMMI and the CMMI for Development constellation, concepts of process improvement, and the history of models used for process improvement and different process improvement approaches.
- Chapter 2, Process Area Components, describes all of the components of the CMMI for Development process areas.[4]
- Chapter 3, Tying It All Together, assembles the model components and explains the concepts of maturity levels and capability levels.
- Chapter 4, Relationships Among Process Areas, provides insight into the meaning and interactions among the CMMI-DEV process areas.
- Chapter 5, Using CMMI Models, describes paths to adoption and the use of CMMI for process improvement and benchmarking of practices in a development organization.
- Chapter 6, Essays and Case Studies, contains essays and case studies contributed by invited authors from a variety of backgrounds and organizations.

Part Two: Generic Goals and Generic Practices, and the Process Areas, contains all of this CMMI model's required and expected components. It also contains related informative components, including subpractices, notes, examples, and example work products.

---

3. An appraisal is an examination of one or more processes by a trained team of professionals using a reference model (e.g., CMMI-DEV) as the basis for determining strengths and weaknesses.

4. A process area is a cluster of related practices in an area that, when implemented collectively, satisfies a set of goals considered important for making improvement in that area. This concept is covered in detail in Chapter 2.

Part Two contains 23 sections. The first section contains the generic goals and practices. The remaining 22 sections each represent one of the CMMI-DEV process areas.

To make these process areas easy to find, they are organized alphabetically by process area acronym. Each section contains descriptions of goals, best practices, and examples.

Part Three: The Appendices and Glossary, consists of four sections:

- Appendix A: References, contains references you can use to locate documented sources of information such as reports, process improvement models, industry standards, and books that are related to CMMI-DEV.
- Appendix B: Acronyms, defines the acronyms used in the model.
- Appendix C: CMMI Version 1.3 Project Participants contains lists of team members who participated in the development of CMMI-DEV V1.3.
- Appendix D: Glossary, defines many of the terms used in CMMI-DEV.

How to Use this Document

Whether you are new to process improvement, new to CMMI, or already familiar with CMMI, Part One can help you understand why CMMI-DEV is the model to use for improving your development processes.

Readers New to Process Improvement

If you are new to process improvement or new to the Capability Maturity Model (CMM) concept, we suggest that you read Chapter 1 first. Chapter 1 contains an overview of process improvement that explains what CMMI is all about.

Next, skim Part Two, including generic goals and practices and specific goals and practices, to get a feel for the scope of the best practices contained in the model. Pay close attention to the purpose and introductory notes at the beginning of each process area.

In Part Three, look through the references in Appendix A and select additional sources you think would be beneficial to read before moving forward with using CMMI-DEV. Read through the acronyms and glossary to become familiar with the language of CMMI. Then, go back and read the details of Part Two.

Readers Experienced with Process Improvement

If you are new to CMMI but have experience with other process improvement models, such as the Software CMM or the Systems Engineering Capability Model (i.e., EIA 731), you will immediately recognize many similarities in their structure and content [EIA 2002a].

We recommend that you read Part One to understand how CMMI is different from other process improvement models. If you have experience with other models, you may want to select which sections to read first. Read Part Two with an eye for best practices you recognize from the models that you have already used. By identifying familiar material, you will gain an understanding of what is new, what has been carried over, and what is familiar from the models you already know.

Next, review the glossary to understand how some terminology can differ from that used in the process improvement models you know. Many concepts are repeated, but they may be called something different.

Readers Familiar with CMMI

If you have reviewed or used a CMMI model before, you will quickly recognize the CMMI concepts discussed and the best practices presented. As always, the improvements that the CMMI Product Team made to CMMI for the V1.3 release were driven by user input. Change requests were carefully considered, analyzed, and implemented.

Some significant improvements you can expect in CMMI-DEV V1.3 include the following:

- High maturity process areas are significantly improved to reflect industry best practices, including a new specific goal and several new specific practices in the process area that was renamed from Organizational Innovation and Deployment (OID) to Organizational Performance Management (OPM).
- Improvements were made to the model architecture that simplify the use of multiple models.
- Informative material was improved, including revising the engineering practices to reflect industry best practice and adding guidance for organizations that use Agile methods.
- Glossary definitions and model terminology were improved to enhance the clarity, accuracy, and usability of the model.

- Level 4 and 5 generic goals and practices were eliminated as well as capability levels 4 and 5 to appropriately focus high maturity on the achievement of business objectives, which is accomplished by applying capability level 1-3 to the high maturity process areas (Causal Analysis and Resolution, Quantitative Project Management, Organizational Performance Management, and Organizational Process Performance).

For a more complete and detailed list of improvements, see http://www.sei.cmu.edu/cmmi/tools/cmmiv1-3/.

Additional Information and Reader Feedback

Many sources of information about CMMI are listed in Appendix A and are also published on the CMMI website—http://www.sei.cmu.edu/cmmi/.

Your suggestions for improving CMMI are welcome. For information on how to provide feedback, see the CMMI website at http://www.sei.cmu.edu/cmmi/tools/cr/. If you have questions about CMMI, send email to cmmi-comments@sei.cmu.edu.

BOOK ACKNOWLEDGMENTS

This book wouldn't be possible without the support of the CMMI user community and the work of a multitude of dedicated people working together on CMMI-based process improvement. Ultimately, without the work of those involved in the CMMI project since it began in 1998, this book would not exist. We would like to specially thank our many CMMI partners who help organizations apply CMMI practices.

The complete CMMI-DEV model is contained in the book, which was created based on more than one thousand change requests submitted by CMMI users. The CMMI Product Team, which included members from different organizations and backgrounds, used these change requests to improve the model to what it is today.

We would also like to acknowledge those who directly contributed to this book. All of these authors were willing to share their insights and experiences and met aggressive deadlines to do so: Steve Baldassano, Victor Basili, Michael Campo, David Card, Bill Curtis, Aldo Dagnino, Kathleen Dangle, Khaled El Emam, Hillel Glazer, Kileen Harrison, Will Hayes, Watts Humphrey, Gargi Keeni, Peter Kraus, Hans Juergen Kugler, Neal Mackertish, Tomoo Matsubara, Judah Mogilensky, James Moore, Joseph Morin, Heather Oppenheimer, Mike Philips, Pat O'Toole, Anne Prem, Robert Rassa, Kevin Schaaff, Michele Shaw, Alex Stall, and Rusty Young. We are delighted that they agreed to contribute their experiences to our book and we hope that you find their insights valuable and applicable to your process improvement activities.

Special thanks go to Addison-Wesley Publishing Partner, Peter Gordon, for his assistance, experience, and advice. We'd also like to thank Kim Boedigheimer, Curt Johnson, Stephane Nakib, and Julie Nahil for their help with the book's publication and promotion.

From Mary Beth Chrissis

I am so very blessed and humbled to be fortunate enough to be part of the third edition of this book. Working on CMMI has allowed me the opportunity to interact with many people. From the SEI Partners who work with the community daily, to the many individuals I've had the privilege to teach, to the people in organizations that believe CMMI will help them improve their business, I've learned so much from you. I'd like you all to know that I realize although my name appears on this book, I'm really just representing all of you. I don't know why I have been given this opportunity, but please know I am greatly appreciative.

I have a very special thank you for my colleagues at the SEI and especially those in the SEPM Program. You've encouraged and supported me. Thanks to Anita Carleton, Mike Phillips, Barbara Tyson, Bob McFeeley, Stacey Cope, Mary Lou Russo, and Barbara Baldwin for all of your day-to-day assistance. I can't forget Bill Peterson who has supported CMMI and the work on this book since its inception.

Version 1.3 wouldn't have been accomplished without the many volunteers who worked on it. I'd like to recognize the training team, particularly Mike Campo and Katie Smith, for spending many hours writing and reviewing the model and training materials. Thanks to Diane Mizukami Williams who had the vision and expertise to improve the CMMI-DEV Intro course. I'd also like to thank Bonnie Bollinger for her sage wisdom and comments. Lastly, thanks to Eric Dorsett, Steve Masters, and Dan Foster for their help with the training materials.

To my coauthors Sandy and Mike, you're the best. Each time we write a book, it is a different experience and I wouldn't want to work with anyone else. Thanks for your patience and understanding during this busy time.

If you know me, you know my family is the center of my life. To my husband, Chuck, and my children, Adam, Pamela, and Kevin, thank you again for supporting me with this book. I love you and I am grateful to have you in my life.

From Mike Konrad

I came to the SEI 23 years ago hoping to contribute to an international initiative that would fundamentally improve the way systems and software are built. CMMI has become that initiative. For this, I thank my many colleagues at the SEI and Industry, past and present.

Over the years I've been honored to work with some of the most talented individuals in systems and software engineering. My favorite teachers have been Roger Bate, Jack Ferguson, Watts Humphrey, and Bill Peterson.

For Version 1.3, I've been particularly honored to work with Jim Armstrong, Richard Basque, Rhonda Brown, Brandon Buteau, Mike Campo, Sandra Cepeda, Mary Beth Chrissis, Mike D'Ambrosa, Eileen Forrester, Brian Gallagher, Will Hayes, Larry Jones, So Norimatsu, Alice Parry, Lynn Penn, Mike Phillips, Karen Richter, Mary Lou Russo, Mary Lynn Russo, Winfried Russwurm, John Scibilia, Sandy Shrum, Kathy Smith, Katie Smith-McGarty, Barbara Tyson, and Rusty Young.

I also continue to learn from my two coauthors, Mary Beth and Sandy; one could not hope for better or more talented coauthors.

With respect to my family, words cannot express my heartfelt thanks to my wife, Patti, and our family, Paul, Jill, Christian, Katie, Alison, Tim, David, and Walter, for their patience while I was working on the book and for sharing their time and insights of the world we all share; to my father, Walter, and my late mother, Renée, for their years of nurturing and sacrifice; and to my sister, Corinne, for her encouragement over the years.

From Sandy Shrum

Working simultaneously on three CMMI books has tested my limits in many ways. Those that have helped me along the journey provided both professional and personal support.

Many thanks to Rhonda Brown and Mike Konrad for their partnership during CMMI model development. They are peerless as team members and friends. Our joint management of the CMMI Core Model Team was not only effective, but enjoyable.

Affectionate thanks to my boyfriend, Jimmy Orsag, for his loving support and for helping me keep my focus and sense of humor through all the hours of work preparing three manuscripts. Heartfelt thanks to my parents, John and Eileen Maruca, for always being there for me no matter what and instilling my strong work ethic.

Finally, thanks to the coauthors of all three CMMI books: Brandon Buteau, Mary Beth Chrissis, Eileen Forrester, Brian Gallagher, Mike Konrad, Mike Phillips, and Karen Richter. They are all terrific to work with. Without their understanding, excellent coordination, and hard work, I would never have been able to participate.

PART ONE

About CMMI for Development

CHAPTER 1

INTRODUCTION

Now more than ever, companies want to deliver products and services better, faster, and cheaper. At the same time, in the high-technology environment of the twenty-first century, nearly all organizations have found themselves building increasingly complex products and services. It is unusual today for a single organization to develop all the components that compose a complex product or service. More commonly, some components are built in-house and some are acquired; then all the components are integrated into the final product or service. Organizations must be able to manage and control this complex development and maintenance process.

The problems these organizations address today involve enterprise-wide solutions that require an integrated approach. Effective management of organizational assets is critical to business success. In essence, these organizations are product and service developers that need a way to manage their development activities as part of achieving their business objectives.

In the current marketplace, maturity models, standards, methodologies, and guidelines exist that can help an organization improve the way it does business. However, most available improvement approaches focus on a specific part of the business and do not take a systemic approach to the problems that most organizations are facing. By focusing on improving one area of a business, these models have unfortunately perpetuated the stovepipes and barriers that exist in organizations.

CMMI for Development (CMMI-DEV) provides an opportunity to avoid or eliminate these stovepipes and barriers. CMMI for Development consists of best practices that address development activities applied to products and services. It addresses practices that cover the product's lifecycle from conception through delivery and maintenance.

The emphasis is on the work necessary to build and maintain the total product.

CMMI-DEV contains 22 process areas. Of those process areas, 16 are core process areas, 1 is a shared process area, and 5 are development specific process areas.[1]

All CMMI-DEV model practices focus on the activities of the developer organization. Five process areas focus on practices specific to development: addressing requirements development, technical solution, product integration, verification, and validation.

About Process Improvement

In its research to help organizations to develop and maintain quality products and services, the Software Engineering Institute (SEI) has found several dimensions that an organization can focus on to improve its business. Figure 1.1 illustrates the three critical dimensions that organizations typically focus on: people, procedures and methods, and tools and equipment.

What holds everything together? It is the processes used in your organization. Processes allow you to align the way you do business.

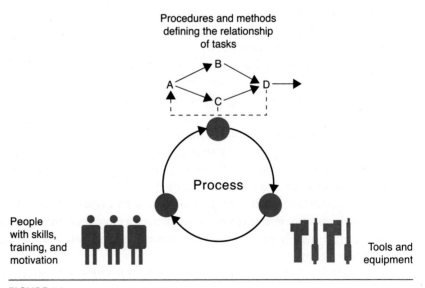

FIGURE 1.1
The Three Critical Dimensions

---

1. A core process area is a process area that is common to all CMMI models. A shared process area is shared by at least two CMMI models, but not all of them.

They allow you to address scalability and provide a way to incorporate knowledge of how to do things better. Processes allow you to leverage your resources and to examine business trends.

This is not to say that people and technology are not important. We are living in a world where technology is changing at an incredible speed. Similarly, people typically work for many companies throughout their careers. We live in a dynamic world. A focus on process provides the infrastructure and stability necessary to deal with an ever-changing world and to maximize the productivity of people and the use of technology to be competitive.

Manufacturing has long recognized the importance of process effectiveness and efficiency. Today, many organizations in manufacturing and service industries recognize the importance of quality processes. Process helps an organization's workforce to meet business objectives by helping them to work smarter, not harder, and with improved consistency. Effective processes also provide a vehicle for introducing and using new technology in a way that best meets the business objectives of the organization.

Looking Ahead

by Watts Humphrey

Nearly 25 years ago when we first started the maturity model work that led to the CMM and CMMI, we took a diagnostic approach. What are the characteristics of organizations that performed good software work? We were following the principle that Tolstoy stated in Anna Karenina.[2]

> "Happy families are all alike; every unhappy family is unhappy in its own way."

In applying the Tolstoy principle to software organizations, we looked for those markers that characterized effective software operations and then formed these characteristics into a maturity model. The logic for the maturity model was that, to do good work, organizations must do everything right. However, since no one could possibly fix all of their problems at once, our strategy was to determine what organizations were doing and compare that to what they

2. Leo Tolstoy, *Anna Karenina*, Modern Library, New York.

should be doing to be a "happy family." Then, using the model as a guide, they should start fixing the omissions and mistakes in the order defined by the model.

Keep Doing the Good Things

Unfortunately, we were not sufficiently clear with our initial guidance, and some people felt that, if they were only trying to get to maturity level 2, they should not do things that were at levels 3, 4, and 5. That is *not* what we meant. Organizations should continue doing all of the "good" things they now are doing and only focus on the problem areas. The objective at level 2 is to address those level 2 things that are missing or inadequate, and fix them first. Then the organization should consider addressing the level 3, 4, and 5 gaps. Again, they should not stop doing any things that work.

The Logic for the Maturity Level 2

The logic that we followed in establishing the maturity levels was as follows. First, organizations cannot do good work, and they certainly cannot improve, if they are in a perpetual state of crisis. Therefore, the first improvement efforts should focus on those things that, if done poorly or not at all, will result in crises. These are planning, configuration management, requirements management, subcontract management, quality assurance, and the like.

The Logic for Maturity Level 3

Second, after the crises are largely controlled and the organization is plan-driven rather than crisis-driven, the next step is learning. How can people learn from each other rather than having to learn from their own mistakes? Again, from Tolstoy's principle, there is an infinite number of ways to fail, so improving by reacting to failures is a never-ending and fruitless struggle. The key is to find out what works best in the organization and to spread that across all groups. Therefore, maturity level 3 focuses on learning-oriented things like process definition, training, and defined ways to make decisions and evaluate alternatives.

The Logic for Maturity Levels 4 and 5

At level 4, the focus turns to quantitative management and quality control, and at level 5, the efforts include continuous improvement, technological innovations, and defect prevention. Unfortunately, we never included an explicit requirement in CMM or CMMI that high-maturity organizations must look outside of their own laboratories to identify best industry practices. Then, after they find these practices, they should measure, evaluate, and prototype them to see if these practices would help improve their operations. This seemed like such an obvious step that we never explicitly required it. However, judging from the slow rate of adoption of new and well-proven software and systems development innovations, such a requirement should have been included in the model.

Continuous Improvement

At this point, of the many organizations that have been evaluated at CMMI level 5, too many have essentially stopped working on improvement. Their objective was to get to level 5 and they are there, so why should they keep improving? This is both an unfortunate and an unacceptable attitude. It is unfortunate because there are many new concepts and methods that these organizations would find beneficial, and it is unacceptable because the essence of level 5 is continuous improvement.

Unfortunately, many organizations have become entangled in the weeds of process improvement and have lost sight of the forest and even of the trees. Six Sigma is a powerful and enormously helpful statistically based method for improvement, but it is easy for people to become so enamored with these sophisticated methods that they lose sight of the objective. This is a mistake. The key is priorities and what will help organizations to improve their business performance. This is where external benchmarking and internal performance measures are needed. Use them to establish improvement priorities and then focus your improvement muscle on those areas that will substantially improve business performance.

Next Steps

While CMMI has been enormously successful, we have learned a great deal in the last 25 years, and there are now important new concepts and methods that were not available when we started. The key new concept concerns **knowledge work**. Peter Drucker, the leading management thinker of the twentieth century, defined knowledge work as work that is done with ideas and concepts rather than with things. While a great deal of today's technical work is knowledge work, large-scale knowledge work is a relatively new phenomenon. Except for software, until recently, the really big projects all concerned hardware systems. Now, however, software work pervades most parts of modern systems, and even the work of hardware designers more closely resembles that of software developers than traditional hardware bread boarding and manufacturing.

To properly manage this new kind of work, new methods are needed, and Drucker enunciated the key new management concept. This is that knowledge work can't be managed with traditional methods; the knowledge workers must manage themselves.[3] The logic behind Drucker's view is compelling, but the story is too extensive to cover in this short perspective. However, there is a growing number of publications that describe knowledge work and how and why new management methods are needed.[4]

In summary, the key point is that software and complex systems development projects are large-scale knowledge work, and the reason such projects have long been troubled is that they have not been managed with suitable methods. The first method that has been designed to follow Drucker's knowledge-management principles is the Team Software Process (TSP), but there will almost certainly be more such methods in the future.

Using the TSP to guide software and systems development projects turns out to be highly effective, and TSP projects are typically delivered on schedule, within budget, and with substantially improved quality and productivity.[5] To assist CMMI users in continuously improving their performance, the SEI has defined a new CMMI-based strategy and a family of practices to guide them in evaluating and piloting these methods. This method is called CMMI-AIM (Accelerated Improvement Method), and it is currently in use by a growing number of organizations.

Conclusions

As we continue refining our processes and methods to address the needs and practices of creative teams and people, new opportunities will keep showing up for broadening the scope of our processes and including new methods and technologies as they become available. Because many of these advances will be new to most users, users will need specific guidance on what these new methods are and how to best use them. The SEI strategy has been to provide this guidance for each new family of methods as it becomes available and is proven in practice.

3. Peter Drucker, Knowledge-Worker Productivity: the Biggest Challenge, California Management Review, Winter 1999, 41, 2, ABI/INFORM Global.

4. Watts S. Humphrey, "Why Can't We Manage Large Projects?" *CrossTalk*, July/August 2010, pp. 4–7; and Watts S. Humphrey and James W. Over, *Leadership, Teamwork, and Trust: Building a Competitive Software Capability*, Reading, MA: Addison Wesley, 2011.

5. Noopur Davis and Julia Mullaney, Team Software Process (TSP) in Practice, SEI Technical Report CMU/SEI-2003-TR-014, September 2003.

Two examples of such new methods are CMMI- and TSP-related guidance on how to develop secure systems and on how to architect complex systems. As we look to the future, there will be many more opportunities for improving the performance of our systems and software engineering work. The key is to couple these methods into a coherent improvement framework such as TSP-CMMI and to provide the explicit guidance organizations need to obtain the potential benefits of these new methods. To avoid chasing the latest fads, however, organizations should measure their own operations, evaluate where they stand relative to their leading peers and competitors, and focus on those improvements that will measurably improve their business performance.

About Capability Maturity Models

A Capability Maturity Model (CMM), including CMMI, is a simplified representation of the world. CMMs contain the essential elements of effective processes. These elements are based on the concepts developed by Crosby, Deming, Juran, and Humphrey.

In the 1930s, Walter Shewhart began work in process improvement with his principles of statistical quality control [Shewhart 1931]. These principles were refined by W. Edwards Deming [Deming 1986], Phillip Crosby [Crosby 1979], and Joseph Juran [Juran 1988]. Watts Humphrey, Ron Radice, and others extended these principles further and began applying them to software in their work at IBM (International Business Machines) and the SEI [Humphrey 1989]. Humphrey's book, *Managing the Software Process*, provides a description of the basic principles and concepts on which many of the Capability Maturity Models (CMMs) are based.

The SEI has taken the process management premise, "the quality of a system or product is highly influenced by the quality of the process used to develop and maintain it," and defined CMMs that embody this premise. The belief in this premise is seen worldwide in quality movements, as evidenced by the International Organization for Standardization/International Electrotechnical Commission (ISO/IEC) body of standards.

CMMs focus on improving processes in an organization. They contain the essential elements of effective processes for one or more disciplines and describe an evolutionary improvement path from ad hoc, immature processes to disciplined, mature processes with improved quality and effectiveness.

Like other CMMs, CMMI models provide guidance to use when developing processes. CMMI models are not processes or process descriptions. The actual processes used in an organization depend on many factors, including application domains and organization structure and size. In particular, the process areas of a CMMI model typically do not map one to one with the processes used in your organization.

The SEI created the first CMM designed for software organizations and published it in a book, *The Capability Maturity Model: Guidelines for Improving the Software Process* [SEI 1995].

Today, CMMI is an application of the principles introduced almost a century ago to this never-ending cycle of process improvement. The value of this process improvement approach has been confirmed over time. Organizations have experienced increased productivity and quality, improved cycle time, and more accurate and predictable schedules and budgets [Gibson 2006].

Evolution of CMMI

The CMM Integration project was formed to sort out the problem of using multiple CMMs. The combination of selected models into a single improvement framework was intended for use by organizations in their pursuit of enterprise-wide process improvement.

Developing a set of integrated models involved more than simply combining existing model materials. Using processes that promote consensus, the CMMI Product Team built a framework that accommodates multiple constellations.

The first model to be developed was the CMMI for Development model (then simply called "CMMI"). Figure 1.2 illustrates the models that led to CMMI Version 1.3.

Initially, CMMI was one model that combined three source models: the *Capability Maturity Model for Software* (SW-CMM) v2.0 draft C, the *Systems Engineering Capability Model* (SECM) [EIA 2002a], and the *Integrated Product Development Capability Maturity Model* (IPD-CMM) v0.98.

These three source models were selected because of their successful adoption or promising approach to improving processes in an organization.

The first CMMI model (V1.02) was designed for use by development organizations in their pursuit of enterprise-wide process improvement. It was released in 2000. Two years later Version 1.1 was released and four years after that, Version 1.2 was released.

History of CMMs

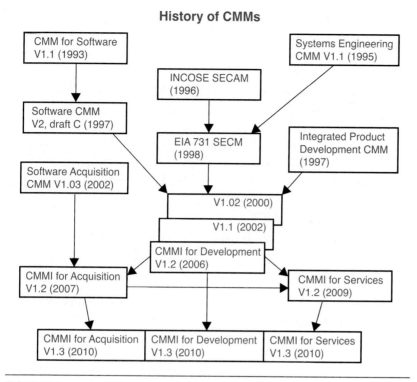

FIGURE 1.2
The History of CMMs[6]

By the time that Version 1.2 was released, two other CMMI models were being planned. Because of this planned expansion, the name of the first CMMI model had to change to become CMMI for Development and the concept of constellations was created.

The CMMI for Acquisition model was released in 2007. Since it built on the CMMI for Development Version 1.2 model, it also was named Version 1.2. Two years later the CMMI for Services model was released. It built on the other two models and also was named Version 1.2.

In 2008 plans were drawn to begin developing Version 1.3, which would ensure consistency among all three models and improve high maturity material in all of the models. Version 1.3 of CMMI for Acquisition [Gallagher 2011, SEI 2010b], CMMI for Development [Chrissis 2011, SEI 2010c], and CMMI for Services [Forrester 2011, SEI 2010a] were released in November 2010.

---

6. EIA 731 SECM is the Electronic Industries Alliance standard 731, or the Systems Engineering Capability Model. INCOSE SECAM is International Council on Systems Engineering Systems Engineering Capability Assessment Model [EIA 2002a].

CMMI: Integration and Improvement Continues

by Bob Rassa

CMMI is almost 15 years old, and has clearly become the worldwide de facto standard for process improvement in the development of systems, including systems engineering, software engineering, design engineering, subcontractor management, and program management. Since the release of CMMI V1.2 (for Development) almost 5 years ago, CMMI has embraced process improvement for Acquisition as well as the delivery of Services.

The full product suite of CMMI-DEV, CMMI-ACQ, and CMMI-SVC covers the complete spectrum of process improvement for the entire business, including commercial and defense industry, governments, and even military organizations. After the initial release of CMMI in November 2000, well over 1,000 Class A appraisals were reported in just four years—very successful numbers by our measures at that time; whereas recently almost 1,400 Class A appraisals were conducted in 2009 alone—quite a significant improvement.

As of January 2006, more than 45,000 individuals had received Introduction to CMMI training. As of July 2010, that number has exceeded more than 117,000 students.

CMMI-DEV has been translated into Japanese, Chinese, French, German, Spanish, and Portuguese. Translation of CMMI-SVC into Arabic is beginning. The success in CMMI recognition and adoption worldwide is undeniable.

The CMMI V1.2 architecture was altered slightly to accommodate two additional CMMI constellations, which we designated CMMI-ACQ (CMMI for Acquisition) and CMMI-SVC (CMMI for Services). CMMI V1.3 focuses on providing some degree of simplification as well as adding more integrity to the overall product suite. V1.3 model improvements have a heavy concentration on the high maturity aspects embodied in levels 4 and 5, in both the model structure as well as the appraisal method.

We learned that there were certain ambiguities within the V1.2 product suite, and the areas affected are now clarified in V1.3 to achieve greater consistency in overall model deployment and appraisal conduct of CMMI. The criteria that are used in the appraisal audit process, which was implemented in 2008, have now been incorporated in the product suite where appropriate. We have also provided clarification on the sampling of "focus programs" in the appraised organization to reduce the complexity and time involved in conducting Class A appraisals, thereby reducing the cost of implementing CMMI.

It has been noted by some that CMMI is only for large organizations, but the data tells a different story. In fact, a large number of small organizations have been appraised and have told us that they reap benefits of CMMI far beyond the investment. A comprehensive Benefits of CMMI report is now on the website of the designated CMMI Steward, the Software Engineering Institute of Carnegie Mellon University (http://www.sei.cmu.edu/cmmi). This report, essentially a compendium of real benefits provided by users, clearly shows positive effects such as reduced defects on delivery, reduced time to identify defects, and more. The data tells us that CMMI is truly state-of-the-art in-process improvement, and the substantive benefits reported confirm this.

However, to be truly effective, CMMI must be applied conscientiously within the organization. When we started the initial development of CMMI, it was well-publicized that its purpose was to integrate the divergent maturity models that existed at the time. We soon realized that the real purpose that should have been communicated as the ultimate benefit of CMMI was that this integrated model would integrate the design and management disciplines in terms of both process and performance.

To achieve this ultimate benefit, care is needed to ensure that integrated processes are put into place within the organization, that such processes are implemented across the enterprise on all new programs and projects, and that such implementation is done in a thorough manner to assure that new programs start out on the right foot.

This book provides the latest expert and detailed guidance for effective CMMI implementation. It covers all the specifics of V1.3 and addresses nuances of interpretation as well as expert advice useful to the new and experienced practitioner.

Hundreds of process improvement experts have contributed to the overall CMMI development and update, and many of them contributed their expertise to this volume for the benefit of the worldwide user community. We trust you will enjoy their work and find it useful as you continue your journey along the path of continuous process improvement.

Remember, great designers and great managers will still likely fail without a proven process framework, and this is what CMMI provides.

CMMI Framework

The CMMI Framework provides the structure needed to produce CMMI models, training, and appraisal components. To allow the use of multiple models within the CMMI Framework, model components are classified as either common to all CMMI models or applicable to a specific model. The common material is called the "CMMI Model Foundation" or "CMF."

The components of the CMF are part of every model generated from the CMMI Framework. Those components are combined with material applicable to an area of interest (e.g., acquisition, development, services) to produce a model.

A "constellation" is defined as a collection of CMMI components that are used to construct models, training materials, and appraisal related documents for an area of interest (e.g., acquisition, development, services). The Development constellation's model is called "CMMI for Development" or "CMMI-DEV."

The Architecture of the CMMI Framework

by Roger Bate
with a postscript by Mike Konrad

Over the years, as the CMMI Product Suite has been used in disparate industries and organizations, it became apparent that CMMI could be applied to all kinds of product development, especially if the terminology was kept general for similar practices.

A further revelation was that the process and project management practices of the model are suitable for a wide range of activities besides product development. This discovery led me to propose that we should enable the expansion of CMMI, including the extension of the scope of CMMI, by creating a new architecture for the CMMI Framework.

This new architecture would accommodate other areas of interest (e.g., Services and Acquisition). I was musing one day about the valuable best practices that were contained in models. I began to think of them as the *stars* of process improvement. I pushed this metaphor a little further to call the collection of components that would be useful in building a model, its training materials, and appraisal documents for an area of interest a *constellation*. This was the beginning of the architecture that was eventually created.

There are two primary objectives for the CMMI Framework architecture:

- Enable the coverage of selected areas of interest to make useful and effective processes.
- Promote maximum commonality of goals and practices across models, training materials, and appraisal methods.

These objectives pull in opposite directions; therefore, the architecture was designed as a bit of a compromise.

The CMMI Framework will be used in the future to accommodate additional content that the user community indicates is desirable. The framework contains components used to construct models and their corresponding training and appraisal materials. The framework is organized so that the models constructed will benefit from common terminology and common practices that have proven to be valuable in previous models.

The CMMI Framework is a collection of all model components, training material components, and appraisal components. These components are organized into groupings, called constellations, which facilitate construction of approved models and preserve the legacy of existing CMM and CMMI models.

In the framework, there are constellations of components that are used to construct models in an area of interest (e.g., Acquisition, Development, and Services). Also in the framework, there is a CMMI model foundation. This foundation is a skeleton model that contains the core model components in a CMMI model structure. The content of the CMMI model foundation is apropos to all areas of interest addressed by the constellations. A CMMI model for a constellation is constructed by inserting additional model components into the CMMI model foundation.

Because the CMMI architecture is designed to encourage preserving as much common material as is reasonable in a multiple constellation environment, the framework contains and controls all CMMI material that can be used to produce any constellation or model.

CMMI models have a defined structure. This structure is designed to provide familiar placement of model components of various constellations and versions. If you look at the structure of a process area, you'll see components including Process Area Name, Category, Maturity Level, Purpose, Introductory Notes, References, and Specific Goals. You will also find that every process area in this model (i.e., CMMI for Development) and all other CMMI models produced from the CMMI Framework have the same structure. This feature helps you to understand quickly where to look for information in any CMMI model.

One of the benefits of having a common architecture and a large portion of common content in the various models is that the effort required to write models, train users, and appraise organizations is greatly reduced. The ability to add model components to the common process areas permits them to expand their scope of coverage to a greater variety of needs. In addition, whole new process areas may be added to provide greater coverage of different areas of interest in the constellations.

CMMI models have a great deal of well-tested content that can be used to guide the creation of high performance processes. The CMMI architecture permits that valuable content to continue to work in different areas of interest, while allowing for innovation and agility in responding to new needs.

You can see that CMMI has grown beyond the *star* practices of the three original source models to *constellations*. This expansion into the galaxy is only possible with a well-thought-out and designed architecture to support it. The CMMI architecture has been designed to provide such support and will grow as needed to continue into the future.

Postscript

Roger passed away in 2009, about two years after this perspective was written for the second edition of this book. Roger's grand vision of constellations and a flexible architecture that established a deep level of commonality among CMMI models was largely realized in the sequential release of the three V1.2 CMMI models published between 2006 and 2009.

One of many anecdotes that reveals Roger's transcending vision and greatness and reflects on the early days of CMMI is when I was contacted by friend and colleague Tomoo Matsubara-san in 1997. He asked me to provide a short opinion piece for his Soapbox column in *IEEE Software* magazine. At the time, we at the SEI were confronted with consternation from many Software CMM transition partners because they felt that we were abandoning the Software CMM product line. Instead, we were pursuing the convergence of the software engineering and systems engineering process improvement communities by creating a product line that both could use.

We hoped such a convergence would not only eliminate the need to separately maintain two models and associated product lines (those for the Software CMM and the EIA 731 Systems Engineering Capability Model), but also would encourage synergism within organizations addressing system-wide performance issues. To me, the Soapbox column provided an opportunity to communicate what we were hoping to accomplish with CMMI, so I suggested to Roger that he write something for Matsubara-san's column on why software engineering would benefit from a "systems engineering" perspective.

This chain of events led to Roger's Soapbox piece, "Do Systems Engineering? Who, Me?"[7] This anecdote typifies Roger's brilliance, ability to span multiple disciplines, and talent for motivating multiple stakeholders with a unifying vision and a shared mission to change the organization's behavior and achieve superior performance.

As mentioned, Roger's vision was largely realized with the release of the Version 1.2 CMMI Product Suite. For V1.3, however, we confronted a challenge that required some modification to Roger's initial vision for the CMMI architecture.

The challenge was the term "project," which commonly refers to an endeavor whose purpose and end are marked by the delivery of something tangible (e.g., a product). This term appeared throughout many of the process areas (PAs) and was generally a good fit for CMMI-ACQ and CMMI-DEV but not for CMMI-SVC. After researching the problem, we devised a solution: for V1.3, we would allow the CMF to vary across constellations in a very limited way. CMF material in CMMI-DEV and CMMI-ACQ could continue to refer to "projects;" whereas in CMMI-SVC, the reference would instead be to "work," "work activities," "services," or similar. In this way, the CMMI user community could continue to use common English terms in a familiar and consistent way while benefitting from a sharing of CMMI terminology and best practices (for 17 PAs) across a broad range of process improvement communities. (This idea was researched by exploratory implementation, a survey, and pilots; and it worked well.)

V1.3 benefits from many synergies. The sequential release of new constellations for V1.2 between 2006 and 2009 provided the opportunity to evaluate what CMF should be—one context at a time. However, in V1.3 development, model material originally proposed

7. Roger R. Bate, "Do Systems Engineering? Who, Me?" *IEEE Software*, vol. 15, no. 4, pp. 65–66, July/Aug. 1998, doi:10.1109/52.687947.

for one area of interest was sometimes extended to all three. Examples include the concept of quality attributes; prioritization of requirements; ontology for products and services; a richer set of examples for measurement and analysis; a sharper focus on what is essential to team performance (i.e., team composition, empowerment, and operational discipline); and alignment of high maturity practices with business objectives enabled by analytics. The V1.3 user may be unaware of these synergies or their sources, but may derive benefit from them.

With V1.3, we've only begun to explore ideas for the future of CMMI. Beyond V1.3, there are lots of promising directions forward, which is only the case because of Roger's original pioneering vision for CMMI. With Roger's passing, his Chief Architect mantle has been passed on to someone many years his junior (me) and I can assure our readers that well into his mid-80s, Roger remained a truly brilliant man, retaining his clear thinking and ear for nuance while maintaining a broad perspective when rendering an opinion; and so I recognize almost as much as anyone how big a space he has left behind. Although he was the one who conceived of the term constellations as a way of thinking about CMMI architecture, to us who knew him well, he was the real star of CMMI.

CMMI for Development

CMMI for Development is a reference model that covers activities for developing both products and services. Organizations from many industries, including aerospace, banking, computer hardware, software, defense, automobile manufacturing, and telecommunications, use CMMI for Development.

CMMI for Development contains practices that cover project management, process management, systems engineering, hardware engineering, software engineering, and other supporting processes used in development and maintenance.

Use professional judgment and common sense to interpret the model for your organization. That is, although the process areas described in this model depict behaviors considered best practices for most users, process areas and practices should be interpreted using an in-depth knowledge of CMMI-DEV, your organizational constraints, and your business environment.

CHAPTER 2

PROCESS AREA COMPONENTS

This chapter describes the components found in each process area and in the generic goals and generic practices. Understanding these components is critical to using the information in Part Two effectively. If you are unfamiliar with Part Two, you may want to skim the Generic Goals and Generic Practices section and a couple of process area sections to get a general feel for the content and layout before reading this chapter.

Core Process Areas and CMMI Models

All CMMI models are produced from the CMMI Framework. This framework contains all of the goals and practices that are used to produce CMMI models that belong to CMMI constellations.

All CMMI models contain 16 core process areas. These process areas cover basic concepts that are fundamental to process improvement in any area of interest (i.e., acquisition, development, services). Some of the material in the core process areas is the same in all constellations. Other material may be adjusted to address a specific area of interest. Consequently, the material in the core process areas may not be exactly the same.

Required, Expected, and Informative Components

Model components are grouped into three categories—required, expected, and informative—that reflect how to interpret them.

Required Components

Required components are CMMI components that are essential to achieving process improvement in a given process area. This achievement must be visibly implemented in an organization's processes. The required components in CMMI are the specific and generic goals. Goal satisfaction is used in appraisals as the basis for deciding whether a process area has been satisfied.

Expected Components

Expected components are CMMI components that describe the activities that are important in achieving a required CMMI component. Expected components guide those who implement improvements or perform appraisals. The expected components in CMMI are the specific and generic practices.

Before goals can be considered to be satisfied, either their practices as described, or acceptable alternatives to them, must be present in the planned and implemented processes of the organization.

Informative Components

Informative components are CMMI components that help model users understand CMMI required and expected components. These components can be example boxes, detailed explanations, or other helpful information. Subpractices, notes, references, goal titles, practice titles, sources, example work products, and generic practice elaborations are informative model components.

The informative material plays an important role in understanding the model. It is often impossible to adequately describe the behavior required or expected of an organization using only a single goal or practice statement. The model's informative material provides information necessary to achieve the correct understanding of goals and practices and thus cannot be ignored.

Components Associated with Part Two

The model components associated with Part Two are summarized in Figure 2.1 to illustrate their relationships.

The following sections provide detailed descriptions of CMMI model components.

Process Areas

A process area is a cluster of related practices in an area that, when implemented collectively, satisfies a set of goals considered important for making improvement in that area. (See the definition of "process area" in the glossary.)

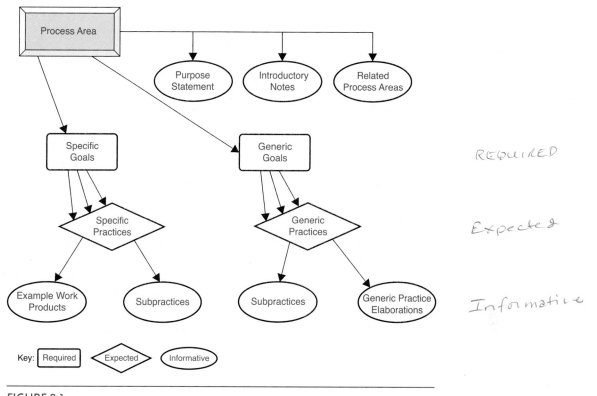

REQUIRED

Expected

Informative

FIGURE 2.1
CMMI Model Components

The 22 process areas are presented in alphabetical order by acronym:

- Causal Analysis and Resolution (CAR)
- Configuration Management (CM)
- Decision Analysis and Resolution (DAR)
- Integrated Project Management (IPM)
- Measurement and Analysis (MA)
- Organizational Process Definition (OPD)
- Organizational Process Focus (OPF)
- Organizational Performance Management (OPM)
- Organizational Process Performance (OPP)
- Organizational Training (OT)
- Product Integration (PI)
- Project Monitoring and Control (PMC)

- Project Planning (PP)
- Process and Product Quality Assurance (PPQA)
- Quantitative Project Management (QPM)
- Requirements Development (RD)
- Requirements Management (REQM)
- Risk Management (RSKM)
- Supplier Agreement Management (SAM)
- Technical Solution (TS)
- Validation (VAL)
- Verification (VER)

Purpose Statements

A purpose statement describes the purpose of the process area and is an informative component.

For example, the purpose statement of the Organizational Process Definition process area is "The purpose of Organizational Process Definition (OPD) is to establish and maintain a usable set of organizational process assets, work environment standards, and rules and guidelines for teams."

Introductory Notes

The introductory notes section of the process area describes the major concepts covered in the process area and is an informative component.

An example from the introductory notes of the Project Monitoring and Control process area is "When actual status deviates significantly from expected values, corrective actions are taken as appropriate."

Related Process Areas

The Related Process Areas section lists references to related process areas and reflects the high-level relationships among the process areas. The Related Process Areas section is an informative component.

An example of a reference found in the Related Process Areas section of the Project Planning process area is "Refer to the Risk Management process area for more information about identifying and analyzing risks and mitigating risks."

Specific Goals

A specific goal describes the unique characteristics that must be present to satisfy the process area. A specific goal is a required model component and is used in appraisals to help determine whether a process area is satisfied. (See the definition of "specific goal" in the glossary.)

For example, a specific goal from the Configuration Management process area is "Integrity of baselines is established and maintained."

Only the statement of the specific goal is a required model component. The title of a specific goal (preceded by the goal number) and notes associated with the goal are considered informative model components.

Generic Goals

Generic goals are called "generic" because the same goal statement applies to multiple process areas. A generic goal describes the characteristics that must be present to institutionalize processes that implement a process area. A generic goal is a required model component and is used in appraisals to determine whether a process area is satisfied. (See the Generic Goals and Generic Practices section in Part Two for a more detailed description of generic goals. See the definition of "generic goal" in the glossary.)

An example of a generic goal is "The process is institutionalized as a defined process."

Only the statement of the generic goal is a required model component. The title of a generic goal (preceded by the goal number) and notes associated with the goal are considered informative model components.

Specific Goal and Practice Summaries

The specific goal and practice summary provides a high-level summary of the specific goals and specific practices. The specific goal and practice summary is an informative component.

Specific Practices

A specific practice is the description of an activity that is considered important in achieving the associated specific goal. The specific practices describe the activities that are expected to result in achievement of the specific goals of a process area. A specific practice is an expected model component. (See the definition of "specific practice" in the glossary.)

For example, a specific practice from the Project Monitoring and Control process area is "Monitor commitments against those identified in the project plan."

Only the statement of the specific practice is an expected model component. The title of a specific practice (preceded by the practice number) and notes associated with the specific practice are considered informative model components.

Example Work Products

The example work products section lists sample outputs from a specific practice. An example work product is an informative model component. (See the definition of "example work product" in the glossary.)

For instance, an example work product for the specific practice "Monitor Project Planning Parameters" in the Project Monitoring and Control process area is "Records of significant deviations."

Subpractices

A subpractice is a detailed description that provides guidance for interpreting and implementing a specific or generic practice. Subpractices can be worded as if prescriptive, but they are actually an informative component meant only to provide ideas that may be useful for process improvement. (See the definition of "subpractice" in the glossary.)

For example, a subpractice for the specific practice "Take Corrective Action" in the Project Monitoring and Control process area is "Determine and document the appropriate actions needed to address identified issues."

Generic Practices

Generic practices are called "generic" because the same practice applies to multiple process areas. The generic practices associated with a generic goal describe the activities that are considered important in achieving the generic goal and contribute to the institutionalization of the processes associated with a process area. A generic practice is an expected model component. (See the definition of "generic practice" in the glossary.)

For example, a generic practice for the generic goal "The process is institutionalized as a managed process" is "Provide adequate resources for performing the process, developing the work products, and providing the services of the process."

Only the statement of the generic practice is an expected model component. The title of a generic practice (preceded by the practice number) and notes associated with the practice are considered informative model components.

Generic Practice Elaborations

Generic practice elaborations appear after generic practices to provide guidance on how the generic practices can be applied uniquely to process areas. A generic practice elaboration is an informative model component. (See the definition of "generic practice elaboration" in the glossary.)

For example, a generic practice elaboration after the generic practice "Establish and maintain an organizational policy for planning and performing the process" for the Project Planning process area is "This policy establishes organizational expectations for estimating the planning parameters, making internal and external commitments, and developing the plan for managing the project."

Additions

Additions are clearly marked model components that contain information of interest to particular users. An addition can be informative material, a specific practice, a specific goal, or an entire process area that extends the scope of a model or emphasizes a particular aspect of its use. There are no additions in the CMMI-DEV model.

Supporting Informative Components

In many places in the model, further information is needed to describe a concept. This informative material is provided in the form of the following components:

- Notes
- Examples
- References

Notes

A note is text that can accompany nearly any other model component. It may provide detail, background, or rationale. A note is an informative model component.

For example, a note that accompanies the specific practice "Implement Action Proposals" in the Causal Analysis and Resolution process area is "Only changes that prove to be of value should be considered for broad implementation."

Examples

An example is a component comprising text and often a list of items, usually in a box, that can accompany nearly any other component

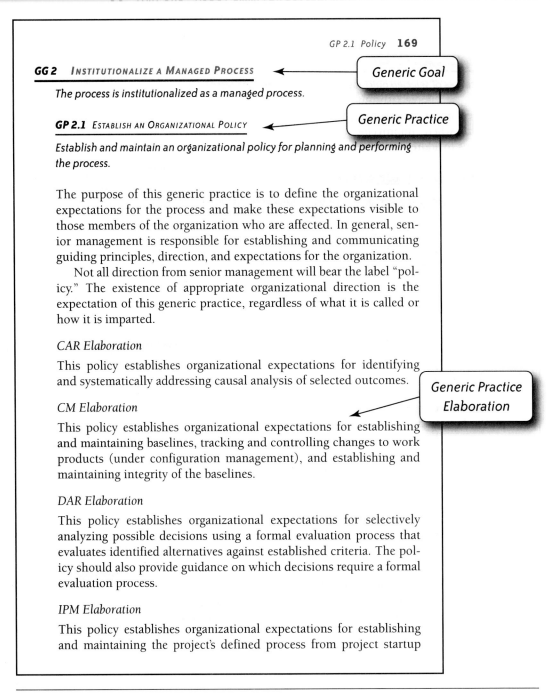

FIGURE 2.4

Sample Page from the Generic Goals and Generic Practices

CHAPTER 3

TYING IT ALL TOGETHER

Now that you have been introduced to the components of CMMI models, you need to understand how they fit together to meet your process improvement needs. This chapter introduces the concept of *levels* and shows how the process areas are organized and used.

CMMI-DEV does not specify that a project or organization must follow a particular process flow or that a certain number of products be developed per day or specific performance targets be achieved. The model does specify that a project or organization should have processes that address development related practices. To determine whether these processes are in place, a project or organization maps its processes to the process areas in this model.

The mapping of processes to process areas enables the organization to track its progress against the CMMI-DEV model as it updates or creates processes. Do not expect that every CMMI-DEV process area will map one to one with your organization's or project's processes.

Understanding Levels

Levels are used in CMMI-DEV to describe an evolutionary path recommended for an organization that wants to improve the processes it uses to develop products or services. Levels can also be the outcome of the rating activity in appraisals.[1] Appraisals can apply to entire organizations or to smaller groups such as a group of projects or a division.

---

1. For more information about appraisals, refer to Appraisal Requirements for CMMI and the Standard CMMI Appraisal Method for Process Improvement Method Definition Document [SEI 2006a, SEI 2006b].

CMMI supports two improvement paths using levels. One path enables organizations to incrementally improve processes corresponding to an individual process area (or group of process areas) selected by the organization. The other path enables organizations to improve a set of related processes by incrementally addressing successive sets of process areas.

These two improvement paths are associated with the two types of levels: capability levels and maturity levels. These levels correspond to two approaches to process improvement called "representations." The two representations are called "continuous" and "staged." Using the continuous representation enables you to achieve "capability levels." Using the staged representation enables you to achieve "maturity levels."

To reach a particular level, an organization must satisfy all of the goals of the process area or set of process areas that are targeted for improvement, regardless of whether it is a capability or a maturity level.

Both representations provide ways to improve your processes to achieve business objectives, and both provide the same essential content and use the same model components.

Structures of the Continuous and Staged Representations

Figure 3.1 illustrates the structures of the continuous and staged representations. The differences between the structures are subtle but significant. The staged representation uses maturity levels to characterize the overall state of the organization's processes relative to the model as a whole, whereas the continuous representation uses capability levels to characterize the state of the organization's processes relative to an individual process area.

What may strike you as you compare these two representations is their similarity. Both have many of the same components (e.g., process areas, specific goals, specific practices), and these components have the same hierarchy and configuration.

What is not readily apparent from the high-level view in Figure 3.1 is that the continuous representation focuses on process area capability as measured by capability levels and the staged representation focuses on overall maturity as measured by maturity levels. This dimension (the capability/maturity dimension) of CMMI is used for benchmarking and appraisal activities, as well as guiding an organization's improvement efforts.

Continuous Representation

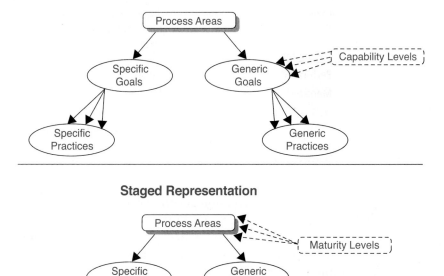

Staged Representation

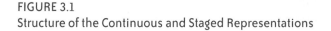

FIGURE 3.1
Structure of the Continuous and Staged Representations

Capability levels apply to an organization's process improvement achievement in individual process areas. These levels are a means for incrementally improving the processes corresponding to a given process area. The four capability levels are numbered 0 through 3.

Maturity levels apply to an organization's process improvement achievement across multiple process areas. These levels are a means of improving the processes corresponding to a given set of process areas (i.e., maturity level). The five maturity levels are numbered 1 through 5.

Table 3.1 compares the four capability levels to the five maturity levels. Notice that the names of two of the levels are the same in both representations (i.e., Managed and Defined). The differences are that there is no maturity level 0; there are no capability levels 4 and 5; and at level 1, the names used for capability level 1 and maturity level 1 are different.

TABLE 3.1   Comparison of Capability and Maturity Levels

Level	*Continuous Representation* *Capability Levels*	*Staged Representation* *Maturity Levels*
Level 0	Incomplete	
Level 1	Performed	Initial
Level 2	Managed	Managed
Level 3	Defined	Defined
Level 4		Quantitatively Managed
Level 5		Optimizing

The continuous representation is concerned with selecting both a particular process area to improve and the desired capability level for that process area. In this context, whether a process is performed or incomplete is important. Therefore, the name "Incomplete" is given to the continuous representation starting point.

The staged representation is concerned with selecting multiple process areas to improve within a maturity level; whether individual processes are performed or incomplete is not the primary focus. Therefore, the name "Initial" is given to the staged representation starting point.

Both capability levels and maturity levels provide a way to improve the processes of an organization and measure how well organizations can and do improve their processes. However, the associated approach to process improvement is different.

Understanding Capability Levels

To support those who use the continuous representation, all CMMI models reflect capability levels in their design and content.

The four capability levels, each a layer in the foundation for ongoing process improvement, are designated by the numbers 0 through 3:

0. Incomplete
1. Performed
2. Managed
3. Defined

A capability level for a process area is achieved when all of the generic goals are satisfied up to that level. The fact that capability levels 2 and 3 use the same terms as generic goals 2 and 3 is intentional because each of these generic goals and practices reflects the meaning of the capability levels of the goals and practices. (See the Generic Goals and Generic Practices section in Part Two for more information about generic goals and practices.) A short description of each capability level follows.

Capability Level 0: Incomplete

An *incomplete* process is a process that either is not performed or is partially performed. One or more of the specific goals of the process area are not satisfied and no generic goals exist for this level since there is no reason to institutionalize a partially performed process.

Capability Level 1: Performed

A capability level 1 process is characterized as a *performed process*. A performed process is a process that accomplishes the needed work to produce work products; the specific goals of the process area are satisfied.

Although capability level 1 results in important improvements, those improvements can be lost over time if they are not institutionalized. The application of institutionalization (the CMMI generic practices at capability levels 2 and 3) helps to ensure that improvements are maintained.

Capability Level 2: Managed

A capability level 2 process is characterized as a *managed process*. A managed process is a performed process that is planned and executed in accordance with policy; employs skilled people having adequate resources to produce controlled outputs; involves relevant stakeholders; is monitored, controlled, and reviewed; and is evaluated for adherence to its process description.

The process discipline reflected by capability level 2 helps to ensure that existing practices are retained during times of stress.

Capability Level 3: Defined

A capability level 3 process is characterized as a *defined process*. A defined process is a managed process that is tailored from the organization's set of standard processes according to the organization's tailoring guidelines; has a maintained process description; and contributes process related experiences to the organizational process assets.

A critical distinction between capability levels 2 and 3 is the scope of standards, process descriptions, and procedures. At capability level 2, the standards, process descriptions, and procedures can be quite different in each specific instance of the process (e.g., on a particular project). At capability level 3, the standards, process descriptions, and procedures for a project are tailored from the organization's set of standard processes to suit a particular project or organizational unit and therefore are more consistent, except for the differences allowed by the tailoring guidelines.

Another critical distinction is that at capability level 3 processes are typically described more rigorously than at capability level 2. A defined process clearly states the purpose, inputs, entry criteria, activities, roles, measures, verification steps, outputs, and exit criteria. At capability level 3, processes are managed more proactively using an understanding of the interrelationships of the process activities and detailed measures of the process and its work products.

Advancing Through Capability Levels

The capability levels of a process area are achieved through the application of generic practices or suitable alternatives to the processes associated with that process area.

Reaching capability level 1 for a process area is equivalent to saying that the processes associated with that process area are *performed processes*.

Reaching capability level 2 for a process area is equivalent to saying that there is a policy that indicates you will perform the process. There is a plan for performing it, resources are provided, responsibilities are assigned, training to perform it is provided, selected work products related to performing the process are controlled, and so on. In other words, a capability level 2 process can be planned and monitored just like any project or support activity.

Reaching capability level 3 for a process area is equivalent to saying that an organizational standard process exists associated with that process area, which can be tailored to the needs of the project. The processes in the organization are now more consistently defined and applied because they are based on organizational standard processes.

After an organization has reached capability level 3 in the process areas it has selected for improvement, it can continue its improvement journey by addressing high maturity process areas (Organizational Process Performance, Quantitative Project Management, Causal Analysis and Resolution, and Organizational Performance Management).

The high maturity process areas focus on improving the performance of those processes already implemented. The high maturity process areas describe the use of statistical and other quantitative techniques to improve organizational and project processes to better achieve business objectives.

When continuing its improvement journey in this way, an organization can derive the most benefit by first selecting the OPP and QPM process areas, and bringing those process areas to capability levels 1, 2, and 3. In doing so, projects and organizations align the selection and analyses of processes more closely with their business objectives.

After the organization attains capability level 3 in the OPP and QPM process areas, the organization can continue its improvement path by selecting the CAR and OPM process areas. In doing so, the organization analyzes the business performance using statistical and other quantitative techniques to determine performance shortfalls, and identifies and deploys process and technology improvements that contribute to meeting quality and process-performance objectives. Projects and the organization use causal analysis to identify and resolve issues affecting performance and promote the dissemination of best practices.

Applying Principles of Empiricism

by Victor R. Basili, Kathleen C. Dangle, and Michele A. Shaw

Thinking Empirically

Thinking empirically about software engineering changes the way you think about process improvement.

Software engineering is an engineering discipline. Like other disciplines, software engineering requires an empirical paradigm that involves observing, building models, analyzing, and experimenting so that we can learn. We need to model the products, the processes, and the cause/effect relationships between them in the context of the organization and the project set. This empirical mindset provides a basis for choosing the appropriate processes, analyzing the effects of those selections, and packaging the resulting knowledge for reuse and evolution; it drives an effective process improvement initiative.

Note: Systems and software engineering have a lot in common; both require human-intensive implementation approaches and fundamentally focus on the issue of design, unlike manufacturing. As such, this empirical thinking can be applied to systems engineering as an underlying approach to improving systems engineering outcomes.

Empirical Principles

There are several principles associated with software engineering. In what follows, we discuss a few of these principles as they relate to process improvement.

P1. Observe your business. Organizations have different characteristics, goals, and cultures; stakeholders have different and competing needs. Well-engineered systems and software depend on many variables and context plays a significant role in defining goals and objectives for what can be and what must be achieved. Organizations must strive to build quantitative and qualitative models to understand the cause and effect relationships between processes and products in the context of the development/maintenance efforts.

How else can these organizations articulate the differences and similarities among projects in the organization so they have a basis for selecting the processes to use to achieve their goals?

P2. Measurement is fundamental. Measurement is a standard abstraction process that allows us to build models or representations of what we observe so we can reason about relationships in context. The use of models in conjunction with experience, judgment, and intuition can guide decision-making. Measurement through models provides a mechanism for an evidence-based investigation so that decisions are supported with facts versus a system of pure beliefs.

P3. Process is a variable. Processes need to be selected and tailored to solve the problem at hand. In order to find the right process for the right situation, organizations must understand the effects of the process under differing conditions. This means a process must be measurable so that its effects can be quantified. It also means organizations must compile evidence that shows what works under what circumstances.

P4. Stakeholders must make their goals explicit. There is a wide range of stakeholders for any project (e.g., customers, end users, contract managers, practitioners, and managers). The organization itself and different stakeholders have different goals and needs. Organizations must make these goals and needs explicit through models and measures so they can be communicated, analyzed, synthesized, evaluated, and used to select and tailor the right processes. Making them explicit allows them to be packaged so they can be remembered and used again.

P5. Learn from experience. Organizations have the opportunity to learn from their experiences and build their core competence in systems and software engineering. For process improvement, the focus should be on learning about processes and how they interact with the environment on each project. This learning is evolutionary and each project should make the organization smarter about how to do the next project. But this learning must be deliberate and explicit or it will not be available for the organization to leverage.

P6. Software Engineering is "big science." Improving software engineering processes must be done through observation and experimentation in the context of where the actual products are being developed. There is a synergistic relationship between practice and research. Industrial, government, and academic organizations must partner to expand and evolve systems and software competencies. There are so many facets to software engineering that it requires multiple talents and differing expertise. We need real-world laboratories that allow us to see the interactions among teams, processes, and products.

The Role of Empiricism in CMMI

At CMMI level 5, process improvement is intended to be an empirically-based activity. Each project is planned and executed using practices that are selected based on the context of the environment, the project needs, and past experiences. A level 5 organization understands the relationship between process and product and is capable of manipulating process to achieve various product characteristics. It is this capability that provides the greatest value from process improvement to the organization.

Empirical thinking shifts the process-improvement mindset from "putting processes in place" to "understanding the effects of processes so that appropriate processes can be adopted." Different and better decisions are made regarding how we choose improvement initiatives (prioritize), how we implement practices, and how we manage efforts in projects and in organizations when our explicit approach is based on empirical principles. That mindset should be in place at the beginning of the process improvement initiative, thereby focusing the effort on the real objectives of the project or the organization, the specific product and process problems, relevant experience with methods, and so on.

Organizations that are effective at implementing process improvement understand and apply empirical principles. Additionally, practices that support these principles are evident within CMMI. CMMI prescribes that data be used to make decisions about process definition at the project level as well as process change at the organizational level. Measurement and learning are catalysts for all of the practices; that is, they provide the bases for why specific practices are selected and how processes are implemented. Systems and software engineering practices are refined and fine-tuned as their effects are better understood.

Some Empirical Techniques That Support CMMI

Many techniques and methods exist to assist organizations and projects realize their goals by implementing CMMI practices. Below are some techniques that the Fraunhofer Center has effectively implemented that you may wish to consider:

Goal/Question/Metric (GQM) Approach—An essential technique for measurement in any context, GQM can support realization of P2 and P4. Originally, GQM was defined for NASA Goddard Space Flight Center to evaluate software defects on a set of projects.[2]

Quality Improvement Paradigm (QIP)—A phased process for organizational improvement that integrates the experience of individual projects with the corporate learning process, and can help realize Empirical Principles P1, P3, and P5. QIP includes characterizing the organization through models, setting goals, choosing appropriate processes for implementation on projects, analyzing results, and packaging the experience for future use in the organization.[3]

Experience Factory (EF)—A concept based on the continual accumulation of project experiences that are essential to organizational and project improvement, EF highlights the logical separation between the project organization and the factory that processes the

---

2. V. Basili, G. Caldiera, and H. D. Rombach, "Goal Question Metric Approach," *Encyclopedia of Software Engineering*, pp. 528–532, John Wiley & Sons, Inc., 1994.

3. V. Basili and G. Caldiera, "Improve Software Quality by Reusing Knowledge and Experience," *Sloan Management Review*, MIT Press, vol. 37(1): 55–64, Fall 1995.

project experiences in an organization experience base to make it reusable. EF can help realize Empirical Principles P1, P2, and P5.[4]

GQM+Strategies—An approach that supports strategic measurement by extending GQM to support goal definition and alignment, strategy development, measurement implementation, and assessment across an enterprise.[5] GQM+Strategies assists the organization in tying together its approach and motivations underlying the implementation of the Empirical Principles.

Adopting these empirical principles early, understanding their role in CMMI, and deliberately selecting techniques to support your effort can have a profound effect on the success of the organization as you embark the process improvement path.

4. V. Basili, G. Caldiera, and H. D. Rombach, "The Experience Factory," *Encyclopedia of Software Engineering*, pp. 469–476, John Wiley & Sons, Inc., 1994.

5. Victor R. Basili, Mikael Lindvall, Myrna Regardie, Carolyn Seaman, Jens Heidrich, Jurgen Munch, Dieter Rombach, and Adam Trendowicz, "Linking Software Development and Business Strategy Through Measurement," *IEEE Computer*, pp. 57–65, April, 2010.

Understanding Maturity Levels

To support those who use the staged representation, all CMMI models reflect maturity levels in their design and content. A maturity level consists of related specific and generic practices for a predefined set of process areas that improve the organization's overall performance.

The maturity level of an organization provides a way to characterize its performance. Experience has shown that organizations do their best when they focus their process improvement efforts on a manageable number of process areas at a time and that those areas require increasing sophistication as the organization improves.

A maturity level is a defined evolutionary plateau for organizational process improvement. Each maturity level matures an important subset of the organization's processes, preparing it to move to the next maturity level. The maturity levels are measured by the achievement of the specific and generic goals associated with each predefined set of process areas.

The five maturity levels, each a layer in the foundation for ongoing process improvement, are designated by the numbers 1 through 5:

1. Initial
2. Managed

3. Defined
4. Quantitatively Managed
5. Optimizing

Remember that maturity levels 2 and 3 use the same terms as capability levels 2 and 3. This consistency of terminology was intentional because the concepts of maturity levels and capability levels are complementary. Maturity levels are used to characterize organizational improvement relative to a set of process areas, and capability levels characterize organizational improvement relative to an individual process area.

Maturity Level 1: Initial

At maturity level 1, processes are usually ad hoc and chaotic. The organization usually does not provide a stable environment to support processes. Success in these organizations depends on the competence and heroics of the people in the organization and not on the use of proven processes. In spite of this chaos, maturity level 1 organizations often produce products and services that work, but they frequently exceed the budget and schedule documented in their plans.

Maturity level 1 organizations are characterized by a tendency to overcommit, abandon their processes in a time of crisis, and be unable to repeat their successes.

Maturity Level 2: Managed

At maturity level 2, the projects have ensured that processes are planned and executed in accordance with policy; the projects employ skilled people who have adequate resources to produce controlled outputs; involve relevant stakeholders; are monitored, controlled, and reviewed; and are evaluated for adherence to their process descriptions. The process discipline reflected by maturity level 2 helps to ensure that existing practices are retained during times of stress. When these practices are in place, projects are performed and managed according to their documented plans.

Also at maturity level 2, the status of the work products are visible to management at defined points (e.g., at major milestones, at the completion of major tasks). Commitments are established among relevant stakeholders and are revised as needed. Work products are appropriately controlled. The work products and services satisfy their specified process descriptions, standards, and procedures.

Maturity Level 3: Defined

At maturity level 3, processes are well characterized and understood, and are described in standards, procedures, tools, and methods. The organization's set of standard processes, which is the basis for maturity level 3, is established and improved over time. These standard processes are used to establish consistency across the organization. Projects establish their defined processes by tailoring the organization's set of standard processes according to tailoring guidelines. (See the definition of "organization's set of standard processes" in the glossary.)

A critical distinction between maturity levels 2 and 3 is the scope of standards, process descriptions, and procedures. At maturity level 2, the standards, process descriptions, and procedures can be quite different in each specific instance of the process (e.g., on a particular project). At maturity level 3, the standards, process descriptions, and procedures for a project are tailored from the organization's set of standard processes to suit a particular project or organizational unit and therefore are more consistent except for the differences allowed by the tailoring guidelines.

Another critical distinction is that at maturity level 3, processes are typically described more rigorously than at maturity level 2. A defined process clearly states the purpose, inputs, entry criteria, activities, roles, measures, verification steps, outputs, and exit criteria. At maturity level 3, processes are managed more proactively using an understanding of the interrelationships of process activities and detailed measures of the process, its work products, and its services.

At maturity level 3, the organization further improves its processes that are related to the maturity level 2 process areas. Generic practices associated with generic goal 3 that were not addressed at maturity level 2 are applied to achieve maturity level 3.

Maturity Level 4: Quantitatively Managed

At maturity level 4, the organization and projects establish quantitative objectives for quality and process performance and use them as criteria in managing projects. Quantitative objectives are based on the needs of the customer, end users, organization, and process implementers. Quality and process performance is understood in statistical terms and is managed throughout the life of projects.

For selected subprocesses, specific measures of process performance are collected and statistically analyzed. When selecting subprocesses for analyses, it is critical to understand the relationships between different subprocesses and their impact on achieving the objectives for quality and process performance. Such an approach helps to ensure that subprocess monitoring using statistical and other quantitative techniques is applied to where it has the most overall value to the business. Process performance baselines and models can be used to help set quality and process performance objectives that help achieve business objectives.

A critical distinction between maturity levels 3 and 4 is the predictability of process performance. At maturity level 4, the performance of projects and selected subprocesses is controlled using statistical and other quantitative techniques, and predictions are based, in part, on a statistical analysis of fine-grained process data.

Maturity Level 5: Optimizing

At maturity level 5, an organization continually improves its processes based on a quantitative understanding of its business objectives and performance needs. The organization uses a quantitative approach to understand the variation inherent in the process and the causes of process outcomes.

Maturity level 5 focuses on continually improving process performance through incremental and innovative process and technological improvements. The organization's quality and process performance objectives are established, continually revised to reflect changing business objectives and organizational performance, and used as criteria in managing process improvement. The effects of deployed process improvements are measured using statistical and other quantitative techniques and compared to quality and process performance objectives. The project's defined processes, the organization's set of standard processes, and supporting technology are targets of measurable improvement activities.

A critical distinction between maturity levels 4 and 5 is the focus on managing and improving organizational performance. At maturity level 4, the organization and projects focus on understanding and controlling performance at the subprocess level and using the results to manage projects. At maturity level 5, the organization is concerned with overall organizational performance using data collected from multiple projects. Analysis of the data identifies shortfalls or gaps in performance. These gaps are used to drive organizational process improvement that generates measurable improvement in performance.

Advancing Through Maturity Levels

Organizations can achieve progressive improvements in their maturity by achieving control first at the project level and continuing to the most advanced level—organization-wide performance management and continuous process improvement—using both qualitative and quantitative data to make decisions.

Since improved organizational maturity is associated with improvement in the range of expected results that can be achieved by an organization, maturity is one way of predicting general outcomes of the organization's next project. For instance, at maturity level 2, the organization has been elevated from ad hoc to disciplined by establishing sound project management. As the organization achieves generic and specific goals for the set of process areas in a maturity level, it increases its organizational maturity and reaps the benefits of process improvement. Because each maturity level forms a necessary foundation for the next level, trying to skip maturity levels is usually counterproductive.

At the same time, recognize that process improvement efforts should focus on the needs of the organization in the context of its business environment and that process areas at higher maturity levels can address the current and future needs of an organization or project.

For example, organizations seeking to move from maturity level 1 to maturity level 2 are frequently encouraged to establish a process group, which is addressed by the Organizational Process Focus process area at maturity level 3. Although a process group is not a necessary characteristic of a maturity level 2 organization, it can be a useful part of the organization's approach to achieving maturity level 2.

This situation is sometimes characterized as establishing a maturity level 1 process group to bootstrap the maturity level 1 organization to maturity level 2. Maturity level 1 process improvement activities may depend primarily on the insight and competence of the process group until an infrastructure to support more disciplined and widespread improvement is in place.

Organizations can institute process improvements anytime they choose, even before they are prepared to advance to the maturity level at which the specific practice is recommended. In such situations, however, organizations should understand that the success of these improvements is at risk because the foundation for their successful institutionalization has not been completed. Processes without the proper foundation can fail at the point they are needed most—under stress.

A defined process that is characteristic of a maturity level 3 organization can be placed at great risk if maturity level 2 management practices are deficient. For example, management may commit to a poorly planned schedule or fail to control changes to baselined requirements. Similarly, many organizations prematurely collect the detailed data characteristic of maturity level 4 only to find the data uninterpretable because of inconsistencies in processes and measurement definitions.

Another example of using processes associated with higher maturity level process areas is in the building of products. Certainly, we would expect maturity level 1 organizations to perform requirements analysis, design, product integration, and verification. However, these activities are not described until maturity level 3, where they are defined as coherent, well-integrated engineering processes. The maturity level 3 engineering process complements a maturing project management capability put in place so that the engineering improvements are not lost by an ad hoc management process.

Process Areas

Process areas are viewed differently in the two representations. Figure 3.2 compares views of how process areas are used in the continuous representation and the staged representation.

The continuous representation enables the organization to choose the focus of its process improvement efforts by choosing those process areas, or sets of interrelated process areas, that best benefit the organization and its business objectives. Although there are some limits on what an organization can choose because of the dependencies among process areas, the organization has considerable freedom in its selection.

To support those who use the continuous representation, process areas are organized into four categories: Process Management, Project Management, Engineering, and Support. These categories emphasize some of the key relationships that exist among the process areas.

Sometimes an informal grouping of process areas is mentioned: high maturity process areas. The four high maturity process areas are: Organizational Process Performance, Quantitative Project Management, Organizational Performance Management, and Causal Analysis and Resolution. These process areas focus on improving the performance of implemented processes that most closely relate to the organization's business objectives.

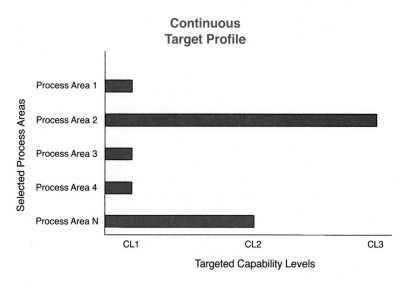

**Continuous
Target Profile**

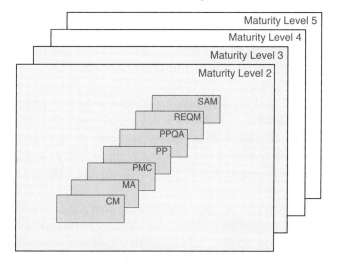

= Groups of process areas chosen for process improvement to achieve maturity level 3

FIGURE 3.2
Process Areas in the Continuous and Staged Representations

Once you select process areas, you must also select how much you would like to mature processes associated with those process areas (i.e., select the appropriate capability level). Capability levels and generic goals and practices support the improvement of processes associated with individual process areas. For example, an organization may wish to reach capability level 2 in one process area and capability level 3 in another. As the organization reaches a capability level, it sets its sights on the next capability level for one of these same process areas or decides to widen its view and address a larger number of process areas. Once it reaches capability level 3 in most of the process areas, the organization can shift its attention to the high maturity process areas and can track the capability of each through capability level 3.

The selection of a combination of process areas and capability levels is typically described in a "target profile." A target profile defines all of the process areas to be addressed and the targeted capability level for each. This profile governs which goals and practices the organization will address in its process improvement efforts.

Most organizations, at minimum, target capability level 1 for the process areas they select, which requires that all of these process areas' specific goals be achieved. However, organizations that target capability levels higher than 1 concentrate on the institutionalization of selected processes in the organization by implementing generic goals and practices.

The staged representation provides a path of improvement from maturity level 1 to maturity level 5 that involves achieving the goals of the process areas at each maturity level. To support those who use the staged representation, process areas are grouped by maturity level, indicating which process areas to implement to achieve each maturity level.

For example, at maturity level 2, there is a set of process areas that an organization would use to guide its process improvement until it could achieve all the goals of all these process areas. Once maturity level 2 is achieved, the organization focuses its efforts on maturity level 3 process areas, and so on. The generic goals that apply to each process area are also predetermined. Generic goal 2 applies to maturity level 2 and generic goal 3 applies to maturity levels 3 through 5.

Table 3.2 provides a list of CMMI-DEV process areas and their associated categories and maturity levels.

TABLE 3.2   Process Areas, Categories, and Maturity Levels

Process Area	Category	Maturity Level
Causal Analysis and Resolution (CAR)	Support	5
Configuration Management (CM)	Support	2
Decision Analysis and Resolution (DAR)	Support	3
Integrated Project Management (IPM)	Project Management	3
Measurement and Analysis (MA)	Support	2
Organizational Process Definition (OPD)	Process Management	3
Organizational Process Focus (OPF)	Process Management	3
Organizational Performance Management (OPM)	Process Management	5
Organizational Process Performance (OPP)	Process Management	4
Organizational Training (OT)	Process Management	3
Product Integration (PI)	Engineering	3
Project Monitoring and Control (PMC)	Project Management	2
Project Planning (PP)	Project Management	2
Process and Product Quality Assurance (PPQA)	Support	2
Quantitative Project Management (QPM)	Project Management	4
Requirements Development (RD)	Engineering	3
Requirements Management (REQM)	Project Management	2
Risk Management (RSKM)	Project Management	3
Supplier Agreement Management (SAM)	Project Management	2
Technical Solution (TS)	Engineering	3
Validation (VAL)	Engineering	3
Verification (VER)	Engineering	3

Equivalent Staging

Equivalent staging is a way to compare results from using the continuous representation to results from using the staged representation. In essence, if you measure improvement relative to selected process areas using capability levels in the continuous representation, how do you translate that work into maturity levels? Is this translation possible?

Up to this point, we have not discussed process appraisals in much detail. The SCAMPI method[6] is used to appraise organizations using CMMI, and one result of an appraisal is a rating [SEI 2011a,

6. The Standard CMMI Appraisal Method for Process Improvement (SCAMPI) method is described in Chapter 5.

Ahern 2005]. If the continuous representation is used for an appraisal, the rating is a "capability level profile." If the staged representation is used for an appraisal, the rating is a "maturity level rating" (e.g., maturity level 3).

A capability level profile is a list of process areas and the corresponding capability level achieved for each. This profile enables an organization to track its capability level by process area. The profile is called an "achievement profile" when it represents the organization's actual progress for each process area. Alternatively, the profile is called a "target profile" when it represents the organization's planned process improvement objectives.

Figure 3.3 illustrates a combined target and achievement profile. The blue portion of each bar represents what has been achieved. The unshaded portion represents what remains to be accomplished to meet the target profile.

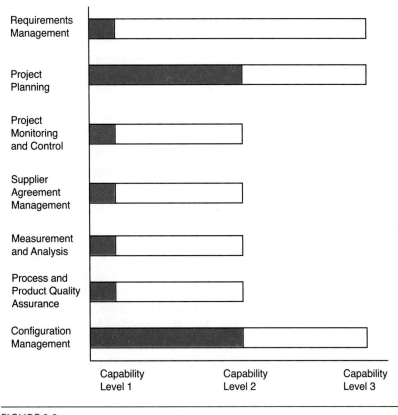

FIGURE 3.3
Example Combined Target and Achievement Profile

An achievement profile, when compared with a target profile, enables an organization to plan and track its progress for each selected process area. Maintaining capability level profiles is advisable when using the continuous representation.

Target staging is a sequence of target profiles that describes the path of process improvement to be followed by the organization. When building target profiles, the organization should pay attention to the dependencies between generic practices and process areas. If a generic practice depends on a process area, either to carry out the generic practice or to provide a prerequisite work product, the generic practice can be much less effective when the process area is not implemented.[7]

Although the reasons to use the continuous representation are many, ratings consisting of capability level profiles are limited in their ability to provide organizations with a way to generally compare themselves with other organizations. Capability level profiles can be used if each organization selects the same process areas; however, maturity levels have been used to compare organizations for years and already provide predefined sets of process areas.

Because of this situation, equivalent staging was created. Equivalent staging enables an organization using the continuous representation to convert a capability level profile to the associated maturity level rating.

The most effective way to depict equivalent staging is to provide a sequence of target profiles, each of which is equivalent to a maturity level rating of the staged representation reflected in the process areas listed in the target profile. The result is a target staging that is equivalent to the maturity levels of the staged representation.

Figure 3.4 shows a summary of the target profiles that must be achieved when using the continuous representation to be equivalent to maturity levels 2 through 5. Each shaded area in the capability level columns represents a target profile that is equivalent to a maturity level.

The following rules summarize equivalent staging:

• To achieve maturity level 2, all process areas assigned to maturity level 2 must achieve capability level 2 or 3.
• To achieve maturity level 3, all process areas assigned to maturity levels 2 and 3 must achieve capability level 3.

---

7. See Table 7.2 in the *Generic Goals and Generic Practices* section of Part Two for more information about the dependencies between generic practices and process areas.

Name	Abbr.	ML	CL1	CL2	CL3
Configuration Management	CM	2	**Target Profile 2**		
Measurement and Analysis	MA	2			
Project Monitoring and Control	PMC	2			
Project Planning	PP	2			
Process and Product Quality Assurance	PPQA	2			
Requirements Management	REQM	2			
Supplier Agreement Management	SAM	2			
Decision Analysis and Resolution	DAR	3	**Target Profile 3**		
Integrated Project Management	IPM	3			
Organizational Process Definition	OPD	3			
Organizational Process Focus	OPF	3			
Organizational Training	OT	3			
Product Integration	PI	3			
Requirements Development	RD	3			
Risk Management	RSKM	3			
Technical Solution	TS	3			
Validation	VAL	3			
Verification	VER	3			
Organizational Process Performance	OPP	4	**Target Profile 4**		
Quantitative Project Management	QPM	4			
Causal Analysis and Resolution	CAR	5	**Target Profile 5**		
Organizational Performance Management	OPM	5			

FIGURE 3.4
Target Profiles and Equivalent Staging

- To achieve maturity level 4, all process areas assigned to maturity levels 2, 3, and 4 must achieve capability level 3.
- To achieve maturity level 5, all process areas must achieve capability level 3.

Achieving High Maturity

When using the staged representation, you attain high maturity when you achieve maturity level 4 or 5. Achieving maturity level 4 involves implementing all process areas for maturity levels 2, 3, and 4. Likewise, achieving maturity level 5 involves implementing all process areas for maturity levels 2, 3, 4, and 5.

When using the continuous representation, you attain high maturity using the equivalent staging concept. High maturity that is equivalent to staged maturity level 4 using equivalent staging is attained when you achieve capability level 3 for all process areas except for Organizational Performance Management (OPM) and Causal Analysis and Resolution (CAR). High maturity that is equivalent to staged maturity level 5 using equivalent staging is attained when you achieve capability level 3 for all process areas.

Using Process Performance Baselines and Process Performance Models to Enable Success

by Michael Campo, Neal Mackertich, and Peter Kraus

Process performance baselines and process performance models are expected CMMI high maturity (maturity levels 4 and 5) artifacts that build on the measurement and analysis activities established at CMMI maturity level 2 to lift an organization from a reactive management state to a proactive management state. At maturity level 2, measurements are analyzed and action taken based on trend analysis or thresholds being crossed. By contrast, the process performance baselines and models developed using high maturity practices enable an organization to predict the ability of its processes to perform in relationship to its business objectives. By aligning process performance and business objectives, process performance baselines and models act as facilitators to organizational and project success. In this essay, we examine the concepts of process performance baselines and models based on our experiences at Raytheon Integrate Defense Systems (IDS).

Before discussing process performance baselines and models, it's important to understand the concept of "quality and process performance objectives." Quality and process performance objectives derived from business objectives are used to leverage value from process performance baselines and models. This connection between quality and process performance objectives, baselines, and models is key. Without it, baselines and models may still provide some benefit to an organization, but not the systematic optimization that comes from using the baselines and models as enabling tools to focus process performance on achievement of business objectives.

In the Measurement and Analysis process area, an organization and its projects develop a measurement system used to support management information needs that are derived from organizational and project objectives. For example, a project with an objective to meet or beat its customer delivery date has an information need to understand its progress toward achieving that milestone. Measures supporting that information need might include schedule performance, productivity, and size. By collecting and analyzing such measures, the project can react to trends that indicate risk to the delivery date. These activities align with the Goal Question Metric (GQM) approach developed by Dr. Victor Basili and others from his work with the United States National Aeronautics and Space Administration.

Quality and process performance objectives build on the GQM approach by explicitly analyzing business, organizational, or project objectives and creating quantified "goals" related to processes that support those objectives. These goals become the quality and process performance objectives. Quality and process performance objectives are typically more strategically aligned than maturity level 2 Measurement and Analysis objectives and are developed from an understanding of historical process performance data. Often, business and organizational objectives may be expressed in nonquantitative terms. For example, "Improve Customer Satisfaction" may be a business objective. In such cases, it may be necessary to derive quality and process performance objectives by asking additional questions, such as "What does it take to improve customer satisfaction?" The answer may be meeting cost, schedule, or quality targets from which quantitative quality and process performance objectives can be established. Individual projects may also establish quality and process performance objectives related to their specific project context, such as objectives related to award fee criteria.

Raytheon IDS has specific business objectives associated with cost and schedule performance. Although many things impact cost and schedule performance on a project, drivers from a process perspective involved improving productivity and reducing rework. Quantitative quality and process performance objectives were established for productivity, defect containment, and defect density in support of the cost and schedule performance objectives. Process performance baselines were then created to understand our ability to achieve the quality and process performance objectives. Historical data related to productivity, defect containment, and defect density was statistically analyzed. Prediction intervals and statistical process control charts were established at both the organizational and individual project levels. Analysis results graphically depict the process performance capability of the organization and its projects as related to the quality and process performance objectives. They represent our process performance baselines.

Process performance baselines are integral enabling management tools. Projects maintain their process performance baselines using ongoing project data as part of their normal ongoing management activity. Process performance baselines are compared against the quality and project performance objectives. Causal analysis is performed and corrective action taken when process performance baselines indicate risk that the quality and process performance objectives may not be achieved. In some cases, analysis involves using statistical techniques to evaluate lower level measures that support a quality and process performance objective. For example, using statistical techniques to analyze peer review data supports quality and process performance objectives related to defect containment and defect density. Organizational process performance baselines are used to maintain quality and process performance objectives by relating current organizational process performance capability to changing business objectives.

The direct relationship between business objectives and quality and process performance objectives, and the use of process performance baselines to quantitatively manage our progress toward achieving these objectives, focused our organization on the characteristics of success. If organizational objectives are subjective (e.g., "Improve customer satisfaction"), projects may become disengaged with those objectives. Making process performance baselines and quality and process performance objectives an integral part of project management clarifies each project's role in business success. The projects become enlisted in a grass-roots effort to help achieve the business objectives. An organization where all individuals recognize their role and responsibility for business success is an organization that is more likely to achieve success.

The versatility of the Goal Question Metric approach further enabled our development and deployment of process performance models in the form of a Goal Question *Model* approach. As with process performance baselines, all process performance model efforts initiate through the linkage and alignment with quality and process performance objectives derived from business objectives. This approach is absolutely critical to effective process performance modeling since without this up-front business alignment, there is a tendency to create elegant models rather than effective models that support business objectives.

Organizational leadership engagement is integral to this process. Development of our Systems Lifecycle Analysis Model (SLAM) process performance model was a direct result of a Raytheon IDS Engineering Leadership expressed concern around the productivity and rework risks associated with accelerated concurrent engineering efforts and their impact on downstream cost performance. This concern naturally led to our generation of questions around what factors related to our concurrent engineering efforts influence our achievement of cost performance, and what controllable subprocesses relate to those factors.

Of specific interest in the development of the SLAM model was the potential statistical relationship between requirements volatility and the degree of requirements—design overlap with that of downstream software and hardware development cost performance. Modeling the relationship between potential input factors and project outcomes involved the use of statistical methods such as regression analysis and Monte Carlo simulation. In the specific case of the SLAM model, a mathematical function of the input factors was reasonably well correlated with the output responses using linear regression techniques (with an adjusted r-squared value = 0.65, p = .000). See Figure 3.5. Additionally collected project data from SLAM piloting and deployment further confirmed the strength of this underlying relationship. The regression equation associated with this statistical correlation was the building block for our SLAM model development efforts.

This is a nice point in our Perspective to reflect on the healthy ingredients of process performance models developed by the Software Engineering Institute:

- Are statistical, probabilistic, or simulation in nature
- Predict interim and/or final project outcomes
- Use controllable factors tied to subprocesses to conduct the prediction
- Model the variation of factors and understand the predicted range or variation of the outcomes
- Enable "what-if" analysis for project planning, dynamic replanning, and problem resolution during project execution
- Connect "upstream" activity with "downstream" activity
- Enable projects to achieve midcourse corrections to ensure project success

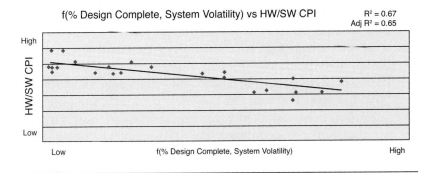

FIGURE 3.5
Relationship of Hardware/Software Cost Performance and Design
Completion/Requirements Volatility

These captured ingredients have served us well in guiding our process performance model development and deployment efforts. The SLAM model leverages the statistical correlation of controllable factors to an outcome prediction in the form of a regression equation. A user-friendly Excel-based interface was then created using Crystal Ball (an industry available software package) to model and statistically generate a cost performance prediction interval using Monte Carlo simulation. See Figure 3.6.

Note that the SLAM model user interface also includes worksheets containing Crystal Ball download instructions, step-by-step guidance for projects on Running SLAM, an Interpreting the Results guide, and a listing of potential mitigation Strategies based on best practices and lessons learned from previous deployment efforts. Information on these worksheets has proven itself to be invaluable

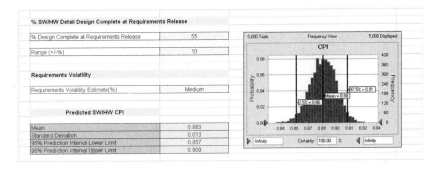

FIGURE 3.6
SLAM Model User Interface

in enabling "what-if" analysis for project planning, dynamic replanning, and problem resolution during project execution.

Projects with aggressive schedules where hardware and software design activities begin prior to requirements release can quantify the associated cost performance risks, determine the requirements volatility level that must be maintained to meet the cost performance objectives, and identify the process changes necessary to manage requirements accordingly. The SLAM model has been effectively used by integrated project teams made up of Systems, Software, Hardware, and Quality Engineering during project planning and execution to predict, manage, and mitigate risk in achieving project cost objectives. Integrated SLAM project deployment has delivered significant cost and cycle time benefits for our programs and has become an integral part of our risk management and decision-making processes.

The SLAM model has helped projects address real issues regarding their ability to meet their cost performance objectives. The success of SLAM promoted further business investment in the process performance modeling of the product development lifecycle. This investment has led to the development of a family of process performance models that support Raytheon IDS cost and schedule business objectives.

Effective development and deployment of process performance baselines and models have significantly improved our process alignment and performance against Raytheon Integrated Defense Systems business and engineering objectives. Resulting efforts in the areas of statistical process management, root cause analysis and corrective action, interdependent execution, and statistically-based risk assessment have resulted in increased productivity, reduced rework, and improved cost and schedule performance. Return-on-investment analysis pertaining to our Raytheon IDS CMMI high maturity efforts has indicated a 24:1 return from our process investment. Process performance baselines and models are the spark that ignited these results and fuels our drive for more.

CHAPTER 4

RELATIONSHIPS AMONG PROCESS AREAS

In this chapter we describe the key relationships among process areas to help you see the organization's view of process improvement and how process areas depend on the implementation of other process areas.

The relationships among multiple process areas, including the information and artifacts that flow from one process area to another—illustrated by the figures and descriptions in this chapter—help you to see a larger view of process implementation and improvement.

Successful process improvement initiatives must be driven by the business objectives of the organization. For example, a common business objective is to reduce the time it takes to get a product to market. The process improvement objective derived from that might be to improve the project management processes to ensure on-time delivery; those improvements rely on best practices in the Project Planning and Project Monitoring and Control process areas.

Although we group process areas in this chapter to simplify the discussion of their relationships, process areas often interact and have an effect on one another regardless of their group, category, or level. For example, the Decision Analysis and Resolution process area (a Support process area at maturity level 3) contains specific practices that address the formal evaluation process used in the Technical Solution process area for selecting a technical solution from alternative solutions.

Being aware of the key relationships that exist among CMMI process areas will help you apply CMMI in a useful and productive way. Relationships among process areas are described in more detail in the references of each process area and specifically in the Related Process Areas section of each process area in Part Two. Refer to Chapter 2 for more information about references.

Process Management

Process Management process areas contain the cross-project activities related to defining, planning, deploying, implementing, monitoring, controlling, appraising, measuring, and improving processes.

The five Process Management process areas in CMMI-DEV are as follows:

- Organizational Process Definition (OPD)
- Organizational Process Focus (OPF)
- Organizational Performance Management (OPM)
- Organizational Process Performance (OPP)
- Organizational Training (OT)

Basic Process Management Process Areas

The Basic Process Management process areas provide the organization with a capability to document and share best practices, organizational process assets, and learning across the organization.

Figure 4.1 provides a bird's-eye view of the interactions among the Basic Process Management process areas and with other process area categories. As illustrated in Figure 4.1, the Organizational Process Focus process area helps the organization to plan, implement, and deploy organizational process improvements based on an understanding of the current strengths and weaknesses of the organization's processes and process assets.

Candidate improvements to the organization's processes are obtained through various sources. These activities include process improvement proposals, measurement of the processes, lessons learned in implementing the processes, and results of process appraisal and product evaluation activities.

The Organizational Process Definition process area establishes and maintains the organization's set of standard processes, work environment standards, and other assets based on the process needs and objectives of the organization. These other assets include descriptions of lifecycle models, process tailoring guidelines, and process related documentation and data.

Projects tailor the organization's set of standard processes to create their defined processes. The other assets support tailoring as well as implementation of the defined processes.

Experiences and work products from performing these defined processes, including measurement data, process descriptions, process

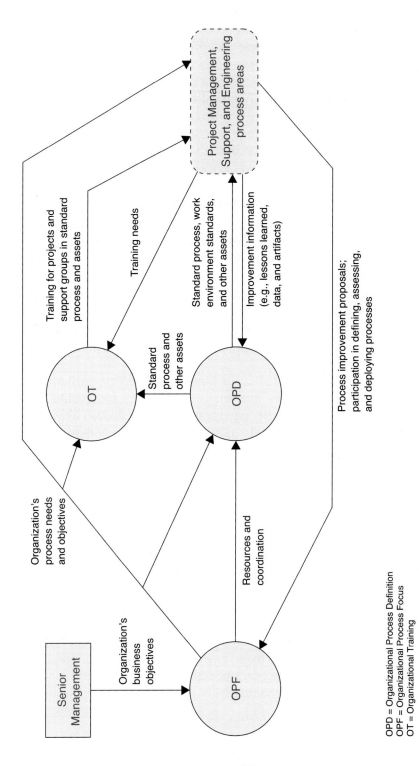

OPD = Organizational Process Definition
OPF = Organizational Process Focus
OT = Organizational Training

FIGURE 4.1
Basic Process Management Process Areas

61

artifacts, and lessons learned, are incorporated as appropriate into the organization's set of standard processes and other assets.

The Organizational Training process area identifies the strategic training needs of the organization as well as the tactical training needs that are common across projects and support groups. In particular, training is developed or obtained to develop the skills required to perform the organization's set of standard processes. The main components of training include a managed training development program, documented plans, staff with appropriate knowledge, and mechanisms for measuring the effectiveness of the training program.

Advanced Process Management Process Areas

The Advanced Process Management process areas provide the organization with an improved capability to achieve its quantitative objectives for quality and process performance.

Figure 4.2 provides a bird's-eye view of the interactions among the Advanced Process Management process areas and with other process area categories. Each of the Advanced Process Management process areas depends on the ability to develop and deploy processes and supporting assets. The Basic Process Management process areas provide this ability.

As illustrated in Figure 4.2, the Organizational Process Performance process area derives quantitative objectives for quality and process performance from the organization's business objectives. The organization provides projects and support groups with common measures, process performance baselines, and process performance models.

These additional organizational assets support composing a defined process that can achieve the project's quality and process performance objectives and support quantitative management. The organization analyzes the process performance data collected from these defined processes to develop a quantitative understanding of product quality, service quality, and process performance of the organization's set of standard processes.

In Organizational Performance Management, process performance baselines and models are analyzed to understand the organization's ability to meet its business objectives and to derive quality and process performance objectives. Based on this understanding, the organization proactively selects and deploys incremental and innovative improvements that measurably improve the organization's performance.

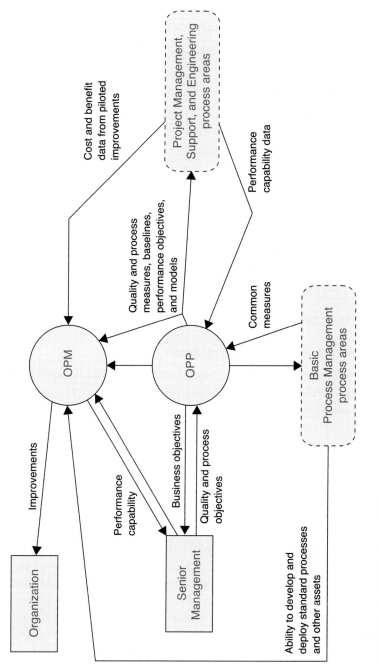

Cost and benefit data from piloted improvements

Project Management, Support, and Engineering process areas

Performance capability data

Quality and process measures, baselines, performance objectives, and models

Common measures

OPM

OPP

Basic Process Management process areas

Improvements

Organization

Performance capability

Business objectives

Quality and process objectives

Senior Management

Ability to develop and deploy standard processes and other assets

OPM = Organizational Performance Management
OPP = Organizational Process Performance

FIGURE 4.2
Advanced Process Management Process Areas

The selection of improvements to deploy is based on a quantitative understanding of the likely benefits and predicted costs of deploying candidate improvements. The organization can also adjust business objectives and quality and process performance objectives as appropriate.

Project Management

Project Management process areas cover the project management activities related to planning, monitoring, and controlling the project.

The seven Project Management process areas in CMMI-DEV are as follows:

- Integrated Project Management (IPM)
- Project Monitoring and Control (PMC)
- Project Planning (PP)
- Quantitative Project Management (QPM)
- Requirements Management (REQM)
- Risk Management (RSKM)
- Supplier Agreement Management (SAM)

Basic Project Management Process Areas

The Basic Project Management process areas address the activities related to establishing and maintaining the project plan, establishing and maintaining commitments, monitoring progress against the plan, taking corrective action, and managing supplier agreements.

Figure 4.3 provides a bird's-eye view of the interactions among the Basic Project Management process areas and with other process area categories. As illustrated in Figure 4.3, the Project Planning process area includes developing the project plan, involving relevant stakeholders, obtaining commitment to the plan, and maintaining the plan.

Planning begins with requirements that define the product and project ("What to Build" in Figure 4.3). The project plan covers the various project management and development activities performed by the project. The project reviews other plans that affect the project from various relevant stakeholders and establishes commitments with those stakeholders for their contributions to the project. For example, these plans cover configuration management, verification, and measurement and analysis.

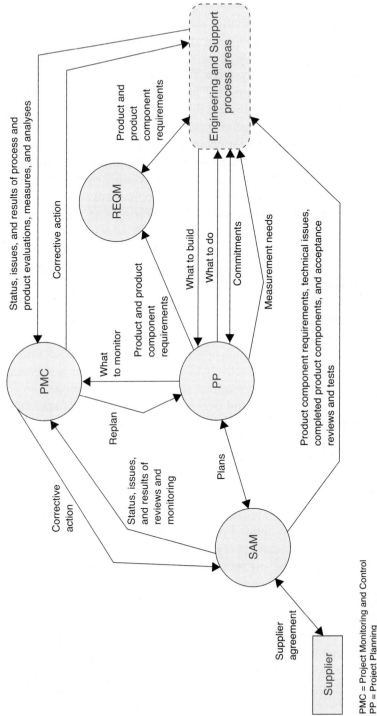

FIGURE 4.3
Basic Project Management Process Areas

PMC = Project Monitoring and Control
PP = Project Planning
REQM = Requirements Management
SAM = Supplier Agreement Management

The Project Monitoring and Control process area contains practices for monitoring and controlling activities and taking corrective action. The project plan specifies the frequency of progress reviews and the measures used to monitor progress. Progress is determined primarily by comparing project status to the plan. When the actual status deviates significantly from the expected values, corrective actions are taken as appropriate. These actions can include replanning, which requires using Project Planning practices.

The Requirements Management process area maintains the requirements. It describes activities for obtaining and controlling requirement changes and ensuring that other relevant plans and data are kept current. It provides traceability of requirements from customer requirements to product requirements to product component requirements.

Requirements Management ensures that changes to requirements are reflected in project plans, activities, and work products. This cycle of changes can affect the Engineering process areas; thus, requirements management is a dynamic and often recursive sequence of events. The Requirements Management process area is fundamental to a controlled and disciplined engineering process.

The Supplier Agreement Management process area addresses the need of the project to acquire those portions of work that are produced by suppliers. Sources of products that can be used to satisfy project requirements are proactively identified. The supplier is selected, and a supplier agreement is established to manage the supplier.

The supplier's progress and performance are tracked as specified in the supplier agreement, and the supplier agreement is revised as appropriate. Acceptance reviews and tests are conducted on the supplier-produced product component.

Advanced Project Management Process Areas

The Advanced Project Management process areas address activities such as establishing a defined process that is tailored from the organization's set of standard processes, establishing the project work environment from the organization's work environment standards, coordinating and collaborating with relevant stakeholders, forming and sustaining teams for the conduct of projects, quantitatively managing the project, and managing risk.

Figure 4.4 provides a bird's-eye view of the interactions among the Advanced Project Management process areas and with other process area categories. Each Advanced Project Management process area depends on the ability to plan, monitor, and control the project. The Basic Project Management process areas provide this ability.

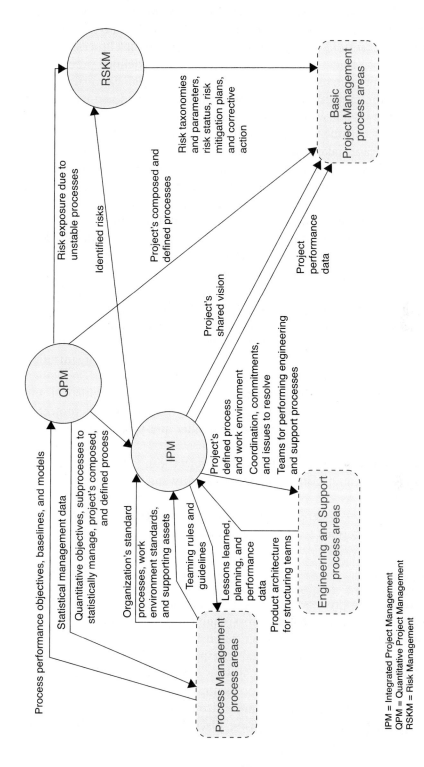

Process performance objectives, baselines, and models

Statistical management data

Quantitative objectives, subprocesses to statistically manage, project's composed, and defined process

Risk exposure due to unstable processes

Identified risks

Project's composed and defined processes

Risk taxonomies and parameters, risk status, risk mitigation plans, and corrective action

Project's shared vision

Project performance data

Project's defined process and work environment

Coordination, commitments, and issues to resolve

Teams for performing engineering and support processes

Organization's standard processes, work environment standards, and supporting assets

Teaming rules and guidelines

Lessons learned, planning, and performance data

Product architecture for structuring teams

RSKM

QPM

IPM

Basic Project Management process areas

Engineering and Support process areas

Process Management process areas

IPM = Integrated Project Management
QPM = Quantitative Project Management
RSKM = Risk Management

FIGURE 4.4
Advanced Project Management Process Areas

The Integrated Project Management process area establishes and maintains the project's defined process that is tailored from the organization's set of standard processes (Organizational Process Definition). The project is managed using the project's defined process.

The project uses and contributes to the organizational process assets, the project's work environment is established and maintained from the organization's work environment standards, and teams are established using the organization's rules and guidelines. The project's relevant stakeholders coordinate their efforts in a timely manner through the identification, negotiation, and tracking of critical dependencies and the resolution of coordination issues.

Although risk identification and monitoring are covered in the Project Planning and Project Monitoring and Control process areas, the Risk Management process area takes a continuing, forward-looking approach to managing risks with activities that include identification of risk parameters, risk assessments, and risk mitigation.

The Quantitative Project Management process area establishes objectives for quality and process performance, composes a defined process that can help achieve those objectives, and quantitatively manages the project. The project's quality and process performance objectives are based on the objectives established by the organization and the customer.

The project's defined process is composed using statistical and other quantitative techniques. Such an analysis enables the project to predict whether it will achieve its quality and process performance objectives.

Based on the prediction, the project can adjust the defined process or can negotiate changes to quality and process performance objectives. As the project progresses, the performance of selected subprocesses is carefully monitored to help evaluate whether the project is on track to achieving its objectives.

Engineering

Engineering process areas cover the development and maintenance activities that are shared across engineering disciplines. The Engineering process areas were written using general engineering terminology so that any technical discipline involved in the product development process (e.g., software engineering, mechanical engineering) can use them for process improvement.

The Engineering process areas also integrate the processes associated with different engineering disciplines into a single product development process, supporting a product oriented process improvement strategy. Such a strategy targets essential business objectives rather than specific technical disciplines. This approach to processes effectively avoids the tendency toward an organizational "stovepipe" mentality.

The Engineering process areas apply to the development of any product or service in the development domain (e.g., software products, hardware products, services, processes).

The five Engineering process areas in CMMI-DEV are as follows:

- Product Integration (PI)
- Requirements Development (RD)
- Technical Solution (TS)
- Validation (VAL)
- Verification (VER)

Figure 4.5 provides a bird's-eye view of the interactions among the five Engineering process areas.

The Requirements Development process area identifies customer needs and translates these needs into product requirements. The set of product requirements is analyzed to produce a high-level conceptual solution. This set of requirements is then allocated to establish an initial set of product component requirements.

Other requirements that help define the product are derived and allocated to product components. This set of product and product component requirements clearly describes the product's performance, quality attributes, design features, verification requirements, etc., in terms the developer understands and uses.

The Requirements Development process area supplies requirements to the Technical Solution process area, where the requirements are converted into the product architecture, product component designs, and product components (e.g., by coding, fabrication). Requirements are also supplied to the Product Integration process area, where product components are combined and interfaces are verified to ensure that they meet the interface requirements supplied by Requirements Development.

The Technical Solution process area develops technical data packages for product components to be used by the Product Integration or Supplier Agreement Management process area. Alternative solutions are examined to select the optimum design based on established criteria. These criteria can be significantly different across

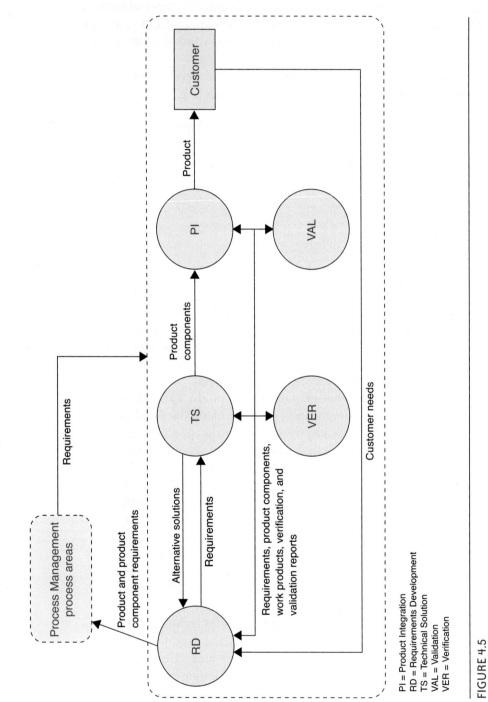

PI = Product Integration
RD = Requirements Development
TS = Technical Solution
VAL = Validation
VER = Verification

FIGURE 4.5
Engineering Process Areas

products, depending on product type, operational environment, performance requirements, support requirements, and cost or delivery schedules. The task of selecting the final solution makes use of the specific practices in the Decision Analysis and Resolution process area.

The Technical Solution process area relies on the specific practices in the Verification process area to perform design verification and peer reviews during design and prior to final build.

The Verification process area ensures that selected work products meet the specified requirements. The Verification process area selects work products and verification methods that will be used to verify work products against specified requirements. Verification is generally an incremental process, starting with product component verification and usually concluding with verification of fully assembled products.

Verification also addresses peer reviews. Peer reviews are a proven method for removing defects early and provide valuable insight into the work products and product components being developed and maintained.

The Validation process area incrementally validates products against the customer's needs. Validation can be performed in the operational environment or in a simulated operational environment. Coordination with the customer on validation requirements is an important element of this process area.

The scope of the Validation process area includes validation of products, product components, selected intermediate work products, and processes. These validated elements can often require reverification and revalidation. Issues discovered during validation are usually resolved in the Requirements Development or Technical Solution process area.

The Product Integration process area contains the specific practices associated with generating an integration strategy, integrating product components, and delivering the product to the customer.

Product Integration uses the specific practices of both Verification and Validation in implementing the product integration process. Verification practices verify the interfaces and interface requirements of product components prior to product integration. Interface verification is an essential event in the integration process. During product integration in the operational environment, the specific practices of the Validation process area are used.

Expanding Capabilities Across the "Constellations"

by Mike Phillips

As we are finishing the details of the current collection of process areas that span three CMMI constellations, this perspective is my opportunity to encourage "continuous thinking." My esteemed mentor as we began and then evolved the CMMI Product Suite was our Chief Architect, Dr. Roger Bate. Roger left us with an amazing legacy. He imagined that organizations could look at a collection of "process areas" and choose ones they might wish to use to facilitate their process improvement journey.

Maturity levels for organizations were acceptable, but not as interesting to him as being able to focus attention on a collection of process areas for business benefit. Small businesses have been the first to see the advantage of this approach, as they often find the full collection of process areas in any constellation daunting. An SEI report, "CMMI Roadmaps," describes some ways to construct thematic approaches to effective use of process areas from the CMMI for Development constellation. This report can be found on the SEI website at http://www.sei.cmu.edu/library/abstracts/reports/08tn010.cfm.

As we created the two new constellations, we took care to refer back to the predecessor collection of process areas in CMMI for Development. For example, in CMMI for Acquisition, we note that some acquisition organizations might need more technical detail in the requirements development effort than what we provided in Acquisition Requirements Development (ARD), and to "reach back" to CMMI-DEV's Requirements Development (RD) process area for more assistance.

In CMMI for Services, we suggest that the Service System Development (SSD) process area is useful when the development efforts are relatively limited, but the full engineering process area category in CMMI-DEV may be useful if major service systems are being created and delivered.

Now with three full constellations to use for process improvement, many additional "refer to" possibilities exist. With the release of the V1.3 Product Suite, we offer the option to declare satisfaction of any of the process areas from the CMMI portfolio. What are some of the more obvious expansions?

We have already mentioned two expansions: ARD using RD and SSD expanded to capture RD, TS, PI, VER, and VAL. What about situations in which most of the development is done outside the organization, but final responsibility for effective systems integration remains with your organization? Perhaps a few of the acquisition PAs would be useful beyond SAM. A simple start would be to investigate using SSAD and AM as a replacement for SAM to get the additional detailed help. And ATM might give some good technical assistance in monitoring the technical progress of the elements being developed by specific partners.

As we add the contributions of CMMI-SVC to the mix, several process areas offer more ways to expand. For example, in V1.2 of CMMI-DEV, we added informative material in Risk Management to address beforehand concerns about continuity of operations after some significant disruption occurs. Now, with CMMI-SVC, we have a full process area, Service Continuity (SCON), to provide robust coverage of continuity concerns. (And for those who need even more coverage, the SEI now has the Resilience Management Model (RMM) to give the greater attention that some financial institutions and similar organizations have expressed as necessary for their process improvement endeavors. For more, see http://www.cert.org/resilience/rmm.html.)

Another expansion worthy of consideration is to include the Service Systems Transition (SST) process area. Organizations that are responsible for development of new systems—and maintenance of existing systems until the new system can be brought to full capability—may find the practices contained in SST to be a useful expansion because the transition part of the product lifecycle has limited coverage in CMMI-DEV. In addition, CMMI-ACQ added two practices to PP and PMC to address planning for and monitoring transition into use, so the CMMI-ACQ versions of these two core process areas might couple nicely with SST.

A topic that challenged the development team for V1.3 was improved coverage of "strategy." Those of us with acquisition experience knew the criticality of an effective acquisition strategy to program success, so the practice was added to the CMMI-ACQ version of PP. In the CMMI-SVC constellation, Strategic Service Management (STSM) has the objective "to get the information needed to make effective strategic decisions about the set of standard services the organization maintains." With minor interpretation, this process area could assist a development organization in determining what types of development projects should be in its product development line. The SVC constellation authors also added a robust strategy establishment practice in the CMMI-SVC version of PP (Work Planning) to "provide the business framework for planning and managing the work."

Two process areas essential for service work were seriously considered for insertion into CMMI-DEV V1.3: Capacity and Availability Management (CAM) and Incident Resolution and Prevention (IRP). In the end, expansion of the CMMI-DEV constellation from 22 to 24 process areas was determined to be less valuable than continuing our efforts to streamline coverage. In any case, these two process areas offer another opportunity for the type of expansion I am exploring in this essay.

Those of you who have experienced appraisals have likely seen the use of target profiles that gather the collection of process areas to be examined. Often these profiles specifically address the necessary collections of process areas associated with maturity levels, but this need not be the case. With the release of V1.3, we have ensured that the reporting system (SCAMPI Appraisal System, or SAS) is robust enough to allow depiction of process areas from multiple CMMI constellations. As use of other architecturally similar SEI models, such as the RMM mentioned above as well as the People CMM, grow in use, we will be able to depict profiles using mixtures of process areas or even practices from multiple models, giving greater value to the process improvement efforts of a growing range of complex organizations.

Recursion and Iteration of Engineering Processes

Most process standards agree that there are two ways that processes can be applied. These two ways are called recursion and iteration.

Recursion occurs when a process is applied to successive levels of system elements within a system structure. The outcomes of one application are used as inputs to the next level in the system structure. For example, the verification process is designed to apply to the entire assembled product, the major product components, and even components of components. How far into the product you apply the verification process depends entirely on the size and complexity of the end product.

Iteration occurs when processes are repeated at the same system level. New information is created by the implementation of one process that feeds that information back into a related process. This new information typically raises questions that must be resolved before completing the processes.

For example, iteration will most likely occur between requirements development and technical solution. Reapplication of the processes can resolve the questions that are raised. Iteration can ensure quality prior to applying the next process.

Engineering processes (e.g., requirements development, verification) are implemented repeatedly on a product to ensure that these engineering processes have been adequately addressed before delivery to the customer. Further, engineering processes are applied to components of the product.

For example, some questions that are raised by processes associated with the Verification and Validation process areas can be resolved by processes associated with the Requirements Development or Product Integration process area. Recursion and iteration of these processes enable the project to ensure quality in all components of the product before it is delivered to the customer.

The project management process areas can likewise be recursive because sometimes projects are nested within projects.

Measurement Makes Improvement Meaningful

by David N. Card

Measurement is an essential component of engineering, management, and process improvement. CMMI defines measurement requirements in Measurement and Analysis, Project Planning, Project Monitoring and Control, Quantitative Project Management, Organizational Process Performance, and, to lesser degrees, in other process areas. Measurement and analysis are two of the five steps in the Six Sigma DMAIC cycle. Lean is based on the application of the mathematical principles of queuing theory to processes. Unless performance can be quantified in terms of productivity, quality, or cycle time, it is hard to gauge improvement, regardless of the improvement approach adopted.

An effective measurement and analysis program is essential to the long-term business success of CMMI users. Measurement is the mechanism by which an organization gains insight into its performance and confronts "goodness." A minimal measurement program may pass an appraisal but will limit the organization's opportunities for real improvement. Moreover, without meaningful feedback, a maturity level is not likely to be maintained.

What roles should measurement and analysis play in an organization? Measurement often is defined in terms of collecting data and thus is distinguished from analysis, the interpretation and use of data. Clearly, the collection of data must be driven by its intended use. As Mark Twain observed, "Data is like garbage. You better know what you are going to do with it, before you start collecting it." Four classes (or levels) of measurement users or decision-making processes may be defined. CMMI introduces these decision-making processes at different maturity levels. Each class of decision-making has a different focus, as described below:

- *Enterprise.* The long-term survival of the organization. The enterprise offers products and/or services in a market. Survival typically means maintaining or increasing profitability and market share. (Organizational Performance Management, a CMMI maturity level 5 process area.)
- *Process.* The efficiency and effectiveness of the organization's means of accomplishing work. The processes of a typical organization may include software engineering, information technology, marketing, and administration. (CMMI maturity levels 4 and 5.)
- *Project.* Realization of a specific product or service for a specific customer or class of customers. Projects use organizational processes and resources to produce products and/or services for the enterprise to market. (CMMI maturity levels 2 and 3.)
- *Product.* Resolution of the technical aspects of the product or service necessary to meet the customer's requirements. Projects manage the resources necessary to deliver the desired product or service. (CMMI maturity level 3.)

As indicated in the preceding descriptions, these areas of concern are inter-related. Moreover, measurement and analysis at all of these levels depend on many of the same sources of data. However, the level of detail and the manner in which the data is analyzed or reported for different purposes may vary.[1]

Measurement specialists often focus on the technical challenges of statistical analysis rather than addressing some of the human and social reasons why measurement systems sometimes fail. Many of

---

1. For a more detailed discussion, see D. Card, "A Practical Framework for Software Measurement and Analysis," Auerbach, *Systems Management Strategies*, October 2000.

these problems are common to organizational change initiatives. Three issues specific to measurement are as follows:

- The cost of data collection and processing is always visible, but the benefits of measurement are not. The benefits depend on what decisions are made based on the data. No decisions—no action—no benefits. Organizations must establish an action orientation.
- Measurement and analysis is new to many software and systems engineers and managers. Training and coaching in these new skills are essential to their successful implementation. As the scope of measurement increases with higher maturity, more sophisticated techniques must be mastered, making training even more critical.
- Measurement provides insight into performance. However, gaining and using that insight may be threatening to those whose performance is measured, and even to those who are just the messengers of performance information. Measurement systems must protect the participants.

All of these issues can, and have been, overcome. CMMI's Measurement and Analysis process area provides a good starting point for introducing measurement into an organization. Building on that with skills and techniques appropriate to the target maturity level and intended uses of measurement, as well as confronting the human issues that are sure to be encountered, facilitates the transition to management by fact, rather than opinion. Without an appropriate and effective measurement program, maturity levels are insignificant assertions.

Support

Support process areas cover the activities that support product development and maintenance. The Support process areas address processes that are used in the context of performing other processes. In general, the Support process areas address processes that are targeted toward the project and can address processes that apply more generally to the organization.

For example, Process and Product Quality Assurance can be used with all the process areas to provide an objective evaluation of the processes and work products described in all the process areas.

The five Support process areas in CMMI-DEV are as follows:

- Causal Analysis and Resolution (CAR)
- Configuration Management (CM)
- Decision Analysis and Resolution (DAR)
- Measurement and Analysis (MA)
- Process and Product Quality Assurance (PPQA)

Basic Support Process Areas

The Basic Support process areas address fundamental support functions that are used by all process areas. Although all Support process areas rely on the other process areas for input, the Basic Support process areas provide support functions that also help implement several generic practices.

Figure 4.6 provides a bird's-eye view of the interactions among the Basic Support process areas and with all other process areas.

The Measurement and Analysis process area supports all process areas by providing specific practices that guide projects and organizations in aligning measurement needs and objectives with a measurement approach that is used to support management information

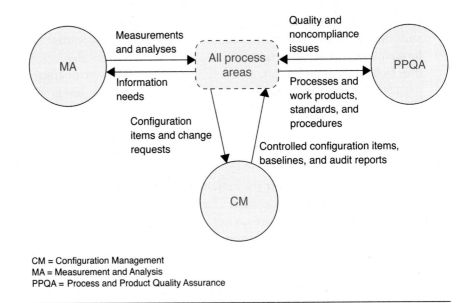

CM = Configuration Management
MA = Measurement and Analysis
PPQA = Process and Product Quality Assurance

FIGURE 4.6
Basic Support Process Areas

needs. The results can be used in making informed decisions and taking appropriate corrective actions.

The Process and Product Quality Assurance process area supports all process areas by providing specific practices for objectively evaluating performed processes, work products, and services against the applicable process descriptions, standards, and procedures, and ensuring that any issues arising from these reviews are addressed.

Process and Product Quality Assurance supports the delivery of high quality products and services by providing the project staff and all levels of management with appropriate visibility into, and feedback on, the processes and associated work products throughout the life of the project.

The Configuration Management process area supports all process areas by establishing and maintaining the integrity of work products using configuration identification, configuration control, configuration status accounting, and configuration audits. The work products placed under configuration management include the products that are delivered to the customer, designated internal work products, acquired products, tools, and other items that are used in creating and describing these work products.

Examples of work products that can be placed under configuration management include plans, process descriptions, requirements, design data, drawings, product specifications, code, compilers, product data files, and product technical publications.

Advanced Support Process Areas

The Advanced Support process areas provide the projects and organization with an improved support capability. Each of these process areas relies on specific inputs or practices from other process areas.

Figure 4.7 provides a bird's-eye view of the interactions among the Advanced Support process areas and with all other process areas.

Using the Causal Analysis and Resolution process area, project members identify causes of selected outcomes and take action to prevent negative outcomes from occurring in the future or to leverage positive outcomes. While the project's defined processes are the initial targets for root cause analysis and action plans, effective process changes can result in process improvement proposals submitted to the organization's set of standard processes.

The Decision Analysis and Resolution process area supports all the process areas by determining which issues should be subjected to a formal evaluation process and then applying a formal evaluation process to them.

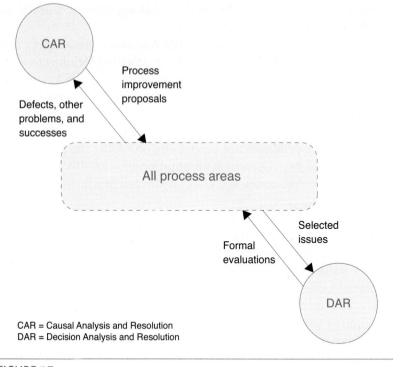

CAR = Causal Analysis and Resolution
DAR = Decision Analysis and Resolution

FIGURE 4.7
Advanced Support Process Areas

People, Process, Technology, and CMMI

by Gargi Keeni

Organizations that have been successful in their process improvement initiatives are known to have taken a holistic approach. Any discussion on process improvement would invariably emphasize the importance of addressing the people, process, and technology (PPT) triad. However, in reality, it is not so common to see synergy between the individuals or groups responsible for these PPT aspects in an organization. Synchronizing the goals of an individual or team with those of the organization is the key for any successful improvement program.

In the context of CMMI, this becomes more evident for the process areas whose activities would have an inherent conflict between individuals/teams priorities and the organization's priorities. Organizations may unknowingly amplify this conflict by having reward and recognition systems in which individual incentives and career goals are only tied to individual/team performance, thereby inhibiting realization of organizational goals.

Let's take an example of an organization that is trying to implement a Process and Product Quality Assurance (PPQA) process. PPQA is a process area at maturity level 2 whose purpose is to provide objective insight into processes and their associated work products.

Now consider each component of the PPT triad:

- *Process.* Though it may seem relatively simple to just define the processes that need to be implemented and with which projects are thus expected to comply, that alone is rarely sufficient to ensure that the intent for the process will be understood or achieved.

  Possible evidence for this is when individuals/teams work overtime to get records in place just before the compliance check is scheduled!

- *People.* Further probing might highlight the fact that an incentive system links the number of noncompliances to the performance of the project leader or project team. This linkage motivates the individual or team to spend nonvalue-adding effort just to ensure that the number of noncompliances is as low as possible.

  The reason for the noncompliance in the first place could have been any of the following:

  - The processes are not suitable for the activities done by the individuals/teams.
  - The process definition is too complicated to be followed.
  - The individuals/teams are not aware of the process and its intent.

  In this case, the organization cannot reap the benefits of the PPQA activities (because the team will "fake it" to "get by" the audit) unless it revisits its people practice of linking the number of noncompliances to the performance of an individual or team. In other words, the organization needs to promote an environment that encourages employee participation in identifying and reporting quality issues (which can include issues with the processes that have been defined as well as noncompliances), which is subpractice 1 of PPQA SP1.1.

- *Technology.* To obtain effective and timely conclusions with respect to the preceding reasons cited for possible noncompliance, organizations need to have systems for tracking and analyzing in near real time the noncompliances and the associated corrective actions. This tracking and analysis, in turn, will provide managers at all levels with appropriate visibility into the processes and work products. However, just procuring a tool for managing noncompliances without proper deployment of processes turns out to be counterproductive in most cases.

Here's what needs to be realized in the situation just described: Objectivity in PPQA evaluations is critical and can be achieved by both independence and the use of criteria; however, the credibility and motivation of the independent entity has a major impact on the quality of PPQA evaluations. In organizations where individuals from other teams conduct the PPQA activities, it is very important to ensure that the right individual is made available for the task. However, as experience says, the right people are usually not available unless the right motivation is provided. If individuals are always evaluated based on the work they do for their team, there is no motivation for them to provide any service external to the team. However, PPQA being a Support PA that runs across the organization, the organization needs to review its incentive measures to provide the right motivation for these activities which are beyond the individuals'/teams' current functions and performance. Incentives that are more fully aligned with organizational objectives will motivate early identification of noncompliances, which in turn will help identify possible problem areas in the processes that the organization is trying to deploy.

As you can see by the PPQA example, it is important to consider all three dimensions of people, process, and technology when addressing any of the activities described in the process areas in CMMI. The PPT impact becomes even more apparent for PAs at higher maturity levels, which have inherently built-in organizational perspectives irrespective of whether it is a large or small organization.

It is essential for an organization to provide an environment that fosters effective deployment of processes. Analysis of the outcome/results on a regular basis provides insights into the effectiveness of the processes and the changes required to meet business objectives.

The PAs at higher maturity levels often directly address people and technology in the practices. However, when implementing these practices, it is important to understand the natural relationships that exist to nurture these behaviors so that an organization can readily adapt to improvement and change, which is necessary in today's environment.

CHAPTER 5

USING CMMI MODELS

The complexity of products today demands an integrated view of how organizations do business. CMMI can reduce the cost of process improvement across enterprises that depend on multiple functions or groups to achieve their objectives.

To achieve this integrated view, the CMMI Framework includes common terminology, common model components, common appraisal methods, and common training materials. This chapter describes how organizations can use the CMMI Product Suite not only to improve their quality, reduce their costs, and optimize their schedules, but also to gauge how well their process improvement program is working.

The Role of Process Standards in Process Definition[†]

by James W. Moore

Suppose you decide to take a physics course at a university. Naturally, you want to get a good grade. You faithfully attend the lectures, read the textbooks, attend the lab sessions, do the homework, take the final examination, and hope for the best outcome. Alternatively, if you can find a willing instructor, you could ask the instructor for a copy of the final exam on the first day of the course. As time permits, you could figure out the answers to the questions and, by the end of the course, turn in your answers to the exam

---

[†] © 2010 The MITRE Corporation. All rights reserved.

[The author's affiliation with The MITRE Corporation is provided for identification purposes only, and is not intended to convey or imply MITRE's concurrence with, or support for, the positions, opinions or viewpoints expressed by the author.]

questions with a request for the corresponding grade. Which of these two approaches is the more effective way to learn physics? We'll return to this question at the end of this article.

There is a long tradition of prescriptive process definition standards, like DoD-Std-2167A, that were intended to tell the software developers what they must do to achieve an acceptable level of professional practice; one conformed to such a standard by implementing processes meeting all of its provisions.[1] In the last dozen or so years, that binary form of pass-fail evaluation has lost favor to a more graded approach of assessing the "maturity" or "capability" of the developer's processes. ISO/IEC 15504, Process Assessment (commonly called SPICE), describes this approach. ISO/IEC 15504 is "agnostic" with respect to the processes being employed. Methods conforming to the standard can be used to assess to any set of processes that are described in a particular stylized manner, called the process reference model. One such process reference model is provided by ISO/IEC/IEEE 12207, Software Lifecycle Processes. Another is provided by ISO/IEC/IEEE 15288, System Lifecycle Processes.

The 15504 standard is used in some nations, but CMMI may have greater recognition in others, especially the U.S. marketplace. Unlike 15504, CMMI provides a great deal of guidance regarding the definition of processes. The criteria that are applied to assess the processes implicitly specify practices that should be embedded in the developer's processes. So this begs the question of whether any other standards are needed for process definition. After all, why not simply implement processes meeting the CMMI criteria and be done with it?

There are four reasons why one should consider using process standards for defining an organization's processes: scope, suitability, communication, and robustness.

First, let's look at scope. Although CMMI is broad, it isn't broad enough for all possible uses. An obvious example is quality management. Although CMMI includes provisions addressing the quality of software products and systems, it does not address the organization-level quality management systems specified by ISO 9001, Quality management systems—Requirements. Because ISO

---

1. Because they were generally over prescriptive, these standards were often "tailored" by modifying their detailed provisions. Of course, conformance to a tailored standard always begs the question of whether the tailoring was done responsibly, or simply consisted of deleting all inconvenient provisions.

9001 conformance is regarded as highly important in many countries, multinational suppliers will find it appropriate to consider that standard in defining their processes—even software and system processes—related to quality. Although less prominent than ISO 9001, there are many other standards describing processes of various kinds. In particular situations, suppliers should consider the provisions of those standards.

The second reason for considering process standards is suitability. It should be obvious that not every organization needs the same set of processes. After all, every organization has some unique characteristics that cause it to differ from its competitors. That competitive advantage should be addressed in organizational processes so that the advantage is relevantly applied to every project of the organization—maintaining its competitive edge. Defining a set of organizational processes (e.g., for software and systems engineering) should consider a number of factors, including:

- Size of the organization
- The nature of the products and services provided by the organization
- The competitive structure of the relevant marketplace
- The nature of the competition
- The regulatory structure that is relevant, including regulatory requirements
- Customs, traditions, and regulation in the relevant industry sector
- The "culture" of the organization, including the degree of regimentation that the workforce will tolerate
- Organizational attitudes toward quality
- The amount of investment capital available for process definition and the extent to which it can be amortized over a base of projects
- The uniformity (or diversity) of anticipated project requirements
- The competitive advantages to be "captured" by the processes
- The form in which documentation (either paper or electronic) is to be captured, saved, and possibly delivered

All of these considerations, and many more, affect the definition of organizational processes, leading to the conclusion that the selection and implementation of cost-effective processes requires a different solution for every organization.

Of course, available process standards do not directly account for all of these factors. They simply provide alternatives to be considered in the overall process definition. In some cases, they describe specific practices that are important in regulatory environments—for example, the Modified Condition Decision Criteria (of RTCA DO-178B, Software Considerations in Airborne Systems and Equipment Certification) that is applied to the testing of avionics systems. More generally, they provide a starting point, a shortcut that allows the process definers to avoid a large volume of relatively straightforward decisions. Perhaps most importantly, they record a baseline of responsible practice, a "safety net," that is overlooked only at some risk.

The third reason for considering process standards is communication. Terminology in software engineering is notoriously vague and flexible—a sign of an emerging profession. This can lead to important misunderstandings: "Oh, when you paid me to 'implement' the software, you meant I should 'test' it also? I didn't include that in the price; you have to pay me extra for that!" Even the consideration of proposals is difficult without a baseline of terminology for comparing processes.

Suppose the buyer asks the supplier what sort of design review practices are performed by the supplier. One possible answer is to provide dozens of pages of proposal prose; another possible answer is for the supplier to say, "We use IEEE Std 1028, Software Reviews." The second answer has the advantage of being succinct, of being precise in terms of what is included, and of being generally accepted as responsible practice.[2] The international standards for lifecycle processes, ISO/IEC/IEEE 12207 and ISO/IEC/IEEE 15288, provide a comprehensive set of processes that span the lifecycles of software products and systems.

If a supplier states that its software development process conforms to that of 12207, a buyer knows the answer to a large number of pertinent questions. To pick only one example, the buyer would know that the software requirements, the architectural design, the detailed design, and the code will all be evaluated for feasibility of operation and maintenance—important downstream activities.

---

2. By the way, I avoid the term *best practice. Responsible practice* is as good as it gets with me. I simply don't believe that any single practice can be regarded as being the best in all possible situations. I believe that most organizations should strive to use responsible practices that are suited to their particular needs. —James W. Moore

The final reason for considering process standards is robustness. Reliance on a single source may lead to defining processes that are inadvertently oriented toward a particular concept of usage. Applying the processes in a different context may lead to unintended results. Despite best attempts at generality, it is impossible to anticipate all possible situations; so it is up to the process designer to consult multiple sources to find processes that are suitable for the particular organization.

The level of prescription is an important consideration here. Those who define processes (including the people who wrote CMMI) necessarily have to make a trade-off of generality versus specificity. Many very good practices were omitted from CMMI because they weren't generally applicable; and many were "watered down" to improve their generality. By consulting multiple sources, including multiple standards, process definers will find practices that are specifically suitable and effective in the intended context even though they were omitted from CMMI because they could not be generalized to the broad CMMI audience. Those who must practice at a more demanding level—e.g., developing safety-critical software—can supplement their baseline processes by applying standards that provide more detailed or stringent treatments of selected practices, e.g., IEEE Std 1012, Software Verification and Validation.

We are now ready to return to the original question of whether a person who wants to learn physics should sit through the course or ask for a copy of the final exam on the first day. The answer to the question: "It depends!" It depends on whether the goal is to gain a broad and useful understanding of physics or to get the highest possible grade with the least possible effort. In business, both answers are reasonable ones depending on the circumstances.

Applying this analogy to the subject at hand, we can conclude (with some cynicism) that if the organization's goal is to attain the highest possible CMMI rating with the smallest possible investment, it is probably appropriate to accept the final exam on the first day of the course—that is, to define a set of organizational processes that directly and straightforwardly address the evaluation criteria of CMMI. On the other hand, if the organization's goal is to define a set of organizational processes that are robust, descriptive, and suitable to the scope and circumstances of the organization—that is, to gain the intended advantages of process improvement—the organization should consult multiple sources, including process definition standards, select suitable ones, and use them as a baseline for defining a cost-effective solution to the organization's needs.

Adopting CMMI

Research has shown that the most powerful initial step to process improvement is to build organizational support through strong senior management sponsorship. To gain the sponsorship of senior management, it is often beneficial to expose them to the performance results experienced by others who have used CMMI to improve their processes [Gibson 2006].

For more information about CMMI performance results, see the SEI website at http://www.sei.cmu.edu/cmmi/research/results/.

The senior manager, once committed as the process improvement sponsor, must be actively involved in the CMMI-based process improvement effort. Activities performed by the senior management sponsor include but are not limited to the following:

* Influence the organization to adopt CMMI
* Choose the best people to manage the process improvement effort
* Monitor the process improvement effort personally
* Be a visible advocate and spokesperson for the process improvement effort
* Ensure that adequate resources are available to enable the process improvement effort to be successful

Given sufficient senior management sponsorship, the next step is establishing a strong, technically competent process group that represents relevant stakeholders to guide process improvement efforts [Ahern 2008, Dymond 2005].

For an organization with a mission to develop software-intensive systems, the process group might include those who represent different disciplines across the organization and other selected members based on the business needs driving improvement. For example, a systems administrator may focus on information technology support, whereas a marketing representative may focus on integrating customers' needs. Both members could make powerful contributions to the process group.

Once your organization decides to adopt CMMI, planning can begin with an improvement approach such as the IDEAL (Initiating, Diagnosing, Establishing, Acting, and Learning) model [McFeeley 1996]. For more information about the IDEAL model, see the SEI Website at http://www.sei.cmu.edu/library/abstracts/reports/96hb001.cfm.

Executive Responsibilities in Process Improvement

by Bill Curtis

We constantly hear that the primary reason process improvement programs fail is from lack of executive leadership. That said, those responsible for facilitating process improvement programs are hard-pressed to specify exactly what they expect from executives. Here are 12 critical actions executives should take to ensure the success of process improvement programs.

1. Take personal responsibility. Executives do not deliver systems to customers. Project managers deliver them. Executives build organizations that deliver systems to customers, and this responsibility cannot be delegated. At the core of Watts Humphrey's Process Maturity Framework that underlies CMMI is a unique model of organizational change and development. Because the responsibility for organizational transformation rests in the executive office, CMMI is a tool for executives to use in improving the performance of their organizations. CMMI will not only transform development practices, but also the organization's culture and the way business results are attained. Executives should not launch an improvement program until they are willing to become personally accountable for its success— or failure.

2. Set realistic goals. Executives must initiate process improvement with a clear statement of the issues driving change and the objectives to be achieved. Slogans such as "Level 2 in 2 years" do little more than reinforce the very behaviors that Level 2 was designed to eliminate. If the improvement objectives are unrealistic, the improvement program will be just one more of the organization's chaotic death march projects. Process improvement programs must model the behaviors that executives want the organization to adopt, especially plan-driven commitments. Schedules for attaining maturity levels should result from planning, not catchy slogans or bonus cycles. Rewards and bonuses should be based on accomplishing planned behavioral or performance improvements, rather than arbitrary dates for appraisal results.

3. Establish an improvement project. Process improvement must be conducted as a project. Executives must assign responsibility for managing the project, provide funding and resources,

approve improvement plans, review status reports, and measure results. The person assigned to lead the improvement project must be a strong role model for other project managers. Executives should ask frequent questions about project plans and the assumptions underlying them. The guidebooks, defined processes, measures, checklists, and other artifacts produced through process improvement are organizational assets. They should be treated as products, albeit for internal use, and be produced with the same project discipline used in producing any other product.

4. Manage change. How many initiatives can dance on the head of a project manager? Many organizations have multiple improvement programs underway simultaneously. In the initial stages of these programs, project managers are the people most affected and are often inundated with the number of changes expected. Executives must determine the amount of change the organization can absorb, prioritize the changes to be made, and shield the organization from improvement overkill. The good news is that some improvement programs such as Six Sigma and CMMI can be synergized, since they both evolved from the concepts initiated by Shewhart and Deming.

5. Align management. Process groups have no power to enforce improvements or change management behavior. If middle managers resist improvements, only executives can force them to align with the program. Executives must build consensus among managers on the objectives and tactics for improvement and hold them accountable for achieving improvement objectives. In particular, middle managers must develop the skills of the project or program managers who report to them. Management steering committees reporting to executives are one way to ensure middle and project managers share responsibility for improvement success.

6. Align incentives. Executives must ensure that incentives are aligned with improvement goals and do not send mixed messages about the behaviors the organization values. Incentives must shift from rewarding heroes to rewarding those whose sound practices avoid the need for heroes. Promotions should go to those who are strong role models of the behaviors the improvement program is trying to instill. Incentives must send a message that management values contributions to building a strong organization just as much as it values individual virtuosity.

7. Establish policies and empower assurance. Policies that merely regurgitate goals from CMMI process areas represent a lost opportunity for executives to communicate their expectations for behavior in their organizations. After policies are established, executives need visibility into compliance. Assurance groups have influence only to the extent that executives enforce policies and address noncompliance. However, the greatest value of assurance groups, and this is subtle in PPQA, is when they serve as mentors to project managers and technical staff on practices that support compliance. Consequently, assurance groups need to be staffed with competent developers and managers so that they are credible in transferring knowledge of best practices across the organization.

8. Involve customers. Unless customers understand how they will benefit from new practices, they may perceive the changes as making projects bureaucratic and inflexible. Consequently, project managers are often trapped in a conflict between their improvement objectives and the demands of their customers. Executives own the relationship with customers and must meet with their peers to explain the improvement strategy and how it will make the development organization a more reliable business partner. Involving customers in improving requirements practices is a good initial step for engaging them in the improvement program.

9. Involve developers. The Process Maturity Framework begins the empowerment of developers by involving them in estimating and planning at Level 2 and it increases their responsibility at each subsequent level. Executives must understand and encourage this cultural transition. They must also ensure that developers are involved in improvement activities because developers have the freshest knowledge of best practices. Developers are also more realistic about how much change they can absorb in an improvement cycle. The role of the process assurance groups is to assist managers and developers in identifying and deploying best practices.

10. Review status. Executives own the organization's commitments. They must approve external commitments and review progress in accomplishing them. Project reviews should not only focus on work status, but also on the progress being made in adopting improvements and of impending risks. Executives highlight their commitment through measurement and should add indicators of improvement progress and results to their

dashboards. Improvement measures should reflect that benefits accrue project by project, rather than in one big bang.

11. Replace laggards. The process group owns responsibility for assisting improvements with the innovators, early adopters, and early and late majority. Executives own the problem of laggards, especially if they are in management. For an improvement program to succeed, executives must be willing to remove even friends for failure to make progress. Successful organizational change programs often end up with different management teams than they started with.

12. Never relent. True leadership begins under stress. With all the pressures generated by demanding business schedules and cost cutting, executives must nevertheless stand firm in driving the improvements they know the organization must make. If they relent under pressure, the organization learns the art of excuses. The ultimate appraisal of maturity is determined by which practices the organization refuses to sacrifice under grinding pressure.

There are other responsibilities executives can assume in supporting process improvement. Nevertheless, these 12 have proven critical since they require executive authority and represent acts of leadership around which the improvement program can galvanize. Executives with little experience in process-disciplined environments are understandably concerned about risking their career on practices that have not contributed significantly in their advancement. Fortunately, there is a growing body of data and community of mature organizations to attest that faith in sensible CMMI-based improvement programs is well placed. It does not take leadership to follow the trodden path. It takes leadership to pursue the promise of new ways.

Your Process Improvement Program

Use the CMMI Product Suite to help establish your organization's process improvement program. Using the product suite for this purpose can be a relatively informal process that involves understanding and applying CMMI best practices to your organization. Or, it can be a formal process that involves extensive training, creation of a process improvement infrastructure, appraisals, and more.

Implementing Engineering Culture for Successful Process Improvement

by Tomoo Matsubara

As most early software professionals, I came from another professional area: mechanical engineering. While I worked at Hitachi's machine factory, which manufactured cranes, pumps, and bulldozers, the factory was in the midst of the Kaizen (i.e., improvement) movement that reduced direct and indirect costs and improved quality. Because the factory was an engineering community, all of the improvement activities were done in an engineering way. Engineers are very practical and don't decide anything without seeing, touching, and measuring things.

The typical problem-solving process used in this environment was to (1) identify problems at the factory floor or in front of real things and phenomena, (2) discuss presumable causes, and (3) conduct experiments and build prototypes.

For mechanical engineers, conducting experiments, measuring things, and drawing charts are a way of life. In this environment, to understand a problem and to observe the progress of improvement, they produced a lot of charts. For efficient and precise fabrication, they developed and applied jigs (i.e., tools used to create specific shapes) and then used small tools for specific fabrication. In some cases, a component with a complex shape, such as convoluted beams for a monorail, were impossible to fabricate without well-designed jigs.

The culture of the factory was very exciting. Designers and workers were friendly and interacted well together. Once a month, there were sports and cultural events such as a lunchtime (one hour) marathon, boat races, and musical concerts. Twice a year, there were safety-work related competitive games such as measuring distances, heights, and weights without using gauges, scales, or other measuring devices. Most of the games involved competition among divisions including design, fabrication, and raw materials (i.e., casting and welding). They were like the "constructive disorders" that Tom DeMarco and Tim Lister wrote about in "Peopleware."[3]

---

3. Tom DeMarco and Timothy Lister, *"Peopleware: Productive Projects and Teams,"* Dorset House, 1999.

After nine years at the machine factory, I moved to a computer factory in 1965. As the general manager of the development organization, I was responsible for developing a banking system. The development organization consisted of hardware makers, software developers, and service providers. I had to anticipate all the risks involved in such a development. One of the biggest potential problems I saw was meeting the systems' high-performance requirements.

To begin meeting these requirements, I provided a scheme that consisted of a series of dynamic steps. These steps were allocated to each of the development groups to use, and measures associated with each of these steps were defined. I performed a drastic triage on the requirements to meet time constraints. In the final stage of development, I had to deal with troubleshooting problems created as the result of being saddled with components developed by different organizations. The system was successfully delivered in 1969.

While I was in charge, I had to determine the causes of problems that occurred among these intricately interacting components and prioritize action items to address them. I learned much about system engineering and other fields of engineering from this task and other real-world experiences and thus became acquainted with a large number of talented individuals having differing expertise.

After a short stint working with banking systems management, I moved again to a software organization called the "software factory" in 1966 immediately after it was formed. It was named by Hitachi's then-CEO Mr. Komai since his philosophy was that software should be treated the same as other industrial products. When I started working at the software factory, it was a culture shock. Everything seemed to be different from the way the machine factory worked or the computer factory worked. I found no experiment-related approach to problem solving, and, in turn, there was minimal use of measurement, numbers, and charts. Designers boldly adopted new ideas and made decisions without using any experiments. Tools are rarely used. What most impressed me was that they didn't boast about their products and systems that they designed and developed.

When Hitachi created its software subsidiary, Hitachi Software Engineering (HSE), in 1970, I was asked to join and plan for its operation. It was just two years later that the term software engineering was coined as a new engineering field at a NATO conference. At that time, HSE initiated its software development with about 200 programmers who had been working at the software factory. These programmers were scattered on multiple projects in manpower contracts with Hitachi. Because nobody had project management skills and experience, "death march" projects were rampant. Top management worried about the company's survival. While we were coping with these incessant problems, we were speculating how to eliminate root causes of problems. Eventually, the company improved its practices enough to deserve to call what it was doing "software engineering."

It was obvious that we needed to train project managers and engineers to give them the power to detect, control, and resolve problems. To do this, management (including me) tried to create a culture of self-reliance, engineering attitude, and systematic thinking. The first thing we did was to better align the people. We gathered the people who were scattered onto various projects and grouped them into teams that were headed by fledgling HSE project managers. Then, I provided these project managers with three types of charts for them to use and trained them how to plot current status of the project on the charts weekly. This approach allowed us to see the project's status and its deviation from target curves for schedule, quality, and cost from a controllability point of view (you can see some of these charts in Tom DeMarco's classic book,[4] *Controlling Software Projects*, and our papers[5]). This idea is based on my belief that most people spontaneously act to take control if he or she realizes the situation. We trained the project managers not only how to plot status on the charts, but also what typically is going on in the project when specific curve patterns appeared. This strategy also succeeded and within a few years we achieved profitable, punctual, and higher quality projects.

Besides these charts, I introduced a lot of mechanisms and systems to help attack problems. I introduced a tool proposal system, borrowed from the idea of applying jigs that I mentioned earlier. We also introduced war game competitions on coding within the software factory. The primary principles behind these ideas are very simple: First, we observed real processes in real projects (i.e., don't decide anything without observation). Second, take an engineering

---

4. Tom DeMarco, "Controlling Software Projects, Management, Measurement & Estimation," Yourdon Inc., 1982.

5. D. Tajima and T. Matsubara, "The Computer Software Industry in Japan," *IEEE Computer*, Vol. 14, no. 5 (May 1981), pp. 89–96.

attitude to deal with any and all phenomena. Finally, think systematically and build-in feedback mechanisms to lead to steady and stable improvement (i.e., all the principles that I experienced at the machine and computer factories). About 30 years after HSE was created, its five divisions achieved CMMI maturity level 3 in 2002 and 2003, and one of them achieved maturity level 5 in 2004. It was one of the earliest such achievements in the world.

Software process is based on software engineering, which is a branch of engineering. However, when I visited some software organizations, I used to be surprised that they lacked engineering expertise as part of software engineering to deal with problems. Developing software requires a complex system in which human beings are critical elements. Consequently, I believe that we must implement appropriate mechanisms for continuous improvement.

Currently, many organizations are coping with integrated process improvement that includes the development of software, hardware, and other related work. To streamline integrated process improvement, an engineering attitude and system-level thinking are common and critical keys.

Selections that Influence Your Program

You must make three selections to apply CMMI to your organization for process improvement:

1. Select a part of the organization.
2. Select a model.
3. Select a representation.

Selecting the projects to be involved in your process improvement program is critical. If you select a group that is too large, it may be too much for the initial improvement effort. The selection should also consider organizational, product, and work homogeneity (i.e., whether the group's members all are experts in the same discipline, whether they all work on the same product or business line, and so on).

Selecting an appropriate model is also essential to a successful process improvement program. The CMMI-DEV model focuses on activities for developing quality products and services. The CMMI-ACQ model focuses on activities for initiating and managing the acquisition of products and services. The CMMI-SVC model focuses on activities for providing quality services to the customer and end users. When selecting a model, appropriate consideration should be given to the primary focus of the organization and projects, as well as to the processes necessary to satisfy business objectives. The lifecycle processes (e.g., conception, design, manufacture, deployment, operations, maintenance, disposal) on which an organization concentrates should also be considered when selecting an appropriate model.

Select the representation (capability or maturity levels) that fits your concept of process improvement. Regardless of which you choose, you can select nearly any process area or group of process areas to guide improvement, although dependencies among process areas should be considered when making such a selection.

As process improvement plans and activities progress, other important selections must be made, including whether to use an appraisal, which appraisal method should be used, which projects should be appraised, how training for staff should be secured, and which staff members should be trained.

CMMI Models

CMMI models describe best practices that organizations have found to be productive and useful to achieving their business objectives. Regardless of your organization, you must use professional judgment when interpreting CMMI best practices for your situation, needs, and business objectives.

This use of judgment is reinforced when you see words such as "adequate," "appropriate," or "as needed" in a goal or practice. These words are used for activities that may not be equally relevant in all situations. Interpret these goals and practices in ways that work for your organization.

Although process areas depict the characteristics of an organization committed to process improvement, you must interpret the process areas using an in-depth knowledge of CMMI, your organization, the business environment, and the specific circumstances involved.

As you begin using a CMMI model to improve your organization's processes, map your real world processes to CMMI process areas. This mapping enables you to initially judge and later track your organization's level of conformance to the CMMI model you are using and to identify opportunities for improvement.

To interpret practices, it is important to consider the overall context in which these practices are used and to determine how well the practices satisfy the goals of a process area in that context. CMMI models do not prescribe nor imply processes that are right for any organization or project. Instead, CMMI describes minimal criteria necessary to plan and implement processes selected by the organization for improvement based on business objectives.

CMMI practices purposely use nonspecific phrases such as "relevant stakeholders," "as appropriate," and "as necessary" to accommodate the needs of different organizations and projects. The specific needs of a project can also differ at various points in its life.

Interpreting CMMI When Using Agile Approaches

CMMI practices are designed to provide value across a range of different situations and thus are stated in general terms. Because CMMI does not endorse any particular approach to development, little information that is approach-specific is provided. Therefore, those who don't have prior experience implementing CMMI in situations similar to the one they are now in may find interpretation non-intuitive.

To help those who use Agile methods to interpret CMMI practices in their environments, notes have been added to selected process areas. These notes are added, usually in the introductory notes, to the following process areas in CMMI-DEV: CM, PI, PMC, PP, PPQA, RD, REQM, RSKM, TS, and VER.

All of the notes begin with the words, "In Agile environments" and are in example boxes to help you to easily recognize them and remind you that these notes are examples of how to interpret practices and therefore are neither necessary nor sufficient for implementing the process area.

Multiple Agile approaches exist. The phrases "Agile environment" and "Agile method" are shorthand for any development or management approach that adheres to the *Manifesto for Agile Development* [Beck 2001].

Such approaches are characterized by the following:

- Direct involvement of the customer in product development
- Use of multiple development iterations to learn about and evolve the product
- Customer willingness to share in the responsibility for decisions and risk

Many development and management approaches can share one or more of these characteristics and yet not be called "Agile." For example, some teams are arguably "Agile" even though the term Agile is not used. Even if you are not using an Agile approach, you might still find value in these notes.

Be cautious when using these notes. Your ultimate interpretation of the process area should fit the specifics of your situation, including your organization's business, project, work group, or team objectives, while fully meeting a CMMI process area's goals and practices. As mentioned earlier, the notes should be taken as examples and are neither necessary nor sufficient to implementing the process area.

Some general background and motivation for the guidance given on Agile development approaches are found in the SEI technical note *CMMI or Agile: Why Not Embrace Both!* [Glazer 2008].

Process Improvement in a Small Company

by Khaled El Emam

In this brief perspective, I will describe how a small company implemented maturity level 2 and 3 processes of a CMMI Staged model. In this case, both the organization (30 staff members) and the organizational unit developing software (a 10-member software development group and a five-member quality assurance group) were small.

Context

TrialStat Corporation develops software used in clinical trials of drug development. A number of FDA regulations apply to both the software and the processes used to develop and maintain that software. Because the software is used to collect and store sensitive personal health information, the security of the application is critical and is usually included in the scope of regulatory audits.

Implementing an Iterative Process

Because of competitive pressures, the release cycle for the application had to be short. A decision was made to adopt an Agile methodology, which promised rapid releases—a release cycle lasting three weeks or less.

At the outset, the three-week release cycle created many problems and resulted in rapid burnout of the development team. The company was at risk of losing key developers, who were unwilling to work overtime and weekends to maintain the rapid release cycle. The short cycle also required curtailing many requirements analysis activities and minimizing quality assurance of the product—both of which were unacceptable.

The development team then experimented with increasing the release interval. After a few attempts, it was decided that a three-month interval was sufficient. This interval was short enough to address the rapidly changing business needs, but long enough to avoid some of the problems encountered with the shorter interval. The longer interval resulted in a development team that was not over-burdened, early and sufficient requirements analysis work, and effective quality assurance.

This process demonstrated that there is no inconsistency between using CMMI and implementing an Agile development process with short release cycles. In fact, it was an advantage to implement process improvements within this framework.

Introducing CMMI Practices Iteratively

Because of the regulated nature of the company's business, a strong process focus (OPD) was necessary from the start. Standard operating procedures documenting all of the engineering and business processes were developed at the same time as project management practices were being implemented. Regular internal audits (PPQA) ensured process compliance.

Because of TrialStat's small size, there was no difference between organizational and project procedures. Training capabilities were not developed in-house, but were outsourced. However, training plans and records were maintained for all staff as part of the company's regulatory requirements (OT).

The iterative development process enabled the continuous introduction of new project practices (in the Project Management, Engineering, and Support process areas), and rapid feedback on their effectiveness. Each iteration represented an opportunity to introduce new processes, a new technology, or expertise (e.g., an individual with specialized skills). After three months, it was possible to determine whether the intervention succeeded and had the desired impact. If it did, it was kept for subsequent iterations. Those that caused problems were either adjusted or eliminated.

This mode of introducing changes imposed some constraints. The interventions could not be large; the development team had to learn, master, and apply them well enough to provide feedback. Therefore, new practices had to be introduced gradually. For example, when peer reviews were introduced, they initially focused only on requirements. Only one or two interventions could be introduced in each iteration. If there were too many interventions, the development team could not focus on delivering features.

Formal CMMI-based process appraisals were not utilized. However, audits against FDA regulations and guidelines were commonly performed by third parties and clients to ensure compliance.

Measurement and Decision Making

The collection and use of metrics for decision making (MA) started from the very beginning of the project, and was subsequently expanded in a series of iterations. First, data on post-release defects were collected. This data was necessary to manage and prioritize defect correction activities and resources. After that system was in place, the metrics related to the ability to meet schedule targets were collected.

Scope management was the next issue. Because the delivery date of each iteration was fixed, flexibility involved controlling the scope. Features scheduled for each iteration were sized for a three-month cycle. In some cases, features were split and implemented over multiple releases. The challenge was coming up with an appropriate approach to measuring the size of the requirements early. Currently, using the number of use cases to measure the size of requirements has worked well in this environment.

The measurement of size and complexity became the subsequent focus of measurement. As the system grew, it became critical to manage its size and complexity. One approach used was to refactor specific parts of the system to reduce complexity.

Lessons Learned

There were surprisingly few fundamental changes needed to apply CMMI in a regulated environment. Many of the practices required in larger settings still applied. Because the company operates in a regulated environment, executive and investor support for process improvement existed from the outset. Therefore, in a different environment, additional effort may be required to obtain such support.

The iterative approach to implementing process improvements allowed the organization to incrementally and continuously improve its practices, and provided a rapid feedback mechanism to evaluate process changes. As more metrics are collected, it will become possible to quantitatively evaluate the improvements.

Process documentation proved helpful for this small organization, making it easier to integrate new staff and ensure that they contributed sooner. Without that documentation, corporate growth would have been more painful. The people typically attracted to a small organization are not necessarily process oriented. Process documentation contributed to establishing clear ground rules for new staff and enforcing a process-oriented corporate culture.

Requirements development and requirements management processes ensured predictability. These processes were addressed early in the improvement effort and served as a foundation for other engineering processes. For a company in the early stages of market penetration, it is critical that the requirements are right for each iteration.

Measurement began, and was needed, from the start. As the organization's practices matured, the types of things that were measured changed, as did the types of decisions made based on that data.

The experience of TrialStat has demonstrated that CMMI can work well in a small organizational setting. Process improvement in a small setting requires a gradual and incremental approach to introducing change to ensure that the organization is not overburdened with an amount of change that affects its ability to deliver its product. A pure Agile approach did not seem to work well; however, with some modification and in combination with CMMI, some Agile practice could be of benefit to the organization.

Using CMMI Appraisals

Many organizations find value in measuring their progress by conducting an appraisal and earning a maturity level rating or a capability level achievement profile. These types of appraisals are typically conducted for one or more of the following reasons:

- To determine how well the organization's processes compare to CMMI best practices and identify areas where improvement can be made
- To inform external customers and suppliers about how well the organization's processes compare to CMMI best practices
- To meet the contractual requirements of one or more customers

Appraisals of organizations using a CMMI model must conform to the requirements defined in the *Appraisal Requirements for CMMI (ARC)* [SEI 2011b] document. Appraisals focus on identifying improvement opportunities and comparing the organization's processes to CMMI best practices.

Appraisal teams use a CMMI model and ARC-conformant appraisal method to guide their evaluation of the organization and their reporting of conclusions. The appraisal results are used (e.g., by a process group) to plan improvements for the organization.

Appraisal Requirements for CMMI

The *Appraisal Requirements for CMMI (ARC)* document describes the requirements for several types of appraisals. A full benchmarking appraisal is defined as a *Class A* appraisal method. Less formal methods are defined as *Class B* or *Class C* methods. The ARC document was designed to help improve consistency across appraisal methods and to help appraisal method developers, sponsors, and users understand the tradeoffs associated with various methods.

Depending on the purpose of the appraisal and the nature of the circumstances, one class may be preferred over the others. Sometimes self assessments, initial appraisals, quick-look or mini appraisals, or external appraisals are appropriate; at other times a formal benchmarking appraisal is appropriate.

A particular appraisal method is declared an ARC Class A, B, or C appraisal method based on the sets of ARC requirements that the method developer addressed when designing the method.

More information about the ARC is available on the SEI website at http://www.sei.cmu.edu/cmmi/tools/appraisals/.

SCAMPI Appraisal Methods

The SCAMPI A appraisal method is the generally accepted method used for conducting ARC Class A appraisals using CMMI models. The *SCAMPI A Method Definition Document* (MDD) defines rules for ensuring the consistency of SCAMPI A appraisal ratings [SEI 2011a]. For benchmarking against other organizations, appraisals must ensure consistent ratings. The achievement of a specific maturity level or the satisfaction of a process area must mean the same thing for different appraised organizations.

The SCAMPI family of appraisals includes Class A, B, and C appraisal methods. The SCAMPI A appraisal method is the officially recognized and most rigorous method. It is the only method that can result in benchmark quality ratings. SCAMPI B and C appraisal methods provide organizations with improvement information that is less formal than the results of a SCAMPI A appraisal, but nonetheless helps the organization to identify improvement opportunities.

More information about SCAMPI methods is available on the SEI website at http://www.sei.cmu.edu/cmmi/tools/appraisals/.

Appraisal Considerations

Choices that affect a CMMI-based appraisal include the following:

- CMMI model
- Appraisal scope, including the organizational unit to be appraised, the CMMI process areas to be investigated, and the maturity level or capability levels to be appraised
- Appraisal method
- Appraisal team leader and team members
- Appraisal participants selected from the appraisal entities to be interviewed
- Appraisal outputs (e.g., ratings, instantiation-specific findings)
- Appraisal constraints (e.g., time spent on site)

The SCAMPI MDD allows the selection of predefined options for use in an appraisal. These appraisal options are designed to help organizations align CMMI with their business needs and objectives.

CMMI appraisal plans and results should always include a description of the appraisal options, model scope, and organizational scope selected. This documentation confirms whether an appraisal meets the requirements for benchmarking.

For organizations that wish to appraise multiple functions or groups, the integrated approach of CMMI enables some economy of scale in model and appraisal training. One appraisal method can provide separate or combined results for multiple functions.

The following appraisal principles for CMMI are the same as those principles used in appraisals for other process improvement models:

- Senior management sponsorship[6]
- A focus on the organization's business objectives
- Confidentiality for interviewees
- Use of a documented appraisal method
- Use of a process reference model (e.g., a CMMI model)
- A collaborative team approach
- A focus on actions for process improvement

---

6. Experience has shown that the most critical factor influencing successful process improvement and appraisals is senior management sponsorship.

CMMI Related Training

Whether your organization is new to process improvement or is already familiar with process improvement models, training is a key element in the ability of organizations to adopt CMMI. An initial set of courses is provided by the SEI and its Partner Network, but your organization may wish to supplement these courses with its own instruction. This approach allows your organization to focus on areas that provide the greatest business value.

The SEI and its Partner Network offer the introductory course, *Introduction to CMMI for Development*. The SEI also offers advanced training to those who plan to become more deeply involved in CMMI adoption or appraisal—for example, those who will guide improvement as part of a process group, those who will lead SCAMPI appraisals, and those who will teach the *Introduction to CMMI for Development* course.

Current information about CMMI related training is available on the SEI website at http://www.sei.cmu.edu/training/.

Improving Industrial Practice

by Hans-Jürgen Kugler

How many software products have a design that can be maintained over the lifetime of the product? How many have a design that exhibits elegance and embodies the principles of good software engineering, as for instance, laid down in Dave Parnas' seminal 1972 paper?[7] How many projects can truly trace the relationship between customer requirements and the features that they are implementing? We now have the second or even third generation of developers—depending on your viewpoint—contributing to or suffering in the software crisis. Do we ever learn? The answer cannot only come from the developer community.

The recent TechRepublic Live 2010 Conference[8] asked, "Buggy Software: Why do we accept it?" The answers made a clear distinction between IT software and other products (e.g., automobiles),

7. D. L. Parnas, "On the Criteria to Be Used in Decomposing Systems into Modules," Communication of the ACM, 15, no. 12 (1972), pp. 1053–1058.

8. TechRepublic Live 2010: The Changing Face of IT conference, Louisville, Kentucky, 30 June to 2 July 2010.

with IT software suffering from a continuous feature increase irrespective of the dangers of increased complexity. This situation does not hold only for the end consumer market, but also for enterprise IT. Mies van der Rohe—"less is more"—must be turning in his grave. Numbers of features are used as apparent market differentiators, since they are easily highlighted. It was even suggested that the user community of the IT movement showed the same signs of a Stockholm Syndrome[9] that hostages may develop.

In a market that does not value product qualities other than cost, it is difficult to develop the urge for quality initiatives. Discipline in *consequently applying known good practices* is often seen as interfering with the time and cost dimensions. A twisted version of Crosby's "quality is free" statement is what seems to drive the actions: There is rarely time to do it right, but always time to do it again.

However, not only IT systems contain software. "Embedded Software Rules"[10] is an article that discusses how software is everywhere: from shavers and most kitchen equipment to airplanes and automobiles. In the automotive industry, 80% to 90% of all in-vehicle innovations are software-driven. Software is the "glue" between functional groups inside and outside the vehicle, but at a cost: 50 to 100 interconnected special purpose computers cooperate in a vehicle running software load measuring in the order of 10^7 lines of code and many thousand (interdependent) calibration parameters. "The *dynaxity* is actually increasing exponentially," according to Prof. Heinecke, CEO of BMW Car IT,[11] where dynaxity is the compound effect of dynamics of change (in market and technology) and complexity of the system under development. The automotive industry is a competitive market, and a market governed by product warranty legislation. Many of the functions of a vehicle are safety relevant, and disciplined and traceable engineering is required.

If the innovative capability of a whole market is affected, individual improvement efforts by companies, however large they may be, are not sufficient. The whole value-creation network needs to be addressed. Many automotive companies have their own strategic improvement initiatives, such as Bosch,[12] with significant positive

---

9. Stockholm Syndrome, Wikipedia, July 2010.

10. S. Ferber, H.-J. Kugler, Robert Bosch GmbH, and KUGLER MAAG CIE GmbH, "Embedded Software Rules," White Paper, 2006.

11. H. Heinecke, "Innovation Development and Community Sources. The Survival Strategy," International SPICE Days, June 2010, Stuttgart.

12. T. Wagner, Robert Bosch GmbH, "Bringing Software on the Road," SEPG 2004, Orlando, Florida, March 2004.

effect.[13] However, industry-wide initiatives are also needed. The automotive industry association (Verband deutscher Automobilindustrie, VDA)[14] issued guidelines, and a software initiative (HIS) was formed by the OEMs.[15] The automotive OEMs focus on the engineering quality of the development process at supplier organisations.

Development projects at suppliers are appraised with respect to process maturity, and the results allow the OEM in question to manage risks better, to develop joint improvement actions, and to increase the urgency and importance of process improvement in the supplier organisation. The model chosen by the HIS is based on "Automotive SPICE"[16] an adaptation of ISO 15504, which is— whilst not equivalent—at least compatible with the continuous representation of CMMI.[17]

CMMI remains the approach of choice for many organisational improvement programmes. Results show that the overall strategy "improve a whole industry" does actually work: whilst software in the early 2000s caused many a driver to resort to walking, these incidents have decreased while process maturity increased[18] and while dynaxity climbed significantly. Dr. Weißbrich, Volkswagen, argued that the active and passive safety features of vehicles show a statistically relevant correlation with the significantly reduced road deaths in Germany.[19] These safety features are realised in software, of course.

In the past, the automotive industry has focussed on its traditional V-shaped iterative development processes, with projects and organisational line function organised in a matrix fashion. Interdependence of projects and the fact that project acquisition, launching, and tear down ("close out") are very dynamic means that stable

---

13. H.-J. Kugler et al., "Critical Success Factors for Software Process Improvement at Bosch GS," Electronic Systems for Vehicles, 11th International Congress, VDI, Baden-Baden, 2003.

14. Verband deutsche Automobilindustrie (German Association of Automotive Industry), VDA Volume 13, Development of Software-Driven Systems – Requirements for Processes and Products, 2004.

15. HIS – Herstellerinitiative Software (OEM Software Initiative by Audi, BMW, Daimler, Porsche and Volkswagen), www.automotive-his.de.

16. Automotive SPICE, www.automotive-his.de.

17. K. Hörmann, "Comparison of CMMI and ISO 15504," KUGLER MAAG CIE White Paper.

18. L. Dittmann, Nutzen von SPICE aus der Sicht eines OEMs, Volkswagen AG, IAA Workshop, Frankfurt, September 2005.

19. Weißbrich, "Spicy Cars—the Value of Automotive SPICE to the German Automotive Industry," International SPICE Days, Stuttgart, June 2010.

teams are more a wish than a reality. Many companies hoped that maturity levels 3 and beyond would provide stability to the organisation, and therefore provide a respite from constant change. *Dynaxity* plays havoc with this. The ability to change, to flexibly adapt to new context conditions, and still run disciplined and traceable processes leading to high-quality products is the market differentiator today.

Model-based development is the mainstay of automotive development methods,[20] but Agile development and Agile project management, Lean and Six Sigma techniques are increasingly used within the context of process improvement programmes, and used with good results, as expected.[21]

No doubt the automotive industry will continue with improving industrial practice. It needs to, in the light of what Lero[22] calls *evolving critical systems*.[23] The market mechanisms enforce that. Open tool platforms adapted to these needs are beginning to take shape[24] and will strengthen consistent application of good practices.

Can the same principles also be applied to different markets or industry domains—for example, medical devices or even ultraportable netbooks? The medical devices market may stand a chance to follow suit, since product warranty legislation applies here too, and since deployment is regulated—and the process plays an important part in the deployment decision. Importance and urgency must be *felt* in a market; only then will its value-creation network exhibit a willingness to change. The pressure of community-based software development on traditional software development may help,[25] provided the rift that exists between many proponents of CMMI and many of those involved in community-based software can be reconciled. In my opinion, this is just a question of time, because the evidence of compatibility exists.

Maybe this is even a moot argument. Experience with the "software car" firmly positions software to be *the* innovation driver. No

---

20. AUTOSAR, www.autosar.org.

21. B. Boehm and R. Turner, "Balancing Agility and Discipline," Addison-Wesley, 7th printing, October 2009.

22. Lero, "Research Area: Evolving Critical Systems," The Irish Software Engineering Research Centre, http://www.lero.ie/research/researchareas/evolvingcriticalsystems.html.

23. L. Coyle et al., "Evolving Critical Systems," *IEEE Computer*, May 2010.

24. B. Lange, "Eclipse auf Rädern," iX 01/2010.

25. H.-J. Kugler, "Open Source Teams entwickeln schneller," Automobil-Elektronik, Dec. 2005.

other "material" has such potential and "weird" (nonNewtonian) properties. Quantum mechanics is the only thing that comes close.[26] Maybe Tom DeMarco was right when he wrote about the end of software engineering:

> Consistency and predictability are still desirable, but they haven't ever been the most important things. . . . We've tortured ourselves over our inability to finish a software project on time and on budget. But . . . this never should have been the supreme goal. The more important goal is transformation, creating software that changes the world or that transforms a company or how it does business. We've been rather successful at transformation, often while operating outside our control envelope.[27]

A very valid point, I find. In this case, the two sides have nothing to argue. Organisational capability, good processes, and individual competence would still be required to learn and improve in achieving this transformation. Heisenberg's uncertainty principle may also prevent us from *objectively controlling* software and its development, because there is no objectivity. But this state does not prevent us from building ecosystems on software platforms that flourish and change the world.

Either way, the future of process improvement, and of the CMMI, looks bright. There is a lot to be done. Let us begin.

---

26. H.-J. Kugler, "What Is Software? An Excursion into Software Physics" Workshop, KUGLER MAAG CIE GmbH, July 2008.

27. T. DeMarco, "Software Engineering – An Idea Whose Time Has Come and Gone?" Viewpoints, *IEEE Software*, June/July 2009.

CHAPTER 6

ESSAYS AND CASE STUDIES

For the third edition of this book, we asked contributors to write short case studies and essays instead of one large case study. The case studies are an excellent mix of experiences involving a variety of organizations and contexts.

Case Studies

The following three case studies each have a unique perspective on using CMMI for Development. The first focuses on how to use the model to achieve maturity level 2 and describes the lessons learned when a process improvement project can change course to achieve its objectives. The second case study follows the experience of an organization that uses CMMI over a long period of time and the competitive advantages it enjoys. The third describes and final case study describes how combining the use of CMMI for Development and Lean Six Sigma can accelerate and improve process improvement.

Switching Tracks: Finding the Right Way to Get to Maturity Level 2

by Heather Oppenheimer and Steve Baldassano

When your customer contract requires that your "software development process must be CMMI Level 2," there's a right way and a wrong way to go about meeting that demand. KNORR Brake tried both ways and has the scars and the rewards to show for it. This is the story of how a very small organization first headed down the wrong track then changed direction—resulting in a successful maturity level 2 appraisal less than nine months later. KNORR Brake Corporation supplies pneumatic and hydraulic braking systems, air conditioning equipment (HVAC), and door operators, as well as repair, overhaul, and maintenance services, for all types of mass transit rail vehicles, including Metro, Light Rail, High-Speed Trains, Commuter Rail, and Monorail. Key characteristics of KNORR Brake products include high reliability, safety, integrated operations and communications, and specialized functionality not available from other vendors.

Of about 250 employees, fewer than 30 are involved in systems and software engineering; the others are employed in the manufacturing facility. Each software project involves one or two highly experienced electrical engineers who develop customized embedded software that is integrated with the hardware at the systems level.

KNORR Brake has maintained ISO-9001-2000 registration since 1994 and must also adhere to IRIS (International Railway Industry Standard) and follow the quality management standards of its parent company, KNORR-Bremse.

The Wrong Route

With such a strong quality management system in place, when a customer required "CMMI Level 2," we thought it would be easy, only requiring the addition of a few new artifacts. No one expected any significant gaps, but if gaps were found, everyone assumed there would be an opportunity to fix minor issues and still achieve the level. Unfortunately, this misunderstanding resulted in a SCAMPI A appraisal that was an expensive way to discover that the organization was rated "mud-sucking, bottom-dwelling Level 1." It also cost the goodwill and enthusiasm of many of the people involved.

Based on our assumption that little or no preparation would be needed, we scheduled our SCAMPI A appraisal almost immediately. Several managers and engineers went to the SEI-authorized Introduction to CMMI course so they could learn what small additions CMMI required them to make to the current quality management system, as well as to meet the requirements for participating as appraisal team members. However, the course examples and model informative material were not very relevant to the world of embedded software and we were still confused about what the model required. Based on the course information and advice from our lead appraiser, we put in place some new processes and procedures, even though none of them provided any value to the business. People were willing to use these new "CMMI processes," but considered them to be useless overhead.

Assuming that all lead appraisers are equivalent, KNORR Brake hired the same lead appraiser who was working with several other subcontractors of the customer. Unfortunately, although he was very experienced and knowledgeable, the lead appraiser tried to assess our implementation of CMMI practices as if KNORR Brake was a large software application development organization—not a group of very small teams developing embedded software.

Although the customer contract specified that "software development must be CMMI Level 2," we assumed that the entire organization would need to comply with the CMMI standard—as if it were ISO or IRIS. As a result, the entire organization, including systems engineering and manufacturing as well as software engineering, was included in the scope of the appraisal. The large scope increased the duration and cost of the appraisal and made it more difficult to find the right evidence of implementation for each practice. At the same time, the areas the customer really cared about were not appraised.

Even though we weren't trying to improve any processes beyond adding some documents, the staff spent hundreds of unplanned hours just preparing for the appraisal, doing things like collecting artifacts. Based on our understanding of the SCAMPI A requirements for "objective evidence," the team wrongly assumed that each practice required at least two unique pieces of evidence; they copied and stored hundreds of documents in Practice Folders within Process Area Directories. Most of the artifacts collected were useless to the appraisal team who ended up looking for all of the evidence again after being unable to make sense of the information so laboriously provided.

The appraisal itself was an agonizing experience. People were nervous about preparation, and then once they were in an interview, they felt like they were on trial. Questions were asked in CMMI-speak rather than in the terminology used in KNORR Brake processes, so the answer was often, "We don't do that" when a particular CMMI practice was something they really did implement. Because no one in KNORR Brake really understood the CMMI model, the assumption was that there was nothing open to question in the lead appraiser's expectation of how practices should be implemented. No one could translate the KNORR Brake processes for embedded software development into CMMI terminology that the lead appraiser would understand. As a result, the organization was rated maturity level 1, the recommendations for addressing gaps weren't useful or implementable, and the whole organization felt that CMMI was a waste of effort.

Switching to the Right Way

Because the contract still required CMMI Level 2 for Software Development, senior management decided to learn more about CMMI and try again. It wasn't easy because we had to overcome some very negative attitudes toward CMMI and SCAMPI in particular, as well as consultants, process improvement, and appraisals in general.

However, this time, we treated the effort as a project, not as an activity to be done in the margins. As long as we had to do it, we decided that we might as well do something useful. We looked at the contract requirement for CMMI Level 2 as an opportunity for understanding KNORR Brake written and unwritten processes and then improving them as needed to add business value.

Senior management demonstrated their commitment by allocating an experienced project manager to manage and facilitate the process improvement effort full-time and granting him the authority and resources necessary to make it happen. This person not only had quality assurance experience, project management experience, and some CMMI training, he was highly respected and trusted by everyone based on his technical experience and skill in delivering a product.

All of the software engineering staff had time allocated to the process improvement program and were involved and engaged in clarifying, understanding, defining, and improving the program lifecycle, operational procedures, work instructions, and the flow and dependencies among them. As an added benefit, the engineers ended up learning a lot from each other, as well as defining processes that worked.

The first step was to look carefully at the contract requirement for CMMI Level 2 to determine exactly where to focus. At the same time, the CMMI Project Manager began to look for a certified lead appraiser to serve as a consultant; someone who would understand the needs and context of a very small organization that does embedded software and who could coach us in interpreting the CMMI model for implementation in that context. The initial phase of the process improvement project included working with the selected consultant to review the contract language to ensure that we really understood what was required, and then to confirm that understanding with the customer. This narrowed the scope of the effort to the software engineering group processes, rather than trying to change the whole enterprise. This approach made the process improvement project more manageable and increased the likelihood of success.

On any journey, whether it's an actual journey by rail or a metaphorical journey of process improvement, it's important to start by understanding where you are and where you want to go. We worked with the new consultant on an in-depth current state analysis to understand the overall KNORR Brake software engineering process architecture, map "what software engineers do and how they do it" to the CMMI model practices to identify possible gaps, and then decide what to do to address those gaps.

CMMI was used as a guide, but all implementation decisions were based on the KNORR Brake process context and culture. A highly interactive version of the SCAMPI B methodology that didn't require the organization to prepare evidence ahead of time was used for the current state analysis to reduce adverse impact on current product development activities without impacting the quality and usefulness of the appraisal results, to increase the learning opportunities during the appraisal, and to be able to tell the customer about process improvement progress in terms of CMMI and their contract requirements.

Over the next several months, the CMMI Project Manager met twice a week for two-hour sessions (lunch provided!) with members of the software engineering group to understand, clarify, and enhance the processes and procedures related to developing embedded software. The CMMI Project Manager reported progress regularly at management status meetings and also met weekly by phone for coaching with the consultant to go over progress, issues, and achievements.

The consultant returned twice for a few days each time to provide customized training and lead hands-on workshop sessions with the team to cover some specific areas of need related to process architecture definition, estimation, risk management, and measurement and analysis. Although everyone was fully engaged with defining processes and procedures, the CMMI Project Manager was responsible for actually documenting them and for ensuring that the KNORR Brake document manager formatted them appropriately and submitted them to the corporate repository correctly.

Our initial focus was to define and document the work flow into the KNORR V-Model (a view of the project lifecycle). When the effort started, program management had monitored only customer document deliverables and three other software engineering tasks: design, code, and test. No one other than software engineers could understand why the software engineering effort and duration estimates were so high, when there appeared to be so little work to do. After we finished, all of the key activities, dependencies, and deliverables were captured in the V-Model; as a result, program management and senior management now had a much better understanding of the software engineering work. CMMI practices in the Requirements Management, Project Planning, Project Monitoring and Control, and Measurement and Analysis processes areas provided guidance for our implementation of the KNORR V-Model.

The KNORR V-Model provided the foundation for an improved and more useful work breakdown structure (WBS), which in turn was used as a starting point for identifying and estimating the factors that impact how much effort each task or deliverable would require. Although the CMMI model informative material and formal training provided many examples of these factors, such as number of functions, source lines of code, and numbers of pages, it turned out that the examples given were not the primary factors affecting effort and schedule estimates in KNORR embedded development.

Engineers knew what factors impacted their effort, but had never captured or shared this tacit knowledge. For example, the amount of work required for customer-deliverable documents is affected by the number of circuit boards and the number of revisions a particular customer is likely to require, rather than the number of pages in a document. With some initial coaching from the consultant, the team was able to determine what factors did make a difference, and then use Wide Band Delphi techniques to estimate typical effort ranges for tasks, depending on the values of those factors and historical effort data for similar activities.

The typical effort ranges were used in the updated project plans and as input to new bids and projects. As a result, KNORR Brake was able to more accurately estimate the cost of new software engineering work, and provide customers with a more accurate prediction of delivery dates. CMMI practices in the Project Planning, Project Monitoring and Control, and Measurement and Analysis process areas helped us implement the new WBS.

After the KNORR V-Model was established, the software project attributes identified, and the WBS completed, the Program Management Schedule was updated to reflect the actual activities, so it was much easier to predict how long a project would take and monitor progress during the project. An additional benefit was that the rest of the organization gained a much better appreciation of the value the software engineering team was providing to the business. Understanding the real project attributes and WBS made a huge improvement in managing our software engineering resources across projects and provided valuable input when bidding new projects.

Some KNORR Brake customers required a Software Requirements Traceability Matrix (SRTM) as a deliverable, but the SRTM was often created after all the work was completed and used to document what existed, rather than a means to manage the work. However, one software engineer had discovered that it was a useful tool, and shared that experience with the other team members during the weekly meetings. The KNORR V-Model was then used to update the structure for the SRTM so that it helps ensure requirements coverage and assessment of the impact of changes throughout a project.

KNORR Brake already had a process for capturing requirements changes that were charged to the customer. However, if a change seemed small or the program manager decided to give it to the customer without charge, it wasn't recorded, and the impact on project schedules, effort, and cost was not assessed. We enhanced and institutionalized the Project Change Request (PCR) process with a new PCR Procedure that requires systems and software engineers to evaluate all changes to determine impact on the schedule, cost, and/or scope and identify any risks related to the change.

We quickly saw the value in the new procedure because several requests that would have been assumed to be small turned into revenue-producing changes, whereas others did not generate a customer charge, but still required replanning of the project resources because they affected the effort and schedule. In conjunction with the KNORR V-Model and the new WBS, CMMI practices in the Requirements Management, Project Planning, Project Monitoring and Control, and Configuration Management process areas helped guide the changes made in the SRTM and the new PCR change request template and procedure.

All of the process and procedure changes interacted synergistically, each supporting and enhancing the others. All either clarified or enhanced the way work was already being done; none added useless overhead. Because the changes were a natural extension of the current processes, it was easy to institutionalize them within the KNORR Quality Management System.

After the process changes were established and as they were becoming institutionalized, the organization began planning for the SCAMPI A appraisal. Working with the consultant, the CMMI Project Manager defined a set of questions to use when interviewing potential lead appraisers to determine whether the candidate would be capable of understanding how CMMI practices can be implemented in a very small organization that creates embedded software. The lead appraiser needed to be able to adapt to the KNORR Brake organizational and process culture, rather than expecting KNORR Brake to do things in a particular way. Because KNORR Brake wanted to have the appraisal before the end of the calendar year, a time that many other organizations are also trying to schedule appraisals, the selection process began in the late summer to increase the likelihood that the lead appraiser chosen would be available when needed.

Each new process advancement and tool improvement was merged into our existing Quality Management System by writing new work instructions and/or operational procedures and storing them in an online repository we call REX (Rail Excellence). This allows both existing and new employees to easily find the appropriate procedures and templates within the context of the process maps that clearly define the development and design lifecycles.

Preparing evidence for the SCAMPI A appraisal turned out to be simple. Because the CMMI Project Manager knew which KNORR Brake processes implemented which CMMI practices, it was just a matter of pointing to the actual work products once they were created. Most of the artifacts selected for evidence had sections that were appropriate for multiple CMMI process areas and practices. The consultant reviewed the evidence with the program manager to make sure the work products selected were appropriate and complete, and that there were clear explanations of the context so that the appraisal team would understand why those particular artifacts were selected. It didn't matter which projects were eventually chosen by the lead appraiser to represent the organization, because the work product links pointed to directory structures that included all projects.

The appraisal was interactive and cooperative rather than confrontational. Work outputs were projected on a screen and the lead appraiser asked participants to explain their work for the entire appraisal team to review. If questions or concerns were raised, they were answered immediately rather than waiting for a separate validation session. Because the appraisal focused on KNORR Brake processes and evaluated CMMI model implementation within that context, rather than focusing on CMMI itself, no one felt threatened and the information was complete and accurate.

The appraisal was finished in less than four days and KNORR Brake software engineering achieved their goal of being rated maturity level 2. Although achieving that rating was certainly important for contractual reasons, perhaps more significantly, staff and management learned that CMMI practices could add value without adding overhead. Members of other functional groups and product lines were asking, "Why do only the software engineers get to do CMMI? We want to do it too!"

Moving Forward (The Journey Continues . . .)

Based on the successful SCAMPI A appraisal with the KNORR Brake Software Development Group and the noticeable value added by the new processes and procedures, the company decided to continue the process improvement effort. The CMMI Project Manager was promoted to a newly formed position as Manager, Business Process Improvement with a mandate from senior staff to make improvements throughout KNORR business and engineering processes. Currently, KNORR has four process improvement teams in action.

One team is extending the Brakes software engineering process improvement work into the domain of HVAC software engineering. The team has already completed tailoring the KNORR V-Model lifecycle and WBS for developing embedded code in the HVAC domain. Project schedules have been updated accordingly with milestones based on a more realistic view of the work required. The HVAC team improved on the Brakes software engineering process with the implementation of a new template for identifying the key project attributes that allows for multiple variations. With this new tool, the HVAC Software Engineer can more accurately characterize the project type, which is a key factor in estimation of effort and schedule.

We are also extending the process improvement work into systems engineering in both the Brakes and HVAC domains. This team is reviewing the systems engineering lifecycle and mapping CMMI practices to the systems engineering process. We are looking at the maturity level 2 process areas, as well as key maturity level 3 process areas where the organization is already strong or where there are issues that need to be addressed in the near term.

Due to the successful process improvement effort completed by the Brakes software engineering group and because the team approach is working extremely well with the newly formed cross-domain software and systems engineering teams, senior management supported formation of a HVAC New Product Design Team that will use CMMI ML2 and ML3 practices in designing new HVAC equipment.

After the systems and software engineering design lifecycles were well understood, we realized that the proposal process needed to be integrated into the overall product lifecycle. A proposal team has completed mapping the entire proposal process and clarifying how it feeds into the systems and software design lifecycle when proposals are awarded. The effort and documentation within the proposal process has proved extremely valuable by providing the framework for future bids as well as helping us predict the resource and time allocation needed for bid preparation itself. In addition, when the contract is awarded, the product and customer details from the bid process are directly transferable into estimates of project size, tasks, and deliverables, thereby saving planning time and effort.

At the end of the year, we will conduct a SCAMPI A that includes systems engineering and software engineering processes for both Brakes and HVAC. We will still use some assistance from an outside consultant to validate our assumptions and decisions, but now that we are able to understand how to apply the CMMI model within the KNORR context, we need much less direct guidance. Based on our experience with process improvement in Brakes software engineering, we predict a high likelihood of success, which will put KNORR at a competitive advantage in our market domain.

Lessons Learned

As a result of travelling first down the wrong track and then down the right one, we have learned some key lessons, which we will apply as we continue on our journey of process improvement:

1. Question assumptions and trust your instincts. Don't assume that you have to do something because CMMI or some expert "requires" it. If it doesn't seem to make any business sense, it probably isn't a good implementation for your current organizational context.
2. When trying to meet contract requirements, use the contract language to help specify organization and model scope for a formal appraisal. Understanding the contract requirements focuses the improvement effort and helps achieve immediate value.
3. Especially if you have had a previous negative experience with process improvement, demonstrate value early and often. When staff and managers see that a change makes their own work easier or more effective, they are more likely to be willing to embrace further changes.
4. Process improvement using CMMI is not something that can be done in the margins. It requires dedicated effort by a respected and trusted project manager as well as involvement and engagement from everyone at every level in the organization.
5. The CMMI model provides value only if it is used as a guide for process improvement, not as a checkbox exercise. Process improvement is not a matter of documenting what "should" be done and forcing everyone to comply, whether or not it provides any business value. Changing the paradigm from "getting by for certification" to "clarifying and improving our processes and using the CMMI model to help" validates what is already being done, makes any changes "stick," and ensures that those changes add business value.

6. All CMMI goals and practices are useful and do not add unnecessary overhead—as long as you interpret them and implement them within your own business and technical context. Within your organizational context, each process improvement will often implement several CMMI practices, and synergy among the improvements increases the benefit of each.

7. A consultant who understands the organizational context can provide guidance in areas where the organization doesn't have expertise and can help the program stay on track. However, process changes need to come from inside the organization for the changes to be institutionalized. Be sure to choose a consultant who will coach rather than prescribe.

8. Choosing a lead appraiser who understands the business context ensures that the appraisal will be valid. If the lead appraiser doesn't really understand the business context and there is no one to help translate between CMMI-ese and the organization's processes and terminology, there's a high likelihood that the appraisal results will be invalid due to miscommunication and you will not achieve your goal.

9. When process improvement activities bring clear business value to one part of the organization, other parts of the organization will ask to get on board too. Success breeds success.

After we switched to the right track for our process improvement journey using CMMI, we have had an enjoyable trip, were able to arrive on schedule, and are looking forward to travelling to the next destination!

Using CMMI as a Basis for Competitive Advantage at ABB

by Aldo Dagnino

ABB is a multinational organization and market leader in power and automation technologies that enable utilities and industries to improve performance while reducing environmental impact. The vast majority of ABB's products consist of complex systems that have both hardware and software components (e.g., robot systems, SCADA systems, relays, control systems, substation automation systems). Some products are purely software (e.g., control systems, substation automation, SCADA systems), whereas others are purely hardware (e.g., power transformers, circuit breakers).

The primary customers of ABB are commercial organizations that are important players in sectors such as utilities, petro-chemicals, pharmaceuticals, automotive, manufacturing, chemical, and oil and gas. Although ABB's customers do not require their suppliers to demonstrate CMMI maturity levels, the company has been utilizing CMMI for almost ten years. CMMI is used for continuous process improvement of the corporation's product development processes. ABB recognized that CMMI provides a good framework for process improvement because it contains industry best practices for the development of complex systems. Following CMMI's principles has helped and continues to help ABB product development business units (BUs) to be leaders in their respective market segments.

Process improvement has been an important element in the history of ABB and can be viewed as a two-stage process. During the first stage, continuous process improvement was promoted by a corporate process organization. The second stage of process improvement was spawned as a result of the positive results observed in stage one and because members of the corporate process improvement organization from stage one moved to several development BUs and became the members primarily responsible for the BUs' process improvement teams.

Adopting CMMI

The official journey for ABB in continuous process improvement of product development began in 1999 when the Software CMM (SW-CMM) based initiative was launched and BUs that developed software products began voluntary participation in the initiative. The name given to this initiative was the ABB Software Process Initiative or ASPI. There were few pilot process improvement projects that "signed up" as participants in the initiative. ASPI was a global and centralized program and a Corporate Software Engineering Process Group (CSEPG) was created to move the initiative forward.

The CSEPG worked in a geographically dispersed fashion with teams in countries where the major software development groups of the corporation were located. The primary objectives of the CSEPG were to develop a group of continuous improvement experts with deep knowledge of the CMM model and to develop the basic methods and tools to be employed at each development BU for improvement activities.

Soon after the initial pilot projects began, it became clear that as ABB's products have a combination of hardware and software components, SW-CMM did not cover practices that fully embraced both types of components. For this reason, adopting CMMI as the framework for continuous process improvement was a natural option. Hence, the CSEPG became a Corporate Engineering Process Group (CEPG). The strategy for the CEPG was to develop deep expertise in CMMI and to promote and increase awareness of the value of CMMI among product development units. The objective was for members of the CEPG to work closely with the product development BUs as trainers, mentors, and coaches to the BU's process improvement team. In this way, the first stage of the continuous process improvement initiative at ABB began.

As the first pilot projects were completed, the number of product development BUs in the corporation interested in CMMI increased by an order of magnitude. Additionally, the experience of the CEPG team working with the initial pilots resulted in a need to develop key robust methods and tools that enabled working more systematically with a larger number of product development BUs. As few development BUs needed to demonstrate a maturity level, the approach taken was to instead demonstrate the economic benefits from making changes to the development processes using CMMI.

Standard Tools and Methods

Thus, standardized internal methods and tools needed to be developed to ensure consistency when engaging multiple product development units. Furthermore, the use of a continuous improvement framework was identified as an important asset. Because development units did not need to demonstrate maturity level, the continuous process improvement activity became cyclic. Cycles were typically one year long and corresponded to the budgeting cycles of the organization. The IDEAL model was selected as a continuous process improvement cycle framework.

The tools and methods developed by the global CEPG team members and then employed during its engagements with product development units in their geographic area of responsibility included primarily the following:

- A tool to assess the readiness of an organization to implement a continuous process improvement initiative
- An internal appraisal methodology, including training and tools
- A methodology to translate the appraisal results into a prioritized process improvement work breakdown structure
- Methods and templates for developing a process improvement plan to manage the improvement activities in the cycle

- A method for measuring the economic benefits associated with the changes made as a result of the process improvement activity
- A data repository that summarized a set of improvement measures for each product development BU engaged
- A repository of lessons learned, good practices, and general knowledge gained in the interactions with product development units

A brief description of these tools and methods and an explanation of their usefulness to implement CMMI are described in the remainder of this case study.

An organization that decides to implement a CMMI continuous process improvement program needs to establish the "right" infrastructure, dedicate human and financial resources, have support from senior management, have a competent change agent, train the organization's members in CMMI, and in general be "ready" for the initiative. A readiness assessment tool and method were developed and are used to quantitatively and qualitatively measure the readiness of an organization to conduct a continuous process improvement program using CMMI.

The readiness assessment is conducted at the beginning of each process improvement cycle and reevaluation is conducted within the cycle as needed. The results of readiness assessments have been used to ensure that senior management, change agents, and the organization are fully committed to the CMMI initiative. When deviations occur, the results of a reassessment show potential areas that need to be addressed to move the CMMI initiative forward.

The use of an internally developed CMMI appraisal methodology and tools has been essential to evaluate and diagnose ABB development BUs against CMMI best practices. This internal appraisal methodology is based on Version 1.1 of the Appraisal Requirements for CMMI (ARC 1.1) and for many years has been used to appraise product development BUs.

The ABB internal appraisal methodology uses both Class B and Class C internal CMMI appraisals. Class B internal CMMI appraisals have been employed primarily when a development organization begins a continuous process improvement cycle and after the improvements made have been institutionalized in the BU. Class C internal CMMI appraisals are used in between Class B appraisals to evaluate one or two CMMI process areas (PAs).

All members of ABB's internal appraisal teams must take the SEI-taught *Introduction to CMMI-DEV* course as well as the ABB appraisal training course. To lead a CMMI internal appraisal, the appraisal leader must have participated in at least three internal Class B appraisals and must have taken the SEI-taught *Intermediate Concepts of CMMI* course. It is also an important and valued requirement that at least one member of the product development BU must participate in the appraisal, because ultimately the development BU will be responsible to move the process improvement project forward.

The results of an internal CMMI appraisal consist of a final presentation that defines the strengths and weaknesses of the organization with respect to CMMI PAs. The final presentation is consolidated by the appraisal team and is delivered by the internal appraisal leader to the participating organization at the end of the appraisal. A second deliverable generated after completing the internal appraisal is a detailed observations document in which observations made by the appraisal team are detailed at the practice level for each PA included in the appraisal activity.

After the appraisal is completed, the observations document is used to generate a work breakdown structure that serves as a basis for the generation of the improvement plan. At this stage, the particular product development BU's annual/biannual objectives play a central role in the selection and prioritization of PAs that will be included in the improvement cycle.

Those PAs that directly contribute to the achievement of the annual/biannual development BU's objectives are selected. For example, a development BU may have as part of its business objectives to reduce the cost of poor quality (COPQ) by 15%. At the same time, the results of the appraisal may show that the BU's process, when compared to the Requirements Development (RD) PA, has many weaknesses that seem to contribute to poor documentation and capture of requirements and hence to a high degree of rework, which raises the COPQ. Under these circumstances, a WBS (work breakdown structure) that addresses what improvement is needed relative to the RD PA is then generated using the observations document. The generation of the process improvement WBS is a difficult task to carry out by the BU's process improvement team and thus the CEPG coach usually works closely with the improvement team to fully develop the WBS.

After the WBS for process improvement has been completed, the process improvement plan (PIP) is developed. The development of the PIP follows closely the practices that the CMMI-DEV recommends in the PP (Project Planning) and PMC (Project Monitoring and Control) process areas, and it serves the purpose of properly managing the process improvement project throughout the cycle.

The CEPG coach works closely with the process improvement project leader in the development BU to define the PIP, but the development BU ultimately "owns" the process improvement plan.

An important aspect of the improvement cycle is defining how to measure the impact of CMMI process improvement activities. As explained previously, each development BU defines annual/biannual business objectives and a subset of the objectives is expected to be affected by process improvement activities. A methodology that measures key performance indicators (KPIs) before the improvements have taken place and after improvements have been institutionalized was developed by the CEPG.

An important aspect of this methodology is the consistency of how the KPIs are measured and at what points in time. Of course, this aspect also has a "rewards and recognition" component that is incorporated to provide incentives to the organization for a continuous process improvement methodology. An interesting result to note in terms of the benefit/cost ratio of several process improvement projects is that ratios in the range of 3:1 to 5:1 have typically been observed. These results mean that for every dollar spent in a process improvement project, the return is typically three to five dollars in terms of cost savings, new market opportunities created, or revenues generated by the development BU.

A database that provided KPIs on the process improvement activities of each product development BU was created and maintained by CEPG members. Typical KPIs included the name of the development BU, how many improvement cycles it had conducted, the types of appraisals conducted, and benefit measures. This database was updated as improvement activities were conducted at each participating development BU.

A CMMI knowledge base was also created and is organized so that it provides a graphic perspective of improvement against CMMI PAs. The objective of this knowledge base is to store and make available to all the corporation good practices implemented by the development BUs engaged in a continuous process improvement program, including artifacts such as templates, lessons learned, answers to frequently asked questions, and any other type of information that can be useful to development BUs.

The First Stage

During the first stage of our continuous process improvement initiative, the previously mentioned tools, methods, and infrastructure were created and employed by the CEPG and participating development BUs. The first stage of the initiative was characterized by the following important elements:

1. A clear business case had to be defined and aligned with the full set of objectives of the development BU carrying out the improvement project.
2. The CEPG was then in a better position to "sell" continuous process improvement to the development BUs.
3. The commitment of a Development BU to continuous process improvement highly depended on the local senior management's background and level of knowledge in software engineering concepts.
4. There was a need to continuously monitor the level of commitment of each development BU to their improvement initiative.
5. There was little need for synchronization of improvement activities, solutions, and tool usage among development units carrying out the improvement initiative.

The Second Stage

Later, several strategic changes were made to the infrastructure used to support continuous process improvement at ABB: the majority of CEPG members were assigned to development BUs and were given the responsibility for that BU's improvement initiative. Concurrently, there was also a realignment in the perspective of senior management to make the continuous process improvement initiative more global. The target of global process improvement is to significantly improve the global reach of corporate product development practices and use common methods and tools where possible.

Today

The global initiative is now firmly grounded in all ABB divisions. The divisions directly own and sustain their improvements. CMMI continues to be the primary framework used for continuous process improvement but the focus is on ensuring attention to lower level practices and standard methods and tools that can be used and customized by all product development units. Internal CMMI appraisals continue to be conducted on a periodic basis.

In summary, ABB has been engaged in a 10-year journey to continually improve its product development processes. The outcomes have continued to be good results, economic benefits, improved morale, and the recognition that the CMMI has been a valuable tool all along the way. Adjustments in the journey were required due to changes brought about by increased globalization of markets and the need to increase the uniformity of process solutions, but the benefits continue.

Leveraging CMMI and LSS to Accelerate the Process Improvement Journey

by Kileen Harrison and Anne Prem

Although Capability Maturity Model Integration (CMMI) and Lean Six Sigma (LSS) are often viewed as competing initiatives, contending for the same process improvement funding and priorities, CMMI and LSS are actually complementary. Implementing these methodologies in tandem can result in a synergistic effect that accelerates and enhances the benefits of process improvement.

The Synergistic Effect

One consideration for how CMMI and LSS relate is to associate CMMI with providing the "what" and LSS as supplying the "how." CMMI identifies "what" activities are expected, but does not specify techniques on how to accomplish those activities. Whereas, LSS identifies "how" activities can be optimized, including specifying tools and techniques. For example, the CMMI model can be leveraged to conduct a gap analysis on an organization's business practices to determine what opportunities for improvement exist. Then, LSS can be applied to provide the organization with tools and techniques for achieving the necessary improvements. Because of their complementary nature, leveraging the two models together can lay a solid foundation for performance-driven improvement that accelerates an overall improvement journey.

Applying the two initiatives together encourages a balance between a focus on process comprehensiveness through CMMI and a focus on business efficiency through LSS. For example, in a typical implementation of CMMI at the managed and defined levels, the focus is on process definition to include all of the necessary elements. Then, improvement and greater efficiency is achieved through process maturity, which is generally associated with advancing through the levels in the model over time. In contrast, LSS is focused on efficiency and greater effectiveness from the onset of the improvement journey. To realize the benefits of this complementary nature, Space and Naval Warfare Systems Command (SPAWAR)

Headquarters Organizational Process Management Office (OPMO) created an approach that utilizes both initiatives, targeting discrete business unit challenges within the organization.

Background Context

SPAWAR is one of the Department of Navy (DoN) major acquisition commands. The SPAWAR Command specifically procures higher-end United States Navy (USN) information technology products and services for the USN fleet and other armed forces. Headquartered in San Diego, Team SPAWAR includes SPAWAR Headquarters, two additional SPAWAR Systems Centers (SSCs), three Program Executive Offices (PEOs), one Joint Program Executive Office (JPEO), and one liaison office located in Washington, D.C. In total, the organization consists of more than 12,000 employees and contractors deployed globally and near the fleet.

Since 2005, SPAWAR Headquarters' OPMO, supported by Booz Allen Hamilton, has been integral in establishing a successful LSS program across Team SPAWAR. Although the two SPAWAR System Centers, focused on engineering, have been engaged with both LSS and CMMI for years and successfully achieved CMMI ratings through formal appraisals, SPAWAR Headquarters' OPMO, a service-focused business unit, began incorporating CMMI in 2008. At that time, OPMO identified a need to integrate CMMI as a process improvement methodology to complement the existing LSS program and the other process improvement tools and techniques they manage and provide throughout Team SPAWAR.

The Challenge

Instilling a culture of process improvement and making positive progress is challenging in any organization and SPAWAR is no exception. The ability to gain and maintain process improvement buy-in from stakeholders within the organization presents an immediate hurdle. Additionally, the government's focus to do more with less while continuing to meet mission objectives provides an additional hurdle. These challenges, coupled with the desire to see tangible results, led to the formation of an approach that leverages both LSS and CMMI.

The Approach

The following paragraphs detail OPMO's approach, including the four major steps the OPMO CMMI assessment team utilizes:

1. Identify Mission Critical Risks
2. Select Relevant CMMI Process Areas
3. Conduct a CMMI Gap Analysis
4. Apply LSS Tools

Step 1: Identify Mission Critical Risks

The OPMO CMMI assessment team initiates the assessment of a business unit by leveraging information contained within a SPAWAR tool referred to as the Policy, Procedures, Processes, Practices & Instructions (P4I) workbook system. Each business unit within SPAWAR is required to update the P4I workbook at least annually. This information is used to identify the business unit's mission, their associated policies and procedures, as well as any risk that may critically impact their mission, thereby creating a snapshot baseline of the business unit's as-is state. The assessment team leverages the risk information identified in the P4I workbook to identify the business unit's possible weaknesses or risk areas. These critical risks are mapped to an associated functional area (e.g., mail processing, records management) to identify a discrete focal area for process improvement activities.

Step 2: Select Relevant CMMI Process Areas

After the focal area is selected, the assessment team conducts interviews with the functional subject matter experts and stakeholders to gain a better understanding of the as-is process. The team also reviews supporting process documentation as well as any other relevant assets or tools. Based on this research, the assessment team selects the CMMI process areas that are most relevant to the focal area. Due to the cross-functional nature of Team SPAWAR's business, the team considers all three of the CMMI constellations (CMMI for Development, CMMI for Acquisition, and CMMI for Services) when selecting the relevant process areas.

The team selects the process areas that have the strongest tie to the specific mission-critical risks identified from the previous step. SPAWAR Headquarters does not currently require attainment of a particular CMMI maturity or capability level. Therefore, the approach focuses on identifying and utilizing key actions or "best practices" from the CMMI models that the business unit can implement to mitigate their mission critical risks and improve operating efficiencies. The improvement actions that result from the best practice assessment assist in building or enhancing the business unit's process framework, which could be leveraged to obtain a CMMI maturity or capability level, if desired.

Step 3: Conduct a CMMI Gap Analysis

Now that the assessment team has reviewed the as-is state and selected the process areas, a detailed gap analysis is conducted. The team leverages an evidence matrix to systematically compare the business unit's targeted functional area's as-is processes against the selected CMMI process areas. As noted previously, because SPAWAR Headquarters does not have a requirement to meet a maturity or capability level, the assessment team focuses on selected process areas to address mission critical risks, rather than using a full CMMI model and appraisal methodology.

Based on the gap analysis, the assessment team documents the findings in a detailed CMMI Assessment Report. The report identifies the business unit's opportunities for improvement, the team's recommendations, and associated benefits. Before delivering the final report, the assessment team validates the findings and recommendations with key stakeholders and subject matter experts from the business unit. These validation activities have proven effective in ensuring accuracy as well as promoting stakeholder buy-in.

Step 4: Apply LSS Tools

Because the CMMI Assessment Reports are detailed and typically contain five to six primary process areas that translate into numerous recommendations for improvement, the business unit typically requires assistance in identifying a "starting point" for addressing the improvement activities. The assessment team helps the business unit to prioritize these activities by using LSS tools, such as the Analytical Hierarchy Process (AHP) and a scoring matrix. Applying these tools provides a quantitative basis to a task (in this case, prioritizing activities) that can be qualitative in nature.

The AHP is a mathematical decision making technique that leverages weighted criteria. Specifically, the business unit identifies four to six criteria that are relevant to their business objectives, such as risk or level of effort. These criteria are compared head-to-head to determine a weight that represents the level of importance of each criterion. Finally, these weights are input into a scoring matrix to objectively prioritize opportunities for improvement. Leveraging the use of the AHP and scoring matrix provides the opportunity to involve the business unit in prioritization and ultimately promotes stakeholder buy-in. This objective methodology also helps build confidence that the most business-critical improvement areas are addressed first.

After a prioritized list of improvements is defined, the top priorities are reviewed to consider the best course of action. A Plan of Action and Milestones is developed, which may include the kickoff of a LSS RIE (Rapid Improvement Event), LSS DMAIC (Define, Measure, Analyze, Improve, Control), or simply a "Just Do It." The as-is process documentation as well as the findings identified from the CMMI gap analysis activities are required inputs to the follow-on LSS events.

Tying It All Together

The assessment team has worked with several different business units. The team and business unit stakeholders have experienced valuable results from the implementation of the CMMI and LSS approach. One specific business unit that the assessment team worked with is SPAWAR's Administrative Services & Support. Their business objectives are to support Team SPAWAR through the establishment of policy, guidance, and oversight for administrative functions including official mail, records management, directives, and correspondence administration.

During the initial analysis activities, the team identified two functional areas that were associated with the business unit's mission critical risks: 1) Official Mail and 2) Records Management. Because Administrative Services & Support's focus is providing these services to SPAWAR, the assessment team selected the CMMI-SVC constellation. In the CMMI-SVC constellation, one of the process areas deemed relevant to the Records Management functional area was Configuration Management. After completing the gap analysis, the assessment team identified various opportunities for improvement and recommendations in regard to Administrative Services & Support's Configuration Management activities.

A sampling of recommendations includes the following:

- Create and maintain one all-inclusive configuration item list of all records managed along with key characteristics (e.g., owner, signature authority, required reviewers, expiration date, update frequency).
- Clearly define the purpose and role of each records management tool and document a process for tool use.
- Identify the authoritative source for managing all records and conduct periodic audits to ensure record integrity is maintained.

After the final CMMI Assessment Report for Records Management was delivered, the business unit and assessment team prioritized the opportunities for improvement using the AHP and scoring matrix in accordance with Step 4 of the approach. Based on this prioritized list, the Administrative Services & Support business unit created a LSS Rapid Improvement Plan that included the following activities:

- Streamline the official document review process.
- Streamline the official document routing process throughout the Command.
- Define a standard configuration management process and associated business rules for use of existing tools to reduce version redundancy and to identify an authoritative source for official documents.

Similarly for Official Mail, in response to the highest priority recommendations for improvement, Step 4 identified the need for a LSS RIE to improve mail handling processes. The LSS RIE resulted in a resolution of duplicative responsibility for mail sorting between an in-house resource and service provider. This resolution eliminated 90% of the in-house resource's workload, which allowed for realignment of the individual's time to focus on reducing backlog in other work areas.

In addition to this specific example of savings realized within the Administrative Services & Support business unit, a few further examples of benefits experienced by other business units include the following:

- Recommendations from a CMMI Assessment Report resulted in the creation of process documentation that will assist with upcoming staff transition activities, including a staff member's retirement.
- Content from the detailed CMMI Assessment Report and the prioritized list of improvement activities were leveraged as critical inputs to a business unit's annual strategic planning session.
- Recommendations from a CMMI Assessment Report are planned to be leveraged to improve quality of contractor deliverables and associated communications.

Lessons Learned and Critical Success Factors

The assessment team has conducted multiple assessments and gained valuable lessons learned feedback as well as knowledge of critical success factors. Two of the most critical challenges that the team faced were the following:

1. Business unit acceptance of ownership for improvement actions
2. Resource availability issues due to major initiatives competing for resources (e.g., Navy Enterprise Resource Planning (ERP) implementation)

The assessment team deployed several techniques to overcome the challenge of business unit ownership. After the assessment was complete, the business unit was responsible to charter and initiate LSS improvement events. However, these activities sometimes required gentle and persistent encouragement from the assessment team to maintain forward progress. In response, the team found that conducting an offsite session was an effective way to build momentum for the improvement activities by allowing individuals to have focused time away from their day-to-day responsibilities.

Additionally, the team found that the use of a RASCI (Responsible, Accountable, Support, Consulted, Informed) chart helped the business unit understand the alignment of resources to roles and provided clear ownership associated with each of the process improvement activities. To mitigate the impact of resource availability issues, the assessment team discovered that communication with senior leadership and managing a realistic schedule were the most critical factors contributing to success. The assessment team kept senior leadership informed throughout the assessment activities; their support and direction were integral to the success of the project.

Clear communication of the CMMI assessment goals was another critical success factor the team recognized. Due to resource constraints and competing priorities, SPAWAR Headquarters determined upfront that the approach would focus on leveraging CMMI best practices and not focus on the achievement of a particular capability or maturity level. By communicating this message early, the assessment team was able to pacify fears and address resistance associated with concern over the level of effort required to reach a particular CMMI maturity or capability level. The assessment team emphasized CMMI "best practices" from the onset of the project to appropriately communicate the scope and focus of the project to the participants.

In conclusion, the sum of CMMI plus LSS does not merely equal the combined benefits of two process improvement approaches; instead, it equals a synergistic result that improves process efficiency and effectiveness faster. A significant factor in achieving maximum benefits of this approach is having participants trained in the appropriate elements of both models and associated nuances. Getting the right resources involved and implementing an approach that leverages both CMMI and LSS can accelerate the realization of process improvement benefits.

Essays

The following essays cover a variety of experiences. The first several essays provide advice for both new and experienced users of CMMI for Development. The fourth essay provides practical advice for hiring a consultant or lead appraiser. The fifth and final essay provides an essay to share with those who are not "sold" on CMMI from a believer that once was skeptical of CMMI's value.

Getting Started in Process Improvement: Tips and Pitfalls

by Judah Mogilensky

So your organization has decided to embark on a process improvement journey. First of all, congratulations on your decision! Perhaps your journey has been triggered by some project disaster you never want to repeat, or perhaps you have realized that taking the next step up in project size and complexity will only lead to success if your processes are strong enough. In any case, you are probably wondering how to get started.

Here's a bad way to start, one that I call "having a process lobotomy." You forget any aspect of process you were doing up to now, and you say, "We have to build everything new, from scratch." I've never seen this work. A much better approach is to recognize that any level of project success you have enjoyed up to now has been based in part on whatever processes, however loose and informal, you have in place. One good strategy is to have a few key people from each current project simply write down, in any form, what they are doing today. Gather these descriptions, noting similarities and differences. Then, convene a meeting of key project people to review the descriptions, identify "best practices" and "lessons learned." (Best practices work; we always want projects to do these. Lessons learned are bad things; we never want projects to do these.) The results of this meeting will be your first documented process description. Your journey will focus on refining this description, adding to it as gaps are identified, and getting people to follow it consistently.

"Well," you say, "we've got very little process in place. There's almost nothing in the CMMI-DEV model that we are doing consistently. Where should we start?" My suggestion is that if you really have almost nothing in place, start with Configuration Management. Every process you undertake, including the writing of your process descriptions, will produce documents, drawings, or some other artifacts. You need to be able to keep track of these, know where they are, know what changes have been made to them, and know what the current versions are. Configuration Management helps you manage your artifacts.

Another good activity to start with is peer reviews. You will be producing descriptions of your processes so that people can follow them consistently and so that you can deliberately and visibly improve them. It's really helpful to have a peer review process documented at a very early stage so that you can use it to peer review the rest of your process descriptions. And later, you will find that performing peer reviews on the products of your projects will be really useful too.

What is the most important factor contributing to success in a process improvement journey? Anyone with experience will give you the same answer: the strength of your sponsorship. The sponsor is the person in the organization with the power and authority to direct that process improvement actions be taken and to provide the resources (funding and people) needed to carry out those actions. However, the strength of sponsorship is not defined just by providing a budget and saying, "Go do it." Rather, sponsors, whether they realize it or not, are constantly sending three types of messages to their organizations: expressed (what they say), demonstrated (what they do), and reinforced (what they reward).

Weak sponsors are those who say they want process improvement—even loudly and publicly—but their own actions and the behaviors that they reward (e.g., badly estimated projects that get into deep trouble but then are saved at the end by late-night heroic efforts) show that they really do not care very much about process improvement. The organization's people will always, in case of conflict, believe the demonstrated and reinforced messages before the expressed messages.

Therefore, one key role of the process group (i.e., the people charged with developing and deploying processes) is to provide feedback to the sponsor about the messages that are being sent and whether they are consistent. This role usually requires some up-front agreement, because upward feedback is not common in most organizations.

What is the next most important success factor? It is an atmosphere that encourages and fosters open and honest feedback from the process users. The only way to tell if processes are working well and helping people is to get comments and feedback from those people. To keep the flow of feedback going, it is vital that the feedback received be acknowledged, valued, and acted on, especially the feedback that says "this is not working for us." Attempts to dismiss or ignore complaints will not cause them to go away, but will only drive the complaints underground where they will be less visible and more damaging.

What are some of the pitfalls to watch out for? There are two that seem to come up frequently: one is loss of sponsor interest, and the other is something that I call "pathological box-checking." The senior executives who generally serve as sponsors tend to live in a very busy, pressure-filled world with short time horizons. Process improvement is a long-term journey with rewards that develop slowly. It is very helpful to set up some regular opportunity, no less often than quarterly, to meet with your sponsor to review progress, celebrate victories, identify obstacles, and provide the upward feedback mentioned earlier. It is also very helpful to build and regularly update your business case, showing the benefits (e.g., cost savings, time savings, better milestone performance, improved delivered quality) of the process improvement effort. Remember, the worse things are when you start, the easier it is to show improvement.

The other pitfall comes about when the objective of achieving some maturity level rating in an appraisal is seen as the primary organizational goal, and anything that interferes with this goal, or puts it at risk, is seen as an obstacle to overcome. This "pathological box-checking" is different from true process improvement in that true process improvement puts the primary emphasis on measurable project performance, measurable business performance, customer satisfaction, employee satisfaction, and continuous improvement. Pathological box-checking, on the other hand, views maturity level ratings as the ultimate objectives and seeks to achieve them even if the result is negative impacts on project performance, business performance, customer and employee satisfaction, and continuous improvement.

Some of the indicators that an organization has gone over to this "dark side" are the following:

- Maturity level targets and associated dates are widely publicized and discussed, but there is little or no corresponding publicity and discussion devoted to project or business performance targets and their associated dates.

- A lot of time and energy is devoted to determining the "minimum acceptable" process implementation that will result in a rating of "satisfied," regardless of the process actually needed by projects or the organization. In severe cases, organizational advocates (perhaps even lawyers) will loudly demand that the lead appraiser point out "where in the model does it explicitly say that I have to do something."

- Because the focus is on achieving maturity level targets as quickly as possible, there is "no time" for broad participation, review, or piloting of new processes. Instead, the processes are developed by a small group, or even imported from outside, and imposed on groups and projects with little regard for suitability or applicability. Objections to these processes are viewed as "resistance to be overcome." Feedback is discouraged; again, there is "no time" to update or revise processes in response to user experiences.

- After a formal appraisal, or perhaps even an informal appraisal, has been conducted and a particular process is rated as "satisfied," changes to that process are effectively (though not explicitly) prohibited. ("If we change it, the lead appraiser might not rate it the same anymore.") In this way, the stated model objective of continuous process improvement is essentially abandoned.

- A final symptom, and perhaps the most serious one, is that effort and energy are devoted to building a "false façade" of documents to present as evidence to a lead appraiser, documents that have little or nothing to do with the actual work being done. The sad thing is that, had an effort like this been put into genuine process improvement instead, the organization would see actual business benefits that "box-checking" will never achieve.

So this brings us to the final question, namely, "How will I know when I have been successful?" Formal appraisals leading to official maturity level ratings (or capability level profiles) can be useful, especially if there is a need to show process progress to higher levels of management or to customers. Even an informal appraisal can provide very useful feedback, and can help make sure that the improvement effort has not missed something important.

However, the real measure of process improvement success is the impact on the business and the impact on its workers. In terms of business impact, look for bottom-line measured improvements in cost and schedule predictability, in project efficiency, and in delivered quality. In terms of impact on workers, look for less pressure, less overtime, more opportunity for people to have real lives outside of work. (One organization expressed it as "reduced late-night pizza orders.") For me, the beauty of process improvement has always been that there is no trade-off between project performance and developer quality of life. The only way to be truly successful is to measurably improve both at the same time.

Avoiding Typical Process Improvement Pitfalls

by Pat O'Toole

When it comes to "process," we commonly encounter three types of people: process zealots, process agnostics, and process atheists. The zealots see "process" as the path to engineering enlightenment—and typically, the *only* path. The agnostics typically don't know, and certainly don't care, whether "process" is a good or a bad thing—just as long as it doesn't get in their way. The process atheists, on the other hand, perceive that the "p word" borders on vulgarity, believing that process hampers creativity, stifles productivity, and ultimately rots the brain—but other than that, process is generally okay for *others* to follow.

One would expect that SCAMPI Lead Appraisers—or as some might call us, "Lead Oppressors"—fall squarely in the process zealot camp. However, after having seen too many organizations inadvertently harm themselves through the misimplementation of CMMI-based processes, I find myself leaning toward agnostic. In this article, I will provide some insight into what I perceive to be the two most common process improvement pitfalls, as well as steps your organization can take to avoid them.

The Alignment Principle: Defining the Word "Improvement"

In my opinion, the greatest single point of failure for most improvement programs is the organization's inability or unwillingness to define the word "improvement" within their own unique business context. In too many organizations, improvement is defined as "achieving Maturity Level X." (The fact that the organization capitalizes "Maturity Level" may indicate that they are paying it undue homage.)

Unfortunately, this misperception elevates the implementation of CMMI-suggested practices to the level of business strategy—a role it was never intended and is ill prepared to fulfill. A better approach is to have senior management establish a comprehensive business strategy and then employ CMMI as one of many tactics that enable the organization to achieve it.

A critical component of this preferred approach is the Alignment Principle. Wouldn't it be wonderful if the business strategy, project objectives, and improvement initiatives were all aligned? By articulating an organizational Alignment Principle, senior management helps to synchronize these three elements.

An organization can use CMMI to help it become the high-quality producer of goods and services in their selected market segment. Alternatively, CMMI might be used to help the organization to become the low-cost producer, or the quickest to market, or the most technically innovative, or the most environmentally friendly, or . . .

Although the model can be used to help an organization achieve any of these strategic positions, the processes employed for each are likely to be vastly different. For example, high quality producers might have checks and balances all along the development life cycle to detect and eliminate defects as close as possible to the point where they were introduced, whereas the quick-to-market leaders would typically have the thinnest layer of process that keeps the project from spiraling out of control.

Therefore, knowing the strategic position that management is trying to achieve for the business is a critical prerequisite to establishing and maintaining processes that will help the organization achieve it. Left to their own devices, an Engineering Process Group (EPG) will build "CMMI-compliant processes." However, given proper direction and motivation from senior management, those same processes will be honed to meet the organization's strategic business objectives. After all, as long as the EPG is going to the trouble of establishing a process infrastructure to achieve maturity level X, wouldn't it be nice if they actually helped the organization accomplish its strategic mission while doing so? (For some, this question borders on insightful rather than rhetorical.)

It seems fairly obvious that if your firm manufactures pace makers, "quality" is the attribute to be maximized. When your primary metric is the "plop factor," you are usually willing to overrun a bit on schedule and cost to reduce the number of field reported defects—especially those reported by the relatives of your former customers.

But you'd be surprised by how few executives can articulate a clear strategy and how little time they invest trying to do so. My favorite consulting engagement of all time stemmed from my first presentation at a major industry conference. After the talk, I was collared by an executive from a 300-person company who asked if I would be willing to facilitate a session in which his company would establish their Alignment Principle. He suggested a three-day offsite meeting in which his boss, the CEO, and the top nine executives in the organization would participate.

After I agreed to help him out, he brought up one little problem— the CEO doesn't listen to consultants! Unfazed, I informed him that I have a way to overcome such an issue—I simply triple my consulting rate. I've determined that if you charge enough money even the biggest of bigwigs *has* to listen!

To start the session, I spent 15 minutes explaining the basic concepts of the Alignment Principle. I then handed each of the 10 attendees a blank index card and asked them to write a single word on the card—"Faster," "Better," "Cheaper," or some other word that best describes the most important attribute for the organization's products and services.

I collected the cards and was dismayed to find 3 cards read "Faster," 3 "Better," 3 "Cheaper," and the last card—the one from the CEO (OK, I kept hers separate) —read "Innovative." After sharing the results with the group, and finding myself somewhat uncertain as to how to proceed, I suggested that we refill our coffee cups.

During the break, the CEO asked if we could speak privately. When we were alone she informed me that my services were no longer required. She said that the exercise pointed out that her Leadership Team obviously did not understand the direction in which she was trying to take the company. Because she had them offsite for three full days, she would invest the time in rectifying this situation. Rather than having a session facilitated by "one of you consultants," she felt that it was necessary for her to demonstrate leadership by taking ownership of the meeting's successful resolution.

As she bid me farewell she concluded with "... and please submit your invoice for the full three days; I will make sure that you are paid promptly." Nine days of pay for about a half hour of work—it don't get no better than that! But I digress ...

Suppose your senior management, like that of the pace-maker company, has just informed you that quality as defined by customer-reported defects is the single most important competitive dimension in the minds of your customers. It's time to craft the Alignment Principle:

"Achieve an annual, sustainable X% reduction in field reported defects without degrading current levels of cost, schedule, and feature variance."

Now the projects know what is most important to senior management, and the EPG knows what it means to help the projects "improve." It's not that cost, schedule, and functionality aren't important; it's just that they are not deemed as critical as customer-perceived quality. And now the EPG can build a process that helps move the organization in that strategic direction.

Avoiding Reverse Exploitation: Focusing on Performance

After you've addressed Pitfall #1—lack of alignment—you'll find that you've simply promoted Pitfall #2—focusing on "implementing the model."

The mantra of process agnostics and atheists is "process = administrivia," and in some misguided organizations, they're right! One might gain insight into the real problem in such organizations by distinguishing among three related concepts: process, process documentation, and process model.

The *process* is the way that work is actually being performed on today's projects. It is nothing more or less than the day-to-day activities carried out by the developers, testers, project managers, and so on as they do their jobs. To say that you are "process adverse" is to contend that all project activity should stop and, unless you're like Wally from Dilbert, this is not a position that most people would advocate.

The *process documentation* is the infrastructure being provided to the projects to help them perform their work in a consistent manner. It's the stuff sitting on the proverbial shelf just waiting to be employed by the projects—process descriptions, procedures, guidelines, templates, forms, metrics, checklists, tailoring guidelines, good case examples, and so on. It *should* provide the projects with a robust set of materials that enables them to conduct their work in the most effective and efficient manner (well, at least in theory!).

Finally, the *process model*, in the current case, the CMMI model, is a collection of good practices that can be exploited by the organization to heighten the probability of achieving success—where success is defined by the Alignment Principle and project-specific customer objectives. Please note the direction of this exploitation—the organization should exploit the model and *not*, as too often happens, the other way around.

How does one avoid reverse exploitation? Let me make three suggestions.

- Recognize that the current projects are enjoying some level of success. Some of them have actually completed and shipped products, right? Some of their customers are reasonably pleased with the work that the projects performed on their behalf, aren't they? Responding "yes" to either question implies that the existing processes (i.e., existing project activities) are working fairly well. The organization should not abandon everything they are currently doing to implement some goofy model just because they are trying to achieve some arbitrary "Maturity Level" (note the caps). Rather, they should determine how best to integrate some of the model's more value-added practices into their existing processes and process documentation to enhance project performance.

  For some organizations, a "find-the-pain, fix-the-pain" approach may be best to kick-start the improvement effort. This approach uses the model like a medical reference guide for addressing chronic project pain. Applying a bit of process aspirin makes a lot more sense than hitting people over the head with a 500+ page book like this and telling them, "Trust me. This is really good for you!"

- To avoid religious warfare among the process zealots, agnostics, and atheists, abandon the term "process improvement" in favor of the term "performance improvement." It's hard for even the most radical process atheist to argue that improving project performance is a bad thing.

- The EPG (retitled from Engineering Process Group to Engineering Performance Group), should change its focus to align with the new name. Rather than obsessing on higher maturity or capability levels—appropriately spelled with lowercase letters—the EPG should focus on helping the projects achieve ever-higher levels of success. Focusing on project performance may not be the quickest path to maturity level X, but it is a sure-fire way to overcome project resistance and actually build momentum and, dare I say, *excitement* for the improvement initiative.

Summary

Now that you've addressed pitfalls #1 and #2, you'll find that you've now promoted pitfalls #3, #4, #5, . . . Truth be told, there is an unlimited number of pitfalls to avoid or overcome as you traverse the ongoing path of performance improvement (most of which, unfortunately, are of your own making).

Someone could write a rather voluminous book describing ways that you could improve project performance. Hold on a second—they already did and you're holding it! Although reading and understanding the model itself is a good start, you also need to recognize that writing process descriptions, procedures, templates, and so on is the *easy* part; doing so in a way that provides value, and getting people to change their behavior as they adopt these new process elements is the really tough part. Just because you build it does *not* mean they will come!

You are strongly encouraged to learn and steal shamelessly from those that have gone before, and are even more strongly encouraged to contribute your experience to the growing body of knowledge for those that are yet to come. Enjoy the journey; the rewards are worth it—provided you don't mess it up!

Ten Missing Links to CMMI Success

by Hillel Glazer

Starting out with CMMI can be particularly daunting to individuals and organizations who don't know what they don't know about CMMI. Often, they set out not knowing they're missing a few bits of information that could make their journeys less arduous and possibly enjoyable. Absent these bits, people find themselves struggling to incorporate CMMI into their work. Between bouts of bashing their heads against the wall, they often find themselves blaming CMMI itself (or some personification of CMMI such as their consultant or lead appraiser), believing there's something clearly "wrong" with the model. Hint: It's not the model.

Whether it's good or bad luck, or some other characteristic of nature, I have had the privilege of working with many companies just starting out with CMMI for the first time. These companies (large or small, traditional or Agile) don't know *what* to expect and they don't *really* understand what using CMMI is all about.

If you are just starting out with CMMI, consider yourselves lucky. You don't have as many bad habits or history to undo. Those experienced with CMMI might find themselves reaching for the Excedrin—realizing, for the first time, the "missing links" to their CMMI challenges. Below, the rather unorthodox approach to using CMMI has resulted in lasting, positive effects.

I must acknowledge my thorough appreciation for the competitive nature of organizations vying for attention and business from customers expecting to see some sort of CMMI "rating" (e.g., "Maturity Level 3"). This is reality. It's a destructive and counterproductive reality because it can cause organizations to pursue CMMI ratings at the expense of people, productivity, and profit. How silly is that? The purpose of incorporating CMMI into your work is to provide a systematic mechanism to improve performance. Increasing overhead, decimating morale and lowering productivity are not "performance improvements." Consider this your first missing link.

Missing Link #1:

CMMI improves performance. Find aspects of your development operation that can stand to improve in terms of time, cost, and quality, and CMMI will make more sense.

Given that CMMI is a framework to improve performance, it stands to reason that success with CMMI comes more easily to those organizations who *want* to improve, can identify aspects of their operation they'd like to improve, and have the culture and leadership to make appropriate changes to facilitate such improvements. Organizations resistant to change (even beneficial changes), who have a culture of blame and mistrust, and whose idea of "measures" starts and ends with top-line sales, are going to find it difficult to use or see any benefit from CMMI. The right culture and leadership will cause the organization's behaviors to align well with CMMI goals. Organizations with the "right" culture and leadership find themselves achieving CMMI ratings without having to think about it.

Missing Link #2:

CMMI alone will not make things much better. For CMMI to work well, it needs: (1) a culture of learning, empowerment, and trust, and (2) leadership with the courage, vision, and direction to eliminate the fear often accompanying changes.

CMMI is unlike any other body of work out there. It's different in how it's supposed to be used, in how we determine how well it's been used. What makes for success with other bodies of work does not necessarily work well with CMMI.

In many parts of our work and personal lives, when we see a virtuous thing to do, we often find ways to adopt it into our daily lives. At first, it takes a conscious effort to get it going; then, if we like it, after awhile it becomes second nature. In fact, we'll naturally find ways to keep doing it and improving what it is that we're doing. In many ways, CMMI is a lot like this, but in some important ways CMMI is different.

Many organizations misconstrue CMMI practices as achievements in and of themselves rather than enablers of long-term results. In other words, they make the *purpose* of incorporating CMMI practices the presence or absence of the practices rather than the business benefits of the practices. Using personal health as an analogy, it's like saying, "Hey! Look at me! I'm eating lettuce! Ignore the cup of blue cheese dressing. I'm eating lettuce!"

Missing Link #3

Don't make it about CMMI. Your efforts with CMMI are to help you improve your business. CMMI practices are not the ends; they're the means to the ends.

CMMI is full of practices. Practices are not processes. Practices are activities that improve processes wherever, whenever, and however they may appear in your organization *in reality*. In fact, it's probably just best to stop thinking about *processes* entirely. Processes confuse people. Just think about *your work*. That leaves us with asking questions like, "What can we do to make our work better?" You can't actually *build anything* by following CMMI. There simply is not enough stuff in it that you can actually follow along to run your operation. You need to have some sort of work flow that *works* for you *first*, and then use CMMI practices to improve it.

Missing Link #4

Know your work. Know how you get stuff done. Then, look into CMMI for ideas on where and how to improve how you get stuff done. That's what CMMI's practices are for—not to define your work, but to refine it.

Speaking of practices, there's frequently much confusion over the coincidental similarity in the names of CMMI process areas to various aspects of how work commonly gets done. The names by which you refer to activities in your work flow may also be words used in CMMI. These activities may be specific tasks, supporting work, or even steps in your development lifecycle. This coincidence does not make everything in CMMI part of your lifecycle. That many activities you do are already in CMMI is testament to the fact that the CMMI is full of smart things to do (and yet there are companies out there that don't do them). However, the converse is not true. If something is in CMMI that you don't think you do, it does *not* mean that you must work them into similarly named parts of your work. More importantly, each practice is an opportunity to leverage activities toward improvement. That they exist in CMMI is more about the role such activities play in improvement, not in defining how work is being done.

Missing Link #5

Don't confuse the names of CMMI process areas with processes you might be using. What separates your conduct of a practice from its appearance in CMMI is a question of whether you're leveraging that practice to improve your work.

Do not pass go. Do not collect $200. Do not even begin to work with CMMI until you completely understand the role and limitations of *models*, how models are used, and the sort of model that CMMI is. All models share certain inalienable characteristics. Foremost is that they're all *fake*. They're not the real thing. They're mere representations of reality, which does not make them *real*. A horse might have 5m² of surface area, but to model the horse we'd probably just represent her as a sphere, cube, or box with 5m² of surface area— depending on the application we're planning to use her in. Horses aren't spheres, but for many models, spheres are good enough.

Good models help us understand complex ideas, test them, and avoid cost and/or danger compared to trying these ideas in the real world. Models are also used to build other things, like object models in software. CMMI is a model for building process performance improvement systems. As such, the *model* isn't the improvement system, it's just a list of characteristics that you use when building *your* improvement system. To describe these characteristics, the model includes examples and other narrative content to inform us of what's meant by the terse summary of characteristics. Then, when benchmarking against CMMI (e.g., in a SCAMPI), what's being investigated is how many of these characteristics your improvement system has compared to the ones listed in the model. The names of the model characteristics in CMMI are goals and practices.

Missing Link #6

CMMI is a model for building improvement systems. Goals and practices in CMMI are the characteristics that help us know whether our system is consistent with the model, and all the "informative" material helps us understand what's meant by the goals and practices. Think: Thousands of words in lieu of pictures.

Earlier I alluded to an experience many of us have shared: the notion of working on bringing some virtuous behavior into our lives, then growing with it until it becomes second nature. CMMI is about improving performance, and we'd eventually like improving performance to be second nature to our work. CMMI provides a systematic way of doing just that, called *generic practices*. Generic practices are CMMI's way of helping organizations systematically make improvement practices part of everyday work.

At first, you need awareness of the practice(s) and with this awareness usually comes some level of accountability. Typically, we make sure someone knows what needs to get done; much like starting a health program by "just doing it." Then, when "just doing it" doesn't cut it, we need to think about it; we'll start to plan ahead, think things through, set aside time and resources, put in checks and balances, get others involved, and get more organized. In other words, we "manage" it; same with the practices in CMMI. As we get even more refined, we'll come up with better definitions for ourselves so we can compare how we're doing to some prior experience. You know the saying, "that which is measured is improved"? It's true.

Missing Link #7

Generic practices are CMMI's way of helping you make performance improvement practices second nature. They're not intended to be separate and unique activities and they're not the same as what you do to make your products. They're what you do to ensure that the way you want things done shows up every day as "business as usual."

OK, so this next "missing link" may be a bit controversial, but it's always worked for me and my clients. When you recognize and apply this thinking, you can avoid all sorts of heartburn. CMMI is easiest to use for experts. In fact, if you think of CMMI's "maturity levels" as follows, it might actually start to make sense:

Put a project management professional and a configuration specialist to work together on a project, and they'll naturally generate practices of maturity level 2. Add an organizational change professional and an experienced engineer to these two, and much (if not all) of maturity level 3 will show up for the team. Add a process modeler and a statistical expert to this high-powered team and it shouldn't be surprising to see maturity level 4 and 5 behaviors appear.

Missing Link #8

Pursue the internal capabilities of project management, engineering, and other described experts and you'll discover the origins of many of the innate features of CMMI. Until you've grown those capabilities, you might want some help.

Many failures en route to realizing benefits with CMMI can be tied to not seeing the complete picture of the organization's processes, how they work together, and how they operate on all project, product, and supporting activities simultaneously and over time. They see very narrow, shallow, and temporary views of their processes, and they often fail to connect their processes to organizational norms, culture, behaviors, or business performance. To complete the picture, define an *architecture* for your processes, including a taxonomy that characterizes the type of work you do and the types of process components (e.g., process descriptions, procedures, guidelines, measures, templates) that you will use to add discipline to your process improvement journey. How much sense does it make to be *ad hoc* in how you pursue improvements?

Missing Link #9

A process architecture and common taxonomy are needed so that you can communicate consistently about your processes, and so that you experience your process as a solution to how you get stuff done. Your processes don't happen in a vacuum or in a different dimension of reality by other people. Treat your process solution using systems thinking and all that it entails.

Understand the origin of CMMI. Specifically, that CMMI has its roots in Lean, TQM, and high performance cultures. CMMI is a systematic, measurable guide to installing the many attributes of these roots. The existence of a guide against which measurable progress can be made does not obviate the validity of the basics. Creating such a guide is not easy, and following it might be tricky, but that doesn't mean you need to be overwhelmed by it. In fact, if you go back to the basic Values, Principles, and Practices of Lean, TQM, and high performance cultures, there's almost nothing in CMMI that will thwart you.

Missing Link #10

Start with the basics. Get grounded—firmly—in what Lean, TQM, and high-performance cultures are all about. Become experts in Lean Systems Thinking, TQM, empowered organizations, and value. CMMI will follow.

I hope these missing links will help you find and complete other links of your own. If I were pressed for a summary of these missing links it would be this: Recognize the psychology and the engineering in performance improvement. Take them both seriously and you'll be fine. Take either lightly and you'll face an uphill struggle.

Good luck on your CMMI journey.

Adopting CMMI: Hiring a CMMI Consultant or Lead Appraiser

by Rawdon Young, Will Hayes, Kevin Schaaff, and Alexander Stall

Many organizations embarking on process improvement initiatives discover that anyone can be called a consultant. There is typically no test, no accrediting organization, or governing body to guide consultants' actions—a person can simply open a business and start providing services.

Many organizations have learned the hard way about the wide range of expertise available. There are differing levels of competence, specialization, and experience. A consultant that is competent in one discipline (e.g., software engineering) or domain (e.g., accounting) may have relatively little to offer in another discipline (e.g., hardware engineering) or domain (e.g., embedded). The experience of individuals offering consulting services must be carefully considered before inviting one of them to help steer the improvement program of an organization. A bad choice can be very costly, have long-term effects on the viability of the program, and affect the credibility of the leadership in an organization.

In this essay, we identify some areas to emphasize when considering prospective consultants and lead appraisers. Our intent is to help maximize the chances that you will hire a professional who can help you achieve your performance goals as well as your goals for process improvement. This essay is based on our own personal experiences as process improvement professionals, as well as observations made during the conduct of quality activities for the CMMI Appraisal Program at the SEI.

Experience Drives Success

"You can't teach experience."—Coaching adage

Experience is perhaps the single most important characteristic of effective CMMI consultants and lead appraisers, and the one that typically distinguishes a particular professional from his or her colleagues and competitors. The content of CMMI constellations and appraisal methods can be gained from careful study of the model documents and through training. However, a real understanding of how they are beneficially applied, and the value that an organization can gain from using them comes from understanding organizations, typically as a result of actually having done that type of work.

But what is experience? By itself, a count of the number of years someone has done something is not sufficient. When looking for an outside expert to help you achieve your performance goals, we have found that the *breadth* of an individual's experience is usually more helpful. Has the professional gained experience by working in or with different organizations, perhaps in different roles? Or, has all of his or her experience been in the same organization, or the same type of work? Stated simply: *"Does the person have X years of experience or 1 year of experience X times?"*

With broad experience, the consultant has a better understanding of how different kinds of organizations work. This greater repertoire aids in diagnosing issues as well as determining a variety of potential solutions. Insight about the drivers within an organization—the underlying pattern of incentives and disincentives—helps in deriving custom solutions to problems. Drawing on a breadth of experience, the consultant or lead appraiser is able to see a greater variety of possibilities and can foresee a variety of plausible patterns of future action in the organization.

Reliance on a narrower range of experience can lead to force-fitting a specific solution because it has worked so well in the past; it might even be used as a selling point for the consultant's business. We have encountered many professionals with "the solution." Very often, "the solution" is based on the techniques they have seen implemented several times within a single organization. Because they have only seen it done in a very narrow context, the approach tends to be less flexible.

Many of these professionals have worked hard to develop "the complete solution" with templates, tools, and training prepackaged and ready to be delivered to the next client. Tailoring this type of solution is often difficult and can result in experimentation that translates into significant effort and risk to the process improvement objectives.

Lead appraisers with narrower experience often struggle with implementations that are unusual or different from what they have seen in the past. Because of this, appraisal teams can arrive at findings that understate the true achievement of the organization, or miss weaknesses that represent significant barriers to achieving performance goals. In the extreme case, a team may identify something as a weakness because it is different than what the lead appraiser has seen in the past, or different than "what the model says."

Remember though that there is a tradeoff of breadth versus depth. As the aphorism goes, "A specialist knows more and more about less and less until he knows everything about nothing and a generalist is someone who knows less and less about more and more until he knows nothing about everything."

How Do We Find the Professional We Need?

The following is advice you should consider when selecting lead appraisers or consultants to help you determine if they have the requisite mix of breadth and depth of experience.

You are looking for both breadth and depth of experience. Breadth comes from working with a variety of different systems, domains, platforms, services, acquisition types, and so on. With this breadth of experience, professionals will have seen a variety of solutions in a variety of situations and thus the tool box of solutions (for consultants) or capability of interpretation (for lead appraisers) they bring to help you is greater than one of less breadth. Depth of experience comes from working hands-on through the entire lifecycle. For example, have they done requirements, design, build, test, and delivery of engineering products and managed projects that did the same? In other words, have they done those things you are hiring them to help you improve or to evaluate against CMMI?

You are looking for someone who understands the work your organization does. It is possible that you will not always be able to hire a consultant who has experience in what your organization does. In these situations, you should hire someone that understands your business. Do prospective lead appraisers or consultants understand the kind of work you do? Do they understand the language of your business, and not just process improvement or appraisal language? In other words, if you are an accounting company, can the consultant or lead appraiser speak cogently and coherently about accounting services? If you develop products using Agile methods, does the consultant or lead appraiser understand the concepts of agility? A good consultant or lead appraiser doesn't necessarily have to be a CPA, a Scrum Master, or a certified expert in your specific domain. However, if you find yourself teaching them an entirely new language or explaining the nature of the competitive market in which the company operates, you should consider the possibility that they do not understand your business context and may have a difficult time developing an effective solution for your organization.

You are looking for someone who balances process improvement and model compliance. When talking to prospective consultants or lead appraisers, try to get an understanding of how they balance process improvement and model compliance. Do they recognize that the process implemented should reflect the work actually being done, and that it should provide positive value to either the performer of the process or to the larger project or organization? Do they understand that changing an organization can be very difficult and time consuming? How can they help you institutionalize the process and not backslide? Key areas of discussion could be building visible and active senior management support, instilling ownership of the process in those required to follow it, identifying consequences for not following the process, identifying rewards for improving the process (not for simply following the process), removing excuses for not following the process, and documenting processes to the level of granularity you need to ensure they are consistently followed.

Beware of consultants and lead appraisers who overemphasize compliance with the model or the standard. A template of "the standard process" that requires little input from projects and staff, a single documented process for all types of projects, or the development of work products simply because "the model says you have to" are not conducive to obtaining value. Worse, they can actually have a negative impact on the success of the organization both in terms of improvement and business objectives. George Box has a quote that summarizes this point nicely, "All models are wrong, some models are useful." Consultants that are unable to help you see the value proposition from the business perspective, or lead appraisers unable to explain the business consequences of a weakness and can only rely on the model, may have insufficient grounding in your context.

On follow-up questions with candidates, try to determine how flexible they are in their process improvement philosophy. Will they insist on remaking your organization to reflect their solution, or are they willing to change their solution to meet the needs of your business?

You are looking for someone who will provide some suggested guidance on how to evaluate your processes effectively. At some point, an organization that undertakes process improvement will probably want (or require) some level of evaluation of how well they have done, whether it be a formal benchmark like a SCAMPI A, or a less formal evaluation of strengths and weaknesses. Lead appraisers or consultants should at least have some approach to these events. Do they view appraisal results as the end goal or as a way to indicate where you can improve? Is their emphasis on improving the performance of the organization or do they focus solely on achieving appraisal results? For lead appraisers, particularly, the ability to explain, with appropriate linkage to business drivers, why an appraisal is valuable to an organization indicates that they have an understanding of how organizations can use appraisals to drive improvements, and not just produce numbers for use in proposals. Similarly, the ability to recognize that not all implementations are identical—sometimes even in the same organization—can mean the difference between a successful, value-added appraisal and a simple exercise to produce a rating number.

You are looking for someone who will provide more than just a "level." None of this is to say that achieving a maturity or capability level is not a worthy goal, but if "Maturity Level x" is the only goal of the consultant you are considering hiring, be aware of the potential impact. You may well achieve the goal (almost any organization can be forced to change behavior for a short time), but your performance probably won't increase and may in fact decrease. It is also likely that the changes won't be institutionalized (i.e., they won't become the habit of the organization) and they will quickly disappear as the organization reverts to its old behaviors after the appraisal.

You are looking for someone who understands the realities of process improvement. Finally, it is usually worthwhile to ask prospective lead appraisers or consultants some questions regarding their experiences related to developing, implementing, and following processes. These questions can provide insight into how well they understand the realities of process improvement. Consider using the following questions:

- Describe situations in the past where you have actually developed processes for an organization.
- Were those processes ever appraised? If so, with what results?
- Have you ever worked in an organization that followed the processes you helped to develop? Have you followed these processes?

Conclusion—Your Mileage May Vary

Of course, no one can guarantee that an organization will truly improve or always derive value from the use of model-based improvement simply because it hired a particular external professional to help along the way. Many other factors affect process improvement initiatives, such as senior management support, the allocation of organizational resources, and the willingness of the leadership in the organization to accept changes—all must be addressed to have a successful improvement effort. However, the right external expert can greatly facilitate the solutions to these complex issues and enhance the likelihood of success.

When seeking to engage an external professional, always remember these two things:

1. It's not just knowing the content of the model or the method; it's knowing how to apply them to a real organization in its context that results in real, valuable process improvement.
2. Past application and experience in multiple contexts helps increase assurance that a consultant or lead appraiser can help you implement a solution that is effective in your situation. A lot of people can do it right once in a specific context, but no two organizations are ever the same; the ability to see the issues from a variety of past experiences is important.

Model content and method structure can be taught and represented in diplomas and certifications, but you can't teach experience. If the only way consultants or lead appraisers can explain their service is by quoting phrases or content from the model or method, proceed with caution. At the end of the day, it's your organization and not theirs that is trying to improve, and process improvement is about competitive advantage, not "checking boxes." If you choose your process consultant or lead appraiser wisely, set measurable objectives, fix real problems relevant to the business of the organization, and demonstrate added value, your process improvement program will be sustained and your efforts will be successful.

From Doubter to Believer: My Journey to CMMI

by Joseph Morin

It was an honor to receive the invitation to contribute an essay for inclusion in this third edition of the CMMI for Development book. It was also somewhat ironic considering that I had mostly avoided involvement with the Process Program[1] during my tenure at the SEI

---

1. The Process Program (now called the Software Engineering Process Management program) is the SEI group that serves as the steward of CMMI and that focuses its work on helping organizations improve their processes as a way of reaching their business objectives.

in the late 80s and early 90s. On the other hand, it now seems appropriate because I have become an outspoken process advocate and enthusiastic contributor to the evolution of the models and appraisal methods over the 16 years since Integrated System Diagnostics was spun off from the SEI as one of its original transition partners.[2] I guess it is true that converts to an idea become its most enthusiastic promoters.

Like many from my generation, involvement in computer science and software engineering was ancillary to my original career objectives. After graduating from Caltech in 1973 with a degree in Astronomy and Physics, I had the enviable opportunity to work as part of the research group responsible for the first three small astronomy satellites.

The mission was to identify and study sources of X-Ray emissions coming from objects in space. To do that, we needed to develop systems and software for the real-time command, control, and communication of the satellites and the on-board instrument packages. The ground based part of these systems utilized computers from Digital Equipment and Data General requiring a mastery of their unique operating systems, assembly languages, and communications interfaces.

We also needed to develop back-end data reduction and analysis systems to extract and understand the scientific data coming from the instruments. These systems involved programming in Fortran and PL/I and becoming an expert in the JCL needed to manipulate the IBM 360/195 at Goddard Space Flight Center as a single user machine from Friday evenings through Monday mornings.

Those were exciting times from the research perspective. We identified many more X-Ray sources than we had anticipated and our work in understanding them led to the first experimental support for the existence of black holes. That said, and much to my surprise, I found myself drawn more and more to the challenges of developing, operating, and maintaining the systems and software than to those associated with the science.

When the opportunity presented itself to join some of my old classmates at Intermetrics, a Cambridge, Massachusetts startup founded by the developers of the guidance, navigation, and control software for NASA's Apollo spacecraft, I enthusiastically made the career change. As had been the case in my field, computers and software were becoming increasingly important in many mission and

---

2. An SEI transition partner is an organization that licenses SEI products to deliver services to clients.

life-critical systems. Computers and software were also becoming increasingly complex.

Improved methods, tools, and techniques for software development and maintenance were a need recognized by policy makers at the highest levels of the U.S. government as well as by developers "in the trenches." Intermetrics contributed to meeting that need through the development of programming languages, compilers, and support software environments for NASA, the U.S. Navy, GM's automotive electronics division, several telecommunications companies, and a number of computer manufacturers.

As we developed systems for these customers, it seemed only natural that we should try to apply best practices to our own work. We adopted the principles and best practices advocated by Fred Brooks and Harlan Mills. We applied some of the empirical techniques coming out of Victor Basili's group at the University of Maryland and used Terry Snyder's Rate Charting technique to track our progress and communicate with management, customers, and other stakeholders.

We actively participated in the R&D and industry standards communities to identify, pilot, and deploy innovative technologies in the performance of our work. It was through this latter activity that I was afforded the privilege of meeting and interacting with a number of the people who would later emerge as key players in the founding and evolution of the SEI and later the CMMI Product Suite. At the time, these colleagues were brought together through the DoD Software Initiative program, which included the development of the Ada programming language and lifecycle support environments that were designed to enforce engineering discipline.

Some years passed before I joined the SEI and had the opportunity to reunite with these respected colleagues. My career had diverged into other niches of computer science and my management responsibilities increased, working in several more startup companies and doing some independent management and marketing consulting for other companies or their venture capital investors. The technological aspect of the work remained fascinating, but the new career direction for me was the challenge that executive management faces in meeting business or mission objectives.

I had seen many good ideas and technologies fall by the wayside or undergo a meteoric rise and fall as a fad. To be successful, organizations need to understand the market and accommodate the wants and needs of stakeholders, including those with competing ideas or technology. Sound plans for piloting and rollout are as important as sound plans for development of systems and software.

Clear communication of achievable expectations within predictable schedule and cost constraints is critical for investors, senior managers, developers, and customers alike. Appropriate training and resources are required to allow personnel to effectively accomplish their roles. Objective measures of quality, progress, and success need to be defined, collected, analyzed, and communicated in ways that enable timely corrective actions and provide a factual basis for key business decisions. All of those factors and others need to be balanced and coordinated to achieve the business objective.

When I received an invitation to join the SEI and work on these issues as part of the Institute's technology transition mission, I eagerly accepted. Groups within the Institute were generating many promising technical ideas. Priscilla Fowler, John Maher, and Cecil Martin were assembling a body of knowledge for successfully managing change in the transition and adoption of innovative technology.

I was thoroughly enjoying applying that body of knowledge in helping the SEI move its ideas into practice with early adopters, particularly in the area of domain-specific system architectures. I was aware of the work in the Process Program but had a lingering prejudice that "real" developers and seasoned managers did not need to be taught what seemed to be common sense presented in broad brush terms.

That viewpoint changed dramatically when I was recruited to be the executive manager in establishing ISD as an SEI spinoff to commercialize the SCE appraisal method. Before I knew it, I was drawn into my first rounds of CBA-IPI assessments and SCE evaluations, predecessors of today's SCAMPI appraisals.

I quickly developed a new appreciation of the model and of the variations in practice implementations across diverse organizations. I realized that my earlier perceptions were woefully misguided. The overall state of the practice was not characterized by the relatively small groups of "heroes" working to implement a clearly shared vision in the startups or R&D centers with which I was most familiar. What had appeared to be common sense was indeed its own extensive body of knowledge that needed to be codified and deployed in the same fashion as the technologies it enabled.

Working with organizations to help them improve their processes has not always been a smooth or easy endeavor. The CMMI Product Development Team deserves special recognition for persevering in the evolution of the model. They have had to reconcile and harmonize myriad viewpoints on what best practice is and how to describe it without being prescriptive. They have weathered uncertainties in funding, aggressive schedules, and changes in emphasis directed by committee.

They have overcome those and other challenges and obstacles to produce a work that can benefit us all. I can attest to those benefits first hand in small organizations applying Agile and Six Sigma techniques in attaining maturity level 5 capability and in large bureaucratic ones more slowly improving predictability and performance as they implement managed and defined processes across the organization.

I encourage you to realize the benefits in your own organization. And for those of you with doubts like me in my earlier days, I encourage you to take a fresh look at what you can gain from this work. I believe that you will find, as I have, that the model captures much of your hard earned knowledge in a way that allows you to effectively communicate and apply that knowledge in improving the performance of your organization.

PART TWO

Generic Goals and Generic Practices, and the Process Areas

GENERIC GOALS AND GENERIC PRACTICES

Overview

This section describes in detail all the generic goals and generic practices of CMMI—model components that directly address process institutionalization. As you address each process area, refer to this section for the details of all generic practices.

Generic practice elaborations appear after generic practices to provide guidance on how the generic practice can be applied uniquely to process areas.

Process Institutionalization

Institutionalization is an important concept in process improvement. When mentioned in the generic goal and generic practice descriptions, institutionalization implies that the process is ingrained in the way the work is performed and there is commitment and consistency to performing (i.e., executing) the process.

An institutionalized process is more likely to be retained during times of stress. When the requirements and objectives for the process change, however, the implementation of the process may also need to change to ensure that it remains effective. The generic practices describe activities that address these aspects of institutionalization.

The degree of institutionalization is embodied in the generic goals and expressed in the names of the processes associated with each goal as indicated in Table 7.1.

Table 7.1   Generic Goals and Process Names

Generic Goal	Progression of Processes
GG 1	Performed process
GG 2	Managed process
GG 3	Defined process

Continued

- Dependencies among the activities, work products, and services of the process
- Resources (e.g., funding, people, tools) needed to perform the process
- Assignment of responsibility and authority
- Training needed for performing and supporting the process
- Work products to be controlled and the level of control to be applied
- Measurement requirements to provide insight into the execution of the process, its work products, and its services
- Involvement of relevant stakeholders
- Activities for monitoring and controlling the process
- Objective evaluation activities of the process
- Management review activities for the process and the work products

Subpractices

1. Define and document the plan for performing the process.

    This plan can be a stand-alone document, embedded in a more comprehensive document, or distributed among multiple documents. In the case of the plan being distributed among multiple documents, ensure that a coherent picture of who does what is preserved. Documents can be hardcopy or softcopy.

2. Define and document the process description.

    The process description, which includes relevant standards and procedures, can be included as part of the plan for performing the process or can be included in the plan by reference.

3. Review the plan with relevant stakeholders and get their agreement.

    This review of the plan includes reviewing that the planned process satisfies the applicable policies, plans, requirements, and standards to provide assurance to relevant stakeholders.

4. Revise the plan as necessary.

CAR Elaboration

This plan for performing the causal analysis and resolution process can be included in (or referenced by) the project plan, which is described in the Project Planning process area. This plan differs from the action proposals and associated action plans described in several specific practices in this process area. The plan called for in this generic practice would address the project's overall causal analysis and resolution process (perhaps tailored from a standard process maintained by the organization). In contrast, the process action proposals and associated action items address the activities needed to address a specific root cause under study.

CM Elaboration

This plan for performing the configuration management process can be included in (or referenced by) the project plan, which is described in the Project Planning process area.

DAR Elaboration

This plan for performing the decision analysis and resolution process can be included in (or referenced by) the project plan, which is described in the Project Planning process area.

IPM Elaboration

This plan for the integrated project management process unites the planning for the project planning and monitor and control processes. The planning for performing the planning related practices in Integrated Project Management is addressed as part of planning the project planning process. This plan for performing the monitor-and-control related practices in Integrated Project Management can be included in (or referenced by) the project plan, which is described in the Project Planning process area.

MA Elaboration

This plan for performing the measurement and analysis process can be included in (or referenced by) the project plan, which is described in the Project Planning process area.

OPD Elaboration

This plan for performing the organizational process definition process can be part of (or referenced by) the organization's process improvement plan.

OPF Elaboration

This plan for performing the organizational process focus process, which is often called "the process improvement plan," differs from the process action plans described in specific practices in this process area. The plan called for in this generic practice addresses the comprehensive planning for all of the specific practices in this process area, from establishing organizational process needs through incorporating process related experiences into organizational process assets.

OPM Elaboration

This plan for performing the organizational performance management process differs from the deployment plans described in a specific practice in this process area. The plan called for in this generic practice addresses the comprehensive planning for all of the specific practices in this process area, from maintaining business objectives to evaluating improvement effects. In contrast, the deployment plans called for in the specific practice would address the planning needed for the deployment of selected improvements.

OPP Elaboration

This plan for performing the organizational process performance process can be included in (or referenced by) the organization's process improvement plan, which is described in the Organizational Process Focus process area. Or it may be documented in a separate plan that describes only the plan for the organizational process performance process.

OT Elaboration

This plan for performing the organizational training process differs from the tactical plan for organizational training described in a specific practice in this process area. The plan called for in this generic practice addresses the comprehensive planning for all of the specific practices in this process area, from establishing strategic training needs through assessing the effectiveness of organizational training. In contrast, the organizational training tactical plan called for in the specific practice of this process area addresses the periodic planning for the delivery of training offerings.

PI Elaboration

This plan for performing the product integration process addresses the comprehensive planning for all of the specific practices in this process area, from the preparation for product integration all the way through to the delivery of the final product.

This plan for performing the product integration process can be part of (or referenced by) the project plan as described in the Project Planning process area.

PMC Elaboration

This plan for performing the project monitoring and control process can be part of (or referenced by) the project plan, as described in the Project Planning process area.

PP Elaboration

Refer to Table 7.2 in Generic Goals and Generic Practices for more information about the relationship between generic practice 2.2 and the Project Planning process area.

PPQA Elaboration

This plan for performing the process and product quality assurance process can be included in (or referenced by) the project plan, which is described in the Project Planning process area.

QPM Elaboration

This plan for performing the quantitative project management process can be included in (or referenced by) the project plan, which is described in the Project Planning process area.

RD Elaboration

This plan for performing the requirements development process can be part of (or referenced by) the project plan as described in the Project Planning process area.

REQM Elaboration

This plan for performing the requirements management process can be part of (or referenced by) the project plan as described in the Project Planning process area.

RSKM Elaboration

This plan for performing the risk management process can be included in (or referenced by) the project plan, which is described in the Project Planning process area. The plan called for in this generic practice addresses the comprehensive planning for all of the specific practices in this process area. In particular, this plan provides the overall approach for risk mitigation, but is distinct from mitigation plans (including contingency plans) for specific risks. In contrast, the risk mitigation plans called for in the specific practices of this process area addresses more focused items such as the levels that trigger risk handling activities.

SAM Elaboration

Portions of this plan for performing the supplier agreement management process can be part of (or referenced by) the project plan as described in the Project Planning process area. Often, however, some portions of the plan reside outside of the project with a group such as contract management.

TS Elaboration

This plan for performing the technical solution process can be part of (or referenced by) the project plan as described in the Project Planning process area.

VAL Elaboration

This plan for performing the validation process can be included in (or referenced by) the project plan, which is described in the Project Planning process area.

VER Elaboration

This plan for performing the verification process can be included in (or referenced by) the project plan, which is described in the Project Planning process area.

GP 2.3 PROVIDE RESOURCES

Provide adequate resources for performing the process, developing the work products, and providing the services of the process.

The purpose of this generic practice is to ensure that the resources necessary to perform the process as defined by the plan are available when they are needed. Resources include adequate funding, appropriate physical facilities, skilled people, and appropriate tools.

The interpretation of the term "adequate" depends on many factors and can change over time. Inadequate resources may be addressed by increasing resources or by removing requirements, constraints, and commitments.

CAR Elaboration

Examples of resources provided include the following:
- Database management systems
- Process modeling tools
- Statistical analysis packages

CM Elaboration

Examples of resources provided include the following:
- Configuration management tools
- Data management tools
- Archiving and reproduction tools
- Database management systems

DAR Elaboration

Examples of resources provided include the following:
- Simulators and modeling tools
- Prototyping tools
- Tools for conducting surveys

IPM Elaboration

Examples of resources provided include the following:
- Problem tracking and trouble reporting packages
- Groupware
- Video conferencing
- Integrated decision database
- Integrated product support environments

MA Elaboration

Staff with appropriate expertise provide support for measurement and analysis activities. A measurement group with such a role may exist.

Examples of resources provided include the following:
- Statistical packages
- Packages that support data collection over networks

OPD Elaboration

A process group typically manages organizational process definition activities. This group typically is staffed by a core of professionals whose primary responsibility is coordinating organizational process improvement.

This group is supported by process owners and people with expertise in various disciplines such as the following:
- Project management
- The appropriate engineering disciplines
- Configuration management
- Quality assurance

> Examples of resources provided include the following:
> - Database management systems
> - Process modeling tools
> - Web page builders and browsers

OPF Elaboration

> Examples of resources provided include the following:
> - Database management systems
> - Process improvement tools
> - Web page builders and browsers
> - Groupware
> - Quality improvement tools (e.g., cause-and-effect diagrams, affinity diagrams, Pareto charts)

OPM Elaboration

> Examples of resources provided include the following:
> - Simulation packages
> - Prototyping tools
> - Statistical packages
> - Dynamic systems modeling
> - Subscriptions to online technology databases and publications
> - Process modeling tools

OPP Elaboration

Special expertise in statistical and other quantitative techniques may be needed to establish process performance baselines for the organization's set of standard processes.

> Examples of resources provided include the following:
> - Database management systems
> - System dynamics models
> - Process modeling tools
> - Statistical analysis packages
> - Problem tracking packages

OT Elaboration

Examples of resources provided include the following:
- Subject matter experts
- Curriculum designers
- Instructional designers
- Instructors
- Training administrators

Special facilities may be required for training. When necessary, the facilities required for the activities in the Organizational Training process area are developed or purchased.

Examples of resources provided include the following:
- Instruments for analyzing training needs
- Workstations to be used for training
- Instructional design tools
- Packages for developing presentation materials

PI Elaboration

Product component interface coordination can be accomplished with an Interface Control Working Group consisting of people who represent external and internal interfaces. Such groups can be used to elicit needs for interface requirements development.

Special facilities may be required for assembling and delivering the product. When necessary, the facilities required for the activities in the Product Integration process area are developed or purchased.

Examples of resources provided include the following:
- Prototyping tools
- Analysis tools
- Simulation tools
- Interface management tools
- Assembly tools (e.g., compilers, make files, joining tools, jigs, fixtures)

PMC Elaboration

> **Examples of resources provided include the following:**
> • Cost tracking systems
> • Effort reporting systems
> • Action item tracking systems
> • Project management and scheduling programs

PP Elaboration

Special expertise, equipment, and facilities in project planning may be required.

> **Special expertise in project planning can include the following:**
> • Experienced estimators
> • Schedulers
> • Technical experts in applicable areas (e.g., product domain, technology)

> **Examples of resources provided include the following:**
> • Spreadsheet programs
> • Estimating models
> • Project planning and scheduling packages

PPQA Elaboration

> **Examples of resources provided include the following:**
> • Evaluation tools
> • Noncompliance tracking tools

QPM Elaboration

Special expertise in statistics and its use in analyzing process performance may be needed to define the analytic techniques used in quantitative management. Special expertise in statistics can also be needed for analyzing and interpreting the measures resulting from statistical analyses; however, teams need sufficient expertise to support a basic understanding of their process performance as they perform their daily work.

> Examples of resources provided include the following:
> - Statistical analysis packages
> - Statistical process and quality control packages
> - Scripts and tools that assist teams in analyzing their own process performance with minimal need for additional expert assistance

RD Elaboration

Special expertise in the application domain, methods for eliciting stakeholder needs, and methods and tools for specifying and analyzing customer, product, and product component requirements may be required.

> Examples of resources provided include the following:
> - Requirements specification tools
> - Simulators and modeling tools
> - Prototyping tools
> - Scenario definition and management tools
> - Requirements tracking tools

REQM Elaboration

> Examples of resources provided include the following:
> - Requirements tracking tools
> - Traceability tools

RSKM Elaboration

> Examples of resources provided include the following:
> - Risk management databases
> - Risk mitigation tools
> - Prototyping tools
> - Modeling and simulation tools

SAM Elaboration

> Examples of resources provided include the following:
> - Preferred supplier lists
> - Requirements tracking tools
> - Project management and scheduling programs

TS Elaboration

Special facilities may be required for developing, designing, and implementing solutions to requirements. When necessary, the facilities required for the activities in the Technical Solution process area are developed or purchased.

Examples of resources provided include the following:
- Design specification tools
- Simulators and modeling tools
- Prototyping tools
- Scenario definition and management tools
- Requirements tracking tools
- Interactive documentation tools

VAL Elaboration

Special facilities may be required for validating the product or product components. When necessary, the facilities required for validation are developed or purchased.

Examples of resources provided include the following:
- Test management tools
- Test case generators
- Test coverage analyzers
- Simulators
- Load, stress, and performance testing tools

VER Elaboration

Special facilities may be required for verifying selected work products. When necessary, the facilities required for the activities in the Verification process area are developed or purchased.

Certain verification methods can require special tools, equipment, facilities, and training (e.g., peer reviews can require meeting rooms and trained moderators; certain verification tests can require special test equipment and people skilled in the use of the equipment).

Examples of resources provided include the following:
- Test management tools
- Test case generators
- Test coverage analyzers
- Simulators

GP 2.4 *ASSIGN RESPONSIBILITY*

Assign responsibility and authority for performing the process, developing the work products, and providing the services of the process.

The purpose of this generic practice is to ensure that there is accountability for performing the process and achieving the specified results throughout the life of the process. The people assigned must have the appropriate authority to perform the assigned responsibilities.

Responsibility can be assigned using detailed job descriptions or in living documents, such as the plan for performing the process. Dynamic assignment of responsibility is another legitimate way to implement this generic practice, as long as the assignment and acceptance of responsibility are ensured throughout the life of the process.

Subpractices

1. Assign overall responsibility and authority for performing the process.
2. Assign responsibility and authority for performing the specific tasks of the process.
3. Confirm that the people assigned to the responsibilities and authorities understand and accept them.

OPF Elaboration

Two groups are typically established and assigned responsibility for process improvement: (1) a management steering committee for process improvement to provide senior management sponsorship, and (2) a process group to facilitate and manage the process improvement activities.

PPQA Elaboration

Responsibility is assigned to those who can perform process and product quality assurance evaluations with sufficient independence and objectivity to guard against subjectivity or bias.

TS Elaboration

Appointing a lead or chief architect that oversees the technical solution and has authority over design decisions helps to maintain consistency in product design and evolution.

GP 2.5 *TRAIN PEOPLE*

Train the people performing or supporting the process as needed.

The purpose of this generic practice is to ensure that people have the necessary skills and expertise to perform or support the process.

Appropriate training is provided to those who will be performing the work. Overview training is provided to orient people who interact with those who perform the work.

> Examples of methods for providing training include self study; self-directed training; self-paced, programmed instruction; formalized on-the-job training; mentoring; and formal and classroom training.

Training supports the successful execution of the process by establishing a common understanding of the process and by imparting the skills and knowledge needed to perform the process.

Refer to the Organizational Training process area for more information about developing skills and knowledge of people so they can perform their roles effectively and efficiently.

CAR Elaboration

> Examples of training topics include the following:
> • Quality management methods (e.g., root cause analysis)

CM Elaboration

> Examples of training topics include the following:
> • Roles, responsibilities, and authority of the configuration management staff
> • Configuration management standards, procedures, and methods
> • Configuration library system

DAR Elaboration

> Examples of training topics include the following:
> • Formal decision analysis
> • Methods for evaluating alternative solutions against criteria

IPM Elaboration

Examples of training topics include the following:

- Tailoring the organization's set of standard processes to meet the needs of the project
- Managing the project based on the project's defined process
- Using the organization's measurement repository
- Using the organizational process assets
- Integrated management
- Intergroup coordination
- Group problem solving

MA Elaboration

Examples of training topics include the following:

- Statistical techniques
- Data collection, analysis, and reporting processes
- Development of goal related measurements (e.g., Goal Question Metric)

OPD Elaboration

Examples of training topics include the following:

- CMMI and other process and process improvement reference models
- Planning, managing, and monitoring processes
- Process modeling and definition
- Developing a tailorable standard process
- Developing work environment standards
- Ergonomics

OPF Elaboration

Examples of training topics include the following:

- CMMI and other process improvement reference models
- Planning and managing process improvement
- Tools, methods, and analysis techniques
- Process modeling
- Facilitation techniques
- Change management

OPM Elaboration

Examples of training topics include the following:
- Cost benefit analysis
- Planning, designing, and conducting pilots
- Technology transition
- Change management

OPP Elaboration

Examples of training topics include the following:
- Process and process improvement modeling
- Statistical and other quantitative methods (e.g., estimating models, Pareto analysis, control charts)

OT Elaboration

Examples of training topics include the following:
- Knowledge and skills needs analysis
- Instructional design
- Instructional techniques (e.g., train the trainer)
- Refresher training on subject matter

PI Elaboration

Examples of training topics include the following:
- Application domain
- Product integration procedures and criteria
- Organization's facilities for integration and assembly
- Assembly methods
- Packaging standards

PMC Elaboration

Examples of training topics include the following:
- Monitoring and control of projects
- Risk management
- Data management

PP Elaboration

Examples of training topics include the following:
- Estimating
- Budgeting
- Negotiating
- Identifying and analyzing risks
- Managing data
- Planning
- Scheduling

PPQA Elaboration

Examples of training topics include the following:
- Application domain
- Customer relations
- Process descriptions, standards, procedures, and methods for the project
- Quality assurance objectives, process descriptions, standards, procedures, methods, and tools

QPM Elaboration

Examples of training topics include the following:
- Basic quantitative (including statistical) analyses that help in analyzing process performance, using historical data, and identifying when corrective action is warranted
- Process modeling and analysis
- Process measurement data selection, definition, and collection

RD Elaboration

Examples of training topics include the following:
- Application domain
- Requirements definition and analysis
- Requirements elicitation
- Requirements specification and modeling
- Requirements tracking

REQM Elaboration

Examples of training topics include the following:
• Application domain
• Requirements definition, analysis, review, and management
• Requirements management tools
• Configuration management
• Negotiation and conflict resolution

RSKM Elaboration

Examples of training topics include the following:
• Risk management concepts and activities (e.g., risk identification, evaluation, monitoring, mitigation)
• Measure selection for risk mitigation

SAM Elaboration

Examples of training topics include the following:
• Regulations and business practices related to negotiating and working with suppliers
• Acquisition planning and preparation
• Commercial off-the-shelf product acquisition
• Supplier evaluation and selection
• Negotiation and conflict resolution
• Supplier management
• Testing and transition of acquired products
• Receiving, storing, using, and maintaining acquired products

TS Elaboration

Examples of training topics include the following:
• Application domain of the product and product components
• Design methods
• Architecture methods
• Interface design
• Unit testing techniques
• Standards (e.g., product, safety, human factors, environmental)

VAL Elaboration

> Examples of training topics include the following:
> • Application domain
> • Validation principles, standards, and methods
> • Intended-use environment

VER Elaboration

> Examples of training topics include the following:
> • Application or service domain
> • Verification principles, standards, and methods (e.g., analysis, demon-
>   stration, inspection, test)
> • Verification tools and facilities
> • Peer review preparation and procedures
> • Meeting facilitation

GP 2.6 CONTROL WORK PRODUCTS

Place selected work products of the process under appropriate levels of control.

The purpose of this generic practice is to establish and maintain the integrity of the selected work products of the process (or their descriptions) throughout their useful life.

The selected work products are specifically identified in the plan for performing the process, along with a specification of the appropriate level of control.

Different levels of control are appropriate for different work products and for different points in time. For some work products, it may be sufficient to maintain version control so that the version of the work product in use at a given time, past or present, is known and changes are incorporated in a controlled manner. Version control is usually under the sole control of the work product owner (which can be an individual, group, or team).

Sometimes, it can be critical that work products be placed under formal or baseline configuration management. This type of control includes defining and establishing baselines at predetermined points. These baselines are formally reviewed and approved, and serve as the basis for further development of the designated work products.

Refer to the Configuration Management process area for more information about establishing and maintaining the integrity of work products using configuration identification, configuration control, configuration status accounting, and configuration audits.

Additional levels of control between version control and formal configuration management are possible. An identified work product can be under various levels of control at different points in time.

CAR Elaboration

> Examples of work products placed under control include the following:
> - Action proposals
> - Action plans
> - Causal analysis and resolution records

CM Elaboration

> Examples of work products placed under control include the following:
> - Access lists
> - Change status reports
> - Change request database
> - CCB meeting minutes
> - Archived baselines

DAR Elaboration

> Examples of work products placed under control include the following:
> - Guidelines for when to apply a formal evaluation process
> - Evaluation reports containing recommended solutions

IPM Elaboration

> Examples of work products placed under control include the following:
> - The project's defined process
> - Project plans
> - Other plans that affect the project
> - Integrated plans
> - Actual process and product measurements collected from the project
> - Project's shared vision
> - Team structure
> - Team charters

MA Elaboration

> Examples of work products placed under control include the following:
> - Measurement objectives
> - Specifications of base and derived measures
> - Data collection and storage procedures
> - Base and derived measurement data sets
> - Analysis results and draft reports
> - Data analysis tools

OPD Elaboration

> Examples of work products placed under control include the following:
> - Organization's set of standard processes
> - Descriptions of lifecycle models
> - Tailoring guidelines for the organization's set of standard processes
> - Definitions of the common set of product and process measures
> - Organization's measurement data
> - Rules and guidelines for structuring and forming teams

OPF Elaboration

> Examples of work products placed under control include the following:
> - Process improvement proposals
> - Organization's approved process action plans
> - Training materials used for deploying organizational process assets
> - Guidelines for deploying the organization's set of standard processes on new projects
> - Plans for the organization's process appraisals

OPM Elaboration

> Examples of work products placed under control include the following:
> - Documented lessons learned from improvement validation
> - Deployment plans
> - Revised improvement measures, objectives, priorities
> - Updated process documentation and training material

OPP Elaboration

> Examples of work products placed under control include the following:
> • Organization's quality and process performance objectives
> • Definitions of the selected measures of process performance
> • Baseline data on the organization's process performance
> • Process performance models

OT Elaboration

> Examples of work products placed under control include the following:
> • Organizational training tactical plan
> • Training records
> • Training materials and supporting artifacts
> • Instructor evaluation forms

PI Elaboration

> Examples of work products placed under control include the following:
> • Acceptance documents for the received product components
> • Evaluated assembled product and product components
> • Product integration strategy
> • Product integration procedures and criteria
> • Updated interface description or agreement

PMC Elaboration

> Examples of work products placed under control include the following:
> • Project schedules with status
> • Project measurement data and analysis
> • Earned value reports

PP Elaboration

> Examples of work products placed under control include the following:
> • Work breakdown structure
> • Project plan
> • Data management plan
> • Stakeholder involvement plan

PPQA Elaboration

Examples of work products placed under control include the following:
- Noncompliance reports
- Evaluation logs and reports

QPM Elaboration

Examples of work products placed under control include the following:
- Subprocesses to be included in the project's defined process
- Operational definitions of the measures, their collection points in the subprocesses, and how the integrity of the measures will be determined
- Collected measurements

RD Elaboration

Examples of work products placed under control include the following:
- Customer functional and quality attribute requirements
- Definition of required functionality and quality attributes
- Product and product component requirements
- Interface requirements

REQM Elaboration

Examples of work products placed under control include the following:
- Requirements
- Requirements traceability matrix

RSKM Elaboration

Examples of work products placed under control include the following:
- Risk management strategy
- Identified risk items
- Risk mitigation plans

SAM Elaboration

Examples of work products placed under control include the following:
- Statements of work
- Supplier agreements
- Memoranda of agreement
- Subcontracts
- Preferred supplier lists

TS Elaboration

Examples of work products placed under control include the following:
- Product, product component, and interface designs
- Technical data packages
- Interface design documents
- Criteria for design and product component reuse
- Implemented designs (e.g., software code, fabricated product components)
- User, installation, operation, and maintenance documentation

---

VAL Elaboration

Examples of work products placed under control include the following:
- Lists of products and product components selected for validation
- Validation methods, procedures, and criteria
- Validation reports

VER Elaboration

Examples of work products placed under control include the following:
- Verification procedures and criteria
- Peer review training material
- Peer review data
- Verification reports

GP 2.7 *IDENTIFY AND INVOLVE RELEVANT STAKEHOLDERS*

Identify and involve the relevant stakeholders of the process as planned.

The purpose of this generic practice is to establish and maintain the expected involvement of relevant stakeholders during the execution of the process.

Involve relevant stakeholders as described in an appropriate plan for stakeholder involvement. Involve stakeholders appropriately in activities such as the following:

- Planning
- Decisions
- Commitments
- Communications
- Coordination
- Reviews
- Appraisals
- Requirements definitions
- Resolution of problems and issues

Refer to the Project Planning process area for more information about planning stakeholder involvement.

The objective of planning stakeholder involvement is to ensure that interactions necessary to the process are accomplished, while not allowing excessive numbers of affected groups and individuals to impede process execution.

Examples of stakeholders that might serve as relevant stakeholders for specific tasks, depending on context, include individuals, teams, management, customers, suppliers, end users, operations and support staff, other projects, and government regulators.

Subpractices

1. Identify stakeholders relevant to this process and their appropriate involvement.

    Relevant stakeholders are identified among the suppliers of inputs to, the users of outputs from, and the performers of the activities in the process. Once the relevant stakeholders are identified, the appropriate level of their involvement in process activities is planned.

2. Share these identifications with project planners or other planners as appropriate.

3. Involve relevant stakeholders as planned.

PI Elaboration

> Examples of measures and work products used in monitoring and controlling include the following:
> - Product component integration profile (e.g., product component assemblies planned and performed, number of exceptions found)
> - Integration evaluation problem report trends (e.g., number written and number closed)
> - Integration evaluation problem report aging (i.e., how long each problem report has been open)
> - Schedule for conduct of specific integration activities

PMC Elaboration

> Examples of measures and work products used in monitoring and controlling include the following:
> - Number of open and closed corrective actions
> - Schedule with status for monthly financial data collection, analysis, and reporting
> - Number and types of reviews performed
> - Review schedule (planned versus actual and slipped target dates)
> - Schedule for collection and analysis of monitoring data

PP Elaboration

> Examples of measures and work products used in monitoring and controlling include the following:
> - Number of revisions to the plan
> - Cost, schedule, and effort variance per plan revision
> - Schedule for development and maintenance of program plans

PPQA Elaboration

> Examples of measures and work products used in monitoring and controlling include the following:
> - Variance of objective process evaluations planned and performed
> - Variance of objective work product evaluations planned and performed
> - Schedule for objective evaluations

QPM Elaboration

> Examples of measures and work products used in monitoring and controlling include the following:
> - Profile of subprocess attributes whose process performance provide insight about the risk to, or are key contributors to, achieving project objectives (e.g., number selected for monitoring through statistical techniques, number currently being monitored, number whose process performance is stable)
> - Number of special causes of variation identified
> - Schedule of data collection, analysis, and reporting activities in a measurement and analysis cycle as it relates to quantitative management activities

RD Elaboration

> Examples of measures and work products used in monitoring and controlling include the following:
> - Cost, schedule, and effort expended for rework
> - Defect density of requirements specifications
> - Schedule for activities to develop a set of requirements

REQM Elaboration

> Examples of measures and work products used in monitoring and controlling include the following:
> - Requirements volatility (percentage of requirements changed)
> - Schedule for coordination of requirements
> - Schedule for analysis of a proposed requirements change

RSKM Elaboration

> Examples of measures and work products used in monitoring and controlling include the following:
> - Number of risks identified, managed, tracked, and controlled
> - Risk exposure and changes to the risk exposure for each assessed risk, and as a summary percentage of management reserve
> - Change activity for risk mitigation plans (e.g., processes, schedule, funding)
>
> *Continues*

Continued

- Occurrence of unanticipated risks
- Risk categorization volatility
- Comparison of estimated versus actual risk mitigation effort and impact
- Schedule for risk analysis activities
- Schedule of actions for a specific mitigation

SAM Elaboration

Examples of measures and work products used in monitoring and controlling include the following:
- Number of changes made to the requirements for the supplier
- Cost and schedule variance in accordance with the supplier agreement
- Schedule for selecting a supplier and establishing an agreement

TS Elaboration

Examples of measures and work products used in monitoring and controlling include the following:
- Cost, schedule, and effort expended for rework
- Percentage of requirements addressed in the product or product component design
- Size and complexity of the product, product components, interfaces, and documentation
- Defect density of technical solutions work products
- Schedule for design activities

VAL Elaboration

Examples of measures and work products used in monitoring and controlling include the following:
- Number of validation activities completed (planned versus actual)
- Validation problem report trends (e.g., number written, number closed)
- Validation problem report aging (i.e., how long each problem report has been open)
- Schedule for a specific validation activity

VER Elaboration

Examples of measures and work products used in monitoring and controlling include the following:

- Verification profile (e.g., the number of verifications planned and performed, and the defects found; or defects categorized by verification method or type)
- Number of defects detected by defect category
- Verification problem report trends (e.g., number written, number closed)
- Verification problem report status (i.e., how long each problem report has been open)
- Schedule for a specific verification activity
- Peer review effectiveness

GP 2.9 OBJECTIVELY EVALUATE ADHERENCE

Objectively evaluate adherence of the process and selected work products against the process description, standards, and procedures, and address non-compliance.

The purpose of this generic practice is to provide credible assurance that the process and selected work products are implemented as planned and adhere to the process description, standards, and procedures. (See the definition of "objectively evaluate" in the glossary.)

Refer to the Process and Product Quality Assurance process area for more information about objectively evaluating processes and work products.

People not directly responsible for managing or performing the activities of the process typically evaluate adherence. In many cases, adherence is evaluated by people in the organization, but external to the process or project, or by people external to the organization. As a result, credible assurance of adherence can be provided even during times when the process is under stress (e.g., when the effort is behind schedule, when the effort is over budget).

CAR Elaboration

Examples of activities reviewed include the following:

- Determining causes of outcomes
- Evaluating results of action plans

Examples of work products reviewed include the following:

- Action proposals selected for implementation
- Causal analysis and resolution records

CM Elaboration

> Examples of activities reviewed include the following:
> • Establishing baselines
> • Tracking and controlling changes
> • Establishing and maintaining the integrity of baselines

> Examples of work products reviewed include the following:
> • Archives of baselines
> • Change request database

DAR Elaboration

> Examples of activities reviewed include the following:
> • Evaluating alternatives using established criteria and methods

> Examples of work products reviewed include the following:
> • Guidelines for when to apply a formal evaluation process
> • Evaluation reports containing recommended solutions

IPM Elaboration

> Examples of activities reviewed include the following:
> • Establishing, maintaining, and using the project's defined process
> • Coordinating and collaborating with relevant stakeholders
> • Using the project's shared vision
> • Organizing teams

> Examples of work products reviewed include the following:
> • Project's defined process
> • Project plans
> • Other plans that affect the project
> • Work environment standards
> • Shared vision statements
> • Team structure
> • Team charters

MA Elaboration

Examples of activities reviewed include the following:
- Aligning measurement and analysis activities
- Providing measurement results

Examples of work products reviewed include the following:
- Specifications of base and derived measures
- Data collection and storage procedures
- Analysis results and draft reports

OPD Elaboration

Examples of activities reviewed include the following:
- Establishing organizational process assets
- Determining rules and guidelines for structuring and forming teams

Examples of work products reviewed include the following:
- Organization's set of standard processes
- Descriptions of lifecycle models
- Tailoring guidelines for the organization's set of standard processes
- Organization's measurement data
- Empowerment rules and guidelines for people and teams
- Organizational process documentation

OPF Elaboration

Examples of activities reviewed include the following:
- Determining process improvement opportunities
- Planning and coordinating process improvement activities
- Deploying the organization's set of standard processes on projects at their startup

Examples of work products reviewed include the following:
- Process improvement plans
- Process action plans
- Process deployment plans
- Plans for the organization's process appraisals

OPM Elaboration

Examples of activities reviewed include the following:
- Analyzing process performance data to determine the organization's ability to meet identified business objectives
- Selecting improvements using quantitative analysis
- Deploying improvements
- Measuring effectiveness of the deployed improvements using statistical and other quantitative techniques

Examples of work products reviewed include the following:
- Improvement proposals
- Deployment plans
- Revised improvement measures, objectives, priorities, and deployment plans
- Updated process documentation and training material

OPP Elaboration

Examples of activities reviewed include the following:
- Establishing process performance baselines and models

Examples of work products reviewed include the following:
- Process performance baselines
- Organization's quality and process performance objectives
- Definitions of the selected measures of process performance

OT Elaboration

Examples of activities reviewed include the following:
- Identifying training needs and making training available
- Providing necessary training

Examples of work products reviewed include the following:
- Organizational training tactical plan
- Training materials and supporting artifacts
- Instructor evaluation forms

PI Elaboration

Examples of activities reviewed include the following:
- Establishing and maintaining a product integration strategy
- Ensuring interface compatibility
- Assembling product components and delivering the product

Examples of work products reviewed include the following:
- Product integration strategy
- Product integration procedures and criteria
- Acceptance documents for the received product components
- Assembled product and product components

PMC Elaboration

Examples of activities reviewed include the following:
- Monitoring project progress and performance against the project plan
- Managing corrective actions to closure

Examples of work products reviewed include the following:
- Records of project progress and performance
- Project review results

PP Elaboration

Examples of activities reviewed include the following:
- Establishing estimates
- Developing the project plan
- Obtaining commitments to the project plan

Examples of work products reviewed include the following:
- WBS
- Project plan
- Data management plan
- Stakeholder involvement plan

PPQA Elaboration

> Examples of activities reviewed include the following:
> • Objectively evaluating processes and work products
> • Tracking and communicating noncompliance issues

> Examples of work products reviewed include the following:
> • Noncompliance reports
> • Evaluation logs and reports

QPM Elaboration

> Examples of activities reviewed include the following:
> • Managing the project using quality and process performance objectives
> • Managing selected subprocesses using statistical and other quantitative techniques

> Examples of work products reviewed include the following:
> • Compositions of the project's defined process
> • Operational definitions of the measures
> • Process performance analyses reports
> • Collected measurements

RD Elaboration

> Examples of activities reviewed include the following:
> • Collecting stakeholder needs
> • Formulating product and product component functional and quality attribute requirements
> • Formulating architectural requirements that specify how product components are organized and designed to achieve particular end-to-end functional and quality attribute requirements
> • Analyzing and validating product and product component requirements

> Examples of work products reviewed include the following:
> • Product requirements
> • Product component requirements
> • Interface requirements
> • Definition of required functionality and quality attributes
> • Architecturally significant quality attribute requirements

REQM Elaboration

Examples of activities reviewed include the following:
- Managing requirements
- Ensuring alignment among project plans, work products, and requirements

Examples of work products reviewed include the following:
- Requirements
- Requirements traceability matrix

RSKM Elaboration

Examples of activities reviewed include the following:
- Establishing and maintaining a risk management strategy
- Identifying and analyzing risks
- Mitigating risks

Examples of work products reviewed include the following:
- Risk management strategy
- Risk mitigation plans

SAM Elaboration

Examples of activities reviewed include the following:
- Establishing and maintaining supplier agreements
- Satisfying supplier agreements

Examples of work products reviewed include the following:
- Plan for supplier agreement management
- Supplier agreements

TS Elaboration

Examples of activities reviewed include the following:
- Selecting product component solutions
- Developing product and product component designs
- Implementing product component designs

Examples of work products reviewed include the following:
- Technical data packages
- Product, product component, and interface designs
- Implemented designs (e.g., software code, fabricated product components)
- User, installation, operation, and maintenance documentation

VAL Elaboration

Examples of activities reviewed include the following:
- Selecting the products and product components to be validated
- Establishing and maintaining validation methods, procedures, and criteria
- Validating products or product components

Examples of work products reviewed include the following:
- Validation methods
- Validation procedures
- Validation criteria

VER Elaboration

Examples of activities reviewed include the following:
- Selecting work products for verification
- Establishing and maintaining verification procedures and criteria
- Performing peer reviews
- Verifying selected work products

Examples of work products reviewed include the following:
- Verification procedures and criteria
- Peer review checklists
- Verification reports

GP 2.10 *REVIEW STATUS WITH HIGHER LEVEL MANAGEMENT*

Review the activities, status, and results of the process with higher level management and resolve issues.

The purpose of this generic practice is to provide higher level management with the appropriate visibility into the process.

Higher level management includes those levels of management in the organization above the immediate level of management responsible for the process. In particular, higher level management can include senior management. These reviews are for managers who provide the policy and overall guidance for the process and not for those who perform the direct day-to-day monitoring and controlling of the process.

Different managers have different needs for information about the process. These reviews help ensure that informed decisions on the planning and performing of the process can be made. Therefore, these reviews are expected to be both periodic and event driven.

OPF Elaboration

These reviews are typically in the form of a briefing presented to the management steering committee by the process group and the process action teams.

Examples of presentation topics include the following:

- Status of improvements being developed by process action teams
- Results of pilots
- Results of deployments
- Schedule status for achieving significant milestones (e.g., readiness for an appraisal, progress toward achieving a targeted organizational maturity level or capability level profile)

OPM Elaboration

These reviews are typically in the form of a briefing presented to higher level management by those responsible for performance improvement.

Examples of presentation topics include the following:

- Improvement areas identified from analysis of current performance compared to business objectives
- Results of process improvement elicitation and analysis activities
- Results from validation activities (e.g., pilots) compared to expected benefits
- Performance data after deployment of improvements
- Deployment cost, schedule, and risk
- Risks of not achieving business objectives

REQM Elaboration

Proposed changes to commitments to be made external to the organization are reviewed with higher level management to ensure that all commitments can be accomplished.

RSKM Elaboration

Reviews of the project risk status are held on a periodic and event driven basis, with appropriate levels of management, to provide visibility into the potential for project risk exposure and appropriate corrective action.

Typically, these reviews include a summary of the most critical risks, key risk parameters (such as likelihood and consequence of the risks), and the status of risk mitigation efforts.

GG 3 INSTITUTIONALIZE A DEFINED PROCESS

The process is institutionalized as a defined process.

GP 3.1 ESTABLISH A DEFINED PROCESS

Establish and maintain the description of a defined process.

The purpose of this generic practice is to establish and maintain a description of the process that is tailored from the organization's set of standard processes to address the needs of a specific instantiation. The organization should have standard processes that cover the process area, as well as have guidelines for tailoring these standard processes to meet the needs of a project or organizational function. With a defined process, variability in how the processes are performed across the organization is reduced and process assets, data, and learning can be effectively shared.

Refer to the Integrated Project Management process area for more information about establishing the project's defined process.

Refer to the Organizational Process Definition process area for more information about establishing standard processes and establishing tailoring criteria and guidelines.

The descriptions of the defined processes provide the basis for planning, performing, and managing the activities, work products, and services associated with the process.

Subpractices

1. Select from the organization's set of standard processes those processes that cover the process area and best meet the needs of the project or organizational function.

2. Establish the defined process by tailoring the selected processes according to the organization's tailoring guidelines.
3. Ensure that the organization's process objectives are appropriately addressed in the defined process.
4. Document the defined process and the records of the tailoring.
5. Revise the description of the defined process as necessary.

GP 3.2 COLLECT PROCESS RELATED EXPERIENCES

Collect process related experiences derived from planning and performing the process to support the future use and improvement of the organization's processes and process assets.

The purpose of this generic practice is to collect process related experiences, including information and artifacts derived from planning and performing the process. Examples of process related experiences include work products, measures, measurement results, lessons learned, and process improvement suggestions. The information and artifacts are collected so that they can be included in the organizational process assets and made available to those who are (or who will be) planning and performing the same or similar processes. The information and artifacts are stored in the organization's measurement repository and the organization's process asset library.

> Examples of relevant information include the effort expended for the various activities, defects injected or removed in a particular activity, and lessons learned.

Refer to the Integrated Project Management process area for more information about contributing to organizational process assets.

Refer to the Organizational Process Definition process area for more information about establishing organizational process assets.

Subpractices

1. Store process and product measures in the organization's measurement repository.

    The process and product measures are primarily those measures that are defined in the common set of measures for the organization's set of standard processes.

2. Submit documentation for inclusion in the organization's process asset library.

3. Document lessons learned from the process for inclusion in the organization's process asset library.

4. Propose improvements to the organizational process assets.

CAR Elaboration

> Examples of process related experiences include the following:
> - Action proposals
> - Number of action plans that are open and for how long
> - Action plan status reports

CM Elaboration

> Examples of process related experiences include the following:
> - Trends in the status of configuration items
> - Configuration audit results
> - Change request aging reports

DAR Elaboration

> Examples process related experiences include the following:
> - Number of alternatives considered
> - Evaluation results
> - Recommended solutions to address significant issues

IPM Elaboration

> Examples of process related experiences include the following:
> - Project's defined process
> - Number of tailoring options exercised by the project to create its defined process
> - Interface coordination issue trends (i.e., number identified, number closed)
> - Number of times the process asset library is accessed for assets related to project planning by project members
> - Records of expenses related to holding face-to-face meetings versus holding meetings using collaborative equipment such as teleconferencing and videoconferencing
> - Project shared vision
> - Team charters

MA Elaboration

Examples of process related experiences include the following:
- Data currency status
- Results of data integrity tests
- Data analysis reports

OPD Elaboration

Examples of process related experiences include the following:
- Submission of lessons learned to the organization's process asset library
- Submission of measurement data to the organization's measurement repository
- Status of the change requests submitted to modify the organization's standard process
- Record of non-standard tailoring requests

OPF Elaboration

Examples of process related experiences include the following:
- Criteria used to prioritize candidate process improvements
- Appraisal findings that address strengths and weaknesses of the organization's processes
- Status of improvement activities against the schedule
- Records of tailoring the organization's set of standard processes and implementing them on identified projects

OPM Elaboration

Examples of process related experiences include the following:
- Lessons learned captured from analysis of process performance data compared to business objectives
- Documented measures of the costs and benefits resulting from implementing and deploying improvements
- Report of a comparison of similar development processes to identify the potential for improving efficiency

OPP Elaboration

Examples of process related experiences include the following:
- Process performance baselines
- Percentage of measurement data that is rejected because of inconsistencies with the process performance measurement definitions

OT Elaboration

Examples of process related experiences include the following:
- Results of training effectiveness surveys
- Training program performance assessment results
- Course evaluations
- Training requirements from an advisory group

PI Elaboration

Examples of process related experiences include the following:
- Records of the receipt of product components, exception reports, confirmation of configuration status, and results of readiness checking
- Percentage of total development effort spent in product integration (actual to date plus estimate to complete)
- Defects found in the product and test environment during product integration
- Problem reports resulting from product integration

PMC Elaboration

Examples of process related experiences include the following:
- Records of significant deviations
- Criteria for what constitutes a deviation
- Corrective action results

PP Elaboration

Examples of process related experiences include the following:
- Project data library structure
- Project attribute estimates
- Risk impacts and probability of occurrence

PPQA Elaboration

Examples of process related experiences include the following:
- Evaluation logs
- Quality trends
- Noncompliance reports
- Status reports of corrective actions
- Cost of quality reports for the project

QPM Elaboration

Examples of process related experiences include the following:
- Records of quantitative management data from the project, including results from the periodic review of the process performance of the sub-processes selected for management against established interim objectives of the project
- Suggested improvements to process performance models

RD Elaboration

Examples of process related experiences include the following:
- List of the requirements for a product that are found to be ambiguous
- Number of requirements introduced at each phase of the project lifecycle
- Lessons learned from the requirements allocation process

REQM Elaboration

Examples of process related experiences include the following:
- Requirements traceability matrix
- Number of unfunded requirements changes after baselining
- Lessons learned in resolving ambiguous requirements

RSKM Elaboration

Examples of process related experiences include the following:
- Risk parameters
- Risk categories
- Risk status reports

SAM Elaboration

> Examples of process related experiences include the following:
> • Results of supplier reviews
> • Trade studies used to select suppliers
> • Revision history of supplier agreements
> • Supplier performance reports

TS Elaboration

> Examples of process related experiences include the following:
> • Results of the make, buy, or reuse analysis
> • Design defect density
> • Results of applying new methods and tools

VAL Elaboration

> Examples of process related experiences include the following:
> • Product component prototype
> • Percentage of time the validation environment is available
> • Number of product defects found through validation per development phase
> • Validation analysis report

VER Elaboration

> Examples of process related experiences include the following:
> • Peer review records that include conduct time and average preparation time
> • Number of product defects found through verification per development phase
> • Verification and analysis report

Applying Generic Practices

Generic practices are components that can be applied to all process areas. Think of generic practices as reminders. They serve the purpose of reminding you to do things right and are expected model components.

GGs & GPs

T/

Ge

GF
Id
Re

For example, consider the generic practice, "Establish and maintain the plan for performing the process" (GP 2.2). When applied to the Project Planning process area, this generic practice reminds you to plan the activities involved in creating the plan for the project. When applied to the Organizational Training process area, this same generic practice reminds you to plan the activities involved in developing the skills and knowledge of people in the organization.

Process Areas that Support Generic Practices

While generic goals and generic practices are the model components that directly address the institutionalization of a process across the organization, many process areas likewise address institutionalization by supporting the implementation of the generic practices. Knowing these relationships will help you effectively implement the generic practices.

Such process areas contain one or more specific practices that when implemented can also fully implement a generic practice or generate a work product that is used in the implementation of a generic practice.

An example is the Configuration Management process area and GP 2.6, "Place selected work products of the process under appropriate levels of control." To implement the generic practice for one or more process areas, you might choose to implement the Configuration Management process area, all or in part, to implement the generic practice.

GF
M
th

Another example is the Organizational Process Definition process area and GP 3.1, "Establish and maintain the description of a defined process." To implement this generic practice for one or more process areas, you should first implement the Organizational Process Definition process area, all or in part, to establish the organizational process assets that are needed to implement the generic practice.

Table 7.2 describes (1) the process areas that support the implementation of generic practices and (2) the recursive relationships between generic practices and their closely related process areas. Both types of relationships are important to remember during process improvement to take advantage of the natural synergies that exist between the generic practices and their related process areas.

GF
Ot
Ev

Given the dependencies that generic practices have on these process areas, and given the more holistic view that many of these process areas provide, these process areas are often implemented early, in whole or in part, before or concurrent with implementing the associated generic practices.

TABLE 7.2   Generic Practice and Process Area Relationships *(Continued)*

Generic Practice	Roles of Process Areas in Implementation of the Generic Practice	How the Generic Practice Recursively Applies to Its Related Process Area(s)[1]
GP 2.10 Review Status with Higher Level Management	**Project Monitoring and Control:** The part of the project monitoring and control process that implements Project Monitoring and Control SP 1.6, "Conduct Progress Reviews," and SP 1.7, "Conduct Milestone Reviews," supports the implementation of GP 2.10 for all project-related process areas, perhaps in full, depending on higher level management involvement in these reviews.	
GP 3.1 Establish a Defined Process	**Integrated Project Management:** The part of the integrated project management process that implements Integrated Project Management SP 1.1, "Establish the Project's Defined Process," can implement GP 3.1 in full for all project-related process areas. **Organizational Process Definition:** For all processes, not just project-related processes, the organizational process definition process establishes the organizational process assets needed to implement GP 3.1.	GP 3.1 applied to the integrated project management process covers establishing defined processes for integrated project management activities.
GP 3.2 Collect Process Related Experiences	**Integrated Project Management:** The part of the integrated project management process that implements Integrated Project Management SP 1.7, "Contribute to the Organizational Process Assets," can implement GP 3.2 in part or full for all project-related process areas. **Organizational Process Focus:** The part of the organizational process focus process that implements Organizational Process Focus SP 3.4, "Incorporate Experiences into the Organizational Process Assets," can implement GP 3.2 in part or full for all process areas. **Organizational Process Definition:** For all processes, the organizational process definition process establishes the organizational process assets needed to implement GP 3.2.	GP 3.2 applied to the integrated project management process covers collecting process related experiences derived from planning and performing integrated project management activities.

There are also a few situations where the result of applying a generic practice to a particular process area would seem to make a whole process area redundant, but, in fact, it does not. It can be natural to think that applying GP 3.1, "Establish a Defined Process," to the Project Planning and Project Monitoring and Control process areas gives the same effect as the first specific goal of Integrated Project Management, "Use the Project's Defined Process."

Although it is true that there is some overlap, the application of the generic practice to these two process areas provides defined processes covering project planning and project monitoring and control activities. These defined processes do not necessarily cover support activities (e.g., configuration management), other project management processes (e.g., integrated project management), or other processes. In contrast, the project's defined process, provided by the Integrated Project Management process area, covers all appropriate processes.

CAUSAL ANALYSIS AND RESOLUTION
A Support Process Area at Maturity Level 5

Purpose

The purpose of Causal Analysis and Resolution (CAR) is to identify causes of selected outcomes and take action to improve process performance.

TIP

CAR helps you establish a disciplined approach to analyzing the causes of outcomes, both positive and negative, of your processes. You can analyze defects or defect trends, problems such as schedule overruns or inter-organizational conflicts, as well as positive outcomes that you want to replicate elsewhere.

Introductory Notes

Causal analysis and resolution improves quality and productivity by preventing the introduction of defects or problems and by identifying and appropriately incorporating the causes of superior process performance.

The Causal Analysis and Resolution process area involves the following activities:

- Identifying and analyzing causes of selected outcomes. The selected outcomes can represent defects and problems that can be prevented from happening in the future or successes that can be implemented in projects or the organization.
- Taking actions to complete the following:
  - Remove causes and prevent the recurrence of those types of defects and problems in the future
  - Proactively analyze data to identify potential problems and prevent them from occurring
  - Incorporate the causes of successes into the process to improve future process performance

Reliance on detecting defects and problems after they have been introduced is not cost effective. It is more effective to prevent defects and problems by integrating Causal Analysis and Resolution activities into each phase of the project.

HINT

Integrating CAR activities into each project phase will help (1) prevent many defects from being introduced and (2) facilitate repetition of those conditions that enable superior performance, thus improving the likelihood of project success.

HINT

You also can apply causal analysis to outcomes of concern to senior management.

HINT

It is impossible to analyze *all* outcomes; instead, focus on outcomes that have the largest risk or present the greatest opportunity.

TIP

Successful implementation of CAR requires significant management commitment and process maturity to ensure that process data is accurately and consistently recorded, causal analysis meetings are adequately supported, and CAR activities are consistently performed across the organization.

X-REF

Causal analysis is mentioned elsewhere in CMMI: in an IPM SP 1.5 subpractice to address causes of selected issues that can affect project objectives; in the notes of OPM SP 1.3 Identify Potential Areas for Improvement; in QPM SP 2.3 Perform Root Cause Analysis; and as an example work product in VER SP 3.2 Analyze Verification Results.

Since similar outcomes may have been previously encountered in other projects or in earlier phases or tasks of the current project, Causal Analysis and Resolution activities are mechanisms for communicating lessons learned among projects.

Types of outcomes encountered are analyzed to identify trends. Based on an understanding of the defined process and how it is implemented, root causes of these outcomes and future implications of them are determined.

Since it is impractical to perform causal analysis on all outcomes, targets are selected by tradeoffs on estimated investments and estimated returns of quality, productivity, and cycle time.

Measurement and analysis processes should already be in place. Existing defined measures can be used, though in some instances new measurement definitions, redefinitions, or clarified definitions may be needed to analyze the effects of a process change.

Refer to the Measurement and Analysis process area for more information about aligning measurement and analysis activities and providing measurement results.

Causal Analysis and Resolution activities provide a mechanism for projects to evaluate their processes at the local level and look for improvements that can be implemented.

When improvements are judged to be effective, the information is submitted to the organizational level for potential deployment in the organizational processes.

The specific practices of this process area apply to a process that is selected for quantitative management. Use of the specific practices of this process area can add value in other situations, but the results may not provide the same degree of impact to the organization's quality and process performance objectives.

Related Process Areas

Refer to the Measurement and Analysis process area for more information about aligning measurement and analysis activities and providing measurement results.

Refer to the Organizational Performance Management process area for more information about selecting and implementing improvements for deployment.

Refer to the Quantitative Project Management process area for more information about quantitatively managing the project to achieve the project's established quality and process performance objectives.

Specific Goal and Practice Summary

SG 1 Determine Causes of Selected Outcomes
  SP 1.1   Select Outcomes for Analysis
  SP 1.2   Analyze Causes
SG 2 Address Causes of Selected Outcomes
  SP 2.1   Implement Action Proposals
  SP 2.2   Evaluate the Effect of Implemented Actions
  SP 2.3   Record Causal Analysis Data

Specific Practices by Goal

SG 1   DETERMINE CAUSES OF SELECTED OUTCOMES

Root causes of selected outcomes are systematically determined.

A root cause is an initiating element in a causal chain which leads to an outcome of interest.

SP 1.1 SELECT OUTCOMES FOR ANALYSIS

Select outcomes for analysis.

This activity could be triggered by an event (reactive) or could be planned periodically, such as at the beginning of a new phase or task (proactive).

> **HINT**
>
> Let your data help you determine which outcomes, if addressed, will realize the most benefit to your organization. Process Performance Baselines (PPBs) and Models (PPMs) may help in this determination.

Example Work Products

1. Data to be used in the initial analysis
2. Initial analysis results data
3. Outcomes selected for further analysis

Subpractices

1. Gather relevant data.

> Examples of relevant data include the following:
> - Defects reported by customers or end users
> - Defects found in peer reviews or testing
> - Productivity measures that are higher than expected
> - Project management problem reports requiring corrective action
> - Process capability problems
> - Earned value measurements by process (e.g., cost performance index)
> - Resource throughput, utilization, or response time measurements
> - Service fulfillment or service satisfaction problems

TIP

It is ineffective to look at every outcome. Therefore, you should establish criteria to help you prioritize and categorize outcomes.

2. Determine which outcomes to analyze further.

When determining which outcomes to analyze further, consider their source, impact, frequency of occurrence, similarity, the cost of analysis, the time and resources needed, safety considerations, etc.

> Examples of methods for selecting outcomes include the following:
> - Pareto analysis
> - Histograms
> - Box and whisker plots for attributes
> - Failure mode and effects analysis (FMEA)
> - Process capability analysis

TIP

An example method for analyzing and categorizing defects is Orthogonal Defect Classification (see Wikipedia), which provides standard taxonomies for classifying defects and their resolution.

3. Formally define the scope of the analysis, including a clear definition of the improvement needed or expected, stakeholders affected, target affected, etc.

> *Refer to the Decision Analysis and Resolution process area for more information about analyzing possible decisions using a formal evaluation process that evaluates identified alternatives against established criteria.*

HINT

To identify actions that address an outcome, you need to understand its root causes.

SP 1.2 ANALYZE CAUSES

Perform causal analysis of selected outcomes and propose actions to address them.

The purpose of this analysis is to define actions that will address selected outcomes by analyzing relevant outcome data and producing action proposals for implementation.

TIP

An action proposal typically documents the outcome to be investigated, its causes, and specific actions that, when taken, will either mitigate the causes to prevent the outcome from reoccurring or increase the likelihood that conditions conducive to superior performance will occur.

Example Work Products

1. Root cause analysis results
2. Action proposal

Subpractices

1. Conduct causal analysis with those who are responsible for performing the task.

Causal analysis is performed, typically in meetings, with those who understand the selected outcome under study. Those who have the best understanding of the selected outcome are typically those who are responsible for performing the task. The analysis is most effective when applied to real time data, as close as possible to the event which triggered the outcome.

X-REF

Action proposals are prioritized, selected, and implemented in SG 2.

Examples of when to perform causal analysis include the following:
- When a stable subprocess does not meet its specified quality and process performance objectives, or when a subprocess needs to be stabilized
- During the task, if and when problems warrant a causal analysis meeting
- When a work product exhibits an unexpected deviation from its requirements
- When more defects than anticipated escape from earlier phases to the current phase
- When process performance exceeds expectations
- At the start of a new phase or task

> **TIP**
>
> There are secondary benefits to causal analysis meetings. Participants develop an appreciation for how upstream activities affect downstream activities, as well as a sense of responsibility and accountability for outcomes that might otherwise remain unanalyzed.

Refer to the Quantitative Project Management process area for more information about performing root cause analysis.

2. Analyze selected outcomes to determine their root causes.

   Analysis of process performance baselines and models can aid in the identification of potential root causes.

   Depending on the type and number of outcomes, it can be beneficial to look at the outcomes in several ways to ensure all potential root causes are investigated. Consider looking at individual outcomes as well as grouping the outcomes.

> **TIP**
>
> In their book *Managing the Unexpected: Assuring High Performance in an Age of Complexity*, Weick and Sutcliffe identify "mindfulness" qualities important in high-reliability organizations including preoccupation with failure and reluctance to simplify. These imply attention to detail when communicating about an individual situation as well as seeking to understand possible systemic causes to a range of apparently unrelated small problems.

Examples of methods to determine root causes include the following:
- Cause-and-effect (fishbone) diagrams
- Check sheets

3. Combine selected outcomes into groups based on their root causes.

   In some cases, outcomes can be influenced by multiple root causes.

> **HINT**
>
> You develop cause-and-effect diagrams using iterative brainstorming (i.e., the "Five Whys"). This process may terminate when it reaches root causes outside the experience of the group or outside the control of its management.

Examples of cause groups or categories include the following:
- Inadequate training and skills
- Breakdown of communication
- Not accounting for all details of a task
- Making mistakes in manual procedures (e.g., keyboard entry)
- Process deficiency

Where appropriate, look for trends or symptoms in or across groupings.

4. Create an action proposal that documents actions to be taken to prevent the future occurrence of similar outcomes or to incorporate best practices into processes.

Process performance models can support cost benefit analysis of action proposals through prediction of impacts and return on investment.

Examples of proposed preventative actions include changes to the following:
- The process in question
- Training
- Tools
- Methods
- Work products

Examples of incorporating best practices include the following:
- Creating activity checklists, which reinforce training or communications related to common problems and techniques for preventing them
- Changing a process so that error-prone steps do not occur
- Automating all or part of a process
- Reordering process activities
- Adding process steps, such as task kickoff meetings to review common problems as well as actions to prevent them

---

An action proposal usually documents the following:
- Originator of the action proposal
- Description of the outcome to be addressed
- Description of the cause
- Cause category
- Phase identified
- Description of the action
- Time, cost, and other resources required to implement the action proposal
- Expected benefits from implementing the action proposal
- Estimated cost of not fixing the problem
- Action proposal category

SG 2   ADDRESS CAUSES OF SELECTED OUTCOMES

Root causes of selected outcomes are systematically addressed.

Projects operating according to a well-defined process systematically analyze where improvements are needed and implement process changes to address root causes of selected outcomes.

SP 2.1 IMPLEMENT ACTION PROPOSALS

Implement selected action proposals developed in causal analysis.

Action proposals describe tasks necessary to address root causes of analyzed outcomes to prevent or reduce the occurrence or recurrence of negative outcomes, or incorporate realized successes. Action plans are developed and implemented for selected action proposals. Only changes that prove to be of value should be considered for broad implementation.

Example Work Products

1. Action proposals selected for implementation
2. Action plans

Subpractices

1. Analyze action proposals and determine their priorities.

Criteria for prioritizing action proposals include the following:
- Implications of not addressing the outcome
- Cost to implement process improvements to address the outcome
- Expected impact on quality

Process performance models can be used to help identify interactions among multiple action proposals.

2. Select action proposals to be implemented.

Refer to the Decision Analysis and Resolution process area for more information about analyzing possible decisions using a formal evaluation process that evaluates identified alternatives against established criteria.

3. Create action plans for implementing the selected action proposals.

Examples of information provided in an action plan include the following:
- Person responsible for implementation
- Detailed description of the improvement
- Description of the affected areas
- People who are to be kept informed of status
- Schedule
- Cost expended
- Next date that status will be reviewed
- Rationale for key decisions
- Description of implementation actions

X-REF

For more information on designing experiments to understand the impact of certain changes, consult good references on Six Sigma and Experimental Design.

HINT

When a resolution has more general applicability, don't document it in a "lessons learned" document; document it in an improvement proposal.

X-REF

For more information on improvements proposals and suggestions, see OPF SP 2.4 and OPM SP 2.1.

HINT

Use the measures associated with a process or subprocess (perhaps supplemented by other measures) to evaluate the effect of changes.

4. Implement action plans.

To implement action plans, the following tasks should be performed:
  * Make assignments.
  * Coordinate the people doing the work.
  * Review the results.
  * Track action items to closure.

Experiments may be conducted for particularly complex changes.

Examples of experiments include the following:
• Using a temporarily modified process
• Using a new tool

Actions may be assigned to members of the causal analysis team, members of the project team, or other members of the organization.

5. Look for similar causes that may exist in other processes and work products and take action as appropriate.

SP 2.2 EVALUATE THE EFFECT OF IMPLEMENTED ACTIONS

Evaluate the effect of implemented actions on process performance.

Refer to the Quantitative Project Management process area for more information about selecting measures and analytic techniques.

Once the changed process is deployed across the project, the effect of changes is evaluated to verify that the process change has improved process performance.

Example Work Products

1. Analysis of process performance and change in process performance

Subpractices

1. Measure and analyze the change in process performance of the project's affected processes or subprocesses.

    This subpractice determines whether the selected change has positively influenced process performance and by how much.

An example of a change in the process performance of the project's defined design process would be a change in the predicted ability of the design to meet the quality and process performance objectives.
Another example would be a change in the defect density of the design documentation, as statistically measured through peer reviews before and after the improvement has been made. On a statistical process control chart, this change in process performance would be represented by an improvement in the mean, a reduction in variation, or both.

Statistical and other quantitative techniques (e.g., hypothesis testing) can be used to compare the before and after baselines to assess the statistical significance of the change.

2. Determine the impact of the change on achieving the project's quality and process performance objectives.

This subpractice determines whether the selected change has positively influenced the ability of the project to meet its quality and process performance objectives by understanding how changes in the process performance data have affected the objectives. Process performance models can aid in the evaluation through prediction of impacts and return on investment.

3. Determine and document appropriate actions if the process or subprocess improvements did not result in expected project benefits.

SP 2.3 RECORD CAUSAL ANALYSIS DATA

Record causal analysis and resolution data for use across projects and the organization.

Example Work Products

1. Causal analysis and resolution records
2. Organizational improvement proposals

Subpractices

1. Record causal analysis data and make the data available so that other projects can make appropriate process changes and achieve similar results.

Record the following:

- Data on outcomes that were analyzed
- Rationale for decisions
- Action proposals from causal analysis meetings
- Action plans resulting from action proposals
- Cost of analysis and resolution activities
- Measures of changes to the process performance of the defined process resulting from resolutions

2. Submit process improvement proposals for the organization when the implemented actions are effective for the project as appropriate.

When improvements are judged to be effective, the information can be submitted to the organizational level for potential inclusion in the organizational processes.

Refer to the Organizational Performance Management process area for more information about selecting improvements.

> **CAR**

> **HINT**
>
> Collect data to know that you are improving project performance relative to your objectives, to know that you have prevented selected problems from reoccurring (or have enabled conditions conducive to superior performance to recur), and to provide sufficient context for organizational evaluation of improvement proposals for possible deployment across the organization (OPM SP 2.2).

CONFIGURATION MANAGEMENT
A Support Process Area at Maturity Level 2

Purpose

The purpose of Configuration Management (CM) is to establish and maintain the integrity of work products using configuration identification, configuration control, configuration status accounting, and configuration audits.

TIP

Because this is a support process area, it is up to the project and organization to decide which work products are subject to CM, and the level of control needed.

CM

Introductory Notes

The Configuration Management process area involves the following activities:

- Identifying the configuration of selected work products that compose baselines at given points in time
- Controlling changes to configuration items
- Building or providing specifications to build work products from the configuration management system
- Maintaining the integrity of baselines
- Providing accurate status and current configuration data to developers, end users, and customers

HINT

CM should capture enough information to identify and maintain the configuration item after those who have developed it have gone.

The work products placed under configuration management include the products that are delivered to the customer, designated internal work products, acquired products, tools, and other items used in creating and describing these work products. (See the definition of "configuration management" in the glossary.)

TIP

Other items may include repair manuals and test results that provide additional insight into the work product.

Examples of work products that can be placed under configuration management include the following:
- Hardware and equipment
- Drawings
- Product specifications
- Tool configurations
- Code and libraries
- Compilers
- Test tools and test scripts
- Installation logs
- Product data files
- Product technical publications
- Plans
- User stories
- Iteration backlogs
- Process descriptions
- Requirements
- Architecture documentation and design data
- Product line plans, processes, and core assets

Acquired products may need to be placed under configuration management by both the supplier and the project. Provisions for conducting configuration management should be established in supplier agreements. Methods to ensure that data are complete and consistent should be established and maintained.

Refer to the Supplier Agreement Management process area for more information about establishing supplier agreements.

HINT

Typically, you determine the levels of granularity during planning. Select the configuration items to define for CM based on technical and business needs.

Configuration management of work products can be performed at several levels of granularity. Configuration items can be decomposed into configuration components and configuration units. Only the term "configuration item" is used in this process area. Therefore, in these practices, "configuration item" may be interpreted as "configuration component" or "configuration unit" as appropriate. (See the definition of "configuration item" in the glossary.)

Baselines provide a stable basis for the continuing evolution of configuration items.

An example of a baseline is an approved description of a product that includes internally consistent versions of requirements, requirement traceability matrices, design, discipline-specific items, and end-user documentation.

Baselines are added to the configuration management system as they are developed. Changes to baselines and the release of work products built from the configuration management system are systematically controlled and monitored via the configuration control, change management, and configuration auditing functions of configuration management.

This process area applies not only to configuration management on projects but also to configuration management of organizational work products such as standards, procedures, reuse libraries, and other shared supporting assets.

Configuration management is focused on the rigorous control of the managerial and technical aspects of work products, including the delivered product or service.

This process area covers the practices for performing the configuration management function and is applicable to all work products that are placed under configuration management.

For product lines, configuration management involves additional considerations due to the sharing of core assets across the products in the product line and across multiple versions of core assets and products. (See the definition of "product line" in the glossary.)

HINT

Review and approve baselines before they are added to (or promoted within) the CM system.

TIP

Anything important enough to ensure its integrity can be subject to CM practices.

CM

In Agile environments, configuration management (CM) is important because of the need to support frequent change, frequent builds (typically daily), multiple baselines, and multiple CM supported workspaces (e.g., for individuals, teams, and even for pair-programming). Agile teams may get bogged down if the organization doesn't: 1) automate CM (e.g., build scripts, status accounting, integrity checking) and 2) implement CM as a single set of standard services. At its start, an Agile team should identify the individual who will be responsible to ensure CM is implemented correctly. At the start of each iteration, CM support needs are re-confirmed. CM is carefully integrated into the rhythms of each team with a focus on minimizing team distraction to get the job done. (See "Interpreting CMMI When Using Agile Approaches" in Part I.)

Related Process Areas

Refer to the Project Monitoring and Control process area for more information about monitoring the project against the plan and managing corrective action to closure.

Refer to the Project Planning process area for more information about developing a project plan.

Specific Goal and Practice Summary

SG 1 Establish Baselines
    SP 1.1   Identify Configuration Items
    SP 1.2   Establish a Configuration Management System
    SP 1.3   Create or Release Baselines
SG 2 Track and Control Changes
    SP 2.1   Track Change Requests
    SP 2.2   Control Configuration Items
SG 3 Establish Integrity
    SP 3.1   Establish Configuration Management Records
    SP 3.2   Perform Configuration Audits

Specific Practices by Goal

SG 1 ESTABLISH BASELINES

Baselines of identified work products are established.

Specific practices to establish baselines are covered by this specific goal. The specific practices under the Track and Control Changes specific goal serve to maintain the baselines. The specific practices of the Establish Integrity specific goal document and audit the integrity of the baselines.

SP 1.1 IDENTIFY CONFIGURATION ITEMS

Identify configuration items, components, and related work products to be placed under configuration management.

Configuration identification is the selection and specification of the following:

- Products delivered to the customer
- Designated internal work products
- Acquired products
- Tools and other capital assets of the project's work environment
- Other items used in creating and describing these work products

Configuration items can include hardware, equipment, and tangible assets as well as software and documentation. Documentation can include requirements specifications and interface documents. Other documents that serve to identify the configuration of the product or service, such as test results, may also be included.

A "configuration item" is an entity designated for configuration management, which may consist of multiple related work products that form a baseline. This logical grouping provides ease of identification and controlled access. The selection of work products for configuration management should be based on criteria established during planning.

Example Work Products

1. Identified configuration items

Subpractices

1. Select configuration items and work products that compose them based on documented criteria.

> Example criteria for selecting configuration items at the appropriate work product level include the following:
> • Work products that can be used by two or more groups
> • Work products that are expected to change over time either because of errors or changes in requirements
> • Work products that are dependent on each other (i.e., a change in one mandates a change in the others)
> • Work products critical to project success

> Examples of work products that may be part of a configuration item include the following:
> • Design
> • Test plans and procedures
> • Test results
> • Interface descriptions
> • Drawings
> • Source code
> • User stories or story cards
> • The declared business case, logic, or value
> • Tools (e.g., compilers)
> • Process descriptions
> • Requirements

2. Assign unique identifiers to configuration items.
3. Specify the important characteristics of each configuration item.

TIP

An example of a group of related work products is a product component and its requirements, design, test case, verification procedure, and verification report.

HINT

When developing your project plan, document what is important for you to control. This part of the plan provides guidance for the project team when identifying configuration items.

HINT

Use criteria to select configuration items to ensure that the selection is consistent and thorough.

CM

HINT

If you use a CM tool, it will sometimes assign unique identifiers to configuration items for you.

> Example characteristics of configuration items include author, document or file type, programming language for software code files, minimum marketable features, and the purpose the configuration item serves.

4. Specify when each configuration item is placed under configuration management.

> Example criteria for determining when to place work products under configuration management include the following:
> • When the work product is ready for test
> • Stage of the project lifecycle
> • Degree of control desired on the work product
> • Cost and schedule limitations
> • Stakeholder requirements

5. Identify the owner responsible for each configuration item.
6. Specify relationships among configuration items.

> Incorporating the types of relationships (e.g., parent-child, dependency) that exist among configuration items into the configuration management structure (e.g., configuration management database) assists in managing the effects and impacts of changes.

SP 1.2 ESTABLISH A CONFIGURATION MANAGEMENT SYSTEM

Establish and maintain a configuration management and change management system for controlling work products.

A configuration management system includes the storage media, procedures, and tools for accessing the system. A configuration management system can consist of multiple subsystems with different implementations that are appropriate for each configuration management environment.

A change management system includes the storage media, procedures, and tools for recording and accessing change requests.

Example Work Products

1. Configuration management system with controlled work products
2. Configuration management system access control procedures
3. Change request database

Subpractices

1. Establish a mechanism to manage multiple levels of control.

   The level of control is typically selected based on project objectives, risk, and resources. Control levels can vary in relation to the project lifecycle, type of system under development, and specific project requirements.

TIP

Not all configuration items require the same level of control. Some may require more control as they move through the project lifecycle.

Example levels of control include the following:
- Uncontrolled: Anyone can make changes.
- Work-in-progress: Authors control changes.
- Released: A designated authority authorizes and controls changes and relevant stakeholders are notified when changes are made.

Levels of control can range from informal control that simply tracks changes made when configuration items are being developed to formal configuration control using baselines that can only be changed as part of a formal configuration management process.

TIP

A formal CM process is typically change-request based and requires extensive tracking and review of all changes.

2. Provide access control to ensure authorized access to the configuration management system.

3. Store and retrieve configuration items in a configuration management system.

4. Share and transfer configuration items between control levels in the configuration management system.

5. Store and recover archived versions of configuration items.

6. Store, update, and retrieve configuration management records.

7. Create configuration management reports from the configuration management system.

8. Preserve the contents of the configuration management system.

HINT

You must find the balance of ensuring all that need access to configuration items have it, but that the need for access is genuine and confirmed.

Examples of preservation functions of the configuration management system include the following:
- Backup and restoration of configuration management files
- Archive of configuration management files
- Recovery from configuration management errors

HINT

Review the CM system regularly to ensure that it is meeting the needs of the projects it serves.

9. Revise the configuration management structure as necessary.

SP 1.3 CREATE OR RELEASE BASELINES

Create or release baselines for internal use and for delivery to the customer.

A baseline is represented by the assignment of an identifier to a configuration item or a collection of configuration items and associated entities at a distinct point in time. As a product or service evolves, multiple baselines can be used to control development and testing. (See the definition of "baseline" in the glossary.)

Hardware products as well as software and documentation should also be included in baselines for infrastructure related configurations (e.g., software, hardware) and in preparation for system tests that include interfacing hardware and software.

One common set of baselines includes the system level requirements, system element level design requirements, and the product definition at the end of development/beginning of production. These baselines are typically referred to respectively as the "functional baseline," "allocated baseline," and "product baseline."

A software baseline can be a set of requirements, design, source code files and the associated executable code, build files, and user documentation (associated entities) that have been assigned a unique identifier.

Example Work Products

1. Baselines
2. Description of baselines

Subpractices

1. Obtain authorization from the CCB before creating or releasing baselines of configuration items.
2. Create or release baselines only from configuration items in the configuration management system.
3. Document the set of configuration items that are contained in a baseline.
4. Make the current set of baselines readily available.

SG 2 TRACK AND CONTROL CHANGES

Changes to the work products under configuration management are tracked and controlled.

The specific practices under this specific goal serve to maintain baselines after they are established by specific practices under the Establish Baselines specific goal.

TIP

CCB authorization should be formal and documented in some way.

TIP

If the baselines released or used do not come from the CM system, the system is not serving its purpose and there is a high risk of losing baseline integrity.

TIP

If the project or organization uses multiple baselines, it is even more critical to ensure that everyone is using the correct baseline.

HINT

To ensure that project members use the CM system, make sure the system is easy to use.

TIP

This goal is typically implemented by establishing a change request system and forming a CCB whose primary role is to review and approve baseline changes.

SP 2.1 TRACK CHANGE REQUESTS

Track change requests for configuration items.

Change requests address not only new or changed requirements but also failures and defects in work products.

Change requests are analyzed to determine the impact that the change will have on the work product, related work products, the budget, and the schedule.

Example Work Products

1. Change requests

Subpractices

1. Initiate and record change requests in the change request database.
2. Analyze the impact of changes and fixes proposed in change requests.

   Changes are evaluated through activities that ensure that they are consistent with all technical and project requirements.

   Changes are evaluated for their impact beyond immediate project or contract requirements. Changes to an item used in multiple products can resolve an immediate issue while causing a problem in other applications.

   Changes are evaluated for their impact on release plans.
3. Categorize and prioritize change requests.

   Emergency requests are identified and referred to an emergency authority if appropriate.

   Changes are allocated to future baselines.
4. Review change requests to be addressed in the next baseline with relevant stakeholders and get their agreement.

   Conduct the change request review with appropriate participants. Record the disposition of each change request and the rationale for the decision, including success criteria, a brief action plan if appropriate, and needs met or unmet by the change. Perform the actions required in the disposition and report results to relevant stakeholders.
5. Track the status of change requests to closure.

   Change requests brought into the system should be handled in an efficient and timely manner. Once a change request has been processed, it is critical to close the request with the appropriate approved action as soon as it is practical. Actions left open result in larger than necessary status lists, which in turn result in added costs and confusion.

TIP

Change requests are formally submitted descriptions of desired modifications to work products. If change requests are not documented consistently, they are difficult to analyze and track.

TIP

A change request system is usually used after an initial baseline is created. A change request system allows you to track every change that is made to work products.

TIP

A database provides a flexible environment for storing and tracking change requests.

TIP

Organizing your change requests enables you to analyze the relationships among them and the order in which these requests should be implemented.

HINT

Track change requests to closure to ensure that if a change request is not addressed, it was not lost or missed.

CM

SP 2.2 CONTROL CONFIGURATION ITEMS

Control changes to configuration items.

Control is maintained over the configuration of the work product baseline. This control includes tracking the configuration of each configuration item, approving a new configuration if necessary, and updating the baseline.

Example Work Products

1. Revision history of configuration items
2. Archives of baselines

Subpractices

1. Control changes to configuration items throughout the life of the product or service.
2. Obtain appropriate authorization before changed configuration items are entered into the configuration management system.

> For example, authorization can come from the CCB, the project manager, product owner, or the customer.

3. Check in and check out configuration items in the configuration management system for incorporation of changes in a manner that maintains the correctness and integrity of configuration items.

> Examples of check-in and check-out steps include the following:
> - Confirming that the revisions are authorized
> - Updating the configuration items
> - Archiving the replaced baseline and retrieving the new baseline
> - Commenting on the changes made to the item
> - Tying changes to related work products such as requirements, user stories, and tests

4. Perform reviews to ensure that changes have not caused unintended effects on the baselines (e.g., ensure that changes have not compromised the safety or security of the system).
5. Record changes to configuration items and reasons for changes as appropriate.

    If a proposed change to the work product is accepted, a schedule is identified for incorporating the change into the work product and other affected areas.

TIP

A revision history usually contains not only what was changed, but also who made the changes, and when and why they were made.

TIP

The life of the product is typically longer than the life of the development project that created it. The responsibility for configuration items may change over time.

HINT

Define authorization procedures so that it is clear how to receive authorization to enter an updated configuration item into the CM system.

TIP

An important part of check in and check out is ensuring that only one copy of a configuration item is authorized for update at one time.

Configuration control mechanisms can be tailored to categories of changes. For example, the approval considerations could be less stringent for component changes that do not affect other components.

Changed configuration items are released after review and approval of configuration changes. Changes are not official until they are released.

SG 3 ESTABLISH INTEGRITY

Integrity of baselines is established and maintained.

The integrity of baselines, established by processes associated with the Establish Baselines specific goal, and maintained by processes associated with the Track and Control Changes specific goal, is addressed by the specific practices under this specific goal.

SP 3.1 ESTABLISH CONFIGURATION MANAGEMENT RECORDS

Establish and maintain records describing configuration items.

Example Work Products

1. Revision history of configuration items
2. Change log
3. Change request records
4. Status of configuration items
5. Differences between baselines

Subpractices

1. Record configuration management actions in sufficient detail so the content and status of each configuration item is known and previous versions can be recovered.
2. Ensure that relevant stakeholders have access to and knowledge of the configuration status of configuration items.

> Examples of activities for communicating configuration status include the following:
> • Providing access permissions to authorized end users
> • Making baseline copies readily available to authorized end users
> • Automatically alerting relevant stakeholders when items are checked in or out or changed, or of decisions made regarding change requests

3. Specify the latest version of baselines.

TIP

Without descriptions of the configuration items, it is difficult and time consuming to understand the status of these items relative to the project plan.

CM

TIP

Version control is an important part of CM. There are different ways to identify versions. A standard way is using sequential numbering.

HINT

When describing the differences between baselines, you should be detailed enough so that users of the baselines can differentiate them easily.

TIP

Audits provide an objective way to know that what is supposed to be controlled is controlled and can be retrieved. Retrieval of accurate information is one of CM's many benefits.

4. Identify the version of configuration items that constitute a particular baseline.

5. Describe differences between successive baselines.

6. Revise the status and history (i.e., changes, other actions) of each configuration item as necessary.

SP 3.2 PERFORM CONFIGURATION AUDITS

Perform configuration audits to maintain the integrity of configuration baselines.

Configuration audits confirm that the resulting baselines and documentation conform to a specified standard or requirement. Configuration item related records can exist in multiple databases or configuration management systems. In such instances, configuration audits should extend to these other databases as appropriate to ensure accuracy, consistency, and completeness of configuration item information. (See the definition of "configuration audit" in the glossary.)

Examples of audit types include the following:

- Functional configuration audits (FCAs): Audits conducted to verify that the development of a configuration item has been completed satisfactorily, that the item has achieved the functional and quality attribute characteristics specified in the functional or allocated baseline, and that its operational and support documents are complete and satisfactory.
- Physical configuration audits (PCAs): Audits conducted to verify that a configuration item, as built, conforms to the technical documentation that defines and describes it.
- Configuration management audits: Audits conducted to confirm that configuration management records and configuration items are complete, consistent, and accurate.

Example Work Products

1. Configuration audit results
2. Action items

Subpractices

TIP

Integrity includes accuracy, consistency, and completeness.

1. Assess the integrity of baselines.
2. Confirm that configuration management records correctly identify configuration items.
3. Review the structure and integrity of items in the configuration management system.

4. Confirm the completeness, correctness, and consistency of items in the configuration management system.

   Completeness, correctness, and consistency of the configuration management system's content are based on requirements as stated in the plan and the disposition of approved change requests.

5. Confirm compliance with applicable configuration management standards and procedures.

6. Track action items from the audit to closure.

TIP

An audit is effective only when all action items from the audit are addressed.

CM

DECISION ANALYSIS AND RESOLUTION
A Support Process Area at Maturity Level 3

Purpose

The purpose of Decision Analysis and Resolution (DAR) is to analyze possible decisions using a formal evaluation process that evaluates identified alternatives against established criteria.

Introductory Notes

The Decision Analysis and Resolution process area involves establishing guidelines to determine which issues should be subject to a formal evaluation process and applying formal evaluation processes to these issues.

A formal evaluation process is a structured approach to evaluating alternative solutions against established criteria to determine a recommended solution.

A formal evaluation process involves the following actions:

- Establishing the criteria for evaluating alternatives
- Identifying alternative solutions
- Selecting methods for evaluating alternatives
- Evaluating alternative solutions using established criteria and methods
- Selecting recommended solutions from alternatives based on evaluation criteria

Rather than using the phrase "alternative solutions to address issues" each time, in this process area, one of two shorter phrases are used: "alternative solutions" or "alternatives."

A formal evaluation process reduces the subjective nature of a decision and provides a higher probability of selecting a solution that meets multiple demands of relevant stakeholders.

DAR

TIP

Examples of nontechnical issues include adding resources and determining delivery approaches for a training class.

While the primary application of this process area is to technical concerns, formal evaluation processes can be applied to many nontechnical issues, particularly when a project is being planned. Issues that have multiple alternative solutions and evaluation criteria lend themselves to a formal evaluation process.

> Trade studies of equipment or software are typical examples of formal evaluation processes.

X-REF

Many of the technical issues that may benefit from a formal evaluation process are addressed in TS, PI, VER, and VAL.

During planning, specific issues requiring a formal evaluation process are identified. Typical issues include selection among architectural or design alternatives, use of reusable or commercial off-the-shelf (COTS) components, supplier selection, engineering support environments or associated tools, test environments, delivery alternatives, and logistics and production. A formal evaluation process can also be used to address a make-or-buy decision, the development of manufacturing processes, the selection of distribution locations, and other decisions.

Guidelines are created for deciding when to use formal evaluation processes to address unplanned issues. Guidelines often suggest using formal evaluation processes when issues are associated with medium-to-high-impact risks or when issues affect the ability to achieve project objectives.

Defining an issue well helps to define the scope of alternatives to be considered. The right scope (i.e., not too broad, not too narrow) will aid in making an appropriate decision for resolving the defined issue.

Formal evaluation processes can vary in formality, type of criteria, and methods employed. Less formal decisions can be analyzed in a few hours, use few criteria (e.g., effectiveness, cost to implement), and result in a one- or two-page report. More formal decisions can require separate plans, months of effort, meetings to develop and approve criteria, simulations, prototypes, piloting, and extensive documentation.

TIP

Tools such as the Analytic Hierarchy Process (AHP), Quality Function Deployment (QFD), the Pugh Method, the Delphi Method, prioritization matrices, cause-and-effect diagrams, decision trees, weighted criteria spreadsheets, and simulations exist to help with weighted decision making.

Both numeric and non-numeric criteria can be used in a formal evaluation process. Numeric criteria use weights to reflect the relative importance of criteria. Non-numeric criteria use a subjective ranking scale (e.g., high, medium, low). More formal decisions can require a full trade study.

A formal evaluation process identifies and evaluates alternative solutions. The eventual selection of a solution can involve iterative activities of identification and evaluation. Portions of identified alternatives can be combined, emerging technologies can change alternatives, and the business situation of suppliers can change during the evaluation period.

A recommended alternative is accompanied by documentation of selected methods, criteria, alternatives, and rationale for the recommendation. The documentation is distributed to relevant stakeholders; it provides a record of the formal evaluation process and rationale, which are useful to other projects that encounter a similar issue.

While some of the decisions made throughout the life of the project involve the use of a formal evaluation process, others do not. As mentioned earlier, guidelines should be established to determine which issues should be subject to a formal evaluation process.

Related Process Areas

Refer to the Integrated Project Management process area for more information about establishing the project's defined process.

Refer to the Risk Management process area for more information about identifying and analyzing risks and mitigating risks.

Specific Goal and Practice Summary

SG 1 Evaluate Alternatives
    SP 1.1   Establish Guidelines for Decision Analysis
    SP 1.2   Establish Evaluation Criteria
    SP 1.3   Identify Alternative Solutions
    SP 1.4   Select Evaluation Methods
    SP 1.5   Evaluate Alternative Solutions
    SP 1.6   Select Solutions

Specific Practices by Goal

SG 1   *EVALUATE ALTERNATIVES*

Decisions are based on an evaluation of alternatives using established criteria.

Issues requiring a formal evaluation process can be identified at any time. The objective should be to identify issues as early as possible to maximize the time available to resolve them.

SP 1.1 ESTABLISH GUIDELINES FOR DECISION ANALYSIS

Establish and maintain guidelines to determine which issues are subject to a formal evaluation process.

Not every decision is significant enough to require a formal evaluation process. The choice between the trivial and the truly important is unclear without explicit guidance. Whether a decision is significant or not is dependent on the project and circumstances and is determined by established guidelines.

Typical guidelines for determining when to require a formal evaluation process include the following:

- A decision is directly related to issues that are medium-to-high-impact risk.
- A decision is related to changing work products under configuration management.
- A decision would cause schedule delays over a certain percentage or amount of time.
- A decision affects the ability of the project to achieve its objectives.
- The costs of the formal evaluation process are reasonable when compared to the decision's impact.
- A legal obligation exists during a solicitation.
- When competing quality attribute requirements would result in significantly different alternative architectures.

Refer to the Risk Management process area for more information about evaluating, categorizing, and prioritizing risks.

Examples of activities for which you may use a formal evaluation process include the following:

- Making decisions involving the procurement of material when 20 percent of the material parts constitute 80 percent of the total material costs
- Making design-implementation decisions when technical performance failure can cause a catastrophic failure (e.g., safety-of-flight item)
- Making decisions with the potential to significantly reduce design risk, engineering changes, cycle time, response time, and production costs (e.g., to use lithography models to assess form and fit capability before releasing engineering drawings and production builds)

Example Work Products

1. Guidelines for when to apply a formal evaluation process

Subpractices

1. Establish guidelines for when to use a formal evaluation process.
2. Incorporate the use of guidelines into the defined process as appropriate.

   Refer to the Integrated Project Management process area for more information about establishing the project's defined process.

HINT

Make sure the guidelines are accessible and understood by everyone in the organization (or project).

SP 1.2 ESTABLISH EVALUATION CRITERIA

Establish and maintain criteria for evaluating alternatives and the relative ranking of these criteria.

Evaluation criteria provide the basis for evaluating alternative solutions. Criteria are ranked so that the highest ranked criteria exert the most influence on the evaluation.

TIP

In some cases, all criteria may be roughly equal and ranking may not be necessary.

This process area is referenced by many other process areas in the model, and many contexts in which a formal evaluation process can be used. Therefore, in some situations you may find that criteria have already been defined as part of another process. This specific practice does not suggest that a second development of criteria be conducted.

A well-defined statement of the issue to be addressed and the decision to be made focuses the analysis to be performed. Such a statement also aids in defining evaluation criteria that minimize the possibility that decisions will be second guessed or that the reason for making the decision will be forgotten. Decisions based on criteria that are explicitly defined and established remove barriers to stakeholder buy-in.

TIP

Documentation helps to provide an understanding of which criteria were considered and how they were ranked.

DAR

Example Work Products

1. Documented evaluation criteria
2. Rankings of criteria importance

Subpractices

1. Define the criteria for evaluating alternative solutions.

   Criteria should be traceable to requirements, scenarios, business case assumptions, business objectives, or other documented sources.

> Typical evaluation methods include the following:
> - Testing
> - Modeling and simulation
> - Engineering studies
> - Manufacturing studies
> - Cost studies
> - Business opportunity studies
> - Surveys
> - Extrapolations based on field experience and prototypes
> - End-user review and comment
> - Judgment provided by an expert or group of experts (e.g., Delphi method)

2. Select evaluation methods based on their ability to focus on the issues at hand without being overly influenced by side issues.

   Results of simulations can be skewed by random activities in the solution that are not directly related to the issues at hand.

3. Determine the measures needed to support the evaluation method.

   Consider the impact on cost, schedule, performance, and risks.

SP 1.5 EVALUATE ALTERNATIVE SOLUTIONS

Evaluate alternative solutions using established criteria and methods.

Evaluating alternative solutions involves analysis, discussion, and review. Iterative cycles of analysis are sometimes necessary. Supporting analyses, experimentation, prototyping, piloting, or simulations may be needed to substantiate scoring and conclusions.

Often, the relative importance of criteria is imprecise and the total effect on a solution is not apparent until after the analysis is performed. In cases where the resulting scores differ by relatively small amounts, the best selection among alternative solutions may not be clear. Challenges to criteria and assumptions should be encouraged.

Example Work Products

1. Evaluation results

Subpractices

1. Evaluate proposed alternative solutions using the established evaluation criteria and selected methods.
2. Evaluate assumptions related to the evaluation criteria and the evidence that supports the assumptions.

3. Evaluate whether uncertainty in the values for alternative solutions affects the evaluation and address these uncertainties as appropriate.

> For instance, if the score varies between two values, is the difference significant enough to make a difference in the final solution set? Does the variation in score represent a high-impact risk? To address these concerns, simulations may be run, further studies may be performed, or evaluation criteria may be modified, among other things.

4. Perform simulations, modeling, prototypes, and pilots as necessary to exercise the evaluation criteria, methods, and alternative solutions.

> Untested criteria, their relative importance, and supporting data or functions can cause the validity of solutions to be questioned. Criteria and their relative priorities and scales can be tested with trial runs against a set of alternatives. These trial runs of a select set of criteria allow for the evaluation of the cumulative impact of criteria on a solution. If trials reveal problems, different criteria or alternatives might be considered to avoid biases.

5. Consider new alternative solutions, criteria, or methods if proposed alternatives do not test well; repeat evaluations until alternatives do test well.

6. Document the results of the evaluation.

> Document the rationale for the addition of new alternatives or methods and changes to criteria, as well as the results of interim evaluations.

SP 1.6 SELECT SOLUTIONS

Select solutions from alternatives based on evaluation criteria.

Selecting solutions involves weighing results from the evaluation of alternatives. Risks associated with the implementation of solutions should be assessed.

Example Work Products

1. Recommended solutions to address significant issues

Subpractices

1. Assess the risks associated with implementing the recommended solution.

> *Refer to the Risk Management process area for more information about identifying and analyzing risks and mitigating risks.*

> Decisions must often be made with incomplete information. There can be substantial risk associated with the decision because of having incomplete information.

When decisions must be made according to a specific schedule, time and resources may not be available for gathering complete information. Consequently, risky decisions made with incomplete information can require re-analysis later. Identified risks should be monitored.

2. Document and communicate to relevant stakeholders the results and rationale for the recommended solution.

It is important to record both why a solution is selected and why another solution was rejected.

INTEGRATED PROJECT MANAGEMENT
A Project Management Process Area at Maturity Level 3

TIP

In the CMMI for Services Model, this process area is called Integrated Work Management.

Purpose

The purpose of Integrated Project Management (IPM) is to establish and manage the project and the involvement of relevant stakeholders according to an integrated and defined process that is tailored from the organization's set of standard processes.

TIP

IPM matures the project management activities described in PP and PMC so that they address the organizational requirements for projects described in OPF and OPD.

Introductory Notes

Integrated Project Management involves the following activities:

- Establishing the project's defined process at project startup by tailoring the organization's set of standard processes
- Managing the project using the project's defined process
- Establishing the work environment for the project based on the organization's work environment standards
- Establishing teams that are tasked to accomplish project objectives
- Using and contributing to organizational process assets
- Enabling relevant stakeholders' concerns to be identified, considered, and, when appropriate, addressed during the project
- Ensuring that relevant stakeholders (1) perform their tasks in a coordinated and timely manner; (2) address project requirements, plans, objectives, problems, and risks; (3) fulfill their commitments; and (4) identify, track, and resolve coordination issues

The integrated and defined process that is tailored from the organization's set of standard processes is called the project's defined process. (See the definition of "project" in the glossary.)

Managing the project's effort, cost, schedule, staffing, risks, and other factors is tied to the tasks of the project's defined process. The implementation and management of the project's defined process are typically described in the project plan. Certain activities may be

TIP

Using IPM to guide project management activities enables project plans to be consistent with project activities because they are both derived from standard processes created by the organization. Further, plans tend to be more reliable and are developed more quickly, and new projects learn more quickly.

IPM

covered in other plans that affect the project, such as the quality assurance plan, risk management strategy, and the configuration management plan.

Since the defined process for each project is tailored from the organization's set of standard processes, variability among projects is typically reduced and projects can easily share process assets, data, and lessons learned.

TIP

It is also easier to share resources (e.g., training and software tools) and to "load balance" staff across projects.

> This process area also addresses the coordination of all activities associated with the project such as the following:
> - Development activities (e.g., requirements development, design, verification)
> - Service activities (e.g., delivery, help desk, operations, customer contact)
> - Acquisition activities (e.g., solicitation, agreement monitoring, transition to operations)
> - Support activities (e.g., configuration management, documentation, marketing, training)

TIP

A proactive approach to integrating plans and coordinating with relevant stakeholders outside the project is a key activity.

The working interfaces and interactions among relevant stakeholders internal and external to the project are planned and managed to ensure the quality and integrity of the overall endeavor. Relevant stakeholders participate as appropriate in defining the project's defined process and the project plan. Reviews and exchanges are regularly conducted with relevant stakeholders to ensure that coordination issues receive appropriate attention and everyone involved with the project is appropriately aware of status, plans, and activities. (See the definition of "relevant stakeholder" in the glossary.) In defining the project's defined process, formal interfaces are created as necessary to ensure that appropriate coordination and collaboration occurs.

This process area applies in any organizational structure, including projects that are structured as line organizations, matrix organizations, or teams. The terminology should be appropriately interpreted for the organizational structure in place.

Related Process Areas

Refer to the Verification process area for more information about performing peer reviews.

Refer to the Measurement and Analysis process area for more information about aligning measurement and analysis activities and providing measurement results.

Refer to the Organizational Process Definition process area for more information about establishing and maintaining a usable set of organizational process assets, work environment standards, and rules and guidelines for teams.

Refer to the Project Monitoring and Control process area for more information about monitoring the project against the plan.

Refer to the Project Planning process area for more information about developing a project plan.

Specific Goal and Practice Summary

SG 1 Use the Project's Defined Process
    SP 1.1   Establish the Project's Defined Process
    SP 1.2   Use Organizational Process Assets for Planning Project Activities
    SP 1.3   Establish the Project's Work Environment
    SP 1.4   Integrate Plans
    SP 1.5   Manage the Project Using Integrated Plans
    SP 1.6   Establish Teams
    SP 1.7   Contribute to Organizational Process Assets
SG 2 Coordinate and Collaborate with Relevant Stakeholders
    SP 2.1   Manage Stakeholder Involvement
    SP 2.2   Manage Dependencies
    SP 2.3   Resolve Coordination Issues

> **TIP**
>
> In Version 1.3, the IPPD material has been removed and SP 1.6 was added to address teams.

Specific Practices by Goal

SG 1   USE THE PROJECT'S DEFINED PROCESS

The project is conducted using a defined process tailored from the organization's set of standard processes.

The project's defined process includes those processes from the organization's set of standard processes that address all processes necessary to acquire, develop, maintain, or deliver the product.

The product related lifecycle processes, such as manufacturing and support processes, are developed concurrently with the product.

> **TIP**
>
> All projects that use IPM have the organization's set of standard processes as a basis to begin planning all project activities.

IPM

SP 1.1   ESTABLISH THE PROJECT'S DEFINED PROCESS

Establish and maintain the project's defined process from project startup through the life of the project.

Refer to the Organizational Process Definition process area for more information about establishing organizational process assets and establishing the organization's measurement repository.

Refer to the Organizational Process Focus process area for more information about deploying organizational process assets and deploying standard processes.

The project's defined process consists of defined processes that form an integrated, coherent lifecycle for the project.

The project's defined process should satisfy the project's contractual requirements, operational needs, opportunities, and constraints. It is designed to provide a best fit for project needs.

A project's defined process is based on the following factors:

- Stakeholder requirements
- Commitments
- Organizational process needs and objectives
- The organization's set of standard processes and tailoring guidelines
- The operational environment
- The business environment

Establishing the project's defined process at project startup helps to ensure that project staff and relevant stakeholders implement a set of activities needed to efficiently establish an initial set of requirements and plans for the project. As the project progresses, the description of the project's defined process is elaborated and revised to better meet project requirements and the organization's process needs and objectives. Also, as the organization's set of standard processes changes, the project's defined process may need to be revised.

Example Work Products

1. The project's defined process

Subpractices

TIP

IPM depends strongly on OPD. It is impossible to implement the specific practices in IPM without having in place the organizational infrastructure described in OPD.

1. Select a lifecycle model from the ones available in organizational process assets.

> **Examples of project characteristics that could affect the selection of lifecycle models include the following:**
> - Size or complexity of the project
> - Project strategy
> - Experience and familiarity of staff with implementing the process
> - Constraints such as cycle time and acceptable defect levels
> - Availability of customers to answer questions and provide feedback on increments
> - Clarity of requirements
> - Customer expectations

2. Select standard processes from the organization's set of standard processes that best fit the needs of the project.

3. Tailor the organization's set of standard processes and other organizational process assets according to tailoring guidelines to produce the project's defined process.

> Sometimes the available lifecycle models and standard processes are inadequate to meet project needs. In such circumstances, the project should seek approval to deviate from what is required by the organization. Waivers are provided for this purpose.
>
> Tailoring can include adapting the organization's common measures and specifying additional measures to meet the information needs of the project.

4. Use other artifacts from the organization's process asset library as appropriate.

Other artifacts can include the following:

- Lessons learned documents
- Templates
- Example documents
- Estimating models

TIP

The organization's set of standard processes are tailored to address the project's specific needs and situation. For example, are stringent quality, safety, or security requirements in place? Is the risk of delivering the wrong product high? Are we working with a new customer, product line, or line of business? Are there stringent schedule constraints?

HINT

Maintain the process asset library to keep it current, or else it could become the dumping ground for all project information and may quickly become unusable.

5. Document the project's defined process.

> The project's defined process covers all of the activities for the project and its interfaces to relevant stakeholders.

Examples of project activities include the following:
- Project planning
- Project monitoring
- Supplier management
- Quality assurance
- Risk management
- Decision analysis and resolution
- Requirements development
- Requirements management
- Configuration management
- Product development and support
- Code review
- Solicitation

TIP

Remember the point from the Introductory Notes that states, "Relevant stakeholders participate as appropriate in defining the project's defined process and the project plan."

IPM

6. Conduct peer reviews of the project's defined process.

> *Refer to the Verification process area for more information about performing peer reviews.*

7. Revise the project's defined process as necessary.

SP 1.2 USE ORGANIZATIONAL PROCESS ASSETS FOR PLANNING PROJECT ACTIVITIES

Use organizational process assets and the measurement repository for estimating and planning project activities.

Refer to the Organizational Process Definition process area for more information about establishing organizational process assets.

When available, use results of previous planning and execution activities as predictors of the relative scope and risk of the effort being estimated.

Example Work Products

1. Project estimates
2. Project plans

Subpractices

1. Use the tasks and work products of the project's defined process as a basis for estimating and planning project activities.

    An understanding of the relationships among tasks and work products of the project's defined process, and of the roles to be performed by relevant stakeholders, is a basis for developing a realistic plan.

2. Use the organization's measurement repository in estimating the project's planning parameters.

> This estimate typically includes the following:
> - Appropriate historical data from this project or similar projects
> - Similarities and differences between the current project and those projects whose historical data will be used
> - Validated historical data
> - Reasoning, assumptions, and rationale used to select the historical data
> - Reasoning of a broad base of experienced project participants

> Examples of parameters that are considered for similarities and differences include the following:
> - Work product and task attributes
> - Application domain
> - Experience of the people
> - Design and development approaches
> - Operational environment

> Examples of data contained in the organization's measurement repository include the following:
> - Size of work products or other work product attributes
> - Effort
> - Cost
> - Schedule
> - Staffing
> - Response time
> - Service capacity
> - Supplier performance
> - Defects

SP 1.3 ESTABLISH THE PROJECT'S WORK ENVIRONMENT

Establish and maintain the project's work environment based on the organization's work environment standards.

An appropriate work environment for a project comprises an infrastructure of facilities, tools, and equipment that people need to perform their jobs effectively in support of business and project objectives. The work environment and its components are maintained at a level of work environment performance and reliability indicated by organizational work environment standards. As required, the project's work environment or some of its components can be developed internally or acquired from external sources.

The project's work environment might encompass environments for product integration, verification, and validation or they might be separate environments.

Refer to the Establish the Product Integration Environment specific practice in the Product Integration process area for more information about establishing and maintaining the product integration environment for the project.

Refer to the Establish the Validation Environment specific practice in the Validation process area for more information about establishing and maintaining the validation environment for the project.

Refer to the Establish the Verification Environment specific practice in the Verification process area for more information about establishing and maintaining the verification environment for the project.

Refer to the Establish Work Environment Standards specific practice in the Organizational Process Definition process area for more information about work environment standards.

TIP

Often, the project's work environment contains components that are common to the organization's overall work environment. Many of these components may be provided by IT or the facilities group.

IPM

Example Work Products

1. Equipment and tools for the project
2. Installation, operation, and maintenance manuals for the project work environment
3. User surveys and results
4. Use, performance, and maintenance records
5. Support services for the project's work environment

Subpractices

TIP

A facilities group can use input from the project to create the work environment.

1. Plan, design, and install a work environment for the project.

    The critical aspects of the project work environment are, like any other product, requirements driven. Functionality and quality attributes of the work environment are explored with the same rigor as is done for any other product development project.

It may be necessary to make tradeoffs among quality attributes, costs, and risks. The following are examples of each:

- Quality attribute considerations can include timely communication, safety, security, and maintainability.
- Costs can include capital outlays, training, a support structure; disassembly and disposal of existing environments; and the operation and maintenance of the environment.
- Risks can include workflow and project disruptions.

Examples of equipment and tools include the following:

- Office software
- Decision support software
- Project management tools
- Test and evaluation equipment
- Requirements management tools and design tools
- Configuration management tools
- Evaluation tools
- Integration tools
- Automated test tools

---

2. Provide ongoing maintenance and operational support for the project's work environment.

    Maintenance and support of the work environment can be accomplished either with capabilities found inside the organization or hired from outside the organization.

> Examples of maintenance and support approaches include the following:
> - Hiring people to perform maintenance and support
> - Training people to perform maintenance and support
> - Contracting maintenance and support
> - Developing expert users for selected tools

3. Maintain the qualification of components of the project's work environment.

   Components include software, databases, hardware, tools, test equipment, and appropriate documentation. Qualification of software includes appropriate certifications. Hardware and test equipment qualification includes calibration and adjustment records and traceability to calibration standards.

4. Periodically review how well the work environment is meeting project needs and supporting collaboration, and take action as appropriate.

> Examples of actions that might be taken include the following:
> - Adding new tools
> - Acquiring additional networks, equipment, training, and support

SP 1.4 INTEGRATE PLANS

Integrate the project plan and other plans that affect the project to describe the project's defined process.

Refer to the Organizational Process Definition process area for more information about establishing organizational process assets and, in particular, establishing the organization's measurement repository.

Refer to the Organizational Process Focus process area for more information about establishing organizational process needs and determining process improvement opportunities.

Refer to the Project Planning process area for more information about developing a project plan.

This specific practice extends the specific practices for establishing and maintaining a project plan to address additional planning activities such as incorporating the project's defined process, coordinating with relevant stakeholders, using organizational process assets, incorporating plans for peer reviews, and establishing objective entry and exit criteria for tasks.

TIP

One of the main differences between IPM and PP is that IPM is more proactive in coordinating with relevant stakeholders, both internal (different teams) and external (organizational functions and support groups) to the project, and is concerned with the integration of plans.

TIP

To help formulate estimates, applicable data may be found in the organization's measurement repository. Additionally, applicable templates, examples, and lessons-learned documents may be found in the organization's process asset library.

IPM

The development of the project plan should account for current and projected needs, objectives, and requirements of the organization, customer, suppliers, and end users as appropriate.

Example Work Products

1. Integrated plans

Subpractices

1. Integrate other plans that affect the project with the project plan.

> Other plans that affect the project plan can include the following:
> - Quality assurance plans
> - Risk management strategy
> - Verification and validation plans
> - Transition to operations and support plans
> - Configuration management plans
> - Documentation plans
> - Staff training plans
> - Facilities and logistics plans

2. Incorporate into the project plan the definitions of measures and measurement activities for managing the project.

> Examples of measures that would be incorporated include the following:
> - Organization's common set of measures
> - Additional project specific measures

> *Refer to the Measurement and Analysis process area for more information about developing and sustaining a measurement capability used to support management information needs.*

3. Identify and analyze product and project interface risks.

> *Refer to the Risk Management process area for more information about identifying and analyzing risks.*

> Examples of product and project interface risks include the following:
> - Incomplete interface descriptions
> - Unavailability of tools, suppliers, or test equipment
> - Unavailability of COTS components
> - Inadequate or ineffective team interfaces

4. Schedule tasks in a sequence that accounts for critical development and delivery factors and project risks.

Examples of factors considered in scheduling include the following:
- Size and complexity of tasks
- Needs of the customer and end users
- Availability of critical resources
- Availability of key staff
- Integration and test issues

---

5. Incorporate plans for performing peer reviews on work products of the project's defined process.

   Refer to the Verification process area for more information about performing peer reviews.

6. Incorporate the training needed to perform the project's defined process in the project's training plans.

   This task typically includes negotiating with the organizational training group on the support they will provide.

   X-REF

   Refer to OT for more information about organizational training.

7. Establish objective entry and exit criteria to authorize the initiation and completion of tasks described in the work breakdown structure (WBS).

   Refer to the Project Planning process area for more information about estimating the scope of the project.

8. Ensure that the project plan is appropriately compatible with the plans of relevant stakeholders.

   Typically the plan and changes to the plan will be reviewed for compatibility.

9. Identify how conflicts will be resolved that arise among relevant stakeholders.

SP 1.5 MANAGE THE PROJECT USING INTEGRATED PLANS

Manage the project using the project plan, other plans that affect the project, and the project's defined process.

Refer to the Organizational Process Definition process area for more information about establishing organizational process assets.

Refer to the Organizational Process Focus process area for more information about establishing organizational process needs, deploying organizational process assets, and deploying standard processes.

Refer to the Project Monitoring and Control process area for more information about providing an understanding of the project's progress so that appropriate

TIP

Walk your talk. The prior SPs established the plan—this SP implements and manages the project against that plan.

IPM

corrective actions can be taken when the project's performance deviates significantly from the plan.

Refer to the Risk Management process area for more information about identifying and analyzing risks and mitigating risks.

Example Work Products

1. Work products created by performing the project's defined process
2. Collected measures (i.e., actuals) and status records or reports
3. Revised requirements, plans, and commitments
4. Integrated plans

Subpractices

1. Implement the project's defined process using the organization's process asset library.

> This task typically includes the following activities:
> - Incorporating artifacts from the organization's process asset library into the project as appropriate
> - Using lessons learned from the organization's process asset library to manage the project

TIP

The organization's process improvement plan is another plan that might affect the project.

2. Monitor and control the project's activities and work products using the project's defined process, project plan, and other plans that affect the project.

> This task typically includes the following activities:
> - Using the defined entry and exit criteria to authorize the initiation and determine the completion of tasks
> - Monitoring activities that could significantly affect actual values of the project's planning parameters
> - Tracking project planning parameters using measurable thresholds that will trigger investigation and appropriate actions
> - Monitoring product and project interface risks
> - Managing external and internal commitments based on plans for tasks and work products of the project's defined process

An understanding of the relationships among tasks and work products of the project's defined process and of the roles to be performed by relevant stakeholders, along with well-defined control mechanisms (e.g., peer reviews), achieves better visibility into project performance and better control of the project.

3. Obtain and analyze selected measurements to manage the project and support organization needs.

   Refer to the Measurement and Analysis process area for more information about obtaining measurement data and analyzing measurement data.

4. Periodically review and align the project's performance with current and anticipated needs, objectives, and requirements of the organization, customer, and end users as appropriate.

   This review includes alignment with organizational process needs and objectives.

Examples of actions that achieve alignment include the following:
- Changing the schedule with appropriate adjustments to other planning parameters and project risks
- Changing requirements or commitments in response to a change in market opportunities or customer and end-user needs
- Terminating the project, iteration, or release

---

5. Address causes of selected issues that can affect project objectives.

   Issues that require corrective action are determined and analyzed as in the Analyze Issues and Take Corrective Actions specific practices of the Project Monitoring and Control process area. As appropriate, the project may periodically review issues previously encountered on other projects or in earlier phases of the project, and conduct causal analysis of selected issues to determine how to prevent recurrence for issues which can significantly affect project objectives. Project process changes implemented as a result of causal analysis activities should be evaluated for effectiveness to ensure that the process change has prevented recurrence and improved performance.

SP 1.6 ESTABLISH TEAMS

Establish and maintain teams.

The project is managed using teams that reflect the organizational rules and guidelines for team structuring, formation, and operation. (See the definition of "team" in the glossary.)

The project's shared vision is established prior to establishing the team structure, which can be based on the WBS. For small organizations, the whole organization and relevant external stakeholders can be treated as a team.

Refer to the Establish Rules and Guidelines for Teams specific practice in the Organizational Process Definition process area for more information about establishing and maintaining organizational rules and guidelines for the structure, formation, and operation of teams.

One of the best ways to ensure coordination and collaboration with relevant stakeholders is to include them on the team.

In a customer environment that requires coordination among multiple product or service development organizations, it is important to establish a team with representation from all parties that affect overall success. Such representation helps to ensure effective collaboration across these organizations, including the timely resolution of coordination issues.

Example Work Products

1. Documented shared vision
2. List of members assigned to each team
3. Team charters
4. Periodic team status reports

Subpractices

1. Establish and maintain the project's shared vision.

   When creating a shared vision, it is critical to understand the interfaces between the project and stakeholders external to the project. The vision should be shared among relevant stakeholders to obtain their agreement and commitment.

2. Establish and maintain the team structure.

   The project WBS, cost, schedule, project risks, resources, interfaces, the project's defined process, and organizational guidelines are evaluated to establish an appropriate team structure, including team responsibilities, authorities, and interrelationships.

3. Establish and maintain each team.

   Establishing and maintaining teams encompasses choosing team leaders and team members and establishing team charters for each team. It also involves providing resources required to accomplish tasks assigned to the team.

4. Periodically evaluate the team structure and composition.

   Teams should be monitored to detect misalignment of work across different teams, mismanaged interfaces, and mismatches of tasks to team members. Take corrective action when team or project performance does not meet expectations.

SP 1.7 *CONTRIBUTE TO ORGANIZATIONAL PROCESS ASSETS*

Contribute process related experiences to organizational process assets.

Refer to the Organizational Process Definition process area for more information about establishing organizational process assets, establishing the organization's measurement repository, and establishing the organization's process asset library.

Refer to the Organizational Process Focus process area for more information about incorporating experiences into organizational process assets.

This specific practice addresses contributing information from processes in the project's defined process to organizational process assets.

TIP

This SP provides feedback to the organization so that the organizational assets can be improved, and data and experiences can be shared with other projects.

Example Work Products

1. Proposed improvements to organizational process assets
2. Actual process and product measures collected from the project
3. Documentation (e.g., exemplary process descriptions, plans, training modules, checklists, lessons learned)
4. Process artifacts associated with tailoring and implementing the organization's set of standard processes on the project

Subpractices

1. Propose improvements to the organizational process assets.
2. Store process and product measures in the organization's measurement repository.

   Refer to the Measurement and Analysis process area for more information about obtaining measurement data.

   Refer to the Project Monitoring and Control process area for more information about monitoring project planning parameters.

   Refer to the Project Planning process area for more information about planning data management.

X-REF

Improvements are proposed using "process improvement proposals." For more information, see OPF SP 1.3.

These process and product measures typically include the following:
- Planning data
- Replanning data

Examples of data recorded by the project include the following:
- Task descriptions
- Assumptions
- Estimates
- Revised estimates
- Definitions of recorded data and measures
- Measures
- Context information that relates the measures to the activities performed and work products produced
- Associated information needed to reconstruct the estimates, assess their reasonableness, and derive estimates for new work

IPM

3. Submit documentation for possible inclusion in the organization's process asset library.

> Examples of documentation include the following:
> - Exemplary process descriptions
> - Training modules
> - Exemplary plans
> - Checklists and templates
> - Project repository shells
> - Tool configurations

4. Document lessons learned from the project for inclusion in the organization's process asset library.

5. Provide process artifacts associated with tailoring and implementing the organization's set of standard processes in support of the organization's process monitoring activities.

> *Refer to the Monitor the Implementation specific practice in the Organizational Process Focus process area for more information about the organization's activities to understand the extent of deployment of standard processes on new and existing projects.*

SG 2 COORDINATE AND COLLABORATE WITH RELEVANT STAKEHOLDERS

X-REF

Relevant stakeholders are identified in GP 2.7 and PP SP 2.6.

Coordination and collaboration between the project and relevant stakeholders are conducted.

SP 2.1 MANAGE STAKEHOLDER INVOLVEMENT

Manage the involvement of relevant stakeholders in the project.

Stakeholder involvement is managed according to the project's integrated plan and defined process.

Refer to the Project Planning process area for more information about planning stakeholder involvement and obtaining plan commitment.

Example Work Products

1. Agendas and schedules for collaborative activities
2. Recommendations for resolving relevant stakeholder issues
3. Documented issues (e.g., issues with stakeholder requirements, product and product component requirements, product architecture, product design)

Subpractices

1. Coordinate with relevant stakeholders who should participate in project activities.

   The relevant stakeholders should already be identified in the project plan.

2. Ensure work products that are produced to satisfy commitments meet the requirements of the recipients.

   Refer to the Verification process area for more information about verifying selected work products.

   The work products produced to satisfy commitments can be services. This task typically includes the following:

   • Reviewing, demonstrating, or testing, as appropriate, each work product produced by relevant stakeholders

   • Reviewing, demonstrating, or testing, as appropriate, each work product produced by the project for other projects with representatives of the projects receiving the work product

   • Resolving issues related to the acceptance of the work products

3. Develop recommendations and coordinate actions to resolve misunderstandings and problems with requirements.

SP 2.2 MANAGE DEPENDENCIES

Participate with relevant stakeholders to identify, negotiate, and track critical dependencies.

Example Work Products

1. Defects, issues, and action items resulting from reviews with relevant stakeholders
2. Critical dependencies
3. Commitments to address critical dependencies
4. Status of critical dependencies

Subpractices

1. Conduct reviews with relevant stakeholders.
2. Identify each critical dependency.
3. Establish need dates and plan dates for each critical dependency based on the project schedule.
4. Review and get agreement on commitments to address each critical dependency with those who are responsible for providing or receiving the work product.
5. Document critical dependencies and commitments.

> **TIP**
>
> These commitments may be external commitments that project staff is addressing.

> **TIP**
>
> Too often, individuals assume critical dependencies identified at the beginning of a project don't change and are someone else's job.

> **TIP**
>
> Ironically, when time and money are limited, integration, coordination, and collaboration activities become more critical. Coordination helps ensure that all involved parties contribute to the product in a timely way to minimize rework and delays.

IPM

> **HINT**
>
> You can facilitate coordination on critical dependencies by determining need and plan dates for each critical dependency and then establishing and managing commitments as described in these subpractices and in PP and PMC.

284 PART TWO THE PROCESS AREAS

> Documentation of commitments typically includes the following:
> - Describing the commitment
> - Identifying who made the commitment
> - Identifying who is responsible for satisfying the commitment
> - Specifying when the commitment will be satisfied
> - Specifying the criteria for determining if the commitment has been satisfied

6. Track the critical dependencies and commitments and take corrective action as appropriate.

   Refer to the Project Monitoring and Control process area for more information about monitoring commitments.

> Tracking critical dependencies typically includes the following:
> - Evaluating the effects of late and early completion for impacts on future activities and milestones
> - Resolving actual and potential problems with responsible parties whenever possible
> - Escalating to the appropriate party the actual and potential problems not resolvable by the responsible individual or group

SP 2.3 RESOLVE COORDINATION ISSUES

Resolve issues with relevant stakeholders.

> Examples of coordination issues include the following:
> - Product and product component requirements and design defects
> - Late critical dependencies and commitments
> - Product level problems
> - Unavailability of critical resources or staff

TIP

These issues are expected to be resolved at the project level. However, because stakeholders may be from outside the project, issues may need to be escalated to the appropriate level of management to be resolved.

Example Work Products

1. Relevant stakeholder coordination issues
2. Status of relevant stakeholder coordination issues

Subpractices

1. Identify and document issues.
2. Communicate issues to relevant stakeholders.
3. Resolve issues with relevant stakeholders.

4. Escalate to appropriate managers the issues not resolvable with relevant stakeholders.

5. Track issues to closure.

6. Communicate with relevant stakeholders on the status and resolution of issues.

MEASUREMENT AND ANALYSIS
A Support Process Area at Maturity Level 2

Purpose

The purpose of Measurement and Analysis (MA) is to develop and sustain a measurement capability used to support management information needs.

HINT

Use this process area whenever you need to measure project progress, product size or quality, or process performance in support of making decisions and taking corrective action.

Introductory Notes

The Measurement and Analysis process area involves the following activities:

TIP

This process area uses the term *objective* both as a noun meaning "a goal to be attained" (first bullet) and as an adjective meaning "unbiased" (fourth bullet).

- Specifying objectives of measurement and analysis so that they are aligned with identified information needs and project, organizational, or business objectives
- Specifying measures, analysis techniques, and mechanisms for data collection, data storage, reporting, and feedback
- Implementing the analysis techniques and mechanisms for data collection, data reporting, and feedback
- Providing objective results that can be used in making informed decisions and taking appropriate corrective action

The integration of measurement and analysis activities into the processes of the project supports the following:

- Objective planning and estimating
- Tracking actual progress and performance against established plans and objectives
- Identifying and resolving process related issues
- Providing a basis for incorporating measurement into additional processes in the future

MA

TIP

Measurement involves everyone. A centralized group, such
as a process group or a measurement group, may provide
help in defining the measures,
the analyses to perform, and
the reporting content and
charts used.

X-REF

It is important to include in
the supplier agreement any
measurement and analysis
activities that you want the
supplier to perform. Refer to
SAM for more information
about supplier activities.

The staff required to implement a measurement capability may or may not be employed in a separate organization-wide program. Measurement capability may be integrated into individual projects or other organizational functions (e.g., quality assurance).

The initial focus for measurement activities is at the project level. However, a measurement capability can prove useful for addressing organization- and enterprise-wide information needs. To support this capability, measurement activities should support information needs at multiple levels, including the business, organizational unit, and project to minimize re-work as the organization matures.

Projects can store project specific data and results in a project specific repository, but when data are to be used widely or are to be analyzed in support of determining data trends or benchmarks, data may reside in the organization's measurement repository.

Measurement and analysis of product components provided by suppliers is essential for effective management of the quality and costs of the project. It is possible, with careful management of supplier agreements, to provide insight into data that support supplier performance analysis.

Measurement objectives are derived from information needs that come from project, organizational, or business objectives. In this process area, when the term "objectives" is used without the "measurement" qualifier, it indicates either project, organizational, or business objectives.

Related Process Areas

Refer to the Requirements Development process area for more information about eliciting, analyzing, and establishing customer, product, and product component requirements.

Refer to the Configuration Management process area for more information about establishing and maintaining the integrity of work products using configuration identification, configuration control, configuration status accounting, and configuration audits.

Refer to the Organizational Process Definition process area for more information about establishing the organization's measurement repository.

Refer to the Project Monitoring and Control process area for more information about monitoring project planning parameters.

Refer to the Project Planning process area for more information about establishing estimates.

Refer to the Quantitative Project Management process area for more information about quantitatively managing the project.

Refer to the Requirements Management process area for more information about maintaining bidirectional traceability of requirements.

Specific Goal and Practice Summary

SG 1 Align Measurement and Analysis Activities
    SP 1.1   Establish Measurement Objectives
    SP 1.2   Specify Measures
    SP 1.3   Specify Data Collection and Storage Procedures
    SP 1.4   Specify Analysis Procedures
SG 2 Provide Measurement Results
    SP 2.1   Obtain Measurement Data
    SP 2.2   Analyze Measurement Data
    SP 2.3   Store Data and Results
    SP 2.4   Communicate Results

Specific Practices by Goal

SG 1   ALIGN MEASUREMENT AND ANALYSIS ACTIVITIES

Measurement objectives and activities are aligned with identified information needs and objectives.

The specific practices under this specific goal can be addressed concurrently or in any order.

- When establishing measurement objectives, experts often think ahead about necessary criteria for specifying measures and analysis procedures. They also think concurrently about the constraints imposed by data collection and storage procedures.
- Often it is important to specify the essential analyses to be conducted before attending to details of measurement specification, data collection, or storage.

SP 1.1 ESTABLISH MEASUREMENT OBJECTIVES

Establish and maintain measurement objectives derived from identified information needs and objectives.

Measurement objectives document the purposes for which measurement and analysis are done and specify the kinds of actions that can be taken based on results of data analyses. Measurement objectives can also identify the change in behavior desired as a result of implementing a measurement and analysis activity.

TIP

When starting a measurement program, an iterative process is usually helpful because you often do not know all of your objectives initially.

HINT

When establishing measurement objectives, ask yourself what question you are answering with the data, why you are measuring something, and how these measurements will affect project behavior.

MA

Measurement objectives may be constrained by existing processes, available resources, or other measurement considerations. Judgments may need to be made about whether the value of the result is commensurate with resources devoted to doing the work.

Modifications to identified information needs and objectives can, in turn, be indicated as a consequence of the process and results of measurement and analysis.

Sources of information needs and objectives can include the following:
• Project plans
• Project performance monitoring
• Interviews with managers and others who have information needs
• Established management objectives
• Strategic plans
• Business plans
• Formal requirements or contractual obligations
• Recurring or other troublesome management or technical problems
• Experiences of other projects or organizational entities
• External industry benchmarks
• Process improvement plans

Example measurement objectives include the following:
• Provide insight into schedule fluctuations and progress
• Provide insight into actual size compared to plan
• Identify unplanned growth
• Evaluate the effectiveness of defect detection throughout the product development lifecycle
• Determine the cost of correcting defects
• Provide insight into actual costs compared to plan
• Evaluate supplier progress against the plan
• Evaluate the effectiveness of mitigating information system vulnerabilities

---

Refer to the Requirements Development process area for more information about eliciting, analyzing, and establishing customer, product, and product component requirements.

Refer to the Project Monitoring and Control process area for more information about monitoring project planning parameters.

Refer to the Project Planning process area for more information about establishing estimates.

Refer to the Requirements Management process area for more information about maintaining bidirectional traceability of requirements.

Example Work Products

1. Measurement objectives

Subpractices

1. Document information needs and objectives.
2. Prioritize information needs and objectives.

    It can be neither possible nor desirable to subject all initially identified information needs to measurement and analysis. Priorities may also need to be set within the limits of available resources.

3. Document, review, and update measurement objectives.

    Carefully consider the purposes and intended uses of measurement and analysis.

    The measurement objectives are documented, reviewed by management and other relevant stakeholders, and updated as necessary. Doing so enables traceability to subsequent measurement and analysis activities, and helps to ensure that analyses will properly address identified information needs and objectives.

    It is important that users of measurement and analysis results be involved in setting measurement objectives and deciding on plans of action. It may also be appropriate to involve those who provide the measurement data.

TIP

Many times, measures are collected and not used. If you have adequate reviews of the objectives, you will minimize the risk of a measure not being used.

4. Provide feedback for refining and clarifying information needs and objectives as necessary.

    Identified information needs and objectives can be refined and clarified as a result of setting measurement objectives. Initial descriptions of information needs may be ambiguous. Conflicts can arise between existing needs and objectives. Precise targets on an already existing measure may be unrealistic.

5. Maintain traceability of measurement objectives to identified information needs and objectives.

    There should always be a good answer to the question, "Why are we measuring this?"

    Of course, measurement objectives can also change to reflect evolving information needs and objectives.

SP 1.2 SPECIFY MEASURES

Specify measures to address measurement objectives.

HINT

When specifying measures, ask yourself which specific measures you will collect.

Measurement objectives are refined into precise, quantifiable measures.
Measurement of project and organizational work can typically be traced to one or more measurement information categories. These categories include the following: schedule and progress, effort and cost, size and stability, and quality.

MA

Measures can be either *base* or *derived*. Data for base measures are obtained by direct measurement. Data for derived measures come from other data, typically by combining two or more base measures.

Examples of commonly used base measures include the following:
- Estimates and actual measures of work product size (e.g., number of pages)
- Estimates and actual measures of effort and cost (e.g., number of person hours)
- Quality measures (e.g., number of defects by severity)
- Information security measures (e.g., number of system vulnerabilities identified)
- Customer satisfaction survey scores

Examples of commonly used derived measures include the following:
- Earned value
- Schedule performance index
- Defect density
- Peer review coverage
- Test or verification coverage
- Reliability measures (e.g., mean time to failure)
- Quality measures (e.g., number of defects by severity/total number of defects)
- Information security measures (e.g., percentage of system vulnerabilities mitigated)
- Customer satisfaction trends

Derived measures typically are expressed as ratios, composite indices, or other aggregate summary measures. They are often more quantitatively reliable and meaningfully interpretable than the base measures used to generate them.

There are direct relationships among information needs, measurement objectives, measurement categories, base measures, and derived measures. This direct relationship is depicted using some common examples in Table 12.1.

Example Work Products

1. Specifications of base and derived measures

Subpractices

1. Identify candidate measures based on documented measurement objectives.

TABLE 12.1   Example Measurement Relationships

Example Project, Organizational, or Business Objectives	Information Need	Measurement Objective	Measurement Information Categories	Example Base Measures	Example Derived Measures
Shorten time to delivery Be first to market the product	What is the estimated delivery time?	Provide insight into schedule fluctuations and progress	Schedule and progress	Estimated and actual start and end dates by task	Milestone performance Percentage of project on time Schedule estimation accuracy
Increase market share by reducing costs of products and services	How accurate are the size and cost estimates?	Provide insight into actual size and costs compared to plan	Size and effort	Estimated and actual effort and size	Productivity
			Effort and cost	Estimated and actual cost	Cost performance Cost variance
Deliver specified functionality	Has scope or project size grown?	Provide insight into actual size compared to plan, identify unplanned growth	Size and stability	Requirements count	Requirements volatility Size estimation accuracy
				Function point count	Estimated vs. actual function points
				Lines of code count	Amount of new, modified, and reused code
Reduce defects in products delivered to the customer by 10% without affecting cost	Where are defects being inserted and detected prior to delivery?	Evaluate the effectiveness of defect detection throughout the product lifecycle	Quality	Number of defects inserted and detected by lifecycle phase Product size	Defect containment by lifecycle phase Defect density
	What is the cost of rework?	Determine the cost of correcting defects	Cost	Number of defects inserted and detected by lifecycle phase Effort hours to correct defects Labor rates	Rework costs
Reduce information system vulnerabilities	What is the magnitude of open system vulnerabilities?	Evaluate the effectiveness of mitigating system vulnerabilities	Information assurance	Number of system vulnerabilities identified and number of system vulnerabilities mitigated	Percentage of system vulnerabilities mitigated

Measurement objectives are refined into measures. Identified candidate measures are categorized and specified by name and unit of measure.

2. Maintain traceability of measures to measurement objectives.

Interdependencies among candidate measures are identified to enable later data validation and candidate analyses in support of measurement objectives.

3. Identify existing measures that already address measurement objectives.

Specifications for measures may already exist, perhaps established for other purposes earlier or elsewhere in the organization.

4. Specify operational definitions for measures.

Operational definitions are stated in precise and unambiguous terms. They address two important criteria:

- Communication: What has been measured, how was it measured, what are the units of measure, and what has been included or excluded?
- Repeatability: Can the measurement be repeated, given the same definition, to get the same results?

5. Prioritize, review, and update measures.

Proposed specifications of measures are reviewed for their appropriateness with potential end users and other relevant stakeholders. Priorities are set or changed, and specifications of measures are updated as necessary.

SP 1.3 *SPECIFY DATA COLLECTION AND STORAGE PROCEDURES*

Specify how measurement data are obtained and stored.

Explicit specification of collection methods helps to ensure that the right data are collected properly. This specification can also help further clarify information needs and measurement objectives.

Proper attention to storage and retrieval procedures helps to ensure that data are available and accessible for future use.

Example Work Products

1. Data collection and storage procedures
2. Data collection tools

Subpractices

1. Identify existing sources of data that are generated from current work products, processes, or transactions.

Existing sources of data may have been identified when specifying the measures. Appropriate collection mechanisms may exist whether or not pertinent data have already been collected.

TIP

Operational definitions are key to effective specification of measures.

X-REF

For additional information on specifying measures, see SEI's Software Engineering Measurement and Analysis website (www.sei.cmu.edu/sema), the Practical Software & Systems Measurement website (www.psmsc.com), and the iSixSigma website (www.isixsigma.com).

TIP

Ensuring appropriate accessibility and maintenance of data integrity are two key concerns related to data storage and retrieval.

2. Identify measures for which data are needed but are not currently available.

3. Specify how to collect and store the data for each required measure.

   Explicit specifications are made of what, how, where, and when data will be collected and stored to ensure its validity and to support later use for analysis and documentation purposes.

Questions to be considered typically include the following:

• Have the frequency of collection and the points in the process where measurements will be made been determined?

• Has the timeline that is required to move measurement results from points of collection to repositories, other databases, or end users been established?

• Who is responsible for obtaining data?

• Who is responsible for data storage, retrieval, and security?

• Have necessary supporting tools been developed or acquired?

---

4. Create data collection mechanisms and process guidance.

   Data collection and storage mechanisms are well integrated with other normal work processes. Data collection mechanisms can include manual or automated forms and templates. Clear, concise guidance on correct procedures is available to those who are responsible for doing the work. Training is provided as needed to clarify processes required for the collection of complete and accurate data and to minimize the burden on those who provide and record data.

5. Support automatic collection of data as appropriate and feasible.

TIP

In today's environment, automation is often used. However, some organizations use several tools and databases to address their measurement needs. You need to manage the compatibility among the tools and databases carefully.

Examples of such automated support include the following:

• Time stamped activity logs

• Static or dynamic analyses of artifacts

---

6. Prioritize, review, and update data collection and storage procedures.

   Proposed procedures are reviewed for their appropriateness and feasibility with those who are responsible for providing, collecting, and storing data. They also may have useful insights about how to improve existing processes or may be able to suggest other useful measures or analyses.

7. Update measures and measurement objectives as necessary.

MA

SP 1.4 SPECIFY ANALYSIS PROCEDURES

Specify how measurement data are analyzed and communicated.

TIP

Often, someone can manipulate data to provide the picture he wants to convey. By specifying the analysis procedures in advance, you can minimize this type of abuse.

Specifying analysis procedures in advance ensures that appropriate analyses will be conducted and reported to address documented measurement objectives (and thereby the information needs and objectives on which they are based). This approach also provides a check that necessary data will, in fact, be collected. Analysis procedures should account for the quality (e.g., age, reliability) of all data that enter into an analysis (whether from the project, organization's measurement repository, or other source). The quality of data should be considered to help select the appropriate analysis procedure and evaluate the results of the analysis.

Example Work Products

1. Analysis specifications and procedures
2. Data analysis tools

Subpractices

1. Specify and prioritize the analyses to be conducted and the reports to be prepared.

    Early on, pay attention to the analyses to be conducted and to the manner in which results will be reported. These analyses and reports should meet the following criteria:

    • The analyses explicitly address the documented measurement objectives.

    • Presentation of results is clearly understandable by the audiences to whom the results are addressed.

    Priorities may have to be set for available resources.

2. Select appropriate data analysis methods and tools.

Issues to be considered typically include the following:

• Choice of visual display and other presentation techniques (e.g., pie charts, bar charts, histograms, radar charts, line graphs, scatter plots, tables)

• Choice of appropriate descriptive statistics (e.g., arithmetic mean, median, mode)

• Decisions about statistical sampling criteria when it is impossible or unnecessary to examine every data element

• Decisions about how to handle analysis in the presence of missing data elements

• Selection of appropriate analysis tools

Descriptive statistics are typically used in data analysis to do the following:

- Examine distributions of specified measures (e.g., central tendency, extent of variation, data points exhibiting unusual variation)
- Examine interrelationships among specified measures (e.g., comparisons of defects by phase of the product's lifecycle, comparisons of defects by product component)
- Display changes over time

Refer to the Select Measures and Analytic Techniques specific practice and Monitor the Performance of Selected Subprocesses specific practice in the Quantitative Project Management process area for more information about the appropriate use of statistical techniques and understanding variation.

3. Specify administrative procedures for analyzing data and communicating results.

TIP

Those responsible for analyzing the data and presenting the results should include those whose activities generated the measurement data or their management whenever possible, with support provided by a process group, QA group, or measurement experts.

Issues to be considered typically include the following:

- Identifying the persons and groups responsible for analyzing the data and presenting the results
- Determining the timeline to analyze the data and present the results
- Determining the venues for communicating the results (e.g., progress reports, transmittal memos, written reports, staff meetings)

4. Review and update the proposed content and format of specified analyses and reports.

All of the proposed content and format are subject to review and revision, including analytic methods and tools, administrative procedures, and priorities. Relevant stakeholders consulted should include end users, sponsors, data analysts, and data providers.

5. Update measures and measurement objectives as necessary.

Just as measurement needs drive data analysis, clarification of analysis criteria can affect measurement. Specifications for some measures may be refined further based on specifications established for data analysis procedures. Other measures may prove unnecessary or a need for additional measures may be recognized.

Specifying how measures will be analyzed and reported can also suggest the need for refining measurement objectives themselves.

6. Specify criteria for evaluating the utility of analysis results and for evaluating the conduct of measurement and analysis activities.

X-REF

Refer to SP 1.1 when refining your measurement objectives.

MA

Criteria for evaluating the utility of the analysis might address the extent to which the following apply:

- The results are provided in a timely manner, understandable, and used for decision making.
- The work does not cost more to perform than is justified by the benefits it provides.

TIP

The criteria are divided into two lists. The first comprises criteria that any organization can use. The second is a bit more sophisticated and might be used by organizations after they establish their measurement program.

Criteria for evaluating the conduct of the measurement and analysis might include the extent to which the following apply:

- The amount of missing data or the number of flagged inconsistencies is beyond specified thresholds.
- There is selection bias in sampling (e.g., only satisfied end users are surveyed to evaluate end-user satisfaction, only unsuccessful projects are evaluated to determine overall productivity).
- Measurement data are repeatable (e.g., statistically reliable).
- Statistical assumptions have been satisfied (e.g., about the distribution of data, about appropriate measurement scales).

SG 2 PROVIDE MEASUREMENT RESULTS

Measurement results, which address identified information needs and objectives, are provided.

TIP

MA provides the foundation for the behavior required in high-maturity organizations. By the time organizations reach maturity level 4, management and staff will use measurement results as part of their daily work.

The primary reason for conducting measurement and analysis is to address identified information needs derived from project, organizational, and business objectives. Measurement results based on objective evidence can help to monitor progress and performance, fulfill obligations documented in a supplier agreement, make informed management and technical decisions, and enable corrective actions to be taken.

SP 2.1 OBTAIN MEASUREMENT DATA

Obtain specified measurement data.

The data necessary for analysis are obtained and checked for completeness and integrity.

Example Work Products

1. Base and derived measurement data sets
2. Results of data integrity tests

Subpractices

1. Obtain data for base measures.

   Data are collected as necessary for previously used and newly specified base measures. Existing data are gathered from project records or elsewhere in the organization.

2. Generate data for derived measures.

   Values are newly calculated for all derived measures.

3. Perform data integrity checks as close to the source of data as possible.

   All measurements are subject to error in specifying or recording data. It is always better to identify these errors and sources of missing data early in the measurement and analysis cycle.

   Checks can include scans for missing data, out-of-bounds data values, and unusual patterns and correlation across measures. It is particularly important to do the following:

   - Test and correct for inconsistency of classifications made by human judgment (i.e., to determine how frequently people make differing classification decisions based on the same information, otherwise known as "inter-coder reliability").

   - Empirically examine the relationships among measures that are used to calculate additional derived measures. Doing so can ensure that important distinctions are not overlooked and that derived measures convey their intended meanings (otherwise known as "criterion validity").

TIP

If too much time has passed, it may be inefficient or even impossible to verify the integrity of a measure or to identify the source of missing data.

SP 2.2 ANALYZE MEASUREMENT DATA

Analyze and interpret measurement data.

Measurement data are analyzed as planned, additional analyses are conducted as necessary, results are reviewed with relevant stakeholders, and necessary revisions for future analyses are noted.

Example Work Products

1. Analysis results and draft reports

Subpractices

1. Conduct initial analyses, interpret results, and draw preliminary conclusions.

   The results of data analyses are rarely self evident. Criteria for interpreting results and drawing conclusions should be stated explicitly.

2. Conduct additional measurement and analysis as necessary and prepare results for presentation.

TIP

Often, someone can misinterpret analyses and draw incorrect conclusions. By specifying criteria for interpreting results in advance, you can minimize the risk of drawing incorrect conclusions.

MA

Results of planned analyses can suggest (or require) additional, unanticipated analyses. In addition, these analyses can identify needs to refine existing measures, to calculate additional derived measures, or even to collect data for additional base measures to properly complete the planned analysis. Similarly, preparing initial results for presentation can identify the need for additional, unanticipated analyses.

3. Review initial results with relevant stakeholders.

It may be appropriate to review initial interpretations of results and the way in which these results are presented before disseminating and communicating them widely.

Reviewing the initial results before their release can prevent needless misunderstandings and lead to improvements in the data analysis and presentation.

Relevant stakeholders with whom reviews may be conducted include intended end users, sponsors, data analysts, and data providers.

4. Refine criteria for future analyses.

Lessons that can improve future efforts are often learned from conducting data analyses and preparing results. Similarly, ways to improve measurement specifications and data collection procedures can become apparent as can ideas for refining identified information needs and objectives.

TIP

Measurement and analysis is a learning process. You will typically go through many cycles before the measures and analyses are fine tuned.

SP 2.3 STORE DATA AND RESULTS

Manage and store measurement data, measurement specifications, and analysis results.

Storing measurement related information enables its timely and cost effective use as historical data and results. The information also is needed to provide sufficient context for interpretation of data, measurement criteria, and analysis results.

Information stored typically includes the following:
- Measurement plans
- Specifications of measures
- Sets of data that were collected
- Analysis reports and presentations
- Retention period for data stored

Stored information contains or refers to other information needed to understand and interpret the measures and to assess them for reasonableness and applicability (e.g., measurement specifications used on different projects when comparing across projects).

Typically, data sets for derived measures can be recalculated and need not be stored. However, it may be appropriate to store summaries based on derived measures (e.g., charts, tables of results, report text).

HINT

Understand what to store, what can be recalculated or reconstructed, and what to discard.

Interim analysis results need not be stored separately if they can be efficiently reconstructed.

Projects can choose to store project specific data and results in a project specific repository. When data are shared across projects, the data can reside in the organization's measurement repository.

Refer to the Configuration Management process area for more information about establishing a configuration management system.

Refer to the Establish the Organization's Measurement Repository specific practice in the Organizational Process Definition process area for more information about establishing the organization's measurement repository.

Example Work Products

1. Stored data inventory

Subpractices

1. Review data to ensure their completeness, integrity, accuracy, and currency.
2. Store data according to data storage procedures.
3. Make stored contents available for use only to appropriate groups and staff members.
4. Prevent stored information from being used inappropriately.

> Examples of ways to prevent the inappropriate use of data and related information include controlling access to data and educating people on the appropriate use of data.

TIP

Inappropriate use of data will seriously undermine the credibility of your MA implementation.

> Examples of the inappropriate use of data include the following:
> - Disclosure of information provided in confidence
> - Faulty interpretations based on incomplete, out-of-context, or otherwise misleading information
> - Measures used to improperly evaluate the performance of people or to rank projects
> - Impugning the integrity of individuals

MA

SP 2.4 COMMUNICATE RESULTS

Communicate results of measurement and analysis activities to all relevant stakeholders.

The results of the measurement and analysis process are communicated to relevant stakeholders in a timely and usable fashion to support decision making and assist in taking corrective action.

Relevant stakeholders include intended end users, sponsors, data analysts, and data providers.

Example Work Products

1. Delivered reports and related analysis results
2. Contextual information or guidance to help interpret analysis results

Subpractices

1. Keep relevant stakeholders informed of measurement results in a timely manner.

   To the extent possible and as part of the normal way they do business, users of measurement results are kept personally involved in setting objectives and deciding on plans of action for measurement and analysis. Users are regularly kept informed of progress and interim results.

   Refer to the Project Monitoring and Control process area for more information about conducting progress reviews.

2. Assist relevant stakeholders in understanding results.

   Results are communicated in a clear and concise manner appropriate to relevant stakeholders. Results are understandable, easily interpretable, and clearly tied to identified information needs and objectives.

   The data analyzed are often not self evident to practitioners who are not measurement experts. The communication of results should be clear about the following:

   • How and why base and derived measures were specified
   • How data were obtained
   • How to interpret results based on the data analysis methods used
   • How results address information needs

Examples of actions taken to help others to understand results include the following:
• Discussing the results with relevant stakeholders
• Providing background and explanation in a document
• Briefing users on results
• Providing training on the appropriate use and understanding of measurement results

---

TIP

An indicator of a mature organization is the daily use of measurement data by both staff and management to guide their activities. This requires effective communication of measurement data and the results of analyses.

TIP

As organizations mature, management and staff should become more comfortable with measurement, be more likely to interpret the analyses correctly, and be able to ask the right questions to help them draw the right conclusions.

ORGANIZATIONAL PROCESS DEFINITION
A Process Management Process Area at Maturity Level 3

Purpose

The purpose of Organizational Process Definition (OPD) is to establish and maintain a usable set of organizational process assets, work environment standards, and rules and guidelines for teams.

Introductory Notes

Organizational process assets enable consistent process execution across the organization and provide a basis for cumulative, long-term benefits to the organization. (See the definition of "organizational process assets" in the glossary.)

The organization's process asset library supports organizational learning and process improvement by allowing the sharing of best practices and lessons learned across the organization. (See the definition of "organizational process assets" in the glossary.)

The organization's set of standard processes also describes standard interactions with suppliers. Supplier interactions are characterized by the following typical items: deliverables expected from suppliers, acceptance criteria applicable to those deliverables, standards (e.g., architecture and technology standards), and standard milestone and progress reviews.

The organization's "set of standard processes" is tailored by projects to create their defined processes. Other organizational process assets are used to support tailoring and implementing defined processes. Work environment standards are used to guide the creation of project work environments. Rules and guidelines for teams are used to aid in their structuring, formation, and operation.

A "standard process" is composed of other processes (i.e., subprocesses) or process elements. A "process element" is the fundamental (i.e., atomic) unit of process definition that describes activities and tasks to consistently perform work. The process architecture provides rules for connecting the process elements of a standard process. The organization's set of standard processes can include multiple process architectures.

(See the definitions of "standard process," "process architecture," "subprocess," and "process element" in the glossary.)

> Organizational process assets can be organized in many ways, depending on the implementation of the Organizational Process Definition process area. Examples include the following:
> - Descriptions of lifecycle models can be part of the organization's set of standard processes or they can be documented separately.
> - The organization's set of standard processes can be stored in the organization's process asset library or it can be stored separately.
> - A single repository can contain both measurements and process related documentation, or they can be stored separately.

Related Process Areas

Refer to the Organizational Process Focus process area for more information about deploying organizational process assets.

Specific Goal and Practice Summary

SG 1 Establish Organizational Process Assets
- SP 1.1   Establish Standard Processes
- SP 1.2   Establish Lifecycle Model Descriptions
- SP 1.3   Establish Tailoring Criteria and Guidelines
- SP 1.4   Establish the Organization's Measurement Repository
- SP 1.5   Establish the Organization's Process Asset Library
- SP 1.6   Establish Work Environment Standards
- SP 1.7   Establish Rules and Guidelines for Teams

Specific Practices by Goal

SG 1 ESTABLISH ORGANIZATIONAL PROCESS ASSETS

A set of organizational process assets is established and maintained.

SP 1.1 ESTABLISH STANDARD PROCESSES

Establish and maintain the organization's set of standard processes.

Standard processes can be defined at multiple levels in an enterprise and they can be related hierarchically. For example, an enterprise can have a set of standard processes that is tailored by individual organizations (e.g., a division, a site) in the enterprise to establish their set of standard processes. The set of standard processes can also be tailored for each of the organization's business areas, product lines, or standard services. Thus the *organization's set of standard processes* can refer to the standard processes established at the organization level and standard processes that may be established at lower levels, although some organizations may have only one level of standard processes. (See the definitions of "standard process" and "organization's set of standard processes" in the glossary.)

Multiple standard processes may be needed to address the needs of different application domains, lifecycle models, methodologies, and tools. The organization's set of standard processes contains process elements (e.g., a work product size estimating element) that may be interconnected according to one or more process architectures that describe relationships among process elements.

The organization's set of standard processes typically includes technical, management, administrative, support, and organizational processes.

The organization's set of standard processes should collectively cover all processes needed by the organization and projects, including those processes addressed by the process areas at maturity level 2.

Example Work Products

1. Organization's set of standard processes

Subpractices

1. Decompose each standard process into constituent process elements to the detail needed to understand and describe the process.

   Each process element covers a closely related set of activities. The descriptions of process elements may be templates to be filled in, fragments to be completed, abstractions to be refined, or complete descriptions to be tailored or used unmodified. These elements are described in such detail that the process, when fully defined, can be consistently performed by appropriately trained and skilled people.

Examples of process elements include the following:
- Template for generating work product size estimates
- Description of work product design methodology

Continues

TIP

Standard processes define the key activities performed in an organization. Some examples of standard processes include requirements elicitation, design, and testing; planning, estimating, monitoring, and control; and product delivery and support.

TIP

The OSSP can include processes that are not directly addressed by CMMI, such as proposal development, project approval, financial management, and procurement.

HINT

Often, organizations look at the exemplar processes from their projects as a starting point to populate the OSSP.

TIP

The objective is to decompose and define the process so that it can be performed consistently across projects but will allow enough flexibility to meet the unique requirements of each project.

OPD

Continued

- Tailorable peer review methodology
- Template for conducting management reviews
- Templates or task flows embedded in workflow tools
- Description of methods for prequalifying suppliers as preferred suppliers

2. Specify the critical attributes of each process element.

Examples of critical attributes include the following:
- Process roles
- Applicable standards
- Applicable procedures, methods, tools, and resources
- Process performance objectives
- Entry criteria
- Inputs
- Verification points (e.g., peer reviews)
- Outputs
- Interfaces
- Exit criteria
- Product and process measures

3. Specify relationships among process elements.

Examples of relationships include the following:
- Order of the process elements
- Interfaces among process elements
- Interfaces with external processes
- Interdependencies among process elements

The rules for describing relationships among process elements are referred to as the "process architecture." The process architecture covers essential requirements and guidelines. Detailed specifications of these relationships are covered in descriptions of defined processes that are tailored from the organization's set of standard processes.

4. Ensure that the organization's set of standard processes adheres to applicable policies, standards, and models.

Adherence to applicable process standards and models is typically demonstrated by developing a mapping from the organization's set of

HINT
Your initial focus should first be on standardizing what you already do well.

standard processes to relevant process standards and models. This mapping is a useful input to future appraisals.

5. Ensure that the organization's set of standard processes satisfies process needs and objectives of the organization.

> *Refer to the Organizational Process Focus process area for more information about establishing organizational process needs.*

6. Ensure that there is appropriate integration among processes that are included in the organization's set of standard processes.

7. Document the organization's set of standard processes.

8. Conduct peer reviews on the organization's set of standard processes.

> *Refer to the Verification process area for more information about performing peer reviews.*

9. Revise the organization's set of standard processes as necessary.

HINT

Break down stovepipes: When capabilities residing in different organizations are routinely needed to understand trade-offs and resolve system-level problems, consider establishing a standard end-to-end process for performing joint work.

> Examples of when the organization's set of standard processes may need to be revised include the following:
> - When improvements to the process are identified
> - When causal analysis and resolution data indicate that a process change is needed
> - When process improvement proposals are selected for deployment across the organization
> - When the organization's process needs and objectives are updated

SP 1.2 ESTABLISH LIFECYCLE MODEL DESCRIPTIONS

Establish and maintain descriptions of lifecycle models approved for use in the organization.

Lifecycle models can be developed for a variety of customers or in a variety of situations, since one lifecycle model may not be appropriate for all situations. Lifecycle models are often used to define phases of the project. Also, the organization can define different lifecycle models for each type of product and service it delivers.

TIP

When managing a project, it is helpful to have a standard description for the phases the project moves through (i.e., project lifecycle model) to organize and assess the adequacy of project activities and to monitor progress.

Example Work Products

1. Descriptions of lifecycle models

Subpractices

1. Select lifecycle models based on the needs of projects and the organization.

> Examples of project lifecycle models include the following:
> • Waterfall or Serial
> • Spiral
> • Evolutionary
> • Incremental
> • Iterative

2. Document descriptions of lifecycle models.

   Lifecycle models can be documented as part of the organization's standard process descriptions or they can be documented separately.

3. Conduct peer reviews on lifecycle models.

   Refer to the Verification process area for more information about performing peer reviews.

4. Revise the descriptions of lifecycle models as necessary.

SP 1.3 ESTABLISH TAILORING CRITERIA AND GUIDELINES

Establish and maintain tailoring criteria and guidelines for the organization's set of standard processes.

Tailoring criteria and guidelines describe the following:

• How the organization's set of standard processes and organizational process assets are used to create defined processes
• Requirements that must be satisfied by defined processes (e.g., the subset of organizational process assets that are essential for any defined process)
• Options that can be exercised and criteria for selecting among options
• Procedures that must be followed in performing and documenting process tailoring

> Examples of reasons for tailoring include the following:
> • Adapting the process to a new product line or work environment
> • Elaborating the process description so that the resulting defined process can be performed
> • Customizing the process for an application or class of similar applications

Flexibility in tailoring and defining processes is balanced with ensuring appropriate consistency of processes across the organization. Flexibility is needed to address contextual variables such as the domain; the nature of the customer; cost, schedule, and quality tradeoffs; the technical difficulty of the work; and the experience of the people implementing the process. Consistency across the organization is needed so that organizational standards, objectives, and strategies are appropriately addressed, and process data and lessons learned can be shared.

TIP

Finding this balance usually takes time, as the organization gains experience from using these assets.

Tailoring is a critical activity that allows controlled changes to processes due to the specific needs of a project or a part of the organization. Processes and process elements that are directly related to critical business objectives should usually be defined as mandatory, but processes and process elements that are less critical or only indirectly affect business objectives may allow for more tailoring.

The amount of tailoring could also depend on the project's lifecycle model, the use of suppliers, and other factors.

Tailoring criteria and guidelines can allow for using a standard process "as is," with no tailoring.

Example Work Products

1. Tailoring guidelines for the organization's set of standard processes

Subpractices

1. Specify selection criteria and procedures for tailoring the organization's set of standard processes.

Examples of criteria and procedures include the following:

- Criteria for selecting lifecycle models from the ones approved by the organization
- Criteria for selecting process elements from the organization's set of standard processes
- Procedures for tailoring selected lifecycle models and process elements to accommodate process characteristics and needs
- Procedures for adapting the organization's common measures to address information needs

---

Examples of tailoring include the following:

- Modifying a lifecycle model
- Combining elements of different lifecycle models
- Modifying process elements
- Replacing process elements
- Reordering process elements

2. Specify the standards used for documenting defined processes.
3. Specify the procedures used for submitting and obtaining approval of waivers from the organization's set of standard processes.
4. Document tailoring guidelines for the organization's set of standard processes.
5. Conduct peer reviews on the tailoring guidelines.

> *Refer to the Verification process area for more information about performing peer reviews.*

6. Revise tailoring guidelines as necessary.

SP 1.4 ESTABLISH THE ORGANIZATION'S MEASUREMENT REPOSITORY

Establish and maintain the organization's measurement repository.

Refer to the Use Organizational Process Assets for Planning Project Activities specific practice in the Integrated Project Management process area for more information about the use of the organization's measurement repository in planning project activities.

The repository contains both product and process measures that are related to the organization's set of standard processes. It also contains or refers to information needed to understand and interpret measures and to assess them for reasonableness and applicability. For example, the definitions of measures are used to compare similar measures from different processes.

Example Work Products

1. Definition of the common set of product and process measures for the organization's set of standard processes
2. Design of the organization's measurement repository
3. Organization's measurement repository (i.e., the repository structure, support environment)
4. Organization's measurement data

Subpractices

1. Determine the organization's needs for storing, retrieving, and analyzing measurements.
2. Define a common set of process and product measures for the organization's set of standard processes.

   Measures in the common set are selected for their ability to provide visibility into processes critical to achieving business objectives and to focus on process elements significantly impacting cost, schedule, and performance within a project and across the organization. The common set of measures can vary for different standard processes.

Measures defined include the ones related to agreement management, some of which may need to be collected from suppliers.

Operational definitions for measures specify procedures for collecting valid data and the point in the process where data will be collected.

Examples of classes of commonly used measures include the following:
- Estimates of work product size (e.g., pages)
- Estimates of effort and cost (e.g., person hours)
- Actual measures of size, effort, and cost
- Test coverage
- Reliability measures (e.g., mean time to failure)
- Quality measures (e.g., number of defects found, severity of defects)
- Peer review coverage

X-REF

Measurement and analysis practices (see MA) are a prerequisite to establishing the organization's measurement repository.

3. Design and implement the measurement repository.

Functions of the measurement repository include the following:

- Supporting effective comparison and interpretation of measurement data among projects
- Providing sufficient context to allow a new project to quickly identify and access data in the repository for similar projects
- Enabling projects to improve the accuracy of their estimates by using their own and other projects' historical data
- Aiding in the understanding of process performance
- Supporting potential statistical management of processes or subprocesses, as needed

4. Specify procedures for storing, updating, and retrieving measures.

Refer to the Measurement and Analysis process area for more information about specifying data collection and storage procedures.

5. Conduct peer reviews on definitions of the common set of measures and procedures for storing, updating, and retrieving measures.

Refer to the Verification process area for more information about performing peer reviews.

6. Enter specified measures into the repository.

Refer to the Measurement and Analysis process area for more information about specifying measures.

7. Make the contents of the measurement repository available for use by the organization and projects as appropriate.

8. Revise the measurement repository, the common set of measures, and procedures as the organization's needs change.

TIP

Entering measurements into a repository is commonly an automated process; however, when not automated, it should be done by the person collecting the measurements.

> Examples of when the common set of measures may need to be revised include the following:
> - New processes are added
> - Processes are revised and new measures are needed
> - Finer granularity of data is required
> - Greater visibility into the process is required
> - Measures are retired

SP 1.5 ESTABLISH THE ORGANIZATION'S PROCESS ASSET LIBRARY

Establish and maintain the organization's process asset library.

> Examples of items to be stored in the organization's process asset library include the following:
> - Organizational policies
> - Process descriptions
> - Procedures (e.g., estimating procedure)
> - Development plans
> - Acquisition plans
> - Quality assurance plans
> - Training materials
> - Process aids (e.g., checklists)
> - Lessons learned reports

Example Work Products

1. Design of the organization's process asset library
2. The organization's process asset library
3. Selected items to be included in the organization's process asset library
4. The catalog of items in the organization's process asset library

Subpractices

1. Design and implement the organization's process asset library, including the library structure and support environment.
2. Specify criteria for including items in the library.
   > Items are selected based primarily on their relationship to the organization's set of standard processes.
3. Specify procedures for storing, updating, and retrieving items.
4. Enter selected items into the library and catalog them for easy reference and retrieval.

5. Make items available for use by projects.
6. Periodically review the use of each item.
7. Revise the organization's process asset library as necessary.

> **TIP**
>
> Library maintenance can quickly become an issue if all documents from every project are stored in the library.

Examples of when the library may need to be revised include the following:
- New items are added
- Items are retired
- Current versions of items are changed

> **TIP**
>
> Some organizations regularly review their PAL contents every 12 to 18 months to decide what to discard or archive.

SP 1.6 ESTABLISH WORK ENVIRONMENT STANDARDS

Establish and maintain work environment standards.

Work environment standards allow the organization and projects to benefit from common tools, training, and maintenance, as well as cost savings from volume purchases. Work environment standards address the needs of all stakeholders and consider productivity, cost, availability, security, and workplace health, safety, and ergonomic factors. Work environment standards can include guidelines for tailoring and the use of waivers that allow adaptation of the project's work environment to meet needs.

> **TIP**
>
> Work environment standards must make sense for your organization, its line of business, the degree of collaboration to be supported, and so on.

> **HINT**
>
> If your organization has a shared vision, your work environment must support it.

Examples of work environment standards include the following:
- Procedures for the operation, safety, and security of the work environment
- Standard workstation hardware and software
- Standard application software and tailoring guidelines for it
- Standard production and calibration equipment
- Process for requesting and approving tailoring or waivers

> **TIP**
>
> Typically, projects have additional requirements for their work environment. This specific practice establishes the standards to be addressed across the organization.

Example Work Products

1. Work environment standards

Subpractices

1. Evaluate commercially available work environment standards appropriate for the organization.
2. Adopt existing work environment standards and develop new ones to fill gaps based on the organization's process needs and objectives.

TIP

Much of the power of teams comes from the excitement that team members share in working together to overcome challenges. However, over time, team members can neglect the needs of their profession and career growth. If this happens across the organization, the organization will gradually lose its core competencies.

TIP

Teams cannot operate as "high-performance teams" if they have to go to management for approval of every action or decision.

TIP

The authority initially given to a newly formed team may be expanded later as project phases are completed and the team demonstrates mature use of the authority granted. The rules for the degree of empowerment should support making such adjustments.

SP 1.7 ESTABLISH RULES AND GUIDELINES FOR TEAMS

Establish and maintain organizational rules and guidelines for the structure, formation, and operation of teams.

Operating rules and guidelines for teams define and control how teams are created and how they interact to accomplish objectives. Team members should understand the standards for work and participate according to those standards.

When establishing rules and guidelines for teams, ensure they comply with all local and national regulations or laws that can affect the use of teams.

Structuring teams involves defining the number of teams, the type of each team, and how each team relates to the others in the structure. Forming teams involves chartering each team, assigning team members and team leaders, and providing resources to each team to accomplish work.

Example Work Products

1. Rules and guidelines for structuring and forming teams
2. Operating rules for teams

Subpractices

1. Establish and maintain empowerment mechanisms to enable timely decision making.

   In a successful teaming environment, clear channels of responsibility and authority are established by documenting and deploying organizational guidelines that clearly define the empowerment of teams.

2. Establish and maintain rules and guidelines for structuring and forming teams.

Organizational process assets can help the project to structure and implement teams. Such assets can include the following:
- Team structure guidelines
- Team formation guidelines
- Team authority and responsibility guidelines
- Guidelines for establishing lines of communication, authority, and escalation
- Team leader selection criteria

---

3. Define the expectations, rules, and guidelines that guide how teams work collectively.

These rules and guidelines establish organizational practices for consistency across teams and can include the following:

- How interfaces among teams are established and maintained
- How assignments are accepted and transferred
- How resources and inputs are accessed
- How work gets done
- Who checks, reviews, and approves work
- How work is approved
- How work is delivered and communicated
- Who reports to whom
- What the reporting requirements (e.g., cost, schedule, performance status), measures, and methods are
- Which progress reporting measures and methods are used

ORGANIZATIONAL PROCESS FOCUS
A Process Management Process Area at Maturity Level 3

Purpose

The purpose of Organizational Process Focus (OPF) is to plan, implement, and deploy organizational process improvements based on a thorough understanding of current strengths and weaknesses of the organization's processes and process assets.

Introductory Notes

The organization's processes include all processes used by the organization and its projects. Candidate improvements to the organization's processes and process assets are obtained from various sources, including the measurement of processes, lessons learned in implementing processes, results of process appraisals, results of product and service evaluation activities, results of customer satisfaction evaluations, results of benchmarking against other organizations' processes, and recommendations from other improvement initiatives in the organization.

Process improvement occurs in the context of the organization's needs and is used to address the organization's objectives. The organization encourages participation in process improvement activities by those who perform the process. The responsibility for facilitating and managing the organization's process improvement activities, including coordinating the participation of others, is typically assigned to a process group. The organization provides the long-term commitment and resources required to sponsor this group and to ensure the effective and timely deployment of improvements.

Careful planning is required to ensure that process improvement efforts across the organization are adequately managed and implemented. Results of the organization's process improvement planning are documented in a process improvement plan.

> **TIP**
>
> As Watts Humphrey said, "If you don't know where you are, a map won't help." Benchmark the processes and practices in your organization before you begin to improve them.

> **TIP**
>
> Although CMMI describes many of the processes that are critical to success, it does not contain everything. Therefore, you may improve processes, such as meeting management and proposal development, which might not be discussed in CMMI.

> **TIP**
>
> Project participation is essential to any process improvement effort.

> **TIP**
>
> Especially in the early phases of process improvement, the process group must visibly demonstrate the organization's investment in process improvement.

The "organization's process improvement plan" addresses appraisal planning, process action planning, pilot planning, and deployment planning. Appraisal plans describe the appraisal timeline and schedule, the scope of the appraisal, resources required to perform the appraisal, the reference model against which the appraisal will be performed, and logistics for the appraisal.

Process action plans usually result from appraisals and document how improvements targeting weaknesses uncovered by an appraisal will be implemented. Sometimes the improvement described in the process action plan should be tested on a small group before deploying it across the organization. In these cases, a pilot plan is generated.

When the improvement is to be deployed, a deployment plan is created. This plan describes when and how the improvement will be deployed across the organization.

Organizational process assets are used to describe, implement, and improve the organization's processes. (See the definition of "organizational process assets" in the glossary.)

Related Process Areas

Refer to the Organizational Process Definition process area for more information about establishing organizational process assets.

Specific Goal and Practice Summary

SG 1 Determine Process Improvement Opportunities
    SP 1.1   Establish Organizational Process Needs
    SP 1.2   Appraise the Organization's Processes
    SP 1.3   Identify the Organization's Process Improvements
SG 2 Plan and Implement Process Actions
    SP 2.1   Establish Process Action Plans
    SP 2.2   Implement Process Action Plans
SG 3 Deploy Organizational Process Assets and Incorporate Experiences
    SP 3.1   Deploy Organizational Process Assets
    SP 3.2   Deploy Standard Processes
    SP 3.3   Monitor the Implementation
    SP 3.4   Incorporate Experiences into Organizational Process Assets

Specific Practices by Goal

SG 1   *DETERMINE PROCESS IMPROVEMENT OPPORTUNITIES*

Strengths, weaknesses, and improvement opportunities for the organization's processes are identified periodically and as needed.

Strengths, weaknesses, and improvement opportunities can be determined relative to a process standard or model such as a CMMI model or ISO standard. Process improvements should be selected to address the organization's needs.

Process improvement opportunities can arise as a result of changing business objectives, legal and regulatory requirements, and results of benchmarking studies.

SP 1.1 ESTABLISH ORGANIZATIONAL PROCESS NEEDS

Establish and maintain the description of process needs and objectives for the organization.

The organization's processes operate in a business context that should be understood. The organization's business objectives, needs, and constraints determine the needs and objectives for the organization's processes. Typically, issues related to customer satisfaction, finance, technology, quality, human resources, and marketing are important process considerations.

> **TIP**
>
> Process improvement must relate directly to the business's objectives.

> The organization's process needs and objectives cover aspects that include the following:
> - Characteristics of processes
> - Process performance objectives, such as time-to-market and delivered quality
> - Process effectiveness

Example Work Products

1. The organization's process needs and objectives

Subpractices

1. Identify policies, standards, and business objectives that are applicable to the organization's processes.

> Examples of standards include the following:
> - ISO/IEC 12207:2008 Systems and Software Engineering – Software Life Cycle Processes [ISO 2008a]
> - ISO/IEC 15288:2008 Systems and Software Engineering – System Life Cycle Processes [ISO 2008b]
> - ISO/IEC 27001:2005 Information technology – Security techniques – Information Security Management Systems – Requirements [ISO/IEC 2005]
>
> *Continues*

Continued

- ISO/IEC 14764:2006 Software Engineering – Software Life Cycle Processes – Maintenance [ISO 2006b]
- ISO/IEC 20000 Information Technology – Service Management [ISO 2005b]
- Assurance Focus for CMMI [DHS 2009]
- NDIA Engineering for System Assurance Guidebook [NDIA 2008]
- Resilience Management Model [SEI 2010d]

2. Examine relevant process standards and models for best practices.
3. Determine the organization's process performance objectives.

   Process performance objectives can be expressed in quantitative or qualitative terms.

   Refer to the Measurement and Analysis process area for more information about establishing measurement objectives.

   Refer to the Organizational Process Performance process area for more information about establishing quality and process performance objectives.

Examples of process performance objectives include the following:
- Achieve a customer satisfaction rating of a certain value
- Ensure product reliability is at least a certain percentage
- Reduce defect insertion rate by a certain percentage
- Achieve a certain cycle time for a given activity
- Improve productivity by a given percentage
- Simplify the requirements approval workflow
- Improve quality of products delivered to customer

4. Define essential characteristics of the organization's processes.

   Essential characteristics of the organization's processes are determined based on the following:

   - Processes currently being used in the organization
   - Standards imposed by the organization
   - Standards commonly imposed by customers of the organization

Examples of process characteristics include the following:
- Level of detail
- Process notation
- Granularity

5. Document the organization's process needs and objectives.
6. Revise the organization's process needs and objectives as needed.

SP 1.2 APPRAISE THE ORGANIZATION'S PROCESSES

Appraise the organization's processes periodically and as needed to maintain an understanding of their strengths and weaknesses.

> Process appraisals can be performed for the following reasons:
> - To identify processes to be improved
> - To confirm progress and make the benefits of process improvement visible
> - To satisfy the needs of a customer-supplier relationship
> - To motivate and facilitate buy-in

The buy-in gained during a process appraisal can be eroded significantly if it is not followed by an appraisal based action plan.

Example Work Products

1. Plans for the organization's process appraisals
2. Appraisal findings that address strengths and weaknesses of the organization's processes
3. Improvement recommendations for the organization's processes

Subpractices

1. Obtain sponsorship of the process appraisal from senior management.

   Senior management sponsorship includes the commitment to have the organization's managers and staff participate in the process appraisal and to provide resources and funding to analyze and communicate findings of the appraisal.

2. Define the scope of the process appraisal.

   Process appraisals can be performed on the entire organization or can be performed on a smaller part of an organization such as a single project or business area.

   The scope of the process appraisal addresses the following:

   - Definition of the organization (e.g., sites, business areas) to be covered by the appraisal
   - Identification of the project and support functions that will represent the organization in the appraisal
   - Processes to be appraised

3. Determine the method and criteria to be used for the process appraisal.

   Process appraisals can occur in many forms. They should address the needs and objectives of the organization, which can change over time.

For example, the appraisal can be based on a process model, such as a CMMI model, or on a national or international standard, such as ISO 9001 [ISO 2008c]. Appraisals can also be based on a benchmark comparison with other organizations in which practices that can contribute to improved organizational performance are identified. The characteristics of the appraisal method may vary, including time and effort, makeup of the appraisal team, and the method and depth of investigation.

4. Plan, schedule, and prepare for the process appraisal.

5. Conduct the process appraisal.

6. Document and deliver the appraisal's activities and findings.

SP 1.3 IDENTIFY THE ORGANIZATION'S PROCESS IMPROVEMENTS

Identify improvements to the organization's processes and process assets.

Example Work Products

1. Analysis of candidate process improvements
2. Identification of improvements for the organization's processes

Subpractices

1. Determine candidate process improvements.

> Candidate process improvements are typically determined by doing the following:
> - Measuring processes and analyzing measurement results
> - Reviewing processes for effectiveness and suitability
> - Assessing customer satisfaction
> - Reviewing lessons learned from tailoring the organization's set of standard processes
> - Reviewing lessons learned from implementing processes
> - Reviewing process improvement proposals submitted by the organization's managers, staff, and other relevant stakeholders
> - Soliciting inputs on process improvements from senior management and other leaders in the organization
> - Examining results of process appraisals and other process related reviews
> - Reviewing results of other organizational improvement initiatives

2. Prioritize candidate process improvements.

    Criteria for prioritization are as follows:

    - Consider the estimated cost and effort to implement the process improvements.

- Evaluate the expected improvement against the organization's improvement objectives and priorities.
- Determine the potential barriers to the process improvements and develop strategies for overcoming these barriers.

Examples of techniques to help determine and prioritize possible improvements to be implemented include the following:
- A cost benefit analysis that compares the estimated cost and effort to implement the process improvements and their associated benefits
- A gap analysis that compares current conditions in the organization with optimal conditions
- Force field analysis of potential improvements to identify potential barriers and strategies for overcoming those barriers
- Cause-and-effect analyses to provide information on the potential effects of different improvements that can then be compared

---

3. Identify and document the process improvements to be implemented.
4. Revise the list of planned process improvements to keep it current.

SG 2 PLAN AND IMPLEMENT PROCESS ACTIONS

Process actions that address improvements to the organization's processes and process assets are planned and implemented.

The successful implementation of improvements requires participation in process action planning and implementation by process owners, those who perform the process, and support organizations.

SP 2.1 ESTABLISH PROCESS ACTION PLANS

Establish and maintain process action plans to address improvements to the organization's processes and process assets.

Establishing and maintaining process action plans typically involves the following roles:
- Management steering committees that set strategies and oversee process improvement activities
- Process groups that facilitate and manage process improvement activities
- Process action teams that define and implement process actions
- Process owners that manage deployment
- Practitioners that perform the process

OPF

TIP

Organizational process assets are those created by the activities in OPD.

TIP

Most of the organization should be involved in these activities.

Stakeholder involvement helps to obtain buy-in on process improvements and increases the likelihood of effective deployment.

Process action plans are detailed implementation plans. These plans differ from the organization's process improvement plan by targeting improvements that were defined to address weaknesses and that were usually uncovered by appraisals.

Example Work Products

1. The organization's approved process action plans

Subpractices

1. Identify strategies, approaches, and actions to address identified process improvements.

    New, unproven, and major changes are piloted before they are incorporated into normal use.

2. Establish process action teams to implement actions.

    The teams and people performing the process improvement actions are called "process action teams." Process action teams typically include process owners and those who perform the process.

3. Document process action plans.

> Process action plans typically cover the following:
> - Process improvement infrastructure
> - Process improvement objectives
> - Process improvements to be addressed
> - Procedures for planning and tracking process actions
> - Strategies for piloting and implementing process actions
> - Responsibility and authority for implementing process actions
> - Resources, schedules, and assignments for implementing process actions
> - Methods for determining the effectiveness of process actions
> - Risks associated with process action plans

4. Review and negotiate process action plans with relevant stakeholders.

5. Revise process action plans as necessary.

SP 2.2 IMPLEMENT PROCESS ACTION PLANS

Implement process action plans.

Example Work Products

1. Commitments among process action teams

2. Status and results of implementing process action plans
3. Plans for pilots

Subpractices

1. Make process action plans readily available to relevant stakeholders.
2. Negotiate and document commitments among process action teams and revise their process action plans as necessary.
3. Track progress and commitments against process action plans.
4. Conduct joint reviews with process action teams and relevant stakeholders to monitor the progress and results of process actions.
5. Plan pilots needed to test selected process improvements.
6. Review the activities and work products of process action teams.
7. Identify, document, and track to closure issues encountered when implementing process action plans.
8. Ensure that results of implementing process action plans satisfy the organization's process improvement objectives.

SG 3 DEPLOY ORGANIZATIONAL PROCESS ASSETS AND INCORPORATE EXPERIENCES

Organizational process assets are deployed across the organization and process related experiences are incorporated into organizational process assets.

The specific practices under this specific goal describe ongoing activities. New opportunities to benefit from organizational process assets and changes to them can arise throughout the life of each project. Deployment of standard processes and other organizational process assets should be continually supported in the organization, particularly for new projects at startup.

SP 3.1 DEPLOY ORGANIZATIONAL PROCESS ASSETS

Deploy organizational process assets across the organization.

Deploying organizational process assets or changes to them should be performed in an orderly manner. Some organizational process assets or changes to them may not be appropriate for use in some parts of the organization (e.g., because of stakeholder requirements, or the current lifecycle phase being implemented). It is therefore important that those who are or will be executing the process, as well as other organization functions (e.g., training, quality assurance), be involved in deployment as necessary.

> **TIP**
>
> IPM, OPF, and OPD are tightly related. OPD defines the organizational assets. OPF manages them, deploys them across the organization, and collects feedback. IPM uses the assets on the project and provides feedback to the organization.

> **HINT**
>
> Be sure to think about retiring the assets and work products that the change replaces.

OPF

Refer to the Organizational Process Definition process area for more information about establishing organizational process assets.

Example Work Products

1. Plans for deploying organizational process assets and changes to them across the organization
2. Training materials for deploying organizational process assets and changes to them
3. Documentation of changes to organizational process assets
4. Support materials for deploying organizational process assets and changes to them

Subpractices

1. Deploy organizational process assets across the organization.

TIP

When planning the deployment of organizational process assets, you may want to consider a staggered release to address the needs of projects at different stages in the lifecycle.

Typical activities performed as a part of the deployment of process assets include the following:

- Identifying organizational process assets that should be adopted by those who perform the process
- Determining how organizational process assets are made available (e.g., via a website)
- Identifying how changes to organizational process assets are communicated
- Identifying resources (e.g., methods, tools) needed to support the use of organizational process assets
- Planning the deployment
- Assisting those who use organizational process assets
- Ensuring that training is available for those who use organizational process assets

---

Refer to the Organizational Training process area for more information about establishing an organizational training capability.

TIP

You may find that you have multiple versions of an asset in use in your organization because of suggested changes. Just like a project, you will need to have change control practices in place for your organizational assets.

2. Document changes to organizational process assets.

Documenting changes to organizational process assets serves two main purposes:

- To enable the communication of changes
- To understand the relationship of changes in the organizational process assets to changes in process performance and results

3. Deploy changes that were made to organizational process assets across the organization.

> Typical activities performed as a part of deploying changes include the following:
> - Determining which changes are appropriate for those who perform the process
> - Planning the deployment
> - Arranging for the support needed for the successful transition of changes

4. Provide guidance and consultation on the use of organizational process assets.

SP 3.2 DEPLOY STANDARD PROCESSES

Deploy the organization's set of standard processes to projects at their startup and deploy changes to them as appropriate throughout the life of each project.

It is important that new projects use proven and effective processes to perform critical early activities (e.g., project planning, receiving requirements, obtaining resources).

Projects should also periodically update their defined processes to incorporate the latest changes made to the organization's set of standard processes when it will benefit them. This periodic update helps to ensure that all project activities derive the full benefit of what other projects have learned.

Refer to the Organizational Process Definition process area for more information about establishing standard processes and establishing tailoring criteria and guidelines.

Example Work Products

1. The organization's list of projects and the status of process deployment on each (i.e., existing and planned projects)
2. Guidelines for deploying the organization's set of standard processes on new projects
3. Records of tailoring and implementing the organization's set of standard processes

Subpractices

1. Identify projects in the organization that are starting up.
2. Identify active projects that would benefit from implementing the organization's current set of standard processes.
3. Establish plans to implement the organization's current set of standard processes on the identified projects.

4. Assist projects in tailoring the organization's set of standard processes to meet their needs.

> Refer to the Integrated Project Management process area for more information about establishing the project's defined process.

5. Maintain records of tailoring and implementing processes on the identified projects.

6. Ensure that the defined processes resulting from process tailoring are incorporated into plans for process compliance audits.

> Process compliance audits are objective evaluations of project activities against the project's defined process.

7. As the organization's set of standard processes is updated, identify which projects should implement the changes.

SP 3.3 MONITOR THE IMPLEMENTATION

Monitor the implementation of the organization's set of standard processes and use of process assets on all projects.

By monitoring implementation, the organization ensures that the organization's set of standard processes and other process assets are appropriately deployed to all projects. Monitoring implementation also helps the organization to develop an understanding of the organizational process assets being used and where they are used in the organization. Monitoring also helps to establish a broader context for interpreting and using process and product measures, lessons learned, and improvement information obtained from projects.

Example Work Products

1. Results of monitoring process implementation on projects
2. Status and results of process compliance audits
3. Results of reviewing selected process artifacts created as part of process tailoring and implementation

Subpractices

1. Monitor the projects' use of organizational process assets and changes to them.

2. Review selected process artifacts created during the life of each project.

> Reviewing selected process artifacts created during the life of a project ensures that all projects are making appropriate use of the organization's set of standard processes.

3. Review results of process compliance audits to determine how well the organization's set of standard processes has been deployed.

Refer to the Process and Product Quality Assurance process area for more information about objectively evaluating processes.

4. Identify, document, and track to closure issues related to implementing the organization's set of standard processes.

SP 3.4 INCORPORATE EXPERIENCES INTO ORGANIZATIONAL PROCESS ASSETS

Incorporate process related experiences derived from planning and performing the process into organizational process assets.

Example Work Products

1. Process improvement proposals
2. Process lessons learned
3. Measurements of organizational process assets
4. Improvement recommendations for organizational process assets
5. Records of the organization's process improvement activities
6. Information on organizational process assets and improvements to them

Subpractices

1. Conduct periodic reviews of the effectiveness and suitability of the organization's set of standard processes and related organizational process assets relative to the process needs and objectives derived from the organization's business objectives.
2. Obtain feedback about the use of organizational process assets.

> **TIP**
>
> Some feedback may be collected as part of QA activities.

3. Derive lessons learned from defining, piloting, implementing, and deploying organizational process assets.
4. Make lessons learned available to people in the organization as appropriate.

    Actions may be necessary to ensure that lessons learned are used appropriately.

> **TIP**
>
> Lessons learned are usually made available through the library established in OPD.

Examples of the inappropriate use of lessons learned include the following:
- Evaluating the performance of people
- Judging process performance or results

Examples of ways to prevent the inappropriate use of lessons learned include the following:
- Controlling access to lessons learned
- Educating people about the appropriate use of lessons learned

---

OPF

5. Analyze measurement data obtained from the use of the organization's common set of measures.

   Refer to the Measurement and Analysis process area for more information about analyzing measurement data.

   Refer to the Organizational Process Definition process area for more information about establishing the organization's measurement repository.

6. Appraise processes, methods, and tools in use in the organization and develop recommendations for improving organizational process assets.

> This appraisal typically includes the following:
> - Determining which processes, methods, and tools are of potential use to other parts of the organization
> - Appraising the quality and effectiveness of organizational process assets
> - Identifying candidate improvements to organizational process assets
> - Determining compliance with the organization's set of standard processes and tailoring guidelines

7. Make the best of the organization's processes, methods, and tools available to people in the organization as appropriate.

8. Manage process improvement proposals.

   Process improvement proposals can address both process and technology improvements.

> The activities for managing process improvement proposals typically include the following:
> - Soliciting process improvement proposals
> - Collecting process improvement proposals
> - Reviewing process improvement proposals
> - Selecting the process improvement proposals to be implemented
> - Tracking the implementation of process improvement proposals

   Process improvement proposals are documented as process change requests or problem reports as appropriate.

   Some process improvement proposals can be incorporated into the organization's process action plans.

9. Establish and maintain records of the organization's process improvement activities.

ORGANIZATIONAL PERFORMANCE MANAGEMENT

A Process Management Process Area at Maturity Level 5

Purpose

The purpose of Organizational Performance Management (OPM) is to proactively manage the organization's performance to meet its business objectives.

TIP

OPM focuses the organization on improving its performance to meet business objectives.

Introductory Notes

The Organizational Performance Management process area enables the organization to manage organizational performance by iteratively analyzing aggregated project data, identifying gaps in performance against the business objectives, and selecting and deploying improvements to close the gaps.

In this process area, the term "improvement" includes all incremental and innovative process and technology improvements, including those improvements made to project work environments. "Improvement" refers to all ideas that would change the organization's processes, technologies, and performance to better meet the organization's business objectives and associated quality and process performance objectives.

TIP

Changes must be measurably better. In early improvement efforts, it is more difficult to determine the effects of changes and whether things have really become better.

Business objectives that this process area might address include the following:

- Improved product quality (e.g., functionality, quality attributes)
- Increased productivity
- Increased process efficiency and effectiveness
- Increased consistency in meeting budget and schedule
- Decreased cycle time
- Greater customer and end-user satisfaction
- Shorter development or production time to change functionality, add new features, or adapt to new technologies

Specific Practices by Goal

SG 1 MANAGE BUSINESS PERFORMANCE

The organization's business performance is managed using statistical and other quantitative techniques to understand process performance shortfalls, and to identify areas for process improvement.

Managing business performance requires the following:

- Maintaining the organization's business objectives
- Understanding the organization's ability to meet the business objectives
- Continually improving processes related to achieving the business objectives

The organization uses defined process performance baselines to determine if the current and projected organizational business objectives are being met. Shortfalls in process performance are identified and analyzed to determine potential areas for process improvement.

Refer to the Organizational Process Performance process area for more information about establishing performance baselines and models.

As the organization improves its process performance or as business strategies change, new business objectives are identified and associated quality and process performance objectives are derived.

Specific goal 2 addresses eliciting and analyzing improvement suggestions that address shortfalls in achieving quality and process performance objectives.

SP 1.1 MAINTAIN BUSINESS OBJECTIVES

Maintain business objectives based on an understanding of business strategies and actual performance results.

Organizational performance data, characterized by process performance baselines, are used to evaluate whether business objectives are realistic and aligned with business strategies. After business objectives have been revised and prioritized by senior management, quality and process performance objectives may need to be created or maintained and re-communicated.

Example Work Products

1. Revised business objectives

X-REF

These three bullets correspond respectively to SPs 1.1, 1.2, and 1.3 through 3.3 (i.e., the rest of the PA).

TIP

In government, NGOs, and non-profit organizations, the term "business performance" may include both "business performance" as well as "mission performance."

TIP

The term *shortfall* in OPM refers to the gap between desired business performance (as characterized in business objectives or quality and process performance objectives [QPPOs]) and actual business performance (as characterized in process performance baselines [PPBs]).

TIP

Without a well defined and communicated set of objectives for the organization, improvements are less likely to be mutually reinforcing and can even be at cross purposes.

TIP

This practice is the responsibility of senior management and should not be delegated.

2. Revised quality and process performance objectives

3. Senior management approval of revised business objectives and quality and process performance objectives

4. Communication of all revised objectives

5. Updated process performance measures

Subpractices

1. Evaluate business objectives periodically to ensure they are aligned with business strategies.

   Senior management is responsible for understanding the marketplace, establishing business strategies, and establishing business objectives.

   Because business strategies and organizational performance evolve, business objectives should be reviewed periodically to determine whether they should be updated. For example, a business objective might be retired when process performance data show that the business objective is being met consistently over time or when the associated business strategy has changed.

2. Compare business objectives with actual process performance results to ensure they are realistic.

   Business objectives can set the bar too high to motivate real improvement. Using process performance baselines helps balance desires and reality.

   If process performance baselines are unavailable, sampling techniques can be used to develop a quantitative basis for comparison in a short period of time.

3. Prioritize business objectives based on documented criteria, such as the ability to win new business, retain existing clients, or accomplish other key business strategies.

4. Maintain quality and process performance objectives to address changes in business objectives.

   Business objectives and quality and process performance objectives will typically evolve over time. As existing objectives are achieved, they will be monitored to ensure they continue to be met, while new business objectives and associated quality and process performance objectives are identified and managed.

   Refer to the Organizational Process Performance process area for more information about establishing quality and process performance objectives.

5. Revise process performance measures to align with quality and process performance objectives.

   Refer to the Organizational Process Performance process area for more information about establishing process performance measures.

TIP

Understanding actual performance is key to establishing realistic objectives with some "stretch" in them (e.g., as in Hoshin planning—see Wikipedia).

X-REF

The business strategy literature is vast, an early milestone being Michael Porter's framework for business strategy development (see "Porter five forces analysis" in Wikipedia). The Christensen and Raynor books mentioned earlier are more recent, addressing how to nurture innovations to create sustained growth. Both books summarize many findings from the broader business strategy literature.

OPM

TIP

Business objectives are refined into QPPOs (e.g., as described in OPP SP 1.1), which then serve as the "touchpoint" between senior management and the organization's performance management and analysis activities as described in the rest of this PA and OPP.

SP 1.2 *ANALYZE PROCESS PERFORMANCE DATA*

Analyze process performance data to determine the organization's ability to meet identified business objectives.

The data that result from applying the process performance measures, which are defined using Organizational Process Performance processes are analyzed to create process performance baselines that help in understanding the current capability of the organization. Comparing process performance baselines to quality and process performance objectives helps the organization to determine its ability to meet business objectives. This data typically are collected from project level process performance data to enable organizational analysis.

Example Work Products

1. Analysis of current capability vs. business objectives
2. Process performance shortfalls
3. Risks associated with meeting business objectives

Subpractices

1. Periodically compare quality and process performance objectives to current process performance baselines to evaluate the ability of the organization to meet its business objectives.

   For example, if cycle time is a critical business need, many different cycle time measures may be collected by the organization. Overall cycle time performance data should be compared to the business objectives to understand if expected performance will satisfy business objectives.

2. Identify shortfalls where the actual process performance is not satisfying the business objectives.
3. Identify and analyze risks associated with not meeting business objectives.
4. Report results of the process performance and risk analyses to organizational leadership.

SP 1.3 *IDENTIFY POTENTIAL AREAS FOR IMPROVEMENT*

Identify potential areas for improvement that could contribute to meeting business objectives.

Potential areas for improvement are identified through a proactive analysis to determine areas that could address process performance

TIP

Is the organization achieving its QPPOs? Where are the shortfalls?

HINT

Poor supplier performance can impact achievement of the QPPOs of the organization. Make sure you clearly understand the contribution of suppliers to achieving your QPPOs and understand where you have direct control of outcomes versus influence.

HINT

Analyses using PPBs, process simulations, and process performance models (PPMs) can assist in evaluating the ability of the organization to meet its business objectives.

TIP

Process performance shortfalls limit the ability of the organization to pursue its chosen business strategies.

TIP

Which areas should the organization target to resolve shortfalls?

shortfalls. Causal Analysis and Resolution processes can be used to diagnose and resolve root causes.

The output from this activity is used to evaluate and prioritize potential improvements, and can result in either incremental or innovative improvement suggestions as described in specific goal 2.

Example Work Products

1. Potential areas for improvement

Subpractices

1. Identify potential improvement areas based on the analysis of process performance shortfalls.

    Performance shortfalls include not meeting productivity, cycle time, or customer satisfaction objectives. Examples of areas to consider for improvement include product technology, process technology, staffing and staff development, team structures, supplier selection and management, and other organizational infrastructures.

2. Document the rationale for the potential improvement areas, including references to applicable business objectives and process performance data.

3. Document anticipated costs and benefits associated with addressing potential improvement areas.

4. Communicate the set of potential improvement areas for further evaluation, prioritization, and use.

SG 2   SELECT IMPROVEMENTS

Improvements are proactively identified, evaluated using statistical and other quantitative techniques, and selected for deployment based on their contribution to meeting quality and process performance objectives.

Improvements to be deployed across the organization are selected from improvement suggestions which have been evaluated for effectiveness in the target deployment environment. These improvement suggestions are elicited and submitted from across the organization to address the improvement areas identified in specific goal 1.

Evaluations of improvement suggestions are based on the following:

- A quantitative understanding of the organization's current quality and process performance

- Satisfaction of the organization's quality and process performance objectives

OPM

- Estimated costs and impacts of developing and deploying the improvements, resources, and funding available for deployment
- Estimated benefits in quality and process performance resulting from deploying the improvements

SP 2.1 ELICIT SUGGESTED IMPROVEMENTS

Elicit and categorize suggested improvements.

This practice focuses on eliciting suggested improvements and includes categorizing suggested improvements as incremental or innovative.

Incremental improvements generally originate with those who do the work (i.e., users of the process or technology). Incremental improvements can be simple and inexpensive to implement and deploy. Incremental improvement suggestions are analyzed, but, if selected, may not need rigorous validation or piloting. Innovative improvements such as new or redesigned processes are more transformational than incremental improvements.

Innovative improvements often arise out of a systematic search for solutions to particular performance issues or opportunities to improve performance. They are identified by those who are trained and experienced with the maturation of particular technologies or whose job it is to track or directly contribute to increased performance.

Innovations can be found externally by actively monitoring innovations used in other organizations or documented in the research literature. Innovations can also be found by looking internally (e.g., by examining project lessons learned). Innovations are inspired by the need to achieve quality and process performance objectives, the need to improve performance baselines, or the external business environment.

> Examples of incremental improvements include the following:
> - Adding an item to a peer review checklist.
> - Combining the technical review and management review for suppliers into a single review.
> - Introducing an incident workaround.
> - Substituting a new component.
> - Making minor updates to a tool.

Examples of innovative improvements typically include additions or major updates to the following:

- Computer and related hardware products
- Transformational support tools
- New or redesigned workflows
- Processes or lifecycle models
- Interface standards
- Reusable components
- Management techniques and methodologies
- Quality improvement techniques and methodologies
- Development techniques and methodologies

Some suggested improvements may be received in the form of a proposal (e.g., an organizational improvement proposal arising from a causal analysis and resolution activity). These suggested improvements will have been analyzed and documented prior to input to Organizational Performance Management processes. When suggested improvements are received as proposals, the proposals are reviewed for completeness and are evaluated as part of the selection process for implementation.

Improvement searches can involve looking outside the organization, deriving innovations from projects using Causal Analysis and Resolution processes, using competitive business intelligence, or analyzing existing organizational performance.

Example Work Products

1. Suggested incremental improvements
2. Suggested innovative improvements

Subpractices

1. Elicit suggested improvements.

   These suggestions document potential improvements to processes and technologies. Managers and staff in the organization as well as customers, end users, and suppliers can submit suggestions. The organization can also search the academic and technology communities for suggested improvements. Some suggested improvements may have been implemented at the project level before being proposed for the organization.

HINT

You can collect suggestions using open-ended mechanisms, surveys, or focus groups.

OPM

Examples of sources for improvements include the following:
- Findings and recommendations from process appraisals
- The organization's quality and process performance objectives
- Analysis of data about customer and end-user problems as well as customer and end-user satisfaction
- Results of process and product benchmarking efforts
- Measured effectiveness of process activities
- Measured effectiveness of project work environments
- Examples of improvements that were successfully adopted elsewhere
- Feedback on previous improvements
- Spontaneous ideas from managers and staff
- Improvement proposals from Causal Analysis and Resolution processes resulting from implemented actions with proven effectiveness
- Analysis of technical performance measures
- Analysis of data on defect causes
- Analysis of project and organizational performance compared to quality and productivity objectives

Refer to the Organizational Process Focus process area for more information about deploying organizational process assets and incorporating experiences.

2. Identify suggested improvements as incremental or innovative.
3. Investigate innovative improvements that may improve the organization's processes and technologies.

Investigating innovative improvements typically involves the following:
- Maintaining awareness of leading relevant technical work and technology trends
- Searching for commercially available innovative improvements
- Collecting proposals for innovative improvements from the projects and the organization
- Reviewing processes and technologies used externally and comparing them to the processes and technologies used in the organization
- Identifying areas where innovative improvements have been used successfully, and reviewing data and documentation of experience using these improvements
- Identifying improvements that integrate new technology into products and project work environments

SP 2.2 ANALYZE SUGGESTED IMPROVEMENTS

Analyze suggested improvements for their possible impact on achieving the organization's quality and process performance objectives.

Suggested improvements are incremental and innovative improvements that are analyzed and possibly selected for validation, implementation, and deployment throughout the organization.

Example Work Products

1. Suggested improvement proposals
2. Selected improvements to be validated

Subpractices

1. Analyze the costs and benefits of suggested improvements.

   Process performance models provide insight into the effect of process changes on process capability and performance.

   Refer to the Organizational Process Performance process area for more information about establishing process performance models.

   Improvement suggestions that have a large cost-to-benefit ratio or that would not improve the organization's processes may be rejected.

Criteria for evaluating costs and benefits include the following:

- Contribution toward meeting the organization's quality and process performance objectives
- Effect on mitigating identified project and organizational risks
- Ability to respond quickly to changes in project requirements, market situations, and the business environment
- Effect on related processes and associated assets
- Cost of defining and collecting data that support the measurement and analysis of the process and technology improvement
- Expected life span of the improvement

---

2. Identify potential barriers and risks to deploying each suggested improvement.

Examples of barriers to deploying improvements include the following:

- Turf guarding and parochial perspectives
- Unclear or weak business rationale
- Lack of short-term benefits and visible successes

Continues

TIP

Elicited improvement suggestions are analyzed (evaluated) for impacts.

X-REF

When analyzing innovations, it is important to consider their potential contribution to business strategy and growth. For more information, refer to the Christensen and Raynor books mentioned near the Related Process Areas section.

TIP

These SP 2.2 subpractices represent the discipline and rigor that is expected of high-maturity organizations and is typically not possible at earlier stages of process improvement.

OPM

TIP

To identify barriers to deployment, it is helpful to understand the organization's attitude toward change and its ability to change. Such knowledge should guide how changes, especially large or complicated ones, are implemented.

Continued

- Unclear picture of what is expected from everyone
- Too many changes at the same time
- Lack of involvement and support from relevant stakeholders

Examples of risk factors that affect the deployment of improvements include the following:

- Compatibility of the improvement with existing processes, values, and skills of potential end users
- Complexity of the improvement
- Difficulty implementing the improvement
- Ability to demonstrate the value of the improvement before widespread deployment
- Justification for large, up-front investments in areas such as tools and training
- Inability to overcome "technology drag" where the current implementation is used successfully by a large and mature installed base of end users

---

3. Estimate the cost, effort, and schedule required for implementing, verifying, and deploying each suggested improvement.

4. Select suggested improvements for validation and possible implementation and deployment based on the evaluations.

   Refer to the Decision Analysis and Resolution process area for more information about analyzing possible decisions using a formal evaluation process that evaluates identified alternatives against established criteria.

TIP

For selected improvement suggestions, an "improvement proposal" incorporates the results of the SP 2.2 subpractices including analyses and evaluations, a plan for implementing the improvement, changes needed, validation method, and success criteria.

5. Document the evaluation results of each selected improvement suggestion in an improvement proposal.

   The proposal should include a problem statement, a plan (including cost and schedule, risk handling, method for evaluating effectiveness in the target environment) for implementing the improvement, and quantitative success criteria for evaluating actual results of the deployment.

6. Determine the detailed changes needed to implement the improvement and document them in the improvement proposal.

7. Determine the validation method that will be used before broad-scale deployment of the change and document it in the improvement proposal.

   - Determining the validation method includes defining the quantitative success criteria that will be used to evaluate results of the validation.

   - Since innovations, by definition, represent a major change with high impact, most innovative improvements will be piloted. Other validation methods, including modeling and simulation can be used as appropriate.

8. Document results of the selection process.

Results of the selection process usually include the following:
- The disposition of each suggested improvement
- The rationale for the disposition of each suggested improvement

---

SP 2.3 VALIDATE IMPROVEMENTS

Validate selected improvements.

Selected improvements are validated in accordance with their improvement proposals.

Examples of validation methods include the following:
- Discussions with stakeholders, perhaps in the context of a formal review
- Prototype demonstrations
- Pilots of suggested improvements
- Modeling and simulation

Pilots can be conducted to evaluate significant changes involving untried, high-risk, or innovative improvements before they are broadly deployed. Not all improvements need the rigor of a pilot. Criteria for selecting improvements for piloting are defined and used. Factors such as risk, transformational nature of change, or number of functional areas affected will determine the need for a pilot of the improvement.

Red-lined or rough-draft process documentation can be made available for use in piloting.

Example Work Products

1. Validation plans
2. Validation evaluation reports
3. Documented lessons learned from validation

Subpractices

1. Plan the validation.

Quantitative success criteria documented in the improvement proposal can be useful when planning validation.

OPM

Validation plans for selected improvements to be piloted should include target projects, project characteristics, a schedule for reporting results, and measurement activities.

2. Review and get relevant stakeholder agreement on validation plans.
3. Consult with and assist those who perform the validation.
4. Create a trial implementation, in accordance with the validation plan, for selected improvements to be piloted.
5. Perform each validation in an environment that is similar to the environment present in a broad scale deployment.
6. Track validation against validation plans.
7. Review and document the results of validation.

Validation results are evaluated using the quantitative criteria defined in the improvement proposal.

Reviewing and documenting results of pilots typically involves the following activities:
- Reviewing pilot results with stakeholders
- Deciding whether to terminate the pilot, rework implementation of the improvement, replan and continue the pilot, or proceed with deployment
- Updating the disposition of improvement proposals associated with the pilot
- Identifying and documenting new improvement proposals as appropriate
- Identifying and documenting lessons learned and problems encountered during the pilot including feedback to the improvement team and changes to the improvement

---

SP 2.4 SELECT AND IMPLEMENT IMPROVEMENTS FOR DEPLOYMENT

Select and implement improvements for deployment throughout the organization based on an evaluation of costs, benefits, and other factors.

Selection of suggested improvements for deployment is based on cost-to-benefit ratios with regard to quality and process performance objectives, available resources, and the results of improvement proposal evaluation and validation activities.

Refer to the Decision Analysis and Resolution process area for more information about analyzing possible decisions using a formal evaluation process that evaluates identified alternatives against established criteria.

Example Work Products

1. Improvements selected for deployment
2. Updated process documentation and training

Subpractices

1. Prioritize improvements for deployment.

   The priority of an improvement is based on an evaluation of its esti-mated cost-to-benefit ratio with regard to the quality and process per-formance objectives as compared to the performance baselines. Return on investment can be used as a basis of comparison.

2. Select improvements to be deployed.

   Selection of improvements to be deployed is based on their priorities, available resources, and results of improvement proposal evaluation and validation activities.

3. Determine how to deploy each improvement.

> Examples of where the improvements may be deployed include the following:
> - Project specific or common work environments
> - Product families
> - Organization's projects
> - Organizational groups

4. Document results of the selection process.

> Results of the selection process usually include the following:
> - The selection criteria for suggested improvements
> - The characteristics of the target projects
> - The disposition of each improvement proposal
> - The rationale for the disposition of each improvement proposal

5. Review any changes needed to implement the improvements.

> Examples of changes needed to deploy an improvement include the following:
> - Process descriptions, standards, and procedures
> - Work environments
> - Education and training
> - Skills
> - Existing commitments
> - Existing activities
> - Continuing support to end users
> - Organizational culture and characteristics

OPM

6. Update the organizational process assets.

> Updating the organizational process assets typically includes reviewing them, gaining approval for them, and communicating them.

Refer to the Organizational Process Definition process area for more information about establishing organizational process assets.

SG 3   DEPLOY IMPROVEMENTS

Measurable improvements to the organization's processes and technologies are deployed and evaluated using statistical and other quantitative techniques.

Once improvements are selected for deployment, a plan for deployment is created and executed. The deployment of improvements is managed and the effects of the improvements are measured and evaluated as to how well they contribute to meeting quality and process performance objectives.

SP 3.1   PLAN THE DEPLOYMENT

Establish and maintain plans for deploying selected improvements.

The plans for deploying selected improvements can be included in the plan for organizational performance management, in improvement proposals, or in separate deployment documents.

This specific practice complements the Deploy Organizational Process Assets specific practice in the Organizational Process Focus process area and adds the use of quantitative data to guide the deployment and to determine the value of improvements.

Refer to the Organizational Process Focus process area for more information about deploying organizational process assets and incorporating experiences.

Example Work Products

1. Deployment plans for selected improvements

Subpractices

1. Determine how each improvement should be adjusted for deployment.

   Improvements identified in a limited context (e.g., for a single improvement proposal) might need to be modified for a selected portion of the organization.

2. Identify strategies that address the potential barriers to deploying each improvement that were defined in the improvement proposals.

3. Identify the target project population for deployment of the improvement.

> Not all projects are good candidates for all improvements. For example, improvements may be targeted to software only projects, COTS integration projects, or operations and support projects.

4. Establish measures and objectives for determining the value of each improvement with respect to the organization's quality and process performance objectives.

> Measures can be based on the quantitative success criteria documented in the improvement proposal or derived from organizational objectives.

TIP

For example, one strategy could be to deploy sets of related improvements incrementally across the organization, so that PPBs and PPMs established in early increments are available for use in later increments.

Examples of measures for determining the value of an improvement include the following:

- Measured improvement in the project's or organization's process performance
- Time to recover the cost of the improvement
- Number and types of project and organizational risks mitigated by the process or technology improvement
- Average time required to respond to changes in project requirements, market situations, and the business environment

---

> Refer to the Measurement and Analysis process area for more information about aligning measurement and analysis activities and providing measurement results.

5. Document the plans for deploying selected improvements.

> The deployment plans should include relevant stakeholders, risk strategies, target projects, measures of success, and schedule.

6. Review and get agreement with relevant stakeholders on the plans for deploying selected improvements.

> Relevant stakeholders include the improvement sponsor, target projects, support organizations, etc.

7. Revise the plans for deploying selected improvements as necessary.

SP 3.2 MANAGE THE DEPLOYMENT

Manage the deployment of selected improvements.

This specific practice can overlap with the Implement Action Proposals specific practice in the Causal Analysis and Resolution process area (e.g., when causal analysis and resolution is used organizationally or across multiple projects).

Example Work Products

1. Updated training materials (to reflect deployed improvements)
2. Documented results of improvement deployment activities
3. Revised improvement measures, objectives, priorities, and deployment plans

Subpractices

1. Monitor the deployment of improvements using deployment plans.
2. Coordinate the deployment of improvements across the organization.

> Coordinating deployment includes the following activities:
> - **Coordinating activities of projects, support groups, and organizational groups for each improvement**
> - **Coordinating activities for deploying related improvements**

3. Deploy improvements in a controlled and disciplined manner.

> Examples of methods for deploying improvements include the following:
> - **Deploying improvements incrementally rather than as a single deployment**
> - **Providing comprehensive consulting to early adopters of improvement in lieu of revised formal training**

4. Coordinate the deployment of improvements into the projects' defined processes as appropriate.

   Refer to the Organizational Process Focus process area for more information about deploying organizational process assets and incorporating experiences.

5. Provide consulting as appropriate to support deployment of improvements.
6. Provide updated training materials or develop communication packages to reflect improvements to organizational process assets.

   Refer to the Organizational Training process area for more information about providing training.

7. Confirm that the deployment of all improvements is completed in accordance with the deployment plan.

8. Document and review results of improvement deployment.

Documenting and reviewing results includes the following:
- Identifying and documenting lessons learned
- Revising improvement measures, objectives, priorities, and deployment plans

---

SP 3.3 EVALUATE IMPROVEMENT EFFECTS

Evaluate the effects of deployed improvements on quality and process performance using statistical and other quantitative techniques.

Refer to the Measurement and Analysis process area for more information about aligning measurement and analysis activities and providing measurement results.

This specific practice can overlap with the Evaluate the Effect of Implemented Actions specific practice in the Causal Analysis and Resolution process area (e.g., when causal analysis and resolution is applied organizationally or across multiple projects).

Example Work Products

1. Documented measures of the effects resulting from deployed improvements

Subpractices

1. Measure the results of each improvement as implemented on the target projects, using the measures defined in the deployment plans.
2. Measure and analyze progress toward achieving the organization's quality and process performance objectives using statistical and other quantitative techniques and take corrective action as needed.

    Refer to the Organizational Process Performance process area for more information about establishing quality and process performance objectives and establishing process performance baselines and models.

TIP
This specific practice looks at measuring the effects of improvements being deployed across the organization. In particular, what is the impact on achieving QPPOs? Is it time to move the "goal post" and introduce new "stretch" QPPOs (see SP 1.1)?

OPM

ORGANIZATIONAL PROCESS PERFORMANCE
A Process Management Process Area at Maturity Level 4

Purpose

The purpose of Organizational Process Performance (OPP) is to establish and maintain a quantitative understanding of the performance of selected processes in the organization's set of standard processes in support of achieving quality and process performance objectives, and to provide process performance data, baselines, and models to quantitatively manage the organization's projects.

Introductory Notes

The Organizational Process Performance process area involves the following activities:

- Establishing organizational quantitative quality and process performance objectives based on business objectives (See the definition of "quality and process performance objectives" in the glossary.)
- Selecting processes or subprocesses for process performance analyses
- Establishing definitions of the measures to be used in process performance analyses (See the definition of "process performance" in the glossary.)
- Establishing process performance baselines and process performance models (See the definitions of "process performance baselines" and "process performance models" in the glossary.)

The collection and analysis of the data and creation of the process performance baselines and models can be performed at different levels of the organization, including individual projects or groups of related projects as appropriate based on the needs of the projects and organization.

OPP

X-REF

The CMMI principle that SPs are agnostic as to who performs them applies here as well. The OPP SPs, including those establishing Process Performance Baselines (PPBs) and Models (PPMs) (SPs 1.4 and 1.5), may in some cases provide more benefit when implemented for an individual project(s).

TIP

A subprocess measure's "central tendency and spread," normalized appropriately (e.g., for work product size), and determined for a set of similar projects, teams, or perhaps just for a single team, together with sufficient contextual data to interpret the individual measurements (to allow subsetting the data from which these statistics are derived), may compose a PPB.

HINT

PPB can be displayed or summarized in different ways, depending on the nature of the data and the contexts from which it arose. These might include control charts, box plots, or histograms.

TIP

This paragraph describes in a simplified way how the organization's PPBs (referred to here as "expected process performance") support the activities described in QPM, which in turn, provide data used to update these PPBs.

The common measures for the organization consist of process and product measures that can be used to characterize the actual performance of processes in the organization's individual projects. By analyzing the resulting measurements, a distribution or range of results can be established that characterize the expected performance of the process when used on an individual project.

Measuring quality and process performance can involve combining existing measures into additional derived measures to provide more insight into overall efficiency and effectiveness at a project or organization level. The analysis at the organization level can be used to study productivity, improve efficiencies, and increase throughput across projects in the organization.

The expected process performance can be used in establishing the project's quality and process performance objectives and can be used as a baseline against which actual project performance can be compared. This information is used to quantitatively manage the project. Each quantitatively managed project, in turn, provides actual performance results that become a part of organizational process assets that are made available to all projects.

Process performance models are used to represent past and current process performance and to predict future results of the process. For example, the latent defects in the delivered product can be predicted using measurements of work product attributes such as complexity and process attributes such as preparation time for peer reviews.

When the organization has sufficient measures, data, and analytical techniques for critical process, product, and service characteristics, it is able to do the following:

- Determine whether processes are behaving consistently or have stable trends (i.e., are predictable)
- Identify processes in which performance is within natural bounds that are consistent across projects and could potentially be aggregated
- Identify processes that show unusual (e.g., sporadic, unpredictable) behavior
- Identify aspects of processes that can be improved in the organization's set of standard processes
- Identify the implementation of a process that performs best

This process area interfaces with and supports the implementation of other high maturity process areas. The assets established and maintained as part of implementing this process area (e.g., the measures to be used to characterize subprocess behavior, process performance baselines, process performance models) are inputs to the quantitative project management, causal analysis and resolution, and organizational performance management processes in support of the analyses described there. Quantitative project management processes provide the quality and process performance data needed to maintain the assets described in this process area.

Related Process Areas

Refer to the Measurement and Analysis process area for more information about specifying measures, obtaining measurement data, and analyzing measurement data.

Refer to the Organizational Performance Management process area for more information about proactively managing the organization's performance to meet its business objectives.

Refer to the Quantitative Project Management process area for more information about quantitatively managing the project to achieve the project's established quality and process performance objectives.

TIP

Mastering the practices in MA is a prerequisite to effectively implementing OPP and QPM. In particular, it is important to evaluate the effectiveness of your measurement system. Are subprocess measures sufficiently accurate and precise to be useful for your intended purposes? Techniques such as ANOVA Gage Repeatability and Reproducibility (GR&R) and Fleiss' kappa (see Wikipedia) may help answer these questions.

X-REF

Another suitable reference is "Measurement and Analysis Infrastructure Diagnostic: Version 1.0: Method Definition Document" by Mark Kasunic. See http://www.sei.cmu.edu/library/abstracts/reports/10tr035.cfm.

OPP

Specific Goal and Practice Summary

SG 1 Establish Performance Baselines and Models
    SP 1.1   Establish Quality and Process Performance Objectives
    SP 1.2   Select Processes
    SP 1.3   Establish Process Performance Measures
    SP 1.4   Analyze Process Performance and Establish Process Performance Baselines
    SP 1.5   Establish Process Performance Models

Specific Practices by Goal

SG 1   ESTABLISH PERFORMANCE BASELINES AND MODELS

Baselines and models, which characterize the expected process performance of the organization's set of standard processes, are established and maintained.

Prior to establishing process performance baselines and models, it is necessary to determine the quality and process performance objectives for those processes (the Establish Quality and Process Performance Objectives specific practice), which processes are suitable to be measured (the Select Processes specific practice), and which measures are useful for determining process performance (the Establish Process Performance Measures specific practice).

The first three practices of this goal are interrelated and often need to be performed concurrently and iteratively to select quality and process performance objectives, processes, and measures. Often, the selection of one quality and process performance objective, process, or measure will constrain the selection of the others. For example, selecting a quality and process performance objective relating to defects delivered to the customer will almost certainly require selecting the verification processes and defect related measures.

The intent of this goal is to provide projects with the process performance baselines and models they need to perform quantitative project management. Many times these baselines and models are collected or created by the organization, but there are circumstances in which a project may need to create the baselines and models for themselves. These circumstances include projects that are not covered by the organization's baselines and models. For these cases the project follows the practices in this goal to create its baselines and models.

SP 1.1 *ESTABLISH QUALITY AND PROCESS PERFORMANCE OBJECTIVES*

Establish and maintain the organization's quantitative objectives for quality and process performance, which are traceable to business objectives.

The organization's quality and process performance objectives can be established for different levels in the organizational structure (e.g., business area, product line, function, project) as well as at different levels in the process hierarchy. When establishing quality and process performance objectives, consider the following:

- Traceability to the organization's business objectives
- Past performance of the selected processes or subprocesses in context (e.g., on projects)
- Multiple attributes of process performance (e.g., product quality, productivity, cycle time, response time)
- Inherent variability or natural bounds of the selected processes or subprocesses

The organization's quality and process performance objectives provide focus and direction to the process performance analysis and quantitative project management activities. However, it should be noted that achieving quality and process performance objectives that are significantly different from current process capability requires use of techniques found in Causal Analysis and Resolution and Organizational Performance Management.

TIP

By ensuring traceability to business objectives, the organization's quality and process performance objectives (QPPOs) become the mechanism for *aligning* the activities described in OPP and QPM with the organization's business objectives.

Example Work Products

1. Organization's quality and process performance objectives

Subpractices

1. Review the organization's business objectives related to quality and
    process performance.

> Examples of business objectives include the following:
> - Deliver products within budget and on time
> - Improve product quality by a specified percent in a specified timeframe
> - Improve productivity by a specified percent in a specified timeframe
> - Maintain customer satisfaction ratings
> - Improve time-to-market for new product or service releases by a specified percent in a specified timeframe
> - Reduce deferred product functionality by a specified percent in a specified timeframe
> - Reduce the rate of product recalls by a specified percent in a specified timeframe
> - Reduce customer total cost of ownership by a specified percent in a specified timeframe
> - Decrease the cost of maintaining legacy products by a specified percent in a specified timeframe

2. Define the organization's quantitative objectives for quality and
    process performance.

    Quality and process performance objectives can be established for
    process or subprocess measurements (e.g., effort, cycle time, defect
    removal effectiveness) as well as for product measurements (e.g., reli-
    ability, defect density) and service measurements (e.g., capacity,
    response times) as appropriate.

HINT

QPPOs can be established at multiple levels of an organization. One approach that aligns the whole organization toward achieving the organization's QPPOs and links QPPOs across all levels is Hoshin Kanri or Hoshin Planning (see Wikipedia).

> Examples of quality and process performance objectives include the following:
> - Achieve a specified defect escape rate, productivity, duration, capacity, or cost target
> - Improve the defect escape rate, productivity, duration, capacity, or cost performance by a specified percent of the process performance baseline in a specified timeframe
> - Improve service level agreement performance by a specified percent of the process performance baseline in a specified timeframe

OPP

4. Revise the selection as necessary.

It may be necessary to revise the selection in the following situations:
- The predictions made by process performance models result in too much variation to make them useful.
- The objectives for quality and process performance change.
- The organization's set of standard processes change.
- The underlying quality and process performance changes.

SP 1.3 ESTABLISH PROCESS PERFORMANCE MEASURES

Establish and maintain definitions of measures to be included in the organization's process performance analyses.

Refer to the Measurement and Analysis process area for more information about specifying measures.

Example Work Products

1. Definitions of selected measures of process performance with rationale for their selection including traceability to selected processes or subprocesses

Subpractices

1. Select measures that reflect appropriate attributes of the selected processes or subprocesses to provide insight into the organization's quality and process performance.

    It is often helpful to define multiple measures for a process or subprocess to understand the impact of changes to the process and avoid sub-optimization. Also, it is often helpful to establish measures for both product and process attributes for the selected process and subprocess, as well as its inputs, outputs, and resources (including people and the skill they bring) consumed.

    The Goal Question Metric paradigm is an approach that can be used to select measures that provide insight into the organization's quality and process performance objectives. It is often useful to analyze how these quality and process performance objectives can be achieved based on an understanding of process performance provided by the selected measures.

> **X-REF**
>
> A commonly heard objection is that it is not possible to measure certain attributes. In his book *How to Measure Anything: Finding the Value of "Intangibles" in Business*, Doug Hubbard provides strategies for how to proceed.

> **X-REF**
>
> The Goal Question Metric (GQM) is a well-known approach to deriving measures that provide insight into issues of interest. See www.cs.umd .edu/~mvz/handouts/gqm.pdf. The SEI's variant of GQM is called the Goal Question Indicator Metric (GQIM). See http://www.sei.cmu.edu/ training/p06.cfm. Also, see the perspective "Applying Principles of Empiricism" in this book for more information about GQM and CMMI (one of that perspective's co-authors is one of the creators of GQM).

Examples of criteria used to select measures include the following:
- Relationship of measures to the organization's quality and process performance objectives
- Coverage that measures provide over the life of the product or service
- Visibility that measures provide into process performance

Continues

Continued

- Availability of measures
- Frequency at which observations of the measure can be collected
- Extent to which measures are controllable by changes to the process or subprocess
- Extent to which measures represent the end users' view of effective process performance

2. Establish operational definitions for the selected measures.

   Refer to the Measurement and Analysis process area for more information about specifying measures.

3. Incorporate selected measures into the organization's set of common measures.

   Refer to the Organizational Process Definition process area for more information about establishing organizational process assets.

4. Revise the set of measures as necessary.

   Measures are periodically evaluated for their continued usefulness and ability to indicate process effectiveness.

SP 1.4 *ANALYZE PROCESS PERFORMANCE AND ESTABLISH PROCESS PERFORMANCE BASELINES*

Analyze the performance of the selected processes, and establish and maintain the process performance baselines.

The selected measures are analyzed to characterize the performance of the selected processes or subprocesses achieved on projects. This characterization is used to establish and maintain process performance baselines. (See the definition of "process performance baseline" in the glossary.) These baselines are used to determine the expected results of the process or subprocess when used on a project under a given set of circumstances.

Process performance baselines are compared to the organization's quality and process performance objectives to determine if the quality and process performance objectives are being achieved.

The process performance baselines are a measurement of performance for the organization's set of standard processes at various levels of detail. The processes that the process performance baselines can address include the following:

- Sequence of connected processes
- Processes that cover the entire life of the project
- Processes for developing individual work products

HINT

To begin systematic collection of these measures from new projects, incorporate them into the organization's set of common measures (OPD SP 1.4).

TIP

QPPOs should motivate superior performance. QPPOs that set the bar too high may demoralize more than they motivate. What does the performance data say about how well a project can do relative to the QPPOs? There is a need for balance between "desires" and "reality."

OPP

There can be several process performance baselines to characterize performance for subgroups of the organization.

Examples of criteria used to categorize subgroups include the following:
- Product line
- Line of business
- Application domain
- Complexity
- Team size
- Work product size
- Process elements from the organization's set of standard processes

---

Tailoring the organization's set of standard processes can significantly affect the comparability of data for inclusion in process performance baselines. Effects of tailoring should be considered in establishing baselines. Depending on the tailoring allowed, separate performance baselines may exist for each type of tailoring.

Refer to the Quantitative Project Management process area for more information about quantitatively managing the project to achieve the project's established quality and process performance objectives.

Example Work Products

1. Analysis of process performance data
2. Baseline data on the organization's process performance

Subpractices

HINT

Record sufficient contextual information with a measurement to enable identification of when it was generated, by whom, and the PPB it should be included in (or regenerating a PPB for a different class of process instances).

1. Collect the selected measurements for the selected processes and subprocesses.

   The process or subprocess in use when the measurement was taken is recorded to enable its use later.

   Refer to the Measurement and Analysis process area for more information about specifying measurement data collection and storage procedures.

2. Analyze the collected measures to establish a distribution or range of results that characterize the expected performance of selected processes or subprocesses when used on a project.

   This analysis should include the stability of the related process or subprocess, and the impacts of associated factors and context. Related factors include inputs to the process and other attributes that can affect the results obtained. The context includes the business context (e.g., domain) and significant tailoring of the organization's set of standard processes.

The measurements from stable subprocesses in projects should be used when possible; other data may not be reliable.

3. Establish and maintain the process performance baselines from collected measurements and analyses.

   Refer to the Measurement and Analysis process area for more information about aligning measurement and analysis activities and providing measurement results.

   Process performance baselines are derived by analyzing collected measures to establish a distribution or range of results that characterize the expected performance for selected processes or subprocesses when used on a project in the organization.

4. Review and get agreement with relevant stakeholders about the process performance baselines.

5. Make the process performance information available across the organization in the measurement repository.

   The organization's process performance baselines are used by projects to estimate the natural bounds for process performance.

6. Compare the process performance baselines to associated quality and process performance objectives to determine if those quality and process performance objectives are being achieved.

   These comparisons should use statistical techniques beyond a simple comparison of the mean to gauge the extent of quality and process performance objective achievement. If the quality and process performance objectives are not being achieved, corrective actions should be considered.

   Refer to the Causal Analysis and Resolution process area for more information about determining causes of selected outcomes.

   Refer to the Organizational Process Focus process area for more information about planning and implementing process actions.

   Refer to the Organizational Performance Management for more information about analyzing process performance data and identifying potential areas for improvement.

7. Revise the process performance baselines as necessary.

Examples of when the organization's process performance baselines may need to be revised include the following:
- When processes change
- When the organization's results change
- When the organization's needs change
- When suppliers' processes change
- When suppliers change

TIP

Unless the process is stable, the data from the process may actually be a mixture of measurements taken from *different* processes. PPBs developed from such data are limited in their usefulness to projects (e.g., estimated natural bounds are likely to be far apart).

HINT

Investigate subgrouping when incorporating data from multiple projects (and teams) into the same PPB. Even if the process is stable within individual projects, its performance across projects may vary so much that the resulting single PPB will be too "wide" to be useful.

HINT

Even when organizational PPBs are established, individual projects may still benefit from establishing their own individual PPBs when they have accumulated sufficient data.

TIP

Ideally, the QPPOs are attainable, but perhaps are a "stretch" beyond the current PPBs. This comparison can help establish feasible objectives. CAR or OPM can also be invoked to help improve process performance.

OPP

TIP

Part of mastering any discipline is developing "nuance" for factors that matter in how a situation will unfold, yet realizing every situation is somewhat different. Although PPMs can never be perfectly accurate, they offer a systematic approach to using the data available in a situation and similar situations to make, scientifically, the best possible judgment or prediction.

HINT

Establish PPMs that provide insight at different points in a project that help it assess progress toward achieving its QPPOs (QPM SP 2.2).

TIP

In general, data-driven approaches to judgment and prediction should, over the long term, perform better than human judgment alone. Perhaps the performance of both should be analyzed and contrasted; then how to best use both can be determined. But in situations unlike those experienced before, neither is likely to perform well.

X-REF

There are now many books on the limitations of human judgment. These include an update to a classic text, *Rational Choice in an Uncertain World: The Psychology of Judgment and Decision Making* by Hastie and Dawes. A more recent book is *The Invisible Gorilla: And Other Ways Our Intuitions Deceive Us* by Chabris and Simons.

SP 1.5 ESTABLISH PROCESS PERFORMANCE MODELS

Establish and maintain process performance models for the organization's set of standard processes.

High maturity organizations generally establish and maintain a set of process performance models at various levels of detail that cover a range of activities that are common across the organization and address the organization's quality and process performance objectives. (See the definition of "process performance model" in the glossary.) Under some circumstances, projects may need to create their own process performance models.

Process performance models are used to estimate or predict the value of a process performance measure from the values of other process, product, and service measurements. These process performance models typically use process and product measurements collected throughout the life of the project to estimate progress toward achieving quality and process performance objectives that cannot be measured until later in the project's life.

Process performance models are used as follows:

- The organization uses them for estimating, analyzing, and predicting the process performance associated with processes in and changes to the organization's set of standard processes.
- The organization uses them to assess the (potential) return on investment for process improvement activities.
- Projects use them for estimating, analyzing, and predicting the process performance of their defined processes.
- Projects use them for selecting processes or subprocesses for use.
- Projects use them for estimating progress toward achieving the project's quality and process performance objectives.

These measures and models are defined to provide insight into and to provide the ability to predict critical process and product characteristics that are relevant to the organization's quality and process performance objectives.

Examples of process performance models include the following:
- System dynamics models
- Regression models
- Complexity models
- Discrete event simulation models
- Monte Carlo simulation models

Refer to the Quantitative Project Management process area for more information about quantitatively managing the project to achieve the project's established quality and process performance objectives.

Example Work Products

1. Process performance models

Subpractices

1. Establish process performance models based on the organization's set of standard processes and process performance baselines.
2. Calibrate process performance models based on the past results and current needs.
3. Review process performance models and get agreement with relevant stakeholders.
4. Support the projects' use of process performance models.
5. Revise process performance models as necessary.

> **Examples of when process performance models may need to be revised include the following:**
> • When processes change
> • When the organization's results change
> • When the organization's quality and process performance objectives change

HINT

Subject matter experts from different relevant disciplines and functions can help identify process and product characteristics important to prediction. A variety of analytic techniques such as ANOVA and sensitivity analysis can also help screen factors for potential inclusion in PPMs. PPBs provide a primary source for the information needed for this analysis.

HINT

Meet with relevant stakeholders to discuss PPMs (e.g., their usefulness and limitations) and what will enable them to make effective use of such models on projects.

TIP

To use PPMs effectively, project staff members and management may need significant support. There may be an initial tendency to dismiss or misuse PPMs or their results.

X-REF

Example PPMs are described in "Approaches to Process Performance Modeling: A Summary from the SEI Series of Workshops on CMMI High Maturity Measurement and Analysis" found at http://www.sei.cmu.edu/library/abstracts/reports/09tr021.cfm.

Experiences from using PPMs are described in "Performance Effects of Measurement and Analysis: Perspectives from CMMI High Maturity Organizations and Appraisers" found at http://www.sei.cmu.edu/library/abstracts/reports/10tr022.cfm.

OPP

of knowledge, and mechanisms for measuring the effectiveness of the training program.

Identifying process training needs is based primarily on the skills required to perform the organization's set of standard processes.

Refer to the Organizational Process Definition process area for more information about establishing standard processes.

TIP

To deploy these processes effectively across the organization, training is typically required.

TIP

Remember, CMMI sets expectations on *what* needs to be done, not *how* to do it. Therefore, each organization must decide what type of training is best for any situation.

Certain skills can be effectively and efficiently imparted through vehicles other than classroom training experiences (e.g., informal mentoring). Other skills require more formalized training vehicles, such as in a classroom, by web-based training, through guided self study, or via a formalized on-the-job training program. The formal or informal training vehicles employed for each situation should be based on an assessment of the need for training and the performance gap to be addressed. The term "training" used throughout this process area is used broadly to include all of these learning options.

Success in training is indicated by the availability of opportunities to acquire the skills and knowledge needed to perform new and ongoing enterprise activities.

Skills and knowledge can be technical, organizational, or contextual. Technical skills pertain to the ability to use equipment, tools, materials, data, and processes required by a project or process. Organizational skills pertain to behavior within and according to the staff members' organization structure, role and responsibilities, and general operating principles and methods. Contextual skills are the self-management, communication, and interpersonal abilities needed to successfully perform work in the organizational and social context of the project and support groups.

Related Process Areas

Refer to the Decision Analysis and Resolution process area for more information about analyzing possible decisions using a formal evaluation process that evaluates identified alternatives against established criteria.

Refer to the Organizational Process Definition process area for more information about establishing organizational process assets.

Refer to the Project Planning process area for more information about planning needed knowledge and skills.

Specific Goal and Practice Summary

SG 1 Establish an Organizational Training Capability
    SP 1.1   Establish Strategic Training Needs
    SP 1.2   Determine Which Training Needs Are the Responsibility of the Organization

SP 1.3   Establish an Organizational Training Tactical Plan
SP 1.4   Establish a Training Capability
SG 2 Provide Training
SP 2.1   Deliver Training
SP 2.2   Establish Training Records
SP 2.3   Assess Training Effectiveness

Specific Practices by Goal

SG 1   ESTABLISH AN ORGANIZATIONAL TRAINING CAPABILITY

A training capability, which supports the roles in the organization, is established and maintained.

The organization identifies training required to develop the skills and knowledge necessary to perform enterprise activities. Once the needs are identified, a training program addressing those needs is developed.

SP 1.1   ESTABLISH STRATEGIC TRAINING NEEDS

Establish and maintain strategic training needs of the organization.

Strategic training needs address long-term objectives to build a capability by filling significant knowledge gaps, introducing new technologies, or implementing major changes in behavior. Strategic planning typically looks two to five years into the future.

> **HINT**
>
> Use strategic training to ensure that the organization continues as a learning organization, strengthens its core competencies, and remains competitive.

Examples of sources of strategic training needs include the following:
- The organization's standard processes
- The organization's strategic business plan
- The organization's process improvement plan
- Enterprise level initiatives
- Skill assessments
- Risk analyses
- Acquisition and supplier management

Example Work Products

1. Training needs
2. Assessment analysis

Subpractices

1. Analyze the organization's strategic business objectives and process improvement plan to identify potential training needs.

2. Document the strategic training needs of the organization.

Examples of categories of training needs include the following:
- Process analysis and documentation
- Engineering (e.g., requirements analysis, design, testing, configuration management, quality assurance)
- Selection and management of suppliers
- Team building
- Management (e.g., estimating, tracking, risk management)
- Leadership
- Disaster recovery and continuity of operations
- Communication and negotiation skills

---

3. Determine the roles and skills needed to perform the organization's set of standard processes.
4. Document the training needed to perform roles in the organization's set of standard processes.
5. Document the training needed to maintain the safe, secure, and continued operation of the business.
6. Revise the organization's strategic needs and required training as necessary.

SP 1.2 DETERMINE WHICH TRAINING NEEDS ARE THE RESPONSIBILITY OF THE ORGANIZATION

Determine which training needs are the responsibility of the organization and which are left to the individual project or support group.

Refer to the Project Planning process area for more information about planning needed knowledge and skills.

TIP

Small organizations may choose to use the practices in this PA to address all of their training. If so, the scope and intent of the practices should be expanded appropriately.

In addition to strategic training needs, organizational training addresses training requirements that are common across projects and support groups. Projects and support groups have the primary responsibility for identifying and addressing their training needs. The organization's training staff is responsible for addressing only common cross-project and support group training needs (e.g., training in work environments common to multiple projects). In some cases, however, the organization's training staff may address additional training needs of projects and support groups, as negotiated with them, in the context of the training resources available and the organization's training priorities.

Example Work Products

1. Common project and support group training needs
2. Training commitments

Subpractices

1. Analyze the training needs identified by projects and support groups.

   Analysis of project and support group needs is intended to identify common training needs that can be most efficiently addressed organization wide. These needs analysis activities are used to anticipate future training needs that are first visible at the project and support group level.

2. Negotiate with projects and support groups on how their training needs will be satisfied.

   The support provided by the organization's training staff depends on the training resources available and the organization's training priorities.

Examples of training appropriately performed by the project or support group include the following:
- Training in the application or service domain of the project
- Training in the unique tools and methods used by the project or support group
- Training in safety, security, and human factors

---

3. Document commitments for providing training support to projects and support groups.

SP 1.3 ESTABLISH AN ORGANIZATIONAL TRAINING TACTICAL PLAN

Establish and maintain an organizational training tactical plan.

The organizational training tactical plan is the plan to deliver the training that is the responsibility of the organization and is necessary for individuals to perform their roles effectively. This plan addresses the near-term execution of training and is adjusted periodically in response to changes (e.g., in needs, in resources) and to evaluations of effectiveness.

TIP
For many organizations, this planning is performed annually, with a review each quarter.

OT

Example Work Products

1. Organizational training tactical plan

Subpractices

1. Establish the content of the plan.

Organizational training tactical plans typically contain the following:
- Training needs
- Training topics
- Schedules based on training activities and their dependencies
- Methods used for training
- Requirements and quality standards for training materials
- Training tasks, roles, and responsibilities
- Required resources including tools, facilities, environments, staffing, skills, and knowledge

---

2. Establish commitments to the plan.

   Documented commitments by those who are responsible for implementing and supporting the plan are essential for the plan to be effective.

3. Revise the plan and commitments as necessary.

SP 1.4 ESTABLISH A TRAINING CAPABILITY

Establish and maintain a training capability to address organizational training needs.

Refer to the Decision Analysis and Resolution process area for more information about analyzing possible decisions using a formal evaluation process that evaluates identified alternatives against established criteria.

Example Work Products

1. Training materials and supporting artifacts

Subpractices

1. Select appropriate approaches to satisfy organizational training needs.

   Many factors may affect the selection of training approaches, including audience specific knowledge, costs, schedule, and the work environment. Selecting an approach requires consideration of the means to provide skills and knowledge in the most effective way possible given the constraints.

Examples of training approaches include the following:
- Classroom training
- Computer aided instruction
- Guided self study
- Formal apprenticeship and mentoring programs
- Facilitated videos
- Chalk talks
- Brown bag lunch seminars
- Structured on-the-job training

---

2. Determine whether to develop training materials internally or to acquire them externally.

   Determine the costs and benefits of internal training development and of acquiring training externally.

Example criteria that can be used to determine the most effective mode of knowledge or skill acquisition include the following:
- Applicability to work or process performance objectives
- Availability of time to prepare for project execution
- Applicability to business objectives
- Availability of in-house expertise
- Availability of training from external sources

Examples of external sources of training include the following:
- Customer provided training
- Commercially available training courses
- Academic programs
- Professional conferences
- Seminars

---

3. Develop or obtain training materials.

   Training can be provided by the project, support groups, the organization, or an external organization. The organization's training staff coordinates the acquisition and delivery of training regardless of its source.

Examples of training materials include the following:
- Courses
- Computer-aided instruction
- Videos

OT

4. Develop or obtain qualified instructors, instructional designers, or mentors.

To ensure that those who develop and deliver internal training have the necessary knowledge and training skills, criteria can be defined to identify, develop, and qualify them. The development of training, including self study and online training, should involve those who have experience in instructional design. In the case of external training, the organization's training staff can investigate how the training provider determines which instructors will deliver the training. This selection of qualified instructors can also be a factor in selecting or continuing to use a training provider.

5. Describe the training in the organization's training curriculum.

Examples of the information provided in training descriptions for each course include the following:
- Topics covered in the training
- Intended audience
- Prerequisites and preparation for participating
- Training objectives
- Length of the training
- Lesson plans
- Completion criteria for the course
- Criteria for granting training waivers

6. Revise training materials and supporting artifacts as necessary.

Examples of situations in which training materials and supporting artifacts may need to be revised include the following:
- Training needs change (e.g., when new technology associated with the training topic is available)
- An evaluation of the training identifies the need for change (e.g., evaluations of training effectiveness surveys, training program performance assessments, instructor evaluation forms)

SG 2   PROVIDE TRAINING

Training for individuals to perform their roles effectively is provided.

When selecting people to be trained, the following should be considered:
- Background of the target population of training participants
- Prerequisite background to receive training

- Skills and abilities needed by people to perform their roles
- Need for cross-discipline training for all disciplines, including project management
- Need for managers to have training in appropriate organizational processes
- Need for training in basic principles of all appropriate disciplines or services to support staff in quality management, configuration management, and other related support functions
- Need to provide competency development for critical functional areas
- Need to maintain competencies and qualifications of staff to operate and maintain work environments common to multiple projects

SP 2.1 DELIVER TRAINING

Deliver training following the organizational training tactical plan.

Example Work Products

1. Delivered training course

Subpractices

1. Select those who will receive the training necessary to perform their roles effectively.

   Training is intended to impart knowledge and skills to people performing various roles in the organization. Some people already possess the knowledge and skills required to perform well in their designated roles. Training can be waived for these people, but care should be taken that training waivers are not abused.

2. Schedule the training, including any resources, as necessary (e.g., facilities, instructors).

   Training should be planned and scheduled. Training is provided that has a direct bearing on work performance expectations. Therefore, optimal training occurs in a timely manner with regard to imminent job performance expectations.

These performance expectations often include the following:
- Training in the use of specialized tools
- Training in procedures that are new to the person who will perform them

---

3. Deliver the training.

   If the training is delivered by a person, then appropriate training professionals (e.g., experienced instructors, mentors) should deliver the training. When possible, training is delivered in settings that closely resemble the actual work environment and includes activities to simulate actual work situations. This approach includes integration of tools, methods, and procedures for competency development. Training is tied to work responsibilities so that on-the-job activities or other outside experiences will reinforce the training within a reasonable time after the training was delivered.

4. Track the delivery of training against the plan.

SP 2.2 ESTABLISH TRAINING RECORDS

Establish and maintain records of organizational training.

TIP

To provide consistent and complete information on each employee, the training records may include all training, whether performed at the organization's level or by a project or support group.

This practice applies to the training performed at the organizational level. Establishment and maintenance of training records for project or support group sponsored training is the responsibility of each individual project or support group.

Example Work Products

1. Training records
2. Training updates to the organizational repository

Subpractices

TIP

To ensure that training records are accurate, you may want to use some CM practices.

1. Keep records of all students who successfully complete each training course or other approved training activity as well as those who are unsuccessful.
2. Keep records of all staff who are waived from training.

   The rationale for granting a waiver should be documented, and both the manager responsible and the manager of the excepted individual should approve the waiver.
3. Keep records of all students who successfully complete their required training.
4. Make training records available to the appropriate people for consideration in assignments.

   Training records may be part of a skills matrix developed by the training organization to provide a summary of the experience and education of people, as well as training sponsored by the organization.

SP 2.3 ASSESS TRAINING EFFECTIVENESS

Assess the effectiveness of the organization's training program.

A process should exist to determine the effectiveness of training (i.e., how well training is meeting the organization's needs).

Examples of methods used to assess training effectiveness include the following:
- Testing in the training context
- Post-training surveys of training participants
- Surveys of manager satisfaction with post-training effects
- Assessment mechanisms embedded in courseware

TIP

Training effectiveness can change over time. Initially, training may be done using one medium or mode of delivery to train large numbers of people and another medium or mode of delivery to deliver ongoing training to new employees or transfers from other departments.

Measures can be taken to assess the benefits of training against both the project's and organization's objectives. Particular attention should be paid to the need for various training methods, such as training teams as integral work units. When used, work or process performance objectives should be unambiguous, observable, verifiable, and shared with course participants. The results of the training effectiveness assessment should be used to revise training materials as described in the Establish a Training Capability specific practice.

Example Work Products

1. Training effectiveness surveys
2. Training program performance assessments
3. Instructor evaluation forms
4. Training examinations

Subpractices

1. Assess in-progress or completed projects to determine whether staff knowledge is adequate for performing project tasks.
2. Provide a mechanism for assessing the effectiveness of each training course with respect to established organizational, project, or individual learning (or performance) objectives.
3. Obtain student evaluations of how well training activities met their needs.

OT

PRODUCT INTEGRATION
An Engineering Process Area at Maturity Level 3

Purpose

The purpose of Product Integration (PI) is to assemble the product from the product components, ensure that the product, as integrated, behaves properly (i.e., possesses the required functionality and quality attributes), and deliver the product.

HINT

To achieve problem-free integration, you need to prepare for product integration activities early in the project.

Introductory Notes

This process area addresses the integration of product components into more complex product components or into complete products.

The scope of this process area is to achieve complete product integration through progressive assembly of product components, in one stage or in incremental stages, according to a defined integration strategy and procedures. Throughout the process areas, where the terms "product" and "product component" are used, their intended meanings also encompass services, service systems, and their components.

A critical aspect of product integration is the management of internal and external interfaces of the products and product components to ensure compatibility among the interfaces. These interfaces are not limited to user interfaces, but also apply to interfaces among components of the product, including internal and external data sources, middleware, and other components that may or may not be within the development organization's control but on which the product relies. Attention should be paid to interface management throughout the project.

Product integration is more than just a one-time assembly of the product components at the conclusion of design and fabrication. Product integration can be conducted incrementally, using an iterative process of assembling product components, evaluating them, and then assembling more product components. It can be conducted using highly automated builds and continuous integration of the

TIP

In some engineering disciplines (e.g., mechanical engineering), the term *assembly* is generally preferred over *integration*. In PI, these two words are used interchangeably.

HINT

Many problems encountered in product integration are due to interface incompatibilities. Therefore, PI also addresses interface management.

PI

completed unit tested product. This process can begin with analysis and simulations (e.g., threads, rapid prototypes, virtual prototypes, physical prototypes) and steadily progress through increasingly more realistic increments until the final product is achieved. In each successive build, prototypes (virtual, rapid, or physical) are constructed, evaluated, improved, and reconstructed based on knowledge gained in the evaluation process. The degree of virtual versus physical prototyping required depends on the functionality of the design tools, the complexity of the product, and its associated risk. There is a high probability that the product, integrated in this manner, will pass product verification and validation. For some products and services, the last integration phase will occur when they are deployed at the intended operational site.

For product lines, products are assembled according to the product line production plan. The product line production plan specifies the assembly process, including which core assets to use and how product line variation is resolved within those core assets.

X-REF

See the definition of "product line" in the glossary.

TIP

Product integration typically proceeds in incremental stages. At each stage, a partial assembly is followed by evaluation. In early stages, prototypes may be used in place of product components that are unavailable. The last stage may integrate the complete product with the end user in the intended environment.

> In Agile environments, product integration is a frequent, often daily, activity. For example, for software, working code is continuously added to the code base in a process called "continuous integration." In addition to addressing continuous integration, the product integration strategy can address how supplier supplied components will be incorporated, how functionality will be built (in layers vs. "vertical slices"), and when to "refactor." The strategy should be established early in the project and be revised to reflect evolving and emerging component interfaces, external feeds, data exchange, and application program interfaces. (See "Interpreting CMMI When Using Agile Approaches" in Part I.)

Related Process Areas

Refer to the Requirements Development process area for more information about identifying interface requirements.

Refer to the Technical Solution process area for more information about designing interfaces using criteria.

Refer to the Validation process area for more information about performing validation.

Refer to the Verification process area for more information about performing verification.

Refer to the Configuration Management process area for more information about tracking and controlling changes.

Refer to the Decision Analysis and Resolution process area for more information about analyzing possible decisions using a formal evaluation process that evaluates identified alternatives against established criteria.

Refer to the Risk Management process area for more information about identifying risks and mitigating risks.

Refer to the Supplier Agreement Management process area for more information about managing the acquisition of products and services from suppliers.

Specific Goal and Practice Summary

SG 1 Prepare for Product Integration
    SP 1.1   Establish an Integration Strategy
    SP 1.2   Establish the Product Integration Environment
    SP 1.3   Establish Product Integration Procedures and Criteria
SG 2 Ensure Interface Compatibility
    SP 2.1   Review Interface Descriptions for Completeness
    SP 2.2   Manage Interfaces
SG 3 Assemble Product Components and Deliver the Product
    SP 3.1   Confirm Readiness of Product Components for Integration
    SP 3.2   Assemble Product Components
    SP 3.3   Evaluate Assembled Product Components
    SP 3.4   Package and Deliver the Product or Product Component

Specific Practices by Goal

SG 1 PREPARE FOR PRODUCT INTEGRATION

Preparation for product integration is conducted.

Preparing for the integration of product components involves establishing an integration strategy, establishing the environment for performing the integration, and establishing integration procedures and criteria. Preparation for integration starts early in the project.

SP 1.1 ESTABLISH AN INTEGRATION STRATEGY

Establish and maintain a product integration strategy.

The product integration strategy describes the approach for receiving, assembling, and evaluating the product components that comprise the product.

> **TIP**
>
> A passive approach to product integration is to wait until product components are ready to integrate to begin assembly and testing. PI recommends a proactive approach that initiates integration activities early in the project and performs integration activities concurrently with the practices of TS and SAM. Such an approach can affect the development schedules of the project and its suppliers.

PI

TIP

There are many possible approaches to receiving, assembling, and evaluating components. An integration strategy should provide a coherent end-to-end approach to accomplishing these activities.

A product integration strategy addresses items such as the following:

- Making product components available for integration (e.g., in what sequence)
- Assembling and evaluating as a single build or as a progression of incremental builds
- Including and testing features in each iteration when using iterative development
- Managing interfaces
- Using models, prototypes, and simulations to assist in evaluating an assembly, including its interfaces
- Establishing the product integration environment
- Defining procedures and criteria
- Making available the appropriate test tools and equipment
- Managing product hierarchy, architecture, and complexity
- Recording results of evaluations
- Handling exceptions

TIP

To be available for integration, product components need to be completed on time. Thus, the nature and timing of integration drives project schedules and when resources need to be available. Therefore, many management and engineering processes depend on the product integration strategy.

The integration strategy should also be aligned with the technical approach described in the Project Planning process area and harmonized with the selection of solutions and the design of product and product components in the Technical Solution process area.

Refer to the Technical Solution process area for more information about selecting product component solutions and implementing the design.

Refer to the Decision Analysis and Resolution process area for more information about analyzing possible decisions using a formal evaluation process that evaluates identified alternatives against established criteria.

Refer to the Project Planning process area for more information about establishing and maintaining plans that define project activities.

Refer to the Risk Management process area for more information about identifying risks and mitigating risks.

Refer to the Supplier Agreement Management process area for more information about managing the acquisition of products and services from suppliers.

The results of developing a product integration strategy are typically documented in a product integration plan, which is reviewed with stakeholders to promote commitment and understanding. Some of the items addressed in a product integration strategy are covered in more detail in the other specific practices and generic practices of this process area (e.g., environment, procedures and criteria, training, roles and responsibilities, involvement of relevant stakeholders).

Example Work Products

1. Product integration strategy
2. Rationale for selecting or rejecting alternative product integration strategies

Subpractices

1. Identify the product components to be integrated.
2. Identify the verifications to be performed during the integration of the product components.

   This identification includes verifications to be performed on interfaces.
3. Identify alternative product component integration strategies.

   Developing an integration strategy can involve specifying and evaluating several alternative integration strategies or sequences.
4. Select the best integration strategy.

   The availability of the following will need to be aligned or harmonized with the integration strategy: product components; the integration environment; test tools and equipment; procedures and criteria; relevant stakeholders; and staff who possess the appropriate skills.
5. Periodically review the product integration strategy and revise as needed.

   Assess the product integration strategy to ensure that variations in production and delivery schedules have not had an adverse impact on the integration sequence or compromised the factors on which earlier decisions were made.
6. Record the rationale for decisions made and deferred.

SP 1.2 ESTABLISH THE PRODUCT INTEGRATION ENVIRONMENT

Establish and maintain the environment needed to support the integration of the product components.

The environment for product integration can either be acquired or developed. To establish an environment, requirements for the purchase or development of equipment, software, or other resources will need to be developed. These requirements are gathered when implementing the processes associated with the Requirements Development process area. The product integration environment can include the reuse of existing organizational resources. The decision to acquire or develop the product integration environment is addressed in the processes associated with the Technical Solution process area.

Refer to the Technical Solution process area for more information about performing make, buy, or reuse analyses.

TIP

Besides product components, the integration strategy can also address integration with test equipment and assembly fixtures.

HINT

At each stage following an assembly, test whether the resulting assembly behaves as expected.

TIP

You can use a formal evaluation process to select an integration strategy or sequence from among alternatives. Criteria for selection can include the impact of the alternative on cost, schedule, performance, and risk.

TIP

Providing an integration environment to support product integration may be a significant endeavor best treated as a project.

PI

TIP

Consider what is required of the integration environment at each stage of integration according to the integration strategy established in SP 1.1.

The environment required at each step of the product integration process can include test equipment, simulators (taking the place of unavailable product components), pieces of real equipment, and recording devices.

Example Work Products

1. Verified environment for product integration
2. Support documentation for the product integration environment

Subpractices

1. Identify the requirements for the product integration environment.
2. Identify verification procedures and criteria for the product integration environment.
3. Decide whether to make or buy the needed product integration environment.

    Refer to the Supplier Agreement Management process area for more information about managing the acquisition of products and services from suppliers.

HINT

Revise the integration environment if the integration strategy significantly changes, additional prototypes and simulations are needed to replace product components that are delivered late, or the understanding of the operational environment changes significantly.

4. Develop an integration environment if a suitable environment cannot be acquired.

    For unprecedented, complex projects, the product integration environment can be a major development. As such, it would involve project planning, requirements development, technical solutions, verification, validation, and risk management.

5. Maintain the product integration environment throughout the project.
6. Dispose of those portions of the environment that are no longer useful.

TIP

This specific practice answers questions such as how to obtain product components to be assembled, how to assemble them, and what testing to perform. Also, criteria are established to answer questions such as when a component is ready for integration, what level of performance is required on each test, and what is acceptable validation and delivery of the final product.

SP 1.3 ESTABLISH PRODUCT INTEGRATION PROCEDURES AND CRITERIA

Establish and maintain procedures and criteria for integration of the product components.

Procedures for the integration of the product components can include such things as the number of incremental iterations to be performed and details of the expected tests and other evaluations to be carried out at each stage.

Criteria can indicate the readiness of a product component for integration or its acceptability.

Procedures and criteria for product integration address the following:

- Level of testing for build components
- Verification of interfaces
- Thresholds of performance deviation
- Derived requirements for the assembly and its external interfaces
- Allowable substitutions of components
- Testing environment parameters
- Limits on cost of testing
- Quality/cost tradeoffs for integration operations
- Probability of proper functioning
- Delivery rate and its variation
- Lead time from order to delivery
- Staff member availability
- Availability of the integration facility/line/environment

Criteria can be defined for how the product components are to be verified and the behaviors (functionality and quality attributes) they are expected to have. Criteria can be defined for how the assembled product components and final integrated product are to be validated and delivered.

Criteria can also constrain the degree of simulation permitted for a product component to pass a test, or can constrain the environment to be used for the integration test.

Pertinent parts of the schedule and criteria for assembly should be shared with suppliers of work products to reduce the occurrence of delays and component failure.

Refer to the Supplier Agreement Management process area for more information about executing the supplier agreement.

TIP

Criteria may impose limits or constraints on how testing is performed.

Example Work Products

1. Product integration procedures
2. Product integration criteria

Subpractices

1. Establish and maintain product integration procedures for the product components.
2. Establish and maintain criteria for product component integration and evaluation.
3. Establish and maintain criteria for validation and delivery of the integrated product.

PI

TIP

The source of many product integration problems lies in incompatible interfaces. SG 2 is designed to help ensure that interfaces are compatible.

X-REF

Because of the importance of interfaces to effective product development, interfaces are addressed in multiple places: Interface requirements is covered in RD SP 2.3, design of interfaces is covered in TS SP 2.3, and ensuring interface compatibility is covered in PI SG 2.

TIP

These reviews should be *periodic* to ensure consistency is maintained between interface descriptions and product components (see Subpractice 3) and that new interfaces are not overlooked.

TIP

Interfaces with environments such as product integration, verification, and validation environments, as well as operational, maintenance, and support environments, should be addressed.

TIP

Interface data is all the data associated with product component interfaces, including requirements, designs, and interface descriptions.

SG 2   ENSURE INTERFACE COMPATIBILITY

The product component interfaces, both internal and external, are compatible.

Many product integration problems arise from unknown or uncontrolled aspects of both internal and external interfaces. Effective management of product component interface requirements, specifications, and designs helps ensure that implemented interfaces will be complete and compatible.

SP 2.1   REVIEW INTERFACE DESCRIPTIONS FOR COMPLETENESS

Review interface descriptions for coverage and completeness.

The interfaces should include, in addition to product component interfaces, all the interfaces with the product integration environment.

Example Work Products

1. Categories of interfaces
2. List of interfaces per category
3. Mapping of the interfaces to the product components and the product integration environment

Subpractices

1. Review interface data for completeness and ensure complete coverage of all interfaces.

   Consider all the product components and prepare a relationship table. Interfaces are usually classified in three main classes: environmental, physical, and functional. Typical categories for these classes include the following: mechanical, fluid, sound, electrical, climatic, electromagnetic, thermal, message, and the human-machine or human interface.

   Examples of interfaces (e.g., for mechanical or electronic components) that can be classified within these three classes include the following:
   - Mechanical interfaces (e.g., weight and size, center of gravity, clearance of parts in operation, space required for maintenance, fixed links, mobile links, shocks and vibrations received from the bearing structure)
   - Noise interfaces (e.g., noise transmitted by the structure, noise transmitted in the air, acoustics)
   - Climatic interfaces (e.g., temperature, humidity, pressure, salinity)

   Continues

Continued

- Thermal interfaces (e.g., heat dissipation, transmission of heat to the bearing structure, air conditioning characteristics)
- Fluid interfaces (e.g., fresh water inlet/outlet, seawater inlet/outlet for a naval/coastal product, air conditioning, compressed air, nitrogen, fuel, lubricating oil, exhaust gas outlet)
- Electrical interfaces (e.g., power supply consumption by network with transients and peak values; nonsensitive control signal for power supply and communications; sensitive signal [e.g., analog links]; disturbing signal [e.g., microwave]; grounding signal to comply with the TEMPEST standard)
- Electromagnetic interfaces (e.g., magnetic field, radio and radar links, optical band link wave guides, coaxial and optical fibers)
- Human-machine interface (e.g., audio or voice synthesis, audio or voice recognition, display [analog dial, liquid crystal display, indicators' light emitting diodes], manual controls [pedal, joystick, track ball, keyboard, push buttons, touch screen])
- Message interfaces (e.g., origination, destination, stimulus, protocols, data characteristics)

TIP

Overlooked or incompletely described interfaces are risks to be identified and managed (RSKM). The realization of these risks in some business situations may lead to safety recalls and be very costly.

HINT

Use these examples (and others) to ensure that all aspects of an interface are addressed in an interface description.

2. Ensure that product components and interfaces are marked to ensure easy and correct connection to the joining product component.

3. Periodically review the adequacy of interface descriptions.

   Once established, the interface descriptions should be periodically reviewed to ensure there is no deviation between the existing descriptions and the products being developed, processed, produced, or bought.

   The interface descriptions for product components should be reviewed with relevant stakeholders to avoid misinterpretations, reduce delays, and prevent the development of interfaces that do not work properly.

TIP

For mechanical or electrical product components, markings can help ensure correct connections.

HINT

Include stakeholders internal and external to the project (e.g., suppliers).

SP 2.2 Manage Interfaces

Manage internal and external interface definitions, designs, and changes for products and product components.

Interface requirements drive the development of the interfaces necessary to integrate product components. Managing product and product component interfaces starts early in the development of the product. The definitions and designs for interfaces affect not only the product components and external systems, but can also affect the verification and validation environments.

HINT

Manage interfaces early in the project to help prevent inconsistencies from arising between product components.

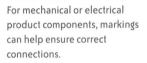

Refer to the Requirements Development process area for more information about identifying interface requirements.

Refer to the Technical Solution process area for more information about designing interfaces using criteria.

Refer to the Configuration Management process area for more information about establishing and maintaining the integrity of work products using configuration identification, configuration control, configuration status accounting, and configuration audits.

Refer to the Manage Requirements Changes specific practice in the Requirements Management process area for more information about managing the changes to the interface requirements.

X-REF

Interface descriptions are typically placed under configuration management (see GP 2.6) so that changes in status are recorded and communicated (see CM SP 3.1).

Management of the interfaces includes maintenance of the consistency of the interfaces throughout the life of the product, compliance with architectural decisions and constraints, and resolution of conflict, noncompliance, and change issues. The management of interfaces between products acquired from suppliers and other products or product components is critical for success of the project.

Refer to the Supplier Agreement Management process area for more information about managing the acquisition of products and services from suppliers.

The interfaces should include, in addition to product component interfaces, all the interfaces with the environment as well as other environments for verification, validation, operations, and support.

The interface changes are documented, maintained, and readily accessible.

Example Work Products

1. Table of relationships among the product components and the external environment (e.g., main power supply, fastening product, computer bus system)
2. Table of relationships among the different product components
3. List of agreed-to interfaces defined for each pair of product components, when applicable
4. Reports from the interface control working group meetings
5. Action items for updating interfaces
6. Application program interface (API)
7. Updated interface description or agreement

TIP

These tables in the example work products are developed as part of the previous specific practice (SP 2.1), but here they have a role in managing interfaces.

TIP

An API is the interface that a computer system, library, or application provides to allow other computer programs to make requests for service and/or exchange data.

Subpractices

1. Ensure the compatibility of the interfaces throughout the life of the product.
2. Resolve conflict, noncompliance, and change issues.

3. Maintain a repository for interface data accessible to project participants.

> A common accessible repository for interface data provides a mechanism to ensure that everyone knows where the current interface data reside and can access them for use.

SG 3 ASSEMBLE PRODUCT COMPONENTS AND DELIVER THE PRODUCT

Verified product components are assembled and the integrated, verified, and validated product is delivered.

Integration of product components proceeds according to the product integration strategy and procedures. Before integration, each product component should be confirmed to be compliant with its interface requirements. Product components are assembled into larger, more complex product components. These assembled product components are checked for correct interoperation. This process continues until product integration is complete. If, during this process, problems are identified, the problem should be documented and a corrective action process initiated.

The timely receipt of needed product components and the involvement of the right people contribute to the successful integration of the product components that compose the product.

SP 3.1 CONFIRM READINESS OF PRODUCT COMPONENTS FOR INTEGRATION

Confirm, prior to assembly, that each product component required to assemble the product has been properly identified, behaves according to its description, and that the product component interfaces comply with the interface descriptions.

Refer to the Verification process area for more information about performing verification.

The purpose of this specific practice is to ensure that the properly identified product component that meets its description can actually be assembled according to the product integration strategy and procedures. The product components are checked for quantity, obvious damage, and consistency between the product component and interface descriptions.

Those who conduct product integration are ultimately responsible for checking to make sure everything is proper with the product components before assembly.

TIP

Although the primary focus of SG 3 is on PI, it summarizes concepts from three PAs: PI, VER, and VAL.

X-REF

If problems are identified before, during, or after an integration stage, an exception report is written (see PMC SG 2).

TIP

The first three specific practices of SG 3 progressively integrate product components in the integration environment using the integration strategy, procedures, and criteria established in SG 1 until the complete product is assembled. The final specific practice is responsible for product packaging, delivery, and installation.

TIP

It may seem as if these practices were written for assembling mechanical or electronic product components, but with the exception of a few notes and subpractices, they also apply more generally, including to software.

PI

Example Work Products

1. Acceptance documents for the received product components
2. Delivery receipts
3. Checked packing lists
4. Exception reports
5. Waivers

Subpractices

1. Track the status of all product components as soon as they become available for integration.
2. Ensure that product components are delivered to the product integration environment in accordance with the product integration strategy and procedures.
3. Confirm the receipt of each properly identified product component.
4. Ensure that each received product component meets its description.
5. Check the configuration status against the expected configuration.
6. Perform a pre-check (e.g., by a visual inspection, using basic measures) of all the physical interfaces before connecting product components together.

SP 3.2 ASSEMBLE PRODUCT COMPONENTS

Assemble product components according to the product integration strategy and procedures.

The assembly activities of this specific practice and the evaluation activities of the next specific practice are conducted iteratively, from the initial product components, through the interim assemblies of product components, to the product as a whole.

Example Work Products

1. Assembled product or product components

Subpractices

1. Ensure the readiness of the product integration environment.
2. Conduct integration in accordance with the product integration strategy, procedures, and criteria.

    Record all appropriate information (e.g., configuration status, serial numbers of the product components, types, calibration date of the meters).
3. Revise the product integration strategy, procedures, and criteria as appropriate.

HINT

Assembly (SP 3.2) and evaluation (SP 3.3) occur at each integration stage. Evaluate the assembled product components before proceeding to the next integration stage.

HINT

If the integration does not proceed as planned (e.g., a product component is not ready for integration), you may have to revise the integration strategy, procedures, criteria, and plans.

SP 3.3 Evaluate Assembled Product Components

Evaluate assembled product components for interface compatibility.

Refer to the Validation process area for more information about performing validation.

Refer to the Verification process area for more information about performing verification.

This evaluation involves examining and testing assembled product components for performance, suitability, or readiness using the product integration procedures, criteria, and environment. It is performed as appropriate for different stages of assembly of product components as identified in the product integration strategy and procedures. The product integration strategy and procedures can define a more refined integration and evaluation sequence than might be envisioned just by examining the product hierarchy or architecture. For example, if an assembly of product components is composed of four less complex product components, the integration strategy will not necessarily call for the simultaneous integration and evaluation of the four units as one. Rather, the four less complex units can be integrated progressively, one at a time, with an evaluation after each assembly operation prior to realizing the more complex product component that matched the specification in the product architecture. Alternatively, the product integration strategy and procedures could have determined that only a final evaluation was the best one to perform.

Example Work Products

1. Exception reports
2. Interface evaluation reports
3. Product integration summary reports

Subpractices

1. Conduct the evaluation of assembled product components following the product integration strategy, procedures, and criteria.
2. Record the evaluation results.

Example results include the following:
- Any adaptation required to the integration procedure or criteria
- Any change to the product configuration (spare parts, new release)
- Evaluation procedure or criteria deviations

TIP

We also addressed interface compatibility in SG 2. Here in SP 3.3, the focus is on evaluating an assembly for interface compatibility. In this practice, the evaluations indicated by the integration procedures and criteria established in SP 1.3 are conducted.

TIP

Integration may be accomplished in multiple stages as opposed to a single stage.

TIP

Evaluations include tests for interface compatibility and of how well the assembled product components interoperate, and may include tests involving end users. Thus, the evaluations may involve both verification and validation.

HINT

Remember to document any adaptation, change, or deviation from the established integration procedure or criteria.

PI

SP 3.4 PACKAGE AND DELIVER THE PRODUCT OR PRODUCT COMPONENT

Package the assembled product or product component and deliver it to the customer.

Refer to the Validation process area for more information about performing validation.

Refer to the Verification process area for more information about performing verification.

The packaging requirements for some products can be addressed in their specifications and verification criteria. This handling of requirements is especially important when items are stored and transported by the customer. In such cases, there can be a spectrum of environmental and stress conditions specified for the package. In other circumstances, factors such as the following can become important:

- Economy and ease of transportation (e.g., containerization)
- Accountability (e.g., shrink wrapping)
- Ease and safety of unpacking (e.g., sharp edges, strength of binding methods, childproofing, environmental friendliness of packing material, weight)

TIP

Depending on the nature of the product, packaging may be relatively straightforward (e.g., distributing software on CDs) or complicated (e.g., packaging and transporting large HVAC systems to office buildings).

The adjustment required to fit product components together in the factory could be different from the one required to fit product components together when installed on the operational site. In that case, the product's logbook for the customer should be used to record such specific parameters.

Example Work Products

1. Packaged product or product components
2. Delivery documentation

Subpractices

1. Review the requirements, design, product, verification results, and documentation to ensure that issues affecting the packaging and delivery of the product are identified and resolved.
2. Use effective methods to package and deliver the assembled product.

> Examples of software packaging and delivery methods include the following:
> - Magnetic tape
> - Diskettes
>
> *Continues*

Continued

• Hardcopy documents
• Compact disks
• Other electronic distribution such as the Internet

3. Satisfy the applicable requirements and standards for packaging and delivering the product.

Examples of requirements and standards include ones for safety, the environment, security, transportability, and disposal.

Examples of requirements and standards for packaging and delivering software include the following:

• Type of storage and delivery media
• Custodians of the master and backup copies
• Required documentation
• Copyrights
• License provisions
• Security of the software

4. Prepare the operational site for installation of the product.

Preparing the operational site can be the responsibility of the customer or end users.

5. Deliver the product and related documentation and confirm receipt.

6. Install the product at the operational site and confirm correct operation.

Installing the product can be the responsibility of the customer or the end users. In some circumstances, little may need to be done to confirm correct operation. In other circumstances, final verification of the integrated product occurs at the operational site.

X-REF

A product installation process (TS SP 3.2) should describe how to prepare a site for product installation.

PI

PROJECT MONITORING AND CONTROL
A Project Management Process Area at Maturity Level 2

Purpose

The purpose of Project Monitoring and Control (PMC) is to provide an understanding of the project's progress so that appropriate corrective actions can be taken when the project's performance deviates significantly from the plan.

Introductory Notes

A project's documented plan is the basis for monitoring activities, communicating status, and taking corrective action. Progress is primarily determined by comparing actual work product and task attributes, effort, cost, and schedule to the plan at prescribed milestones or control levels in the project schedule or WBS. Appropriate visibility of progress enables timely corrective action to be taken when performance deviates significantly from the plan. A deviation is significant if, when left unresolved, it precludes the project from meeting its objectives.

The term "project plan" is used throughout this process area to refer to the overall plan for controlling the project.

When actual status deviates significantly from expected values, corrective actions are taken as appropriate. These actions can require replanning, which can include revising the original plan, establishing new agreements, or including additional mitigation activities in the current plan.

Related Process Areas

Refer to the Measurement and Analysis process area for more information about providing measurement results.

TIP

In the CMMI for Services Model, this process area is called Work Monitoring and Control.

TIP

PP provides the overall plan and PMC tracks activities against the plan.

TIP

Initially, the organization may have a reactive culture. However, as monitoring and control of activities become routine, project managers and staff begin to anticipate problems and success in advance.

TIP

Throughout the other PAs, when corrective action is needed, PMC is referenced.

Refer to the Project Planning process area for more information about establishing and maintaining plans that define project activities.

Specific Goal and Practice Summary

SG 1 Monitor the Project Against the Plan
    SP 1.1   Monitor Project Planning Parameters
    SP 1.2   Monitor Commitments
    SP 1.3   Monitor Project Risks
    SP 1.4   Monitor Data Management
    SP 1.5   Monitor Stakeholder Involvement
    SP 1.6   Conduct Progress Reviews
    SP 1.7   Conduct Milestone Reviews
SG 2 Manage Corrective Action to Closure
    SP 2.1   Analyze Issues
    SP 2.2   Take Corrective Action
    SP 2.3   Manage Corrective Actions

Specific Practices by Goal

SG 1　MONITOR THE PROJECT AGAINST THE PLAN

Actual project progress and performance are monitored against the project plan.

X-REF

The project plan was developed in PP.

SP 1.1　MONITOR PROJECT PLANNING PARAMETERS

Monitor actual values of project planning parameters against the project plan.

Project planning parameters constitute typical indicators of project progress and performance and include attributes of work products and tasks, costs, effort, and schedule. Attributes of the work products and tasks include size, complexity, service level, availability, weight, form, fit, and function. The frequency of monitoring parameters should be considered.

TIP

Actual values are used as "historical data" to provide a basis for estimates in planning.

Monitoring typically involves measuring actual values of project planning parameters, comparing actual values to estimates in the plan, and identifying significant deviations. Recording actual values of project planning parameters includes recording associated contextual information to help understand measures. An analysis of the impact that significant deviations have on determining the corrective actions to take is handled in specific goal 2 and its specific practices in this process area.

Example Work Products

1. Records of project performance
2. Records of significant deviations
3. Cost performance reports

Subpractices

1. Monitor progress against the schedule.

TIP

These subpractices mirror the specific practices in PP.

> Progress monitoring typically includes the following:
> - Periodically measuring the actual completion of activities and milestones
> - Comparing actual completion of activities and milestones against the project plan schedule
> - Identifying significant deviations from the project plan schedule estimates

2. Monitor the project's costs and expended effort.

> Effort and cost monitoring typically includes the following:
> - Periodically measuring the actual effort and costs expended and staff assigned
> - Comparing actual effort, costs, staffing, and training to the project plan budget and estimates
> - Identifying significant deviations from the project plan budget and estimates

3. Monitor the attributes of work products and tasks.

   Refer to the Measurement and Analysis process area for more information about developing and sustaining a measurement capability used to support management information needs.

   Refer to the Project Planning process area for more information about establishing estimates of work product and task attributes.

> Monitoring the attributes of work products and tasks typically includes the following:
> - Periodically measuring the actual attributes of work products and tasks, such as size, complexity, or service levels (and changes to these attributes)
> - Comparing the actual attributes of work products and tasks (and changes to these attributes) to the project plan estimates
> - Identifying significant deviations from the project plan estimates

4. Monitor resources provided and used.

Refer to the Project Planning process area for more information about planning the project's resources.

Examples of resources include the following:
- Physical facilities
- Computers, peripherals, and software
- Networks
- Security environment
- Project staff
- Processes

---

5. Monitor the knowledge and skills of project staff.

Refer to the Project Planning process area for more information about planning needed knowledge and skills.

Monitoring the knowledge and skills of project staff typically includes the following:
- Periodically measuring the acquisition of knowledge and skills by project staff
- Comparing the actual training obtained to that documented in the project plan
- Identifying significant deviations from the project plan estimates

---

6. Document significant deviations in project planning parameters.

SP 1.2 MONITOR COMMITMENTS

Monitor commitments against those identified in the project plan.

Example Work Products

1. Records of commitment reviews

Subpractices

1. Regularly review commitments (both external and internal).
2. Identify commitments that have not been satisfied or are at significant risk of not being satisfied.
3. Document the results of commitment reviews.

TIP

Situations may prevent appropriate follow-through with commitments, especially in an immature organization. Therefore, it is necessary to monitor commitments and take corrective action when commitments change.

SP 1.3 MONITOR PROJECT RISKS

Monitor risks against those identified in the project plan.

Refer to the Project Planning process area for more information about identifying project risks.

Refer to the Risk Management process area for more information about identifying potential problems before they occur so that risk handling activities can be planned and invoked as needed across the life of the product or project to mitigate adverse impacts on achieving objectives.

TIP

SP 1.3 checks the status of the risks that were identified in PP. This practice is reactive and involves minimal risk management activities. For more complete and proactive handling of project risks, refer to RSKM.

Example Work Products

1. Records of project risk monitoring

Subpractices

1. Periodically review the documentation of risks in the context of the project's current status and circumstances.

2. Revise the documentation of risks as additional information becomes available.

   As projects progress (especially projects of long duration or continuous operation), new risks arise. It is important to identify and analyze these new risks. For example, software, equipment, and tools in use can become obsolete; or key staff can gradually lose skills in areas of particular long-term importance to the project and organization.

3. Communicate the risk status to relevant stakeholders.

> Examples of risk status include the following:
> • A change in the probability that the risk occurs
> • A change in risk priority

SP 1.4 MONITOR DATA MANAGEMENT

Monitor the management of project data against the project plan.

Refer to the Plan Data Management specific practice in the Project Planning process area for more information about identifying types of data to be managed and how to plan for their management.

Data management activities should be monitored to ensure that data management requirements are being satisfied. Depending on the results of monitoring and changes in project requirements, situation, or status, it may be necessary to re-plan the project's data management activities.

Example Work Products

1. Records of data management

Subpractices

1. Periodically review data management activities against their description in the project plan.
2. Identify and document significant issues and their impacts.

> An example of a significant issue is when stakeholders do not have the access to project data they need to fulfill their roles as relevant stakeholders.

3. Document results of data management activity reviews.

SP 1.5 MONITOR STAKEHOLDER INVOLVEMENT

Monitor stakeholder involvement against the project plan.

Refer to the Plan Stakeholder Involvement specific practice in the Project Planning process area for more information about identifying relevant stakeholders and planning appropriate involvement with them.

TIP

In some plans, a specific stakeholder may be identified; whereas other stakeholders will be identified by role such as quality assurance representative.

Stakeholder involvement should be monitored to ensure that appropriate interactions occur. Depending on the results of monitoring and changes in project requirements, situation, or status, it may be necessary to re-plan stakeholder involvement.

> In Agile environments, the sustained involvement of customer and potential end users in the project's product development activities can be crucial to project success; thus, customer and end-user involvement in project activities should be monitored. (See "Interpreting CMMI When Using Agile Approaches" in Part I.)

Example Work Products

1. Records of stakeholder involvement

Subpractices

1. Periodically review the status of stakeholder involvement.
2. Identify and document significant issues and their impacts.
3. Document the results of stakeholder involvement status reviews.

SP 1.6 CONDUCT PROGRESS REVIEWS

Periodically review the project's progress, performance, and issues.

A "project's progress" is the project's status as viewed at a particular time when the project activities performed so far and their results and impacts are reviewed with relevant stakeholders (especially project representatives and project management) to determine whether there are significant issues or performance shortfalls to be addressed.

Progress reviews are project reviews to keep relevant stakeholders informed. These project reviews can be informal and may not be specified explicitly in project plans.

Example Work Products

1. Documented project review results

Subpractices

1. Regularly communicate status on assigned activities and work products to relevant stakeholders.

   Managers, staff, customers, end users, suppliers, and other relevant stakeholders are included in reviews as appropriate.

2. Review the results of collecting and analyzing measures for controlling the project.

   The measurements reviewed can include measures of customer satisfaction.

   Refer to the Measurement and Analysis process area for more information about aligning measurement and analysis activities and providing measurement results.

3. Identify and document significant issues and deviations from the plan.

4. Document change requests and problems identified in work products and processes.

   Refer to the Configuration Management process area for more information about tracking and controlling changes.

5. Document the results of reviews.

6. Track change requests and problem reports to closure.

SP 1.7 CONDUCT MILESTONE REVIEWS

Review the project's accomplishments and results at selected project milestones.

Refer to the Establish the Budget and Schedule specific practice in the Project Planning process area for more information about identifying major milestones.

> **TIP**
> Progress reviews are held regularly (e.g., weekly, monthly, or quarterly).

> **TIP**
> Milestones are major events in a project. If you are using a project lifecycle model, milestones may be predetermined.

PMC

Milestones are pre-planned events or points in time at which a thorough review of status is conducted to understand how well stakeholder requirements are being met. (If the project includes a developmental milestone, then the review is conducted to ensure that the assumptions and requirements associated with that milestone are being met.) Milestones can be associated with the overall project or a particular service type or instance. Milestones can thus be event based or calendar based.

Milestone reviews are planned during project planning and are typically formal reviews.

Progress reviews and milestone reviews need not be held separately. A single review can address the intent of both. For example, a single pre-planned review can evaluate progress, issues, and performance up through a planned time period (or milestone) against the plan's expectations.

Depending on the project, "project startup" and "project close-out" could be phases covered by milestone reviews.

Example Work Products

1. Documented milestone review results

Subpractices

1. Conduct milestone reviews with relevant stakeholders at meaningful points in the project's schedule, such as the completion of selected phases.

    Managers, staff, customers, end users, suppliers, and other relevant stakeholders are included in milestone reviews as appropriate.
2. Review commitments, the plan, status, and risks of the project.
3. Identify and document significant issues and their impacts.
4. Document results of the review, action items, and decisions.
5. Track action items to closure.

SG 2   MANAGE CORRECTIVE ACTION TO CLOSURE

HINT

Managing corrective action to closure is critical. It is not enough to identify the action item; you must confirm that it has been completed.

Corrective actions are managed to closure when the project's performance or results deviate significantly from the plan.

SP 2.1   ANALYZE ISSUES

Collect and analyze issues and determine corrective actions to address them.

Example Work Products

1. List of issues requiring corrective actions

Subpractices

1. Gather issues for analysis.

   Issues are collected from reviews and the execution of other processes.

Examples of issues to be gathered include the following:

- Issues discovered when performing technical reviews, verification, and validation
- Significant deviations in project planning parameters from estimates in the project plan
- Commitments (either internal or external) that have not been satisfied
- Significant changes in risk status
- Data access, collection, privacy, or security issues
- Stakeholder representation or involvement issues
- Product, tool, or environment transition assumptions (or other customer or supplier commitments) that have not been achieved

---

2. Analyze issues to determine the need for corrective action.

   Refer to the Establish the Budget and Schedule specific practice in the Project Planning process area for more information about corrective action criteria.

   Corrective action is required when the issue, if left unresolved, may prevent the project from meeting its objectives.

SP 2.2 TAKE CORRECTIVE ACTION

Take corrective action on identified issues.

Example Work Products

1. Corrective action plans

Subpractices

1. Determine and document the appropriate actions needed to address identified issues.

   Refer to the Project Planning process area for more information about developing a project plan.

Examples of potential actions include the following:
- Modifying the statement of work
- Modifying requirements

Continues

TIP

In some cases, the corrective action can be to monitor the situation. A corrective action does not always result in a complete solution to the problem.

Continued

- Revising estimates and plans
- Renegotiating commitments
- Adding resources
- Changing processes
- Revising project risks

2. Review and get agreement with relevant stakeholders on the actions to be taken.
3. Negotiate changes to internal and external commitments.

SP 2.3 MANAGE CORRECTIVE ACTIONS

Manage corrective actions to closure.

Example Work Products

1. Corrective action results

Subpractices

1. Monitor corrective actions for their completion.
2. Analyze results of corrective actions to determine the effectiveness of the corrective actions.
3. Determine and document appropriate actions to correct deviations from planned results from performing corrective actions.

    Lessons learned as a result of taking corrective action can be inputs to planning and risk management processes.

PROJECT PLANNING
A Project Management Process Area at Maturity Level 2

Purpose

The purpose of Project Planning (PP) is to establish and maintain plans that define project activities.

Introductory Notes

One of the keys to effectively managing a project is project planning. The Project Planning process area involves the following activities:

- Developing the project plan
- Interacting with relevant stakeholders appropriately
- Getting commitment to the plan
- Maintaining the plan

Planning includes estimating the attributes of work products and tasks, determining the resources needed, negotiating commitments, producing a schedule, and identifying and analyzing project risks. Iterating through these activities may be necessary to establish the project plan. The project plan provides the basis for performing and controlling project activities that address commitments with the project's customer. (See the definition of "project" in the glossary.)

The project plan is usually revised as the project progresses to address changes in requirements and commitments, inaccurate estimates, corrective actions, and process changes. Specific practices describing both planning and replanning are contained in this process area.

The term "project plan" is used throughout this process area to refer to the overall plan for controlling the project. The project plan can be a stand-alone document or be distributed across multiple documents. In either case, a coherent picture of who does what should be included. Likewise, monitoring and control can be centralized or

TIP

In the CMMI for Services Model, this process area is called Work Planning.

TIP

In planning, you determine the requirements to be fulfilled, the tasks to perform, and the resources and coordination required. This information is the basis for obtaining the needed resources and commitments.

TIP

The plan is a declaration that the work has been rationally thought through and requests for resources are credible. If you ask management to commit resources, they want to know it is worth the investment. A project plan helps you convince them.

TIP

Project planning is not just for large projects. Research with the Personal Software Process (PSP) has demonstrated that individuals working on tasks lasting only a few hours increase overall quality and productivity by making time to plan.

X-REF

PMC addresses tracking of project activities in the plan.

distributed, as long as at the project level a coherent picture of project status can be maintained.

For product lines, there are multiple sets of work activities that would benefit from the practices of this process area. These work activities include the creation and maintenance of the core assets, developing products to be built using the core assets, and orchestrating the overall product line effort to support and coordinate the operations of the inter-related work groups and their activities.

> In Agile environments, performing incremental development involves planning, monitoring, controlling, and re-planning more frequently than in more traditional development environments. While a high-level plan for the overall project or work effort is typically established, teams will estimate, plan, and carry out the actual work an increment or iteration at a time. Teams typically do not forecast beyond what is known about the project or iteration, except for anticipating risks, major events, and large-scale influences and constraints. Estimates reflect iteration and team specific factors that influence the time, effort, resources, and risks to accomplish the iteration. Teams plan, monitor, and adjust plans during each iteration as often as it takes (e.g., daily). Commitments to plans are demonstrated when tasks are assigned and accepted during iteration planning, user stories are elaborated or estimated, and iterations are populated with tasks from a maintained backlog of work. (See "Interpreting CMMI When Using Agile Approaches" in Part I.)

Related Process Areas

Refer to the Requirements Development process area for more information about eliciting, analyzing, and establishing customer, product, and product component requirements.

Refer to the Technical Solution process area for more information about selecting, designing, and implementing solutions to requirements.

Refer to the Measurement and Analysis process area for more information about specifying measures.

Refer to the Requirements Management process area for more information about managing requirements.

Refer to the Risk Management process area for more information about identifying and analyzing risks and mitigating risks.

Specific Goal and Practice Summary

SG 1 Establish Estimates
    SP 1.1   Estimate the Scope of the Project
    SP 1.2   Establish Estimates of Work Product and Task Attributes
    SP 1.3   Define Project Lifecycle Phases
    SP 1.4   Estimate Effort and Cost

SG 2 Develop a Project Plan
    SP 2.1   Establish the Budget and Schedule
    SP 2.2   Identify Project Risks
    SP 2.3   Plan Data Management
    SP 2.4   Plan the Project's Resources
    SP 2.5   Plan Needed Knowledge and Skills
    SP 2.6   Plan Stakeholder Involvement
    SP 2.7   Establish the Project Plan

SG 3 Obtain Commitment to the Plan
    SP 3.1   Review Plans That Affect the Project
    SP 3.2   Reconcile Work and Resource Levels
    SP 3.3   Obtain Plan Commitment

Specific Practices by Goal

SG 1 ESTABLISH ESTIMATES

Estimates of project planning parameters are established and maintained.

Project planning parameters include all information needed by the project to perform necessary planning, organizing, staffing, directing, coordinating, reporting, and budgeting.

Estimates of planning parameters should have a sound basis to instill confidence that plans based on these estimates are capable of supporting project objectives.

Factors to consider when estimating these parameters include project requirements, including product requirements, requirements imposed by the organization, requirements imposed by the customer, and other requirements that affect the project

Documentation of the estimating rationale and supporting data is needed for stakeholder review and commitment to the plan and for maintenance of the plan as the project progresses.

X-REF

SG 1 focuses on providing estimates of project planning parameters; actual values are monitored in PMC SP 1.1.

TIP

Project planning parameters are a key to managing a project. Planning parameters primarily include size, effort, and cost.

TIP

The basis for estimates can include historical data, the judgment of experienced estimators, and other factors.

HINT

Use this rationale to help justify to management why you need resources and why the effort and schedule estimates are appropriate.

PP

SP 1.1 *ESTIMATE THE SCOPE OF THE PROJECT*

Establish a top-level work breakdown structure (WBS) to estimate the scope of the project.

The WBS evolves with the project. A top-level WBS can serve to structure initial estimating. The development of a WBS divides the overall project into an interconnected set of manageable components.

Typically, the WBS is a product, work product, or task oriented structure that provides a scheme for identifying and organizing the logical units of work to be managed, which are called "work packages." The WBS provides a reference and organizational mechanism for assigning effort, schedule, and responsibility and is used as the underlying framework to plan, organize, and control the work done on the project.

Some projects use the term "contract WBS" to refer to the portion of the WBS placed under contract (possibly the entire WBS). Not all projects have a contract WBS (e.g., internally funded development).

Example Work Products

1. Task descriptions
2. Work package descriptions
3. WBS

Subpractices

1. Develop a WBS.

   The WBS provides a scheme for organizing the project's work. The WBS should permit the identification of the following items:
   - Risks and their mitigation tasks
   - Tasks for deliverables and supporting activities
   - Tasks for skill and knowledge acquisition
   - Tasks for the development of needed support plans, such as configuration management, quality assurance, and verification plans
   - Tasks for the integration and management of nondevelopmental items

2. Define the work packages in sufficient detail so that estimates of project tasks, responsibilities, and schedule can be specified.

   The top-level WBS is intended to help gauge the project work effort for tasks and organizational roles and responsibilities. The amount of detail in the WBS at this level helps in developing realistic schedules, thereby minimizing the need for management reserve.

3. Identify products and product components to be externally acquired.

   Refer to the Supplier Agreement Management process area for more information about managing the acquisition of products and services from suppliers.

4. Identify work products to be reused.

SP 1.2 ESTABLISH ESTIMATES OF WORK PRODUCT AND TASK ATTRIBUTES

Establish and maintain estimates of work product and task attributes.

Size is the primary input to many models used to estimate effort, cost, and schedule. Models can also be based on other attributes such as service level, connectivity, complexity, availability, and structure.

> Examples of attributes to estimate include the following:
> - Number and complexity of requirements
> - Number and complexity of interfaces
> - Volume of data
> - Number of functions
> - Function points
> - Source lines of code
> - Number of classes and objects
> - Team velocity and complexity
> - Number of pages
> - Number of inputs and outputs
> - Number of technical risk items
> - Number of database tables
> - Number of fields in data tables
> - Architecture elements
> - Experience of project participants
> - Amount of code to be reused versus created
> - Number of logic gates for integrated circuits
> - Number of parts (e.g., printed circuit boards, components, mechanical parts)
> - Physical constraints (e.g., weight, volume)
> - Geographic dispersal of project members
> - Proximity of customers, end users, and suppliers
> - How agreeable or difficult the customer is
> - Quality and "cleanliness" of the existing code base

X-REF

Reuse is also addressed in TS.

PP

HINT

Learn to quantify the resources needed for particular tasks by associating size measures with each type of work product and building historical data. By collecting historical data from projects, you can learn how measured size relates to the resources consumed by tasks. This knowledge can then be used when planning the next project.

X-REF

For more information on estimating, see Richard D. Stutzke, *Estimating Software-Intensive Systems: Projects, Products, and Processes*, SEI Series in Software Engineering, 2005.

TIP

This list purposely provides a lengthy list of examples. Rarely would you see all of these attributes addressed in any plan.

The estimates should be consistent with project requirements to determine the project's effort, cost, and schedule. A relative level of difficulty or complexity should be assigned for each size attribute.

Example Work Products

1. Size and complexity of tasks and work products
2. Estimating models
3. Attribute estimates
4. Technical approach

Subpractices

1. Determine the technical approach for the project.

   The technical approach defines a top-level strategy for development of the product. It includes decisions on architectural features, such as distributed or client/server; state-of-the-art or established technologies to be applied, such as robotics, composite materials, or artificial intelligence; and the functionality and quality attributes expected in the final products, such as safety, security, and ergonomics.

2. Use appropriate methods to determine the attributes of the work products and tasks to be used to estimate resource requirements.

   Methods for determining size and complexity should be based on validated models or historical data.

   The methods for determining attributes evolve as the understanding of the relationship of product characteristics to attributes increases.

3. Estimate the attributes of work products and tasks.

> Examples of work products for which size estimates are made include the following:
> - Deliverable and nondeliverable work products
> - Documents and files
> - Operational and support hardware, firmware, and software

SP 1.3 DEFINE PROJECT LIFECYCLE PHASES

Define project lifecycle phases on which to scope the planning effort.

The determination of a project's lifecycle phases provides for planned periods of evaluation and decision making. These periods are normally defined to support logical decision points at which the appropriateness of continued reliance on the project plan and strategy is determined and significant commitments are made concerning resources. Such points provide planned events at which project course corrections and determinations of future scope and cost can be made.

Understanding the project lifecycle is crucial in determining the scope of the planning effort and the timing of initial planning, as well as the timing and criteria (critical milestones) for replanning.

The project lifecycle phases need to be defined depending on the scope of requirements, the estimates for project resources, and the nature of the project. Larger projects can contain multiple phases, such as concept exploration, development, production, operations, and disposal. Within these phases, subphases may be needed. A development phase can include subphases such as requirements analysis, design, fabrication, integration, and verification. The determination of project phases typically includes selection and refinement of one or more development models to address interdependencies and appropriate sequencing of the activities in the phases.

Depending on the strategy for development, there can be intermediate phases for the creation of prototypes, increments of capability, or spiral model cycles. In addition, explicit phases for "project startup" and "project close-out" can be included.

Example Work Products

1. Project lifecycle phases

SP 1.4 *ESTIMATE EFFORT AND COST*

Estimate the project's effort and cost for work products and tasks based on estimation rationale.

Estimates of effort and cost are generally based on results of analysis using models or historical data applied to size, activities, and other planning parameters. Confidence in these estimates is based on rationale for the selected model and the nature of the data. There can be occasions when available historical data do not apply, such as when efforts are unprecedented or when the type of task does not fit available models. For example, an effort can be considered unprecedented if the organization has no experience with such a product or task.

Unprecedented efforts are more risky, require more research to develop reasonable bases of estimate, and require more management reserve. The uniqueness of the project should be documented when using these models to ensure a common understanding of any assumptions made in the initial planning phases.

TIP

For example, in waterfall development, at the end of the requirements analysis phase, the requirements are evaluated to assess consistency, completeness, and feasibility, and to decide whether the project is ready (from a technical and risk perspective) to commit resources to the design phase.

X-REF

An example of a parametric software cost estimation model is COCOMO II (see http://sunset.usc.edu/csse/research/COCOMOII/cocomo_main.html).

TIP

Unprecedented efforts require an iterative or spiral development model that provides frequent opportunities for feedback used to resolve issues or risks and to plan the next iteration.

Example Work Products

1. Estimation rationale
2. Project effort estimates
3. Project cost estimates

Subpractices

1. Collect models or historical data to be used to transform the attributes of work products and tasks into estimates of labor hours and costs.

   Many parametric models have been developed to help estimate cost and schedule. The use of these models as the sole source of estimation is not recommended because these models are based on historical project data that may or may not be pertinent to the project. Multiple models and methods can be used to ensure a high level of confidence in the estimate.

   Historical data should include the cost, effort, and schedule data from previously executed projects and appropriate scaling data to account for differing sizes and complexity.

2. Include supporting infrastructure needs when estimating effort and cost.

   The supporting infrastructure includes resources needed from a development and sustainment perspective for the product.

   Consider the infrastructure resource needs in the development environment, the test environment, the production environment, the operational environment, or any appropriate combination of these environments when estimating effort and cost.

Examples of infrastructure resources include the following:
- Critical computer resources (e.g., memory, disk and network capacity, peripherals, communication channels, the capacities of these resources)
- Engineering environments and tools (e.g., tools for prototyping, testing, integration, assembly, computer-aided design [CAD], simulation)
- Facilities, machinery, and equipment (e.g., test benches, recording devices)

---

3. Estimate effort and cost using models, historical data, or a combination of both.

> **HINT**
>
> If you are using only one parametric model, make sure it is calibrated to your project's characteristics.

> **TIP**
>
> Scaling can be reliable when applied from experiences similar to the one at hand.

Examples of effort and cost inputs used for estimating typically include the following:

- Estimates provided by an expert or group of experts (e.g., Delphi method, Extreme Programming's Planning Game)
- Risks, including the extent to which the effort is unprecedented
- Critical competencies and roles needed to perform the work
- Travel
- WBS
- Selected project lifecycle model and processes
- Lifecycle cost estimates
- Skill levels of managers and staff needed to perform the work
- Knowledge, skill, and training needs
- Direct labor and overhead
- Service agreements for call centers and warranty work
- Level of security required for tasks, work products, hardware, software, staff, and work environment
- Facilities needed (e.g., office and meeting space and workstations)
- Product and product component requirements
- Size estimates of work products, tasks, and anticipated changes
- Cost of externally acquired products
- Capability of manufacturing processes
- Engineering facilities needed
- Capability of tools provided in engineering environment
- Technical approach

TIP

The common phrase "walk the talk" is often used when talking about how a project is conducted. The project plan is "the talk."

PP

SG 2 DEVELOP A PROJECT PLAN

A project plan is established and maintained as the basis for managing the project.

A project plan is a formal, approved document used to manage and control the execution of the project. It is based on project requirements and established estimates.

The project plan should consider all phases of the project lifecycle. Project planning should ensure that all plans affecting the project are consistent with the overall project plan.

TIP

In some cases, each project phase may have a more detailed and focused plan of its own, in addition to the overall project plan. Also, a detailed plan typically is provided for each iteration of development focused on particular requirements issues, design issues, or other risks.

TIP

Plans that may affect the project plan include configuration management plans, quality assurance plans, the organization's process improvement plan, and the organization's training plan.

SP 2.1 ESTABLISH THE BUDGET AND SCHEDULE

Establish and maintain the project's budget and schedule.

The project's budget and schedule are based on developed estimates and ensure that budget allocation, task complexity, and task dependencies are appropriately addressed.

Event driven, resource-limited schedules have proven to be effective in dealing with project risk. Identifying accomplishments to be demonstrated before initiation of an event provides some flexibility in the timing of the event, a common understanding of what is expected, a better vision of the state of the project, and a more accurate status of the project's tasks.

Example Work Products

1. Project schedules
2. Schedule dependencies
3. Project budget

Subpractices

1. Identify major milestones.

   Milestones are pre-planned events or points in time at which a thorough review of status is conducted to understand how well stakeholder requirements are being met. (If the project includes a developmental milestone, then the review is conducted to ensure that the assumptions and requirements associated with that milestone are being met.) Milestones can be associated with the overall project or a particular service type or instance. Milestones can thus be event based or calendar based. If calendar based, once agreed, milestone dates are often difficult to change.

2. Identify schedule assumptions.

   When schedules are initially developed, it is common to make assumptions about the duration of certain activities. These assumptions are frequently made on items for which little if any estimation data are available. Identifying these assumptions provides insight into the level of confidence (i.e., uncertainties) in the overall schedule.

3. Identify constraints.

   Factors that limit the flexibility of management options should be identified as early as possible. The examination of the attributes of work products and tasks often bring these issues to the surface. Such attributes can include task duration, resources, inputs, and outputs.

4. Identify task dependencies.

   Frequently, the tasks for a project or service can be accomplished in some ordered sequence that minimizes the duration. This sequencing involves the identification of predecessor and successor tasks to determine optimal ordering.

> Examples of tools and inputs that can help determine optimal ordering of task activities include the following:
> - Critical Path Method (CPM)
> - Program Evaluation and Review Technique (PERT)
> - Resource limited scheduling
> - Customer priorities
> - Marketable features
> - End-user value

5. Establish and maintain the budget and schedule.

> Establishing and maintaining the project's budget and schedule typically includes the following:
> - Defining the committed or expected availability of resources and facilities
> - Determining the time phasing of activities
> - Determining a breakout of subordinate schedules
> - Defining dependencies among activities (predecessor or successor relationships)
> - Defining schedule activities and milestones to support project monitoring and control
> - Identifying milestones, releases, or increments for the delivery of products to the customer
> - Defining activities of appropriate duration
> - Defining milestones of appropriate time separation
> - Defining a management reserve based on the confidence level in meeting the schedule and budget
> - Using appropriate historical data to verify the schedule
> - Defining incremental funding requirements
> - Documenting project assumptions and rationale

6. Establish corrective action criteria.

Criteria are established for determining what constitutes a significant deviation from the project plan. A basis for gauging issues and problems is necessary to determine when corrective action should be taken. Corrective actions can lead to replanning, which may include revising the original plan, establishing new agreements, or including mitigation activities in the current plan. The project plan defines

HINT

Establish corrective action criteria early in the project to ensure that issues are addressed appropriately and consistently.

when (e.g., under what circumstances, with what frequency) the criteria will be applied and by whom.

SP 2.2 IDENTIFY PROJECT RISKS

Identify and analyze project risks.

Refer to the Monitor Project Risks specific practice in the Project Monitoring and Control process area for more information about risk monitoring activities.

Refer to the Risk Management process area for more information about identifying potential problems before they occur so that risk handling activities can be planned and invoked as needed across the life of the product or project to mitigate adverse impacts on achieving objectives.

Risks are identified or discovered and analyzed to support project planning. This specific practice should be extended to all plans that affect the project to ensure that appropriate interfacing is taking place among all relevant stakeholders on identified risks.

Project planning risk identification and analysis typically include the following:
- Identifying risks
- Analyzing risks to determine the impact, probability of occurrence, and time frame in which problems are likely to occur
- Prioritizing risks

Example Work Products

1. Identified risks
2. Risk impacts and probability of occurrence
3. Risk priorities

Subpractices

1. Identify risks.

   The identification of risks involves the identification of potential issues, hazards, threats, vulnerabilities, and so on that could negatively affect work efforts and plans. Risks should be identified and described understandably before they can be analyzed and managed properly. When identifying risks, it is a good idea to use a standard method for defining risks. Risk identification and analysis tools can be used to help identify possible problems.

Examples of risk identification and analysis tools include the following:
- Risk taxonomies
- Risk assessments
- Checklists
- Structured interviews
- Brainstorming
- Process, project, and product performance models
- Cost models
- Network analysis
- Quality factor analysis

2. Document risks.
3. Review and obtain agreement with relevant stakeholders on the completeness and correctness of documented risks.
4. Revise risks as appropriate.

Examples of when identified risks may need to be revised include the following:
- When new risks are identified
- When risks become problems
- When risks are retired
- When project circumstances change significantly

SP 2.3 PLAN DATA MANAGEMENT

Plan for the management of project data.

Data are forms of documentation required to support a project in all of its areas (e.g., administration, engineering, configuration management, finance, logistics, quality, safety, manufacturing, procurement). The data can take any form (e.g., reports, manuals, notebooks, charts, drawings, specifications, files, correspondence). The data can exist in any medium (e.g., printed or drawn on various materials, photographs, electronic, multimedia).

Data can be deliverable (e.g., items identified by a project's contract data requirements) or data can be nondeliverable (e.g., informal data, trade studies, analyses, internal meeting minutes, internal design review documentation, lessons learned, action items). Distribution can take many forms, including electronic transmission.

TIP

Selecting a standard form can facilitate communication and understanding.

TIP

Providing a reason for the data being collected encourages cooperation from those providing the data.

TIP

The data management plan defines the data necessary for the project, who owns it, where it is stored, and how it is used. Also, it may specify what happens to the data after the project terminates.

TIP

Data privacy and security should be considered, but may not be an applicable consideration for certain types of projects.

X-REF

Measurement data is a subset of project data. See MA SPs 1.3 and 2.3 for more information on collecting, storing, and controlling access to measurement data.

X-REF

These requirements are often developed when you are eliciting stakeholder needs and developing customer requirements, which is addressed in RD SP1.1 and SP1.2.

Data requirements for the project should be established for both data items to be created and their content and form, based on a common or standard set of data requirements. Uniform content and format requirements for data items facilitate understanding of data content and help with consistent management of data resources.

The reason for collecting each document should be clear. This task includes the analysis and verification of project deliverables and nondeliverables, data requirements, and customer supplied data. Often, data are collected with no clear understanding of how they will be used. Data are costly and should be collected only when needed.

Example Work Products

1. Data management plan
2. Master list of managed data
3. Data content and format description
4. Lists of data requirements for acquirers and suppliers
5. Privacy requirements
6. Security requirements
7. Security procedures
8. Mechanisms for data retrieval, reproduction, and distribution
9. Schedule for the collection of project data
10. List of project data to be collected

Subpractices

1. Establish requirements and procedures to ensure privacy and the security of data.

   Not everyone will have the need or clearance necessary to access project data. Procedures should be established to identify who has access to which data as well as when they have access to which data.

2. Establish a mechanism to archive data and to access archived data.

   Accessed information should be in an understandable form (e.g., electronic or computer output from a database) or represented as originally generated.

3. Determine the project data to be identified, collected, and distributed.

4. Determine the requirements for providing access to and distribution of data to relevant stakeholders.

   A review of other elements of the project plan can help to determine who requires access to or receipt of project data as well as which data are involved.

5. Decide which project data and plans require version control or other levels of configuration control and establish mechanisms to ensure project data are controlled.

X-REF

Levels of control are addressed in CM SP1.2.

SP 2.4 *Plan the Project's Resources*

Plan for resources to perform the project.

TIP

This practice addresses *all* resources, not just personnel.

Defining project resources (e.g., labor, equipment, materials, methods) and quantities needed to perform project activities builds on initial estimates and provides additional information that can be applied to expand the WBS used to manage the project.

The top-level WBS developed earlier as an estimation mechanism is typically expanded by decomposing these top levels into work packages that represent single work units that can be separately assigned, performed, and tracked. This subdivision is done to distribute management responsibility and provide better management control.

Each work package in the WBS should be assigned a unique identifier (e.g., number) to permit tracking. A WBS can be based on requirements, activities, work products, services, or a combination of these items. A dictionary that describes the work for each work package in the WBS should accompany the work breakdown structure.

TIP

The WBS established in SP 1.1 is expanded to help identify roles as well as staffing, process, facility, and tool requirements; assign work; obtain commitment to perform the work; and track it to completion. Automated tools can help you with this activity.

Example Work Products

1. Work packages
2. WBS task dictionary
3. Staffing requirements based on project size and scope
4. Critical facilities and equipment list
5. Process and workflow definitions and diagrams
6. Project administration requirements list
7. Status reports

Subpractices

1. Determine process requirements.

   The processes used to manage a project are identified, defined, and coordinated with all relevant stakeholders to ensure efficient operations during project execution.

2. Determine communication requirements.

   These requirements address the kinds of mechanisms to be used for communicating with customers, end users, project staff, and other relevant stakeholders.

TIP

At maturity level 3, the organization is typically the main source of process requirements, standard processes, and process assets that aid in their use (see OPD).

3. Determine staffing requirements.

   The staffing of a project depends on the decomposition of project requirements into tasks, roles, and responsibilities for accomplishing project requirements as laid out in the work packages of the WBS.

   Staffing requirements should consider the knowledge and skills required for each identified position as defined in the Plan Needed Knowledge and Skills specific practice.

4. Determine facility, equipment, and component requirements.

   Most projects are unique in some way and require a set of unique assets to accomplish project objectives. The determination and acquisition of these assets in a timely manner are crucial to project success.

TIP

Some items (e.g., unusual skills) take time to obtain, and need for these should be identified early.

   It is best to identify lead-time items early to determine how they will be addressed. Even when required assets are not unique, compiling a list of all facilities, equipment, and parts (e.g., number of computers for the staff working on the project, software applications, office space) provides insight into aspects of the scope of an effort that are often overlooked.

5. Determine other continuing resource requirements.

   Beyond determining processes, reporting templates, staffing, facilities, and equipment, there may be a continuing need for other types of resources to effectively carry out project activities, including the following:

   • Consumables (e.g., electricity, office supplies)

   • Access to intellectual property

   • Access to transportation (for people and equipment)

   The requirements for such resources are derived from the requirements found in (existing and future) agreements (e.g., customer agreements, service agreements, supplier agreements), the project's strategic approach, and the need to manage and maintain the project's operations for a period of time.

TIP

This practice addresses the training that is specific to the project.

SP 2.5 PLAN NEEDED KNOWLEDGE AND SKILLS

Plan for knowledge and skills needed to perform the project.

Refer to the Organizational Training process area for more information about developing skills and knowledge of people so they can perform their roles effectively and efficiently.

TIP

At maturity level 2, the organization may not be capable of providing much training for its projects. Each project might address all of its knowledge and skill needs. At maturity level 3, the organization takes responsibility for addressing common training needs (e.g., training in the organization's set of standard processes).

Knowledge delivery to projects involves training project staff and acquiring knowledge from outside sources.

Staffing requirements are dependent on the knowledge and skills available to support the execution of the project.

Example Work Products

1. Inventory of skill needs
2. Staffing and new hire plans
3. Databases (e.g., skills, training)
4. Training plans

TIP

Either the project or the organization can maintain these example work products.

Subpractices

1. Identify the knowledge and skills needed to perform the project.
2. Assess the knowledge and skills available.
3. Select mechanisms for providing needed knowledge and skills.

HINT

Consider all knowledge and skills required for the project, not just the technical aspects.

> Example mechanisms include the following:
> • In-house training (both organizational and project)
> • External training
> • Staffing and new hires
> • External skill acquisition

TIP

If a skill is needed for the current project, but is not expected to be needed for future projects, external skill acquisition may be the best choice. However, if the skill needed for the project is expected to continue, training existing employees or hiring a new employee should be explored.

The choice of in-house training or outsourced training for needed knowledge and skills is determined by the availability of training expertise, the project's schedule, and business objectives.

4. Incorporate selected mechanisms into the project plan.

SP 2.6 PLAN STAKEHOLDER INVOLVEMENT

Plan the involvement of identified stakeholders.

Stakeholders are identified from all phases of the project lifecycle by identifying the people and functions that should be represented in the project and describing their relevance and the degree of interaction for project activities. A two-dimensional matrix with stakeholders along one axis and project activities along the other axis is a convenient format for accomplishing this identification. Relevance of the stakeholder to the activity in a particular project phase and the amount of interaction expected would be shown at the intersection of the project phase activity axis and the stakeholder axis.

For inputs of stakeholders to be useful, careful selection of relevant stakeholders is necessary. For each major activity, identify stakeholders who are affected by the activity and those who have expertise that is needed to conduct the activity. This list of relevant stakeholders will probably change as the project moves through phases of the project lifecycle. It is important, however, to ensure that relevant

X-REF

Identifying and involving relevant stakeholders is also addressed in PMC SP 1.5, IPM, and GP 2.7.

HINT

For each project phase, identify stakeholders important to the success of that phase and their role (e.g., implementer, reviewer, or consultant). Arrange this information into a matrix to aid in communication, obtain their commitment (SP 3.3), and monitor status (PMC SP 1.5).

TIP

Not all stakeholders identified will be relevant stakeholders. Only a limited number of stake-holders are selected for inter-action with the project as work progresses.

stakeholders in the latter phases of the lifecycle have early input to requirements and design decisions that affect them.

> Examples of the type of material that should be included in a plan for stakeholder interaction include the following:
> - List of all relevant stakeholders
> - Rationale for stakeholder involvement
> - Relationships among stakeholders
> - Resources (e.g., training, materials, time, funding) needed to ensure stakeholder interaction
> - Schedule for the phasing of stakeholder interaction
> - Roles and responsibilities of relevant stakeholders with respect to the project, by project lifecycle phase
> - Relative importance of the stakeholder to the success of the project, by project lifecycle phase

Implementing this specific practice relies on shared or exchanged information with the previous Plan Needed Knowledge and Skills specific practice.

Example Work Products

1. Stakeholder involvement plan

SP 2.7 ESTABLISH THE PROJECT PLAN

Establish and maintain the overall project plan.

HINT

Most project plans change over time as requirements are better understood, so plan how and when you will maintain the plan.

A documented plan that addresses all relevant planning items is nec-essary to achieve the mutual understanding and commitment of indi-viduals, groups, and organizations that execute or support the plans.

The plan generated for the project defines all aspects of the effort, tying together the following in a logical manner:

TIP

The plan document should reflect the project's status as requirements and the project environment change.

TIP

A documented plan communi-cates resources needed, expec-tations, and commitments; contains a game plan for rele-vant stakeholders, including the project team (SP 3.3); and is the basis for managing the project.

- Project lifecycle considerations
- Project tasks
- Budgets and schedules
- Milestones
- Data management
- Risk identification
- Resource and skill requirements
- Stakeholder identification and interaction
- Infrastructure considerations

Infrastructure considerations include responsibility and authority relationships for project staff, management, and support organizations.

Lifecycle considerations can include coverage of later phases of the product or service life (that might be beyond the life of the project), especially transition to another phase or party (e.g., transition to manufacturing, training, operations, a service provider).

For software, the planning document is often referred to as one of the following:
- Software development plan
- Software project plan
- Software plan

For hardware, the planning document is often referred to as a hardware development plan. Development activities in preparation for production can be included in the hardware development plan or defined in a separate production plan.

Examples of plans that have been used in the U.S. Department of Defense community include the following:
- Integrated Master Plan—an event driven plan that documents significant accomplishments with pass/fail criteria for both business and technical elements of the project and that ties each accomplishment to a key project event.
- Integrated Master Schedule—an integrated and networked multi-layered schedule of project tasks required to complete the work effort documented in a related Integrated Master Plan.
- Systems Engineering Management Plan—a plan that details the integrated technical effort across the project.
- Systems Engineering Master Schedule—an event based schedule that contains a compilation of key technical accomplishments, each with measurable criteria, requiring successful completion to pass identified events.
- Systems Engineering Detailed Schedule—a detailed, time dependent, task oriented schedule that associates dates and milestones with the Systems Engineering Master Schedule.

Example Work Products

1. Overall project plan

SG 3 OBTAIN COMMITMENT TO THE PLAN

Commitments to the project plan are established and maintained.

To be effective, plans require commitment by those who are responsible for implementing and supporting the plan.

SP 3.1 REVIEW PLANS THAT AFFECT THE PROJECT

Review all plans that affect the project to understand project commitments.

Plans developed in other process areas typically contain information similar to that called for in the overall project plan. These plans can provide additional detailed guidance and should be compatible with and support the overall project plan to indicate who has the authority, responsibility, accountability, and control. All plans that affect the project should be reviewed to ensure they contain a common understanding of the scope, objectives, roles, and relationships that are required for the project to be successful. Many of these plans are described by the Plan the Process generic practice.

Example Work Products

1. Record of the reviews of plans that affect the project

SP 3.2 RECONCILE WORK AND RESOURCE LEVELS

Adjust the project plan to reconcile available and estimated resources.

To establish a project that is feasible, obtain commitment from relevant stakeholders and reconcile differences between estimates and available resources. Reconciliation is typically accomplished by modifying or deferring requirements, negotiating more resources, finding ways to increase productivity, outsourcing, adjusting the staff skill mix, or revising all plans that affect the project or its schedules.

Example Work Products

1. Revised methods and corresponding estimating parameters (e.g., better tools, the use of off-the-shelf components)
2. Renegotiated budgets
3. Revised schedules
4. Revised requirements list
5. Renegotiated stakeholder agreements

TIP

Before making a commitment, a project member analyzes what it will take to meet that commitment. Project members who make commitments should continually evaluate their ability to meet their commitments, communicate immediately to those affected when they cannot meet their commitments, and mitigate the impacts of being unable to meet their commitments.

TIP

Commitments are a recurring theme in CMMI. Requirements are committed to in REQM, documented and reconciled in PP, monitored in PMC, and addressed more thoroughly in IPM.

HINT

Beware of commitments that are given freely. A favorite quote that applies is "How bad do you want it? That is how bad you will get it!" If you do not allow commitments to be made freely, staff most likely will try to provide the commitment you want to hear instead of a well-thought out answer that is accurate.

TIP

Because resource availability can change, such reconciliation will likely need to be done multiple times during the life of the project.

SP 3.3 OBTAIN PLAN COMMITMENT

Obtain commitment from relevant stakeholders responsible for performing and supporting plan execution.

Obtaining commitment involves interaction among all relevant stakeholders, both internal and external to the project. The individual or group making a commitment should have confidence that the work can be performed within cost, schedule, and performance constraints. Often, a provisional commitment is adequate to allow the effort to begin and to permit research to be performed to increase confidence to the appropriate level needed to obtain a full commitment.

Example Work Products

1. Documented requests for commitments
2. Documented commitments

Subpractices

1. Identify needed support and negotiate commitments with relevant stakeholders.

   The WBS can be used as a checklist for ensuring that commitments are obtained for all tasks.

   The plan for stakeholder interaction should identify all parties from whom commitment should be obtained.

2. Document all organizational commitments, both full and provisional, ensuring the appropriate level of signatories.

   Commitments should be documented to ensure a consistent mutual understanding and for project tracking and maintenance. Provisional commitments should be accompanied by a description of risks associated with the relationship.

3. Review internal commitments with senior management as appropriate.

4. Review external commitments with senior management as appropriate.

   Management can have the necessary insight and authority to reduce risks associated with external commitments.

5. Identify commitments regarding interfaces between project elements and other projects and organizational units so that these commitments can be monitored.

   Well-defined interface specifications form the basis for commitments.

TIP

Commitments are a two-way form of communication.

TIP

In maturity level 1 organizations, management often communicates a different picture of the project than the staff does. This inconsistency indicates that commitments were not obtained.

PP

TIP

Documenting commitments makes clear the responsibilities of those involved with the project.

TIP

A commitment not documented is a commitment not made (memories are imperfect and thus unreliable).

TIP

Senior management must be informed of external commitments (especially those with customers, end users, and suppliers), as they can expose the organization to unnecessary risk.

X-REF

For more information on managing commitments, dependencies, and coordination issues among relevant stakeholders, see IPM SG 2. For more information on identifying and managing interfaces, see PI SG 2.

PROCESS AND PRODUCT QUALITY ASSURANCE
A Support Process Area at Maturity Level 2

Purpose

The purpose of Process and Product Quality Assurance (PPQA) is to provide staff and management with objective insight into processes and associated work products.

TIP

PPQA is often referred to as the "eyes and ears" of the organization. It ensures that the organization's policies, practices, and processes are followed.

Introductory Notes

The Process and Product Quality Assurance process area involves the following activities:

- Objectively evaluating performed processes and work products against applicable process descriptions, standards, and procedures
- Identifying and documenting noncompliance issues
- Providing feedback to project staff and managers on the results of quality assurance activities
- Ensuring that noncompliance issues are addressed

TIP

The phrase "process descriptions, standards, and procedures" is used in PPQA (and GP 2.9) to represent management's expectations as to how project work will be performed. The applicable process descriptions, standards, and procedures are typically identified during project planning.

The Process and Product Quality Assurance process area supports the delivery of high-quality products by providing project staff and managers at all levels with appropriate visibility into, and feedback on, processes and associated work products throughout the life of the project.

The practices in the Process and Product Quality Assurance process area ensure that planned processes are implemented, while the practices in the Verification process area ensure that specified requirements are satisfied. These two process areas can on occasion address the same work product but from different perspectives. Projects should take advantage of the overlap to minimize duplication of effort while taking care to maintain separate perspectives.

Objectivity in process and product quality assurance evaluations is critical to the success of the project. (See the definition of "objectively

TIP

Objectivity is required. Independence is not required but is often the means used to assure objectivity.

evaluate" in the glossary.) Objectivity is achieved by both independence and the use of criteria. A combination of methods providing evaluations against criteria by those who do not produce the work product is often used. Less formal methods can be used to provide broad day-to-day coverage. More formal methods can be used periodically to assure objectivity.

TIP

For less mature organizations, formal audits conducted by a separate QA group may be best. Implementing peer reviews as an objective evaluation method (second bullet) requires care; see upcoming notes and example box.

> Examples of ways to perform objective evaluations include the following:
> - Formal audits by organizationally separate quality assurance organizations
> - Peer reviews, which can be performed at various levels of formality
> - In-depth review of work at the place it is performed (i.e., desk audits)
> - Distributed review and comment of work products
> - Process checks built into the processes such as a fail-safe for processes when they are done incorrectly (e.g., Poka-Yoke)

Traditionally, a quality assurance group that is independent of the project provides objectivity. However, another approach may be appropriate in some organizations to implement the process and product quality assurance role without that kind of independence.

TIP

When an independent approach is not used, it is important to be able to demonstrate how the objectivity was achieved.

> For example, in an organization with an open, quality oriented culture, the process and product quality assurance role can be performed, partially or completely, by peers and the quality assurance function can be embedded in the process. For small organizations, this embedded approach might be the most feasible approach.

If quality assurance is embedded in the process, several issues should be addressed to ensure objectivity. Everyone performing quality assurance activities should be trained in quality assurance. Those who perform quality assurance activities for a work product should be separate from those who are directly involved in developing or maintaining the work product. An independent reporting channel to the appropriate level of organizational management should be available so that noncompliance issues can be escalated as necessary.

> For example, when implementing peer reviews as an objective evaluation method, the following issues should be addressed:
> - Members are trained and roles are assigned for people attending the peer reviews.
> - A member of the peer review who did not produce this work product is assigned to perform the quality assurance role.
>
> *Continues*

> *Continued*
>
> • Checklists based on process descriptions, standards, and procedures are available to support the quality assurance activity.
> • Noncompliance issues are recorded as part of the peer review report and are tracked and escalated outside the project when necessary.

Quality assurance should begin in the early phases of a project to establish plans, processes, standards, and procedures that will add value to the project and satisfy the requirements of the project and organizational policies. Those who perform quality assurance activities participate in establishing plans, processes, standards, and procedures to ensure that they fit project needs and that they will be usable for performing quality assurance evaluations. In addition, processes and associated work products to be evaluated during the project are designated. This designation can be based on sampling or on objective criteria that are consistent with organizational policies, project requirements, and project needs.

When noncompliance issues are identified, they are first addressed in the project and resolved there if possible. Noncompliance issues that cannot be resolved in the project are escalated to an appropriate level of management for resolution.

This process area applies to evaluations of project activities and work products, and to organizational (e.g., process group, organizational training) activities and work products. For organizational activities and work products, the term "project" should be appropriately interpreted.

HINT

Start QA early in your project.

TIP

For organizations just beginning to establish QA, sampling is usually 100%. However, as an organization becomes more experienced in QA, it becomes possible to select a smaller sample of the processes and work products to evaluate without compromising QA effectiveness.

> In Agile environments, teams tend to focus on immediate needs of the iteration rather than on longer term and broader organizational needs. To ensure that objective evaluations are perceived to have value and are efficient, discuss the following early: (1) how objective evaluations are to be done, (2) which processes and work products will be evaluated, (3) how results of evaluations will be integrated into the team's rhythms (e.g., as part of daily meetings, checklists, peer reviews, tools, continuous integration, retrospectives). (See "Interpreting CMMI When Using Agile Approaches" in Part I.)

Related Process Areas

Refer to the Verification process area for more information about ensuring that selected work products meet their specified requirements.

Specific Goal and Practice Summary

SG 1 Objectively Evaluate Processes and Work Products
    SP 1.1   Objectively Evaluate Processes
    SP 1.2   Objectively Evaluate Work Products
SG 2 Provide Objective Insight
    SP 2.1   Communicate and Resolve Noncompliance Issues
    SP 2.2   Establish Records

Specific Practices by Goal

SG 1   OBJECTIVELY EVALUATE PROCESSES AND WORK PRODUCTS

Adherence of the performed process and associated work products to applicable process descriptions, standards, and procedures is objectively evaluated.

SP 1.1   OBJECTIVELY EVALUATE PROCESSES

Objectively evaluate selected performed processes against applicable process descriptions, standards, and procedures.

Objectivity in quality assurance evaluations is critical to the success of the project. A description of the quality assurance reporting chain and how it ensures objectivity should be defined.

Example Work Products

1. Evaluation reports
2. Noncompliance reports
3. Corrective actions

Subpractices

TIP

Quality is everyone's job. It is important that everyone in the organization be comfortable identifying and openly discussing quality concerns.

1. Promote an environment (created as part of project management) that encourages staff participation in identifying and reporting quality issues.
2. Establish and maintain clearly stated criteria for evaluations.

    The intent of this subpractice is to provide criteria, based on business needs, such as the following:

    • What will be evaluated
    • When or how often a process will be evaluated
    • How the evaluation will be conducted
    • Who must be involved in the evaluation

3. Use the stated criteria to evaluate selected performed processes for adherence to process descriptions, standards, and procedures.

4. Identify each noncompliance found during the evaluation.

5. Identify lessons learned that could improve processes.

SP 1.2 OBJECTIVELY EVALUATE WORK PRODUCTS

Objectively evaluate selected work products against applicable process descriptions, standards, and procedures.

Example Work Products

1. Evaluation reports
2. Noncompliance reports
3. Corrective actions

Subpractices

1. Select work products to be evaluated based on documented sampling criteria if sampling is used.

   Work products can include services produced by a process whether the recipient of the service is internal or external to the project or organization.

2. Establish and maintain clearly stated criteria for the evaluation of selected work products.

   The intent of this subpractice is to provide criteria, based on business needs, such as the following:

   • What will be evaluated during the evaluation of a work product
   • When or how often a work product will be evaluated
   • How the evaluation will be conducted
   • Who must be involved in the evaluation

3. Use the stated criteria during evaluations of selected work products.

4. Evaluate selected work products at selected times.

Examples of when work products can be evaluated against process descriptions, standards, or procedures include the following:
• Before delivery to the customer
• During delivery to the customer
• Incrementally, when it is appropriate
• During unit testing
• During integration
• When demonstrating an increment

---

5. Identify each case of noncompliance found during evaluations.

6. Identify lessons learned that could improve processes.

HINT

If you are using a traditional QA approach that involves a QA group, assign that group the responsibility for sharing new best practices with projects during project planning.

HINT

You can embed objective evaluations of work products in some verification activities — particularly peer reviews — although doing so requires care. (See the Introductory Notes for more information.)

PPQA

HINT

Subpractice 4 recommends evaluation of work products at different times and from different perspectives. The important point is that you think broadly about what will best give you the objective insight you need during your project.

TIP

Reports and feedback from QA help the organization identify what is and is not working.

SG 2   PROVIDE OBJECTIVE INSIGHT

Noncompliance issues are objectively tracked and communicated, and resolution is ensured.

SP 2.1   COMMUNICATE AND RESOLVE NONCOMPLIANCE ISSUES

Communicate quality issues and ensure the resolution of noncompliance issues with the staff and managers.

HINT

Noncompliance issues may be common in low-maturity organizations and should be addressed at the lowest possible level. Don't "criminalize" those responsible for noncompliance.

Noncompliance issues are problems identified in evaluations that reflect a lack of adherence to applicable standards, process descriptions, or procedures. The status of noncompliance issues provides an indication of quality trends. Quality issues include noncompliance issues and trend analysis results.

When noncompliance issues cannot be resolved in the project, use established escalation mechanisms to ensure that the appropriate level of management can resolve the issue. Track noncompliance issues to resolution.

Example Work Products

1. Corrective action reports
2. Evaluation reports
3. Quality trends

Subpractices

1. Resolve each noncompliance with the appropriate members of the staff if possible.
2. Document noncompliance issues when they cannot be resolved in the project.

TIP

In some cases, organizational requirements and project requirements conflict. Such situations can require noncompliance issues to be escalated to a level that includes the project as well as QA.

> Examples of ways to resolve noncompliance in the project include the following:
> • Fixing the noncompliance
> • Changing the process descriptions, standards, or procedures that were violated
> • Obtaining a waiver to cover the noncompliance

3. Escalate noncompliance issues that cannot be resolved in the project to the appropriate level of management designated to receive and act on noncompliance issues.

4. Analyze noncompliance issues to see if there are quality trends that can be identified and addressed.
5. Ensure that relevant stakeholders are aware of results of evaluations and quality trends in a timely manner.
6. Periodically review open noncompliance issues and trends with the manager designated to receive and act on noncompliance issues.
7. Track noncompliance issues to resolution.

SP 2.2 ESTABLISH RECORDS

Establish and maintain records of quality assurance activities.

Example Work Products

1. Evaluation logs
2. Quality assurance reports
3. Status reports of corrective actions
4. Reports of quality trends

Subpractices

1. Record process and product quality assurance activities in sufficient detail so that status and results are known.
2. Revise the status and history of quality assurance activities as necessary.

HINT

QA activities are often unappreciated. To address this issue, consider reporting a *compliance percentage* rather than the number of noncompliance issues for projects. This puts a positive spin on QA and may encourage friendly competition.

PPQA

TIP

Records provide a way to identify trends in QA activities (including noncompliance issues) that allow the organization to identify where additional guidance or process changes are needed.

QUANTITATIVE PROJECT MANAGEMENT
A Project Management Process Area at Maturity Level 4

TIP

In the CMMI for Services Model, this process area is called Quantitative Work Management.

Purpose

The purpose of Quantitative Project Management (QPM) is to quantitatively manage the project to achieve the project's established quality and process performance objectives.

TIP

QPM helps a project migrate from using the rear view mirror to manage the project to using predictive, forward-looking approaches to help steer the project to success.

Introductory Notes

The Quantitative Project Management process area involves the following activities:

TIP

When asked to state why QPM is important, one colleague replied, "The enterprise needs data for the next generation!"

- Establishing and maintaining the project's quality and process performance objectives
- Composing a defined process for the project to help to achieve the project's quality and process performance objectives
- Selecting subprocesses and attributes critical to understanding performance and that help to achieve the project's quality and process performance objectives
- Selecting measures and analytic techniques to be used in quantitative management
- Monitoring the performance of selected subprocesses using statistical and other quantitative techniques
- Managing the project using statistical and other quantitative techniques to determine whether or not the project's objectives for quality and process performance are being satisfied
- Performing root cause analysis of selected issues to address deficiencies in achieving the project's quality and process performance objectives

TIP

Although CMMI does not define who performs the SPs of a PA, the activities described in QPM are often best performed by those who actually execute the project's defined process as they are in the best position to understand the details of the situation they are in. Access to those with special expertise in measurement and quantitative techniques (e.g., Six Sigma black belts) can, however, be beneficial.

Organizational process assets used to achieve high maturity, including quality and process performance objectives, selected processes, measures, baselines, and models, are established using organizational process performance processes and used in quantitative project

TIP

When effectively implemented, QPM empowers individuals and teams by enabling them to accurately estimate (make predictions) and thus make sounder commitments based on these estimates (predictions).

QPM

X-REF

QPM and OPP are tightly coupled process areas. Each produces work products used by the other. Refer to OPP extensively when considering how to implement QPM.

management processes. The project can use organizational process performance processes to define additional objectives, measures, baselines, and models as needed to effectively analyze and manage performance. The measures, measurements, and other data resulting from quantitative project management processes are incorporated into the organizational process assets. In this way, the organization and its projects derive benefit from assets improved through use.

The project's defined process is a set of interrelated subprocesses that form an integrated and coherent process for the project. The Integrated Project Management practices describe establishing the project's defined process by selecting and tailoring processes from the organization's set of standard processes. (See the definition of "defined process" in the glossary.)

Quantitative Project Management practices, unlike Integrated Project Management practices, help you to develop a quantitative understanding of the expected performance of processes or subprocesses. This understanding is used as a basis for establishing the project's defined process by evaluating alternative processes or subprocesses for the project and selecting the ones that will best achieve the quality and process performance objectives.

Establishing effective relationships with suppliers is also important to the successful implementation of this process area. Establishing effective relationships can involve establishing quality and process performance objectives for suppliers, determining the measures and analytic techniques to be used to gain insight into supplier progress and performance, and monitoring progress toward achieving those objectives.

An essential element of quantitative management is having confidence in predictions (i.e., the ability to accurately predict the extent to which the project can fulfill its quality and process performance objectives). Subprocesses to be managed through the use of statistical and other quantitative techniques are chosen based on the needs for predictable process performance.

Another essential element of quantitative management is understanding the nature and extent of the variation experienced in process performance and recognizing when the project's actual performance may not be adequate to achieve the project's quality and process performance objectives.

Thus, quantitative management includes statistical thinking and the correct use of a variety of statistical techniques. (See the definition of "quantitative management" in the glossary.)

TIP

By "statistical thinking," we mean using statistical techniques as tools in appropriate ways to assess the variation in the performance of a process, to investigate its causes, and to recognize from the data when the process is not performing as it should. (See the definition of "statistical techniques" in the glossary.)

Statistical and other quantitative techniques are used to develop an understanding of the actual performance or to predict the performance of processes. Such techniques can be applied at multiple levels, from a focus on individual subprocesses to analyses that span lifecycle phases, projects, and support functions. Non-statistical techniques provide a less rigorous but still useful set of approaches that together with statistical techniques help the project to understand whether or not quality and process performance objectives are being satisfied and to identify any needed corrective actions.

This process area applies to managing a project. Applying these concepts to managing other groups and functions can help to link different aspects of performance in the organization to provide a basis for balancing and reconciling competing priorities to address a broader set of business objectives.

TIP

An important term is "statistical and other quantitative techniques." (See its definition in the glossary.) High maturity organizations and projects leverage an understanding of what factors matter in an unfolding situation to control its future course. Statistical and other quantitative techniques provide the insight needed to accomplish this, thus helping "steer" the project toward achieving its objectives.

> Examples of other groups and functions that could benefit from using this process area include the following:
> - Quality assurance or quality control functions
> - Process definition and improvement
> - Internal research and development functions
> - Risk identification and management functions
> - Technology scouting functions
> - Market research
> - Customer satisfaction assessment
> - Problem tracking and reporting

Related Process Areas

Refer to the Causal Analysis and Resolution process area for more information about identifying causes of selected outcomes and taking action to improve process performance.

Refer to the Integrated Project Management process area for more information about establishing the project's defined process.

Refer to the Measurement and Analysis process area for more information about aligning measurement and analysis activities and providing measurement results.

Refer to the Organizational Process Definition process area for more information about establishing organizational process assets.

Refer to the Organizational Performance Management process area for more information about proactively managing the organization's performance to meet its business objectives.

X-REF

See *How to Measure Anything: Finding the Value of "Intangibles" in Business* by Douglas W. Hubbard (John Wiley & Sons, Inc.).

X-REF

See *Moving Up the CMMI Capability and Maturity Levels Using Simulation* by David M. Raffo and Wayne Wakeland (found at http://www.sei.cmu.edu/reports/08tr002.pdf).

X-REF

See *Understanding Variation: The Key to Managing Chaos* (Second Edition) by Donald J. Wheeler (SPC Press, Inc.).

QPM

Refer to the Organizational Process Performance process area for more information about establishing and maintaining a quantitative understanding of the performance of selected processes in the organization's set of standard processes in support of achieving quality and process performance objectives, and providing process performance data, baselines, and models to quantitatively manage the organization's projects.

Refer to the Project Monitoring and Control process area for more information about providing an understanding of the project's progress so that appropriate corrective actions can be taken when the project's performance deviates significantly from the plan.

Refer to the Supplier Agreement Management process area for more information about managing the acquisition of products and services from suppliers.

Specific Goal and Practice Summary

SG 1 Prepare for Quantitative Management
    SP 1.1   Establish the Project's Objectives
    SP 1.2   Compose the Defined Process
    SP 1.3   Select Subprocesses and Attributes
    SP 1.4   Select Measures and Analytic Techniques
SG 2 Quantitatively Manage the Project
    SP 2.1   Monitor the Performance of Selected Subprocesses
    SP 2.2   Manage Project Performance
    SP 2.3   Perform Root Cause Analysis

Specific Practices by Goal

SG 1   *PREPARE FOR QUANTITATIVE MANAGEMENT*

Preparation for quantitative management is conducted.

Preparation activities include establishing quantitative objectives for the project, composing a defined process for the project that can help to achieve those objectives, selecting subprocesses and attributes critical to understanding performance and achieving the objectives, and selecting measures and analytic techniques that support quantitative management.

These activities may need to be repeated when needs and priorities change, when there is an improved understanding of process performance, or as part of risk mitigation or corrective action.

HINT

You can perform SPs 1.1 through 1.4 concurrently and iteratively.

SP 1.1 ESTABLISH THE PROJECT'S OBJECTIVES

Establish and maintain the project's quality and process performance objectives.

When establishing the project's quality and process performance objectives, think about the processes that will be included in the project's defined process and what the historical data indicate regarding their process performance. These considerations, along with others such as technical capability, will help in establishing realistic objectives for the project.

The project's objectives for quality and process performance are established and negotiated at an appropriate level of detail (e.g., for individual product components, subprocesses, project teams) to permit an overall evaluation of the objectives and risks at the project level. As the project progresses, project objectives can be updated as the project's actual performance becomes known and more predictable, and to reflect changing needs and priorities of relevant stakeholders.

Example Work Products

1. The project's quality and process performance objectives
2. Assessment of the risk of not achieving the project's objectives

Subpractices

1. Review the organization's objectives for quality and process performance.

    This review ensures that project members understand the broader business context in which the project operates. The project's objectives for quality and process performance are developed in the context of these overarching organizational objectives.

    Refer to the Organizational Process Performance process area for more information about establishing quality and process performance objectives.

2. Identify the quality and process performance needs and priorities of the customer, suppliers, end users, and other relevant stakeholders.

    Typically, the identification of relevant stakeholders' needs will begin early (e.g., during development of the statement of work). Needs are further elicited, analyzed, refined, prioritized, and balanced during requirements development.

TIP

Generally, these objectives are established early during project planning as customer requirements relating to product quality, service quality, and process performance are being established and analyzed.

X-REF

Quality and process performance objectives (QPPOs) should satisfy certain criteria such as "SMART criteria." SMART is an abbreviation for specific, measurable, attainable, relevant, and time-bound (see Wikipedia for more information).

TIP

The project's QPPOs are based, in part, on those of the organization. This approach helps to ensure that the project's QPPOs are aligned with those of the organization.

QPM

Examples of quality and process performance attributes for which needs and priorities might be identified include the following:
- Duration
- Predictability
- Reliability
- Maintainability
- Usability
- Timeliness
- Functionality
- Accuracy

3. Define and document measurable quality and process performance objectives for the project.

Defining and documenting objectives for the project involve the following:

- Incorporating appropriate organizational quality and process performance objectives
- Writing objectives that reflect the quality and process performance needs and priorities of the customer, end users, and other relevant stakeholders
- Determining how each objective will be achieved
- Reviewing the objectives to ensure they are sufficiently specific, measurable, attainable, relevant, and time-bound

Examples of measurable quality attributes include the following:
- Mean time between failures
- Number and severity of defects in the released product
- Critical resource utilization
- Number and severity of customer complaints concerning the provided service

Examples of measurable process performance attributes include the following:
- Cycle time
- Percentage of rework time
- Percentage of defects removed by product verification activities (perhaps by type of verification, such as peer reviews and testing)
- Defect escape rates
- Number and severity of defects found (or incidents reported) in first year following product delivery (or start of service)

Examples of project quality and process performance objectives include:
- Maintain change request backlog size below a target value.
- Improve velocity in an Agile environment to a target value by a target date.
- Reduce idle time by x% by a target date.
- Maintain schedule slippage below a specified percent.
- Reduce the total lifecycle cost by a specified percent by a target date.
- Reduce defects in products delivered to the customer by 10% without affecting cost.

4. Derive interim objectives to monitor progress toward achieving the project's objectives.

   Interim objectives can be established for attributes of selected lifecycle phases, milestones, work products, and subprocesses.

   Since process performance models characterize relationships among product and process attributes, these models can be used to help derive interim objectives that guide the project toward achieving its objectives.

5. Determine the risk of not achieving the project's quality and process performance objectives.

   The risk is a function of the established objectives, the product architecture, the project's defined process, availability of needed knowledge and skills, etc. Process performance baselines and models can be used to evaluate the likelihood of achieving a set of objectives and provide guidance in negotiating objectives and commitments. The assessment of risk can involve various project stakeholders and can be conducted as part of the conflict resolution described in the next subpractice.

6. Resolve conflicts among the project's quality and process performance objectives (e.g., if one objective cannot be achieved without compromising another).

   Process performance models can help to identify conflicts and help to ensure that the resolution of conflicts does not introduce new conflicts or risks.

   Resolving conflicts involves the following activities:
   - Setting relative priorities for objectives
   - Considering alternative objectives in light of long-term business strategies as well as short-term needs
   - Involving the customer, end users, senior management, project management, and other relevant stakeholders in tradeoff decisions
   - Revising objectives as necessary to reflect results of conflict resolution

7. Establish traceability to the project's quality and process performance objectives from their sources.

Examples of sources of objectives include the following:
- Requirements
- The organization's quality and process performance objectives
- The customer's quality and process performance objectives
- Business objectives
- Discussions with customers and potential customers
- Market surveys
- Product Architecture

An example of a method to identify and trace these needs and priorities is Quality Function Deployment (QFD).

---

8. Define and negotiate quality and process performance objectives for suppliers.
9. Revise the project's quality and process performance objectives as necessary.

SP 1.2 COMPOSE THE DEFINED PROCESS

Using statistical and other quantitative techniques, compose a defined process that enables the project to achieve its quality and process performance objectives.

Refer to the Integrated Project Management process area for more information about establishing the project's defined process.

Refer to the Organizational Process Definition process area for more information about establishing organizational process assets.

Refer to the Organizational Process Performance process area for more information about establishing performance baselines and models.

Composing the project's defined process goes beyond the process selection and tailoring described in the Integrated Project Management process area. It involves identifying alternatives to one or more processes or subprocesses, performing quantitative analysis of performance and selecting the alternatives that are best able to help the project to achieve its quality and process performance objectives.

Example Work Products

1. Criteria used to evaluate alternatives for the project
2. Alternative subprocesses
3. Subprocesses to be included in the project's defined process
4. Assessment of risk of not achieving the project's objectives

Subpractices

1. Establish the criteria to use in evaluating process alternatives for the project.

> Criteria can be based on the following:
> - Quality and process performance objectives
> - Availability of process performance data and the relevance of the data to evaluating an alternative
> - Familiarity with an alternative or with alternatives similar in composition
> - Existence of process performance models that can be used in evaluating an alternative
> - Product line standards
> - Project lifecycle models
> - Stakeholder requirements
> - Laws and regulations

2. Identify alternative processes and subprocesses for the project.

   Identifying alternatives can include one or more of the following:
   - Analyzing organizational process performance baselines to identify candidate subprocesses that would help achieve the project's quality and process performance objectives
   - Identifying subprocesses from the organization's set of standard processes as well as tailored processes in the process asset library that can help to achieve the objectives
   - Identifying processes from external sources (e.g., such as other organizations, professional conferences, academic research)
   - Adjusting the level or depth of intensity with which a subprocess is applied (as described in further detail in a subpractice that follows)

   Adjusting the level or depth of intensity with which the subprocesses are applied can involve the following choices:
   - Number and type of peer reviews to be held and when
   - Amount of effort or calendar time devoted to particular tasks
   - Number and selection of people involved

- Skill level requirements for performing specific tasks
- Selective application of specialized construction or verification techniques
- Reuse decisions and associated risk mitigation strategies
- The product and process attributes to be measured
- Sampling rate for management data

Refer to the Integrated Project Management process area for more information about using organizational process assets for planning project activities.

HINT

When project subprocesses interact with supplier or end-user subprocesses, the dynamics may not be obvious. Use process simulation in concert with PPMs to uncover hidden behavior and unintended consequences.

X-REF

For more information about process simulation, see the Raffo and Wakeland report mentioned earlier.

3. Analyze the interaction of alternative subprocesses to understand relationships among the subprocesses, including their attributes.

    An analysis of the interaction will provide insight into the relative strengths and weaknesses of particular alternatives. This analysis can be supported by a calibration of the organization's process performance models with process performance data (e.g., as characterized in process performance baselines).

    Additional modeling may be needed if existing process performance models cannot address significant relationships among the alternative subprocesses under consideration and there is high risk of not achieving objectives.

4. Evaluate alternative subprocesses against the criteria.

    Use historical data, process performance baselines, and process performance models as appropriate to assist in evaluating alternatives against the criteria. These evaluations can include use of a sensitivity analysis particularly in high risk situations.

    Refer to the Decision Analysis and Resolution process area for more information about evaluating alternatives.

5. Select the alternative subprocesses that best meet the criteria.

    It may be necessary to iterate through the activities described in the previous subpractices several times before confidence is achieved that the best available alternatives have been identified.

6. Evaluate the risk of not achieving the project's quality and process performance objectives.

    An analysis of risk associated with the selected alternative defined process can lead to identifying new alternatives to be evaluated, as well as areas requiring more management attention.

    Refer to the Risk Management process area for more information about identifying and analyzing risks.

Examples of graphical displays include the following:
- Scatterplots
- Histograms
- Box and whiskers plots
- Run charts
- Ishikawa diagrams

Examples of other techniques used to analyze process performance include the following:
- Tally sheets
- Classification schemas (e.g., Orthogonal Defect Classification)

7. Determine what process performance baselines and models may be needed to support identified analyses.

In some situations, the set of baselines and models provided as described in Organizational Process Performance may be inadequate to support quantitative project management. This situation can happen when the objectives, processes, stakeholders, skill levels, or environment for the project are different from other projects for which baselines and models were established.

As the project progresses, data from the project can serve as a more representative data set for establishing missing or a project specific set of process performance baselines and models.

Hypothesis testing comparing project data to prior historical data can confirm the need to establish additional baselines and models specific to the project.

8. Instrument the organizational or project support environment to support collection, derivation, and analysis of measures.

This instrumentation is based on the following:
- Description of the organization's set of standard processes
- Description of the project's defined process
- Capabilities of the organizational or project support environment

9. Revise measures and statistical analysis techniques as necessary.

SG 2   QUANTITATIVELY MANAGE THE PROJECT

The project is quantitatively managed.

Quantitatively managing the project involves the use of statistical and other quantitative techniques to do the following:
- Monitor the selected subprocesses using statistical and other quantitative techniques

QPM

> **TIP**
>
> We prepare for quantitative management in SG 1. We perform quantitative management in SG 2. Under some circumstances, it may be necessary to revisit the practices under SG 1 (e.g., to address changes to QPPOs or select a superior subprocess alternative).

- Determine whether or not the project's quality and process performance objectives are being satisfied
- Perform root cause analysis of selected issues to address deficiencies

SP 2.1 MONITOR THE PERFORMANCE OF SELECTED SUBPROCESSES

Monitor the performance of selected subprocesses using statistical and other quantitative techniques.

The intent of this specific practice is to use statistical and other quantitative techniques to analyze variation in subprocess performance and to determine actions necessary to achieve each subprocess's quality and process performance objectives.

Example Work Products

1. Natural bounds of process performance for each selected subprocess attribute
2. The actions needed to address deficiencies in the process stability or capability of each selected subprocess

Subpractices

1. Collect data, as defined by the selected measures, on the subprocesses as they execute.
2. Monitor the variation and stability of the selected subprocesses and address deficiencies.

   This analysis involves evaluating measurements in relation to the natural bounds calculated for each selected measure and identifying outliers or other signals of potential non-random behavior, determining their causes and preventing or mitigating the effects of their recurrence (i.e., addressing special causes of variation).

   During such analysis, be sensitive to the sufficiency of the data and to shifts in process performance that can affect the ability to achieve or maintain process stability.

   Analytic techniques for identifying outliers or signals include statistical process control charts, prediction intervals, and analysis of variance. Some of these techniques involve graphical displays.

   Other deficiencies in process performance to consider include when variation is too large to have confidence that the subprocess is stable, or too great to assess its capability (next subpractice) of achieving the objectives established for each selected attribute.

3. Monitor the capability and performance of the selected subprocesses and address deficiencies.

   The intent of this subpractice is to identify what actions to take to help the subprocess achieve its quality and process performance objectives. Be sure that the subprocess performance is stable relative to the selected measures (previous subpractice) before comparing its capability to its quality and process performance objectives.

Examples of actions that can be taken when the performance of a selected subprocess fails to satisfy its objectives include the following:

- Improving the implementation of the existing subprocess to reduce its variation or improve its performance (i.e., addressing common causes of variation)
- Identifying and implementing an alternative subprocess through identifying and adopting new process elements, subprocesses, and technologies that may help better align with objectives
- Identifying risks and risk mitigation strategies for each deficiency in subprocess capability
- Renegotiating or re-deriving objectives for each selected attribute of a subprocess so that they can be met by the subprocess

Some actions can involve the use of root cause analysis, which is further described in SP 2.3.

Refer to the Project Monitoring and Control process area for more information about managing corrective action to closure.

SP 2.2 MANAGE PROJECT PERFORMANCE

Manage the project using statistical and other quantitative techniques to determine whether or not the project's objectives for quality and process performance will be satisfied.

Refer to the Measurement and Analysis process area for more information about aligning measurement and analysis activities and providing measurement results.

Refer to the Organizational Performance Management process area for more information about managing business performance.

This specific practice is project focused and uses multiple inputs to predict if the project's quality and process performance objectives will be satisfied. Based on this prediction, risks associated with not meeting the project's quality and process performance objectives are identified and managed, and actions to address deficiencies are defined as appropriate.

Key inputs to this analysis include the individual subprocess stability and capability data derived from the previous specific practice, as well as performance data from monitoring other subprocesses, risks, and suppliers' progress.

Example Work Products

1. Predictions of results to be achieved relative to the project's quality and process performance objectives
2. Graphical displays and data tabulations for other subprocesses, which support quantitative management
3. Assessment of risks of not achieving the project's quality and process performance objectives
4. Actions needed to address deficiencies in achieving project objectives

Subpractices

1. Periodically review the performance of subprocesses.

   Stability and capability data from monitoring selected subprocesses, as described in SP2.1, are a key input into understanding the project's overall ability to meet quality and process performance objectives.

   In addition, subprocesses not selected for their impact on project objectives can still create problems or risks for the project and thus some level of monitoring for these subprocesses may be desired as well. Analytic techniques involving the use of graphical displays can also prove to be useful to understanding subprocess performance.

2. Monitor and analyze suppliers' progress toward achieving their quality and process performance objectives.
3. Periodically review and analyze actual results achieved against established interim objectives.

> **TIP**
>
> PPMs (OPP SP 1.5) calibrated with project-specific data or PPBs can help the project determine whether it will be able to achieve its QPPOs.

4. Use process performance models calibrated with project data to assess progress toward achieving the project's quality and process performance objectives.

   Process performance models are used to assess progress toward achieving objectives that cannot be measured until a future phase in the project lifecycle. Objectives can either be interim objectives or overall objectives.

> An example is the use of process performance models to predict the latent defects in work products in future phases or in the delivered product.

   Calibration of process performance models is based on the results obtained from performing the activities described in the previous subpractices and specific practices.

5. Identify and manage risks associated with achieving the project's quality and process performance objectives.

   Refer to the Risk Management process area for more information about identifying and analyzing risks and mitigating risks.

> Example sources of risks include the following:
> - Subprocesses having inadequate performance or capability
> - Suppliers not achieving their quality and process performance objectives
> - Lack of visibility into supplier capability
> - Inaccuracies in the process performance models used for predicting performance
> - Deficiencies in predicted process performance (estimated progress)
> - Other identified risks associated with identified deficiencies

6. Determine and implement actions needed to address deficiencies in achieving the project's quality and process performance objectives.

> The intent of this subpractice is to identify and implement the right set of actions, resources, and schedule to place the project back on a path toward achieving its objectives.

> Examples of actions that can be taken to address deficiencies in achieving the project's objectives include the following:
> - Changing quality and process performance objectives so that they are within the expected range of the project's defined process
> - Improving the implementation of the project's defined process
> - Adopting new subprocesses and technologies that have the potential for satisfying objectives and managing associated risks
> - Identifying the risk and risk mitigation strategies for deficiencies
> - Terminating the project

> Some actions can involve the use of root cause analysis, which is addressed in the next specific practice.

> *Refer to the Project Monitoring and Control process area for more information about managing corrective action to closure.*

> When corrective actions result in changes to attributes or measures related to adjustable factors in a process performance model, the model can be used to predict the effects of the actions. When undertaking critical corrective actions in high risk situations, a process performance model can be created to predict the effects of the change.

SP 2.3 PERFORM ROOT CAUSE ANALYSIS

Perform root cause analysis of selected issues to address deficiencies in achieving the project's quality and process performance objectives.

Issues to address include deficiencies in subprocess stability and capability, and deficiencies in project performance relative to its objectives.

TIP

The deficiencies mentioned in the SP statement are those arising out of the analyses described in SP 2.1 (subprocess performance deficiencies) and SP 2.2 (predicted deficiencies in achieving project QPPOs).

QPM

Root cause analysis of selected issues is best performed shortly after the problem is first identified, while the event is still recent enough to be carefully investigated.

The formality of and effort required for a root cause analysis can vary greatly and can be determined by such factors as the stakeholders who are involved; the risk or opportunity that is present; the complexity of the situation; the frequency with which the situation could recur; the availability of data, baselines, and models that can be used in the analysis; and how much time has passed since the events triggering the deficiency.

In the case of a subprocess that exhibits too much variation, is performed rarely, and involves different stakeholders, it could take weeks or months to identify root causes.

Likewise, the actions to take can range significantly in terms of effort and time needed to determine, plan, and implement them.

It is often difficult to know how much time is needed unless an initial analysis of the deficiencies is undertaken.

Refer to the Causal Analysis and Resolution process area for more information about identifying causes of selected outcomes and taking action to improve process performance.

Refer to the Measurement and Analysis process area for more information about aligning measurement and analysis activities and providing measurement results.

Example Work Products

1. Subprocess and project performance measurements and analyses (including statistical analyses) recorded in the organization's measurement repository
2. Graphical displays of data used to understand subprocess and project performance and performance trends
3. Identified root causes and potential actions to take

Subpractices

1. Perform root cause analysis, as appropriate, to diagnose process performance deficiencies.

   Process performance baselines and models are used in diagnosing deficiencies; identifying possible solutions; predicting future project and process performance; and evaluating potential actions as appropriate.

   The use of process performance models in predicting future project and process performance is described in a subpractice of the previous specific practice.

X-REF

Although an Ishikawa diagram (i.e., fishbone diagram) is a common tool for simple root cause analysis, deficiencies affecting achievement of the project's QPPOs often require more in-depth analysis. In addition to the use of PPBs and PPMs, consider tools such as the Current Reality Tree from the Theory of Constraints. For more information, visit the Goldratt Institute at www.goldratt.com/ or consult Wikipedia.

2. Identify and analyze potential actions.
3. Implement selected actions.
4. Assess the impact of the actions on subprocess performance.

    This assessment of impact can include an evaluation of the statistical significance of the impacts resulting from the actions taken to improve process performance

REQUIREMENTS DEVELOPMENT
An Engineering Process Area at Maturity Level 3

Purpose

The purpose of Requirements Development (RD) is to elicit, analyze, and establish customer, product, and product component requirements.

TIP

REQM works alongside RD to manage requirements, changes to requirements, and traceability and to ensure alignment of work products as requirements are developed.

Introductory Notes

This process area describes three types of requirements: customer requirements, product requirements, and product component requirements. Taken together, these requirements address the needs of relevant stakeholders, including needs pertinent to various product lifecycle phases (e.g., acceptance testing criteria) and product attributes (e.g., responsiveness, safety, reliability, maintainability). Requirements also address constraints caused by the selection of design solutions (e.g., integration of commercial off-the-shelf products, use of a particular architecture pattern).

All development projects have requirements. Requirements are the basis for design. The development of requirements includes the following activities:

TIP

Customer needs can prescribe particular solutions (e.g., a client-server application) in addition to describing the problem to be solved.

- Elicitation, analysis, validation, and communication of customer needs, expectations, and constraints to obtain prioritized customer requirements that constitute an understanding of what will satisfy stakeholders
- Collection and coordination of stakeholder needs
- Development of the lifecycle requirements of the product
- Establishment of the customer functional and quality attribute requirements
- Establishment of initial product and product component requirements consistent with customer requirements

TIP

See the definition of "quality attributes" in the glossary. Quality attribute requirements are nonfunctional requirements.

RD

TIP

See the definition of "service system" in the glossary. For more information about developing service systems, see the Service System Development process area of the CMMI for Services model.

TIP

As long as they continue to be maintained, requirements provide value to those supporting the product throughout its life. For example, requirements remind implementers, maintainers, and trainers of what the product is supposed to do so that their actions contribute to requirements satisfaction.

TIP

See the definitions of "derived requirements" and "allocated requirements" in the glossary.

TIP

For more on recursion, see "Recursion and Iteration of Engineering Processes" in section 4.

TIP

Requirements validation is intended to uncover critical stakeholder needs, expectations, interfaces, and constraints. The practices in VAL may provide additional insight into how RD validation activities can be performed.

TIP

Safety, security, and affordability are quality attributes. Note that they may have different implications for different phases of the product's life and for different stakeholders.

- This process area addresses all customer requirements rather than only product level requirements because the customer can also provide specific design requirements.

Customer requirements are further refined into product and product component requirements. In addition to customer requirements, product and product component requirements are derived from the selected design solutions. Throughout the process areas, where the terms "product" and "product component" are used, their intended meanings also encompass services, service systems, and their components.

Requirements are identified and refined throughout the phases of the product lifecycle. Design decisions, subsequent corrective actions, and feedback during each phase of the product's lifecycle are analyzed for impact on derived and allocated requirements.

The Requirements Development process area includes three specific goals. The Develop Customer Requirements specific goal addresses defining a set of customer requirements to use in the development of product requirements. The Develop Product Requirements specific goal addresses defining a set of product or product component requirements to use in the design of products and product components. The Analyze and Validate Requirements specific goal addresses the analysis of customer, product, and product component requirements to define, derive, and understand the requirements. The specific practices of the third specific goal are intended to assist the specific practices in the first two specific goals. The processes associated with the Requirements Development process area and processes associated with the Technical Solution process area can interact recursively with one another.

Analyses are used to understand, define, and select the requirements at all levels from competing alternatives. These analyses include the following:

- Analysis of needs and requirements for each product lifecycle phase, including needs of relevant stakeholders, the operational environment, and factors that reflect overall customer and end-user expectations and satisfaction, such as safety, security, and affordability
- Development of an operational concept
- Definition of the required functionality and quality attributes

This definition of required functionality and quality attributes describes what the product is to do. (See the definition of "definition of required functionality and quality attributes" in the glossary.) This definition can include descriptions, decompositions, and a partitioning of the functions (or in object oriented analysis what has been referred to as "services" or "methods") of the product.

In addition, the definition specifies design considerations or constraints on how the required functionality will be realized in the product. Quality attributes address such things as product availability; maintainability; modifiability; timeliness, throughput, and responsiveness; reliability; security; and scalability. Some quality attributes will emerge as architecturally significant and thus drive the development of the product architecture.

Such analyses occur recursively at successively more detailed layers of a product's architecture until sufficient detail is available to enable detailed design, acquisition, and testing of the product to proceed. As a result of the analysis of requirements and the operational concept (including functionality, support, maintenance, and disposal), the manufacturing or production concept produces more derived requirements, including consideration of the following:

- Constraints of various types
- Technological limitations
- Cost and cost drivers
- Time constraints and schedule drivers
- Risks
- Consideration of issues implied but not explicitly stated by the customer or end user
- Factors introduced by the developer's unique business considerations, regulations, and laws

A hierarchy of logical entities (e.g., functions and subfunctions, object classes and subclasses; processes; other architectural entities) is established through iteration with the evolving operational concept. Requirements are refined, derived, and allocated to these logical entities. Requirements and logical entities are allocated to products, product components, people, or associated processes. In the case of iterative or incremental development, the requirements are also allocated to iterations or increments.

Involvement of relevant stakeholders in both requirements development and analysis gives them visibility into the evolution of requirements. This activity continually assures them that the requirements are being properly defined.

For product lines, engineering processes (including requirements development) may be applied to at least two levels in the organization.

> **TIP**
>
> The term "definition of required functionality and quality attributes" is new in CMMI V1.3. It extends the concept "definition of required functionality" to include quality attributes, recognizing that architectural tradeoffs can span both.

RD

X-REF

See the definition of "product line" in the glossary.

TIP

The discipline implied by the practices in RD may help projects—not just those employing Agile methods—adequately attend to the needs of other stakeholders, other lifecycle phases, and needed quality attributes so that critical needs and risks are not overlooked or forgotten.

At an organizational or product line level, a "commonality and variation analysis" is performed to help elicit, analyze, and establish core assets for use by projects within the product line. At the project level, these core assets are then used as per the product line production plan as part of the project's engineering activities.

In Agile environments, customer needs and ideas are iteratively elicited, elaborated, analyzed, and validated. Requirements are documented in forms such as user stories, scenarios, use cases, product backlogs, and the results of iterations (working code in the case of software). Which requirements will be addressed in a given iteration is driven by an assessment of risk and by the priorities associated with what is left on the product backlog. What details of requirements (and other artifacts) to document is driven by the need for coordination (among team members, teams, and later iterations) and the risk of losing what was learned. When the customer is on the team, there can still be a need for separate customer and product documentation to allow multiple solutions to be explored. As the solution emerges, responsibilities for derived requirements are allocated to the appropriate teams. (See "Interpreting CMMI When Using Agile Approaches" in Part I.)

Related Process Areas

Refer to the Product Integration process area for more information about ensuring interface compatibility.

Refer to the Technical Solution process area for more information about selecting product component solutions and developing the design.

Refer to the Validation process area for more information about validating product or product components.

Refer to the Verification process area for more information about verifying selected work products.

Refer to the Configuration Management process area for more information about tracking and controlling changes.

Refer to the Requirements Management process area for more information about managing requirements.

Refer to the Risk Management process area for more information about identifying and analyzing risks.

Specific Goal and Practice Summary

SG 1 Develop Customer Requirements
    SP 1.1   Elicit Needs
    SP 1.2   Transform Stakeholder Needs into Customer Requirements

SG 2 Develop Product Requirements
    SP 2.1   Establish Product and Product Component Requirements
    SP 2.2   Allocate Product Component Requirements
    SP 2.3   Identify Interface Requirements

SG 3 Analyze and Validate Requirements
    SP 3.1   Establish Operational Concepts and Scenarios
    SP 3.2   Establish a Definition of Required Functionality and Quality Attributes
    SP 3.3   Analyze Requirements
    SP 3.4   Analyze Requirements to Achieve Balance
    SP 3.5   Validate Requirements

Specific Practices by Goal

SG 1 DEVELOP CUSTOMER REQUIREMENTS

Stakeholder needs, expectations, constraints, and interfaces are collected and translated into customer requirements.

The needs of stakeholders (e.g., customers, end users, suppliers, builders, testers, manufacturers, logistics support staff) are the basis for determining customer requirements. The stakeholder needs, expectations, constraints, interfaces, operational concepts, and product concepts are analyzed, harmonized, refined, and elaborated for translation into a set of customer requirements.

Frequently, stakeholder needs, expectations, constraints, and interfaces are poorly identified or conflicting. Since stakeholder needs, expectations, constraints, and limitations should be clearly identified and understood, an iterative process is used throughout the life of the project to accomplish this objective. To facilitate the required interaction, a surrogate for the end user or customer is frequently involved to represent their needs and help resolve conflicts. The customer relations or marketing part of the organization as well as members of the development team from disciplines such as human engineering or support can be used as surrogates. Environmental, legal, and other constraints should be considered when creating and resolving the set of customer requirements.

TIP

In some situations, project work is authorized through a supplier agreement that documents the requirements (see SAM SP 1.3). Additional effort may be needed to determine a more refined and complete set of customer requirements.

TIP

Some stakeholder needs are rarely communicated in an official document. They are communicated in documentation, conversations, meetings, demonstrations, and so on. Therefore, this information must be translated into requirements that the project and stakeholders can agree to.

HINT

Rarely does a customer know exactly what he needs. Prototypes or an iterative development process can sometimes help you more effectively learn the requirements for the product.

RD

SP 1.1 *ELICIT NEEDS*

Elicit stakeholder needs, expectations, constraints, and interfaces for all phases of the product lifecycle.

X-REF

In the case of product lines or product families, SP 1.1 is sometimes implemented across the product line or product family. See the penultimate paragraph of the RD Intro Notes for more information.

HINT

Determine what the product must do and how it should behave. Also determine what is required to produce it, license it, market it, distribute it, install it, train end users, repair it, maintain it, migrate to new versions, support its use, retire it, and dispose of it.

Eliciting goes beyond collecting requirements by proactively identifying additional requirements not explicitly provided by customers. Additional requirements should address the various product lifecycle activities and their impact on the product.

Examples of techniques to elicit needs include the following:
- Technology demonstrations
- Interface control working groups
- Technical control working groups
- Interim project reviews
- Questionnaires, interviews, and scenarios (operational, sustainment, and development) obtained from end users
- Operational, sustainment, and development walkthroughs and end-user task analysis
- Quality attribute elicitation workshops with stakeholders
- Prototypes and models
- Brainstorming
- Quality Function Deployment
- Market surveys
- Beta testing
- Extraction from sources such as documents, standards, or specifications
- Observation of existing products, environments, and workflow patterns
- Use cases
- User stories
- Delivering small incremental "vertical slices" of product functionality
- Business case analysis
- Reverse engineering (for legacy products)
- Customer satisfaction surveys

Examples of sources of requirements that may not be identified by the customer include the following:
- Business policies
- Standards
- Previous architectural design decisions and principles
- Business environmental requirements (e.g., laboratories, testing and other facilities, information technology infrastructure)

Continues

Continued

- Technology
- Legacy products or product components (reuse product components)
- Regulatory statutes

Example Work Products

1. Results of requirements elicitation activities

Subpractices

1. Engage relevant stakeholders using methods for eliciting needs, expectations, constraints, and external interfaces.

SP 1.2 TRANSFORM STAKEHOLDER NEEDS INTO CUSTOMER REQUIREMENTS

Transform stakeholder needs, expectations, constraints, and interfaces into prioritized customer requirements.

The various inputs from the relevant stakeholders should be consolidated, missing information should be obtained, and conflicts should be resolved as customer requirements are developed and prioritized. The customer requirements can include needs, expectations, and constraints with regard to verification and validation.

> **TIP**
>
> Neither the acquirer nor the project should abrogate or diminish project responsibility to implement appropriate verifications and validations.

In some situations, the customer provides a set of requirements to the project, or the requirements exist as an output of a previous project's activities. In these situations, the customer requirements could conflict with the relevant stakeholders' needs, expectations, constraints, and interfaces and will need to be transformed into the recognized set of customer requirements after appropriate resolution of conflicts.

Relevant stakeholders representing all phases of the product's lifecycle should include business as well as technical functions. In this way, concepts for all product related lifecycle processes are considered concurrently with the concepts for the products. Customer requirements result from informed decisions on the business as well as technical effects of their requirements.

Example Work Products

1. Prioritized customer requirements
2. Customer constraints on the conduct of verification
3. Customer constraints on the conduct of validation

RD

TIP

Prioritization also provides guidance when making architectural tradeoffs and ensures priorities are not later overlooked or forgotten.

X-REF

The Kano model is an approach to classifying and prioritizing functionality and attributes according to their impact on customer perceptions of quality. One source of information on the Kano model is the Wikipedia website (en.wikipedia.org/wiki/Kano_model).

TIP

See the definitions of "product lifecycle" and "architecture" in the glossary.

Subpractices

1. Translate stakeholder needs, expectations, constraints, and interfaces into documented customer requirements.

2. Establish and maintain a prioritization of customer functional and quality attribute requirements.

   Having prioritized customer requirements helps to determine project, iteration, or increment scope. This prioritization ensures that functional and quality attribute requirements critical to the customer and other stakeholders are addressed quickly.

3. Define constraints for verification and validation.

SG 2 DEVELOP PRODUCT REQUIREMENTS

Customer requirements are refined and elaborated to develop product and product component requirements.

Customer requirements are analyzed in conjunction with the development of the operational concept to derive more detailed and precise sets of requirements called "product and product component requirements." Product and product component requirements address the needs associated with each product lifecycle phase. Derived requirements arise from constraints; consideration of issues implied but not explicitly stated in the customer requirements baseline; factors introduced by the selected architecture, product lifecycle, and design; and the developer's unique business considerations. The requirements are reexamined with each successive, lower level set of requirements and architecture, and the preferred product concept is refined.

The requirements are allocated to product functions and product components including objects, people, and processes. In the case of iterative or incremental development, the requirements are also allocated to iterations or increments based on customer priorities, technology issues, and project objectives. The traceability of requirements to functions, objects, tests, issues, or other entities is documented. The allocated requirements and functions (or other logical entities) are the basis for the synthesis of the technical solution; however, as the architecture is defined or emerges, it serves as the ultimate basis for directing the allocation of requirements to the solution. As internal components are developed, additional interfaces are defined and interface requirements are established.

Refer to the Requirements Management process area for more information about maintaining bidirectional traceability of requirements.

SP 2.1 *ESTABLISH PRODUCT AND PRODUCT COMPONENT REQUIREMENTS*

Establish and maintain product and product component requirements, which are based on the customer requirements.

The customer functional and quality attribute requirements can be expressed in the customer's terms and can be nontechnical descriptions. The product requirements are the expression of these requirements in technical terms that can be used for design decisions. An example of this translation is found in the first House of Quality Function Deployment, which maps customer desires into technical parameters. For instance, "solid sounding door" may be mapped to size, weight, fit, dampening, and resonant frequencies.

Product and product component requirements address the satisfaction of customer, business, and project objectives and associated attributes, such as effectiveness and affordability.

Derived requirements also address the needs of other lifecycle phases (e.g., production, operations, disposal) to the extent compatible with business objectives.

The modification of requirements due to approved requirement changes is covered by the "maintain" aspect of this specific practice; whereas, the administration of requirement changes is covered by the Requirements Management process area.

Refer to the Requirements Management process area for more information about managing requirements.

Example Work Products

1. Derived requirements
2. Product requirements
3. Product component requirements
4. Architectural requirements, which specify or constrain the relationships among product components

Subpractices

1. Develop requirements in technical terms necessary for product and product component design.
2. Derive requirements that result from design decisions.

    Refer to the Technical Solution process area for more information about selecting product component solutions and developing the design.

    Selection of a technology brings with it additional requirements. For instance, use of electronics requires additional technology specific requirements such as electromagnetic interference limits.

TIP

Recursion is built into SP 2.1. Product requirements are associated with the top level of the product hierarchy. Product component requirements are recursively developed for each lower level in parallel with the recursive development of TS.

X-REF

There are many sources of information on QFD, including the iSixSigma website (www.isixsigma.com) and the Quality Function Deployment Institute website (www.qfdi.org).

TIP

The wording in SP 2.1, "... maintain product and product-component requirements," should be interpreted to cover the modification of requirements, not the administration of such changes (REQM SP 1.3).

RD

X-REF

For sources of information on architecture patterns, see x-ref for TS SP 2.1.

Architectural decisions, such as selection of architecture patterns, introduce additional derived requirements for product components. For example, the Layers Pattern will constrain dependencies between certain product components.

3. Develop architectural requirements capturing critical quality attributes and quality attribute measures necessary for establishing the product architecture and design.

TIP

Architecture requirements express the product qualities and performance points that are critical to customer satisfaction (also see TS SP 2.1).

Examples of quality attribute measures include the following:
- Respond within 1 second
- System is available 99% of the time
- Implement a change with no more than one staff week of effort

4. Establish and maintain relationships between requirements for consideration during change management and requirements allocation.

Refer to the Requirements Management process area for more information about maintaining bidirectional traceability of requirements.

Relationships between requirements can aid in evaluating the impact of changes.

SP 2.2 ALLOCATE PRODUCT COMPONENT REQUIREMENTS

Allocate the requirements for each product component.

Refer to the Technical Solution process area for more information about selecting product component solutions.

TIP

Other examples of shared requirements include a constraint on memory that is to be met by a collection of components and a safety requirement that is to be achieved by the components of a product.

TIP

Sometimes, a provisional allocation of a higher-level requirement to product components is made, but is later revised to account for the unique or emerging capabilities of individual suppliers, teams, or new COTS products.

The product architecture provides the basis for allocating product requirements to product components. The requirements for product components of the defined solution include allocation of product performance; design constraints; and fit, form, and function to meet requirements and facilitate production. In cases where a higher level requirement specifies a quality attribute that will be the responsibility of more than one product component, the quality attribute can sometimes be partitioned for unique allocation to each product component as a derived requirement, however, other times the shared requirement should instead be allocated directly to the architecture. For example, allocation of shared requirements to the architecture would describe how a performance requirement (e.g., on responsiveness) is budgeted among components so as to account in an end-to-end manner for realization of the requirement. This concept of shared requirements can extend to other architecturally significant quality attributes (e.g., security, reliability).

Example Work Products

1. Requirement allocation sheets
2. Provisional requirement allocations
3. Design constraints
4. Derived requirements
5. Relationships among derived requirements

Subpractices

1. Allocate requirements to functions.
2. Allocate requirements to product components and the architecture.
3. Allocate design constraints to product components and the architecture.
4. Allocate requirements to delivery increments.
5. Document relationships among allocated requirements.

    Relationships include dependencies in which a change in one requirement can affect other requirements.

SP 2.3 IDENTIFY INTERFACE REQUIREMENTS

Identify interface requirements.

Interfaces between functions (or between objects or other logical entities) are identified. Interfaces can drive the development of alternative solutions described in the Technical Solution process area.

Refer to the Product Integration process area for more information about ensuring interface compatibility.

Interface requirements between products or product components identified in the product architecture are defined. They are controlled as part of product and product component integration and are an integral part of the architecture definition.

Example Work Products

1. Interface requirements

Subpractices

1. Identify interfaces both external to the product and internal to the product (e.g., between functional partitions or objects).

    As the design progresses, the product architecture will be altered by technical solution processes, creating new interfaces between product components and components external to the product.

    Interfaces with product related lifecycle processes should also be identified.

TIP

Because of the importance of interfaces to effective product development, interfaces are addressed in multiple places: Interface requirements is covered in RD SP 2.3, design of interfaces is covered in TS SP 2.3, and ensuring interface compatibility is covered in PI SG 2.

TIP

Identifying the interfaces for which requirements will be developed is not a one-time event, but may continue for as long as design progresses or in response to changes.

RD

> Examples of these interfaces include interfaces with test equipment, transportation systems, support systems, and manufacturing facilities.

2. Develop the requirements for the identified interfaces.

    Refer to the Technical Solution process area for more information about designing interfaces using criteria.

    Requirements for interfaces are defined in terms such as origination, destination, stimulus, data characteristics for software, and electrical and mechanical characteristics for hardware.

SG 3 ANALYZE AND VALIDATE REQUIREMENTS

The requirements are analyzed and validated.

The specific practices of the Analyze and Validate Requirements specific goal support the development of the requirements in both the Develop Customer Requirements specific goal and the Develop Product Requirements specific goal. The specific practices associated with this specific goal cover analyzing and validating the requirements with respect to the end user's intended environment.

Analyses are performed to determine what impact the intended operational environment will have on the ability to satisfy the stakeholders' needs, expectations, constraints, and interfaces. Considerations, such as feasibility, mission needs, cost constraints, potential market size, and acquisition strategy, should all be taken into account, depending on the product context. Architecturally significant quality attributes are identified based on mission and business drivers. A definition of required functionality and quality attributes is also established. All specified usage modes for the product are considered.

The objectives of the analyses are to determine candidate requirements for product concepts that will satisfy stakeholder needs, expectations, and constraints and then to translate these concepts into requirements. In parallel with this activity, the parameters that will be used to evaluate the effectiveness of the product are determined based on customer input and the preliminary product concept.

Requirements are validated to increase the probability that the resulting product will perform as intended in the use environment.

TIP

The purpose of requirements validation is to make sure you have a clear understanding of what the customer wants and needs. Often, this understanding evolves over time and requires a series of requirements validation activities.

TIP

Requirements analyses examine requirements from different perspectives (e.g., feasibility, cost, and risk) and often use different abstractions (e.g., process, functional, data flow, entity-relationship, state diagrams, and temporal).

HINT

Technical performance parameters (TPPs) can be used to help in assessing or predicting quality attributes, cost, schedule, risk, etc.

X-REF

For more information about technical performance parameters, see "Using CMMI to Improve Earned Value Management" (www.sei.cmu.edu/publications/documents/02.reports/02tn016.html).

SP 3.1 *ESTABLISH OPERATIONAL CONCEPTS AND SCENARIOS*

Establish and maintain operational concepts and associated scenarios.

A scenario is typically a sequence of events that may occur in the development, use, or sustainment of the product, which is used to make explicit some of the functional or quality attribute needs of the stakeholders. In contrast, an operational concept for a product usually depends on both the design solution and the scenario. For example, the operational concept for a satellite based communications product is quite different from one based on landlines. Since the alternative solutions have not usually been defined when preparing the initial operational concepts, conceptual solutions are developed for use when analyzing the requirements. The operational concepts are refined as solution decisions are made and lower level detailed requirements are developed.

Just as a design decision for a product can become a requirement for a product component, the operational concept can become the scenarios (requirements) for product components. Operational concepts and scenarios are evolved to facilitate the selection of product component solutions that, when implemented, will satisfy the intended use of the product or facilitate its development and sustainment. Operational concepts and scenarios document the interaction of the product components with the environment, end users, and other product components, regardless of engineering discipline. They should be documented for all modes and states within operations, product development, deployment, delivery, support (including maintenance and sustainment), training, and disposal.

Scenarios can be developed to address operational, sustainment, development, or other event sequences.

> **HINT**
>
> Think of an operational concept as a *picture* that portrays the product, end user, and other entities in the intended environment. Think of a scenario as a *story* describing a sequence of events and end-user and product interactions. An operational concept provides a context for developing or evaluating a set of scenarios.

> **TIP**
>
> Operational concepts and scenarios are a way to demonstrate or bring to life what the requirements are trying to capture.

Example Work Products

1. Operational concept
2. Product or product component development, installation, operational, maintenance, and support concepts
3. Disposal concepts
4. Use cases
5. Timeline scenarios
6. New requirements

Subpractices

1. Develop operational concepts and scenarios that include operations, installation, development, maintenance, support, and disposal as appropriate.

Identify and develop scenarios, consistent with the level of detail in the stakeholder needs, expectations, and constraints in which the proposed product or product component is expected to operate.

Augment scenarios with quality attribute considerations for the functions (or other logical entities) described in the scenario.

2. Define the environment in which the product or product component will operate, including boundaries and constraints.

3. Review operational concepts and scenarios to refine and discover requirements.

Operational concept and scenario development is an iterative process. The reviews should be held periodically to ensure that they agree with the requirements. The review can be in the form of a walk-through.

4. Develop a detailed operational concept, as products and product components are selected, that defines the interaction of the product, the end user, and the environment, and that satisfies the operational, maintenance, support, and disposal needs.

<table>
<tr><td>X-REF</td></tr>
<tr><td>Component selection is further described in TS.</td></tr>
</table>

SP 3.2 ESTABLISH A DEFINITION OF REQUIRED FUNCTIONALITY AND QUALITY ATTRIBUTES

Establish and maintain a definition of required functionality and quality attributes.

One approach to defining required functionality and quality attributes is to analyze scenarios using what some have called a "functional analysis" to describe what the product is intended to do. This functional description can include actions, sequence, inputs, outputs, or other information that communicates the manner in which the product will be used. The resulting description of functions, logical groupings of functions, and their association with requirements is referred to as a functional architecture. (See the definitions of "functional analysis" and "functional architecture" in the glossary.)

<table>
<tr><td>TIP</td></tr>
<tr><td>As the activities described in RD and TS progress, the definition of required functionality and quality attributes is refined to reflect decisions made.</td></tr>
</table>

Such approaches have evolved in recent years through the introduction of architecture description languages, methods, and tools to more fully address and characterize the quality attributes, allowing a richer (e.g., multi-dimensional) specification of constraints on how the defined functionality will be realized in the product, and facilitating additional analyses of the requirements and technical solutions. Some quality attributes will emerge as architecturally significant and thus drive the development of the product architecture. These quality attributes often reflect cross-cutting concerns that may not be allocatable to lower level elements of a solution. A clear understanding of the quality attributes and their importance based on mission or business needs is an essential input to the design process.

Example Work Products

1. Definition of required functionality and quality attributes
2. Functional architecture
3. Activity diagrams and use cases
4. Object oriented analysis with services or methods identified
5. Architecturally significant quality attribute requirements

Subpractices

1. Determine key mission and business drivers.
2. Identify desirable functionality and quality attributes.

   Functionality and quality attributes can be identified and defined through an analysis of various scenarios with relevant stakeholders as described in the previous specific practice.

3. Determine architecturally significant quality attributes based on key mission and business drivers.
4. Analyze and quantify functionality required by end users.

   This analysis can involve considering the sequencing of time critical functions.

5. Analyze requirements to identify logical or functional partitions (e.g., subfunctions).
6. Partition requirements into groups, based on established criteria (e.g., similar functionality, similar quality attribute requirements, coupling), to facilitate and focus the requirements analysis.
7. Allocate customer requirements to functional partitions, objects, people, or support elements to support the synthesis of solutions.
8. Allocate requirements to functions and subfunctions (or other logical entities).

SP 3.3 ANALYZE REQUIREMENTS

Analyze requirements to ensure that they are necessary and sufficient.

In light of the operational concept and scenarios, the requirements for one level of the product hierarchy are analyzed to determine whether they are necessary and sufficient to meet the objectives of higher levels of the product hierarchy. The analyzed requirements then provide the basis for more detailed and precise requirements for lower levels of the product hierarchy.

As requirements are defined, their relationship to higher level requirements and the higher level definition of required functionality and quality attributes should be understood. Also, the key requirements used to track progress are determined. For instance, the

> **TIP**
>
> Requirements analyses help answer questions such as whether all requirements are necessary, whether any are missing, whether they are consistent with one other, and whether they can be implemented and verified.

> **X-REF**
>
> When analyzing requirements, look at some of the characteristics described in REQM SP 1.1 Subpractice 2 to understand the many factors that can be considered.

RD

TIP

The relationships among requirements up and down the product hierarchy are investigated and recorded (see REQM SP 1.4).

weight of a product or size of a software product can be monitored through development based on its risk or its criticality to the customer.

Refer to the Verification process area for more information about establishing verification procedures and criteria.

Example Work Products

1. Requirements defects reports
2. Proposed requirements changes to resolve defects
3. Key requirements
4. Technical performance measures

Subpractices

HINT

As conflicts are removed, inform the relevant stakeholders of changes that affect the requirements they provided.

1. Analyze stakeholder needs, expectations, constraints, and external interfaces to organize them into related subjects and remove conflicts.
2. Analyze requirements to determine whether they satisfy the objectives of higher level requirements.
3. Analyze requirements to ensure that they are complete, feasible, realizable, and verifiable.

    While design determines the feasibility of a particular solution, this subpractice addresses knowing which requirements affect feasibility.

TIP

In these subpractices, you determine whether the requirements serve as an adequate basis for product development and how to track progress in achieving key requirements.

4. Identify key requirements that have a strong influence on cost, schedule, performance, or risk.
5. Identify technical performance measures that will be tracked during the development effort.

    Refer to the Measurement and Analysis process area for more information about developing and sustaining a measurement capability used to support management information needs.

6. Analyze operational concepts and scenarios to refine the customer needs, constraints, and interfaces and to discover new requirements.

    This analysis can result in more detailed operational concepts and scenarios as well as supporting the derivation of new requirements.

SP 3.4 ANALYZE REQUIREMENTS TO ACHIEVE BALANCE

Analyze requirements to balance stakeholder needs and constraints.

TIP

Often, the wish list is too large. It is necessary to understand the tradeoffs and what is truly important.

Stakeholder needs and constraints can address such things as cost, schedule, product or project performance, functionality, priorities, reusable components, maintainability, or risk.

Example Work Products

1. Assessment of risks related to requirements

Subpractices

1. Use proven models, simulations, and prototyping to analyze the balance of stakeholder needs and constraints.

   Results of the analyses can be used to reduce the cost of the product and the risk in developing the product.

2. Perform a risk assessment on the requirements and definition of required functionality and quality attributes.

   Refer to the Risk Management process area for more information about identifying and analyzing risks.

3. Examine product lifecycle concepts for impacts of requirements on risks.

4. Assess the impact of the architecturally significant quality attribute requirements on the product and product development costs and risks.

   When the impact of requirements on costs and risks seems to outweigh the perceived benefit, relevant stakeholders should be consulted to determine what changes may be needed.

   As an example, a really tight response time requirement or a high availability requirement could prove expensive to implement. Perhaps the requirement could be relaxed once the impacts (e.g., on cost) are understood.

SP 3.5 VALIDATE REQUIREMENTS

Validate requirements to ensure the resulting product will perform as intended in the end user's environment.

Requirements validation is performed early in the development effort with end users to gain confidence that the requirements are capable of guiding a development that results in successful final validation. This activity should be integrated with risk management activities. Mature organizations will typically perform requirements validation in a more sophisticated way using multiple techniques and will broaden the basis of the validation to include other stakeholder needs and expectations.

TIP

Requirements validation should begin early and should be repeated to limit the risk of having inadequate requirements.

RD

> Examples of techniques used for requirements validation include the following:
> - Analysis
> - Simulations
> - Prototyping
> - Demonstrations

Example Work Products

1. Record of analysis methods and results

Subpractices

1. Analyze the requirements to determine the risk that the resulting product will not perform appropriately in its intended use environment.

2. Explore the adequacy and completeness of requirements by developing product representations (e.g., prototypes, simulations, models, scenarios, storyboards) and by obtaining feedback about them from relevant stakeholders.

   Refer to the Validation process area for more information about preparing for validation and validating product or product components.

3. Assess the design as it matures in the context of the requirements validation environment to identify validation issues and expose unstated needs and customer requirements.

TIP

Requirements validation in this SP and product validation in VAL have the same goal, though different perspectives. Requirements validation focuses on the adequacy and completeness of the requirements. VAL focuses on predicting at multiple points in product development how well the product will satisfy user needs.

REQUIREMENTS MANAGEMENT

A Project Management Process Area at Maturity Level 2

Purpose

The purpose of Requirements Management (REQM) is to manage requirements of the project's products and product components and to ensure alignment between those requirements and the project's plans and work products.

X-REF

REQM does not address eliciting or developing requirements. For more information on these topics, refer to the RD process area.

Introductory Notes

Requirements management processes manage all requirements received or generated by the project, including both technical and nontechnical requirements as well as requirements levied on the project by the organization.

In particular, if the Requirements Development process area is implemented, its processes will generate product and product component requirements that will also be managed by the requirements management processes.

Throughout the process areas, where the terms "product" and "product component" are used, their intended meanings also encompass services, service systems, and their components.

When the Requirements Management, Requirements Development, and Technical Solution process areas are all implemented, their associated processes can be closely tied and be performed concurrently.

The project takes appropriate steps to ensure that the set of approved requirements is managed to support the planning and execution needs of the project. When a project receives requirements from an approved requirements provider, these requirements are reviewed with the requirements provider to resolve issues and prevent misunderstanding before requirements are incorporated into project plans. Once the requirements provider and the requirements receiver reach an agreement, commitment to the requirements is obtained from project participants. The project manages changes to

TIP

REQM addresses *all requirements* handled by the project, thus providing a stable foundation for project planning, development, testing, and delivery.

TIP

Nontechnical requirements include requirements that address cost and schedule.

TIP

RD develops requirements, TS implements them, and REQM manages them from development through implementation.

TIP

Requirements providers can include customers, end users, suppliers, management, regulatory agencies, or standards bodies.

REQM

TIP

Managing changes to requirements ensures that all parts of the project are working on the most current set of requirements.

TIP

Bidirectional traceability, explained in SP 1.4, is a concept that is critical to implementing RD and TS.

requirements as they evolve and identifies inconsistencies that occur among plans, work products, and requirements.

Part of managing requirements is documenting requirements changes and their rationale and maintaining bidirectional traceability between source requirements, all product and product component requirements, and other specified work products. (See the definition of "bidirectional traceability" in the glossary.)

All projects have requirements. In the case of maintenance activities, changes are based on changes to the existing requirements, design, or implementation. In projects that deliver increments of product capability, the changes can also be due to evolving customer needs, technology maturation and obsolescence, and standards evolution. In both cases, the requirements changes, if any, might be documented in change requests from the customer or end users, or they might take the form of new requirements received from the requirements development process. Regardless of their source or form, activities that are driven by changes to requirements are managed accordingly.

TIP

In maintenance projects, requirements changes still need to be managed, regardless of their source.

TIP

The practices and principles in a process area are often more broadly applicable than first imagined. REQM is often valuable to an organization's training department, quality assurance group, marketing group, and so on.

In Agile environments, requirements are communicated and tracked through mechanisms such as product backlogs, story cards, and screen mock-ups. Commitments to requirements are either made collectively by the team or an empowered team leader. Work assignments are regularly (e.g., daily, weekly) adjusted based on progress made and as an improved understanding of the requirements and solution emerge. Traceability and consistency across requirements and work products is addressed through the mechanisms already mentioned as well as during start-of-iteration or end-of-iteration activities such as "retrospectives" and "demo days." (See "Interpreting CMMI When Using Agile Approaches" in Part I.)

Related Process Areas

Refer to the Requirements Development process area for more information about eliciting, analyzing, and establishing customer, product, and product component requirements.

Refer to the Technical Solution process area for more information about selecting, designing, and implementing solutions to requirements.

Refer to the Configuration Management process area for more information about establishing baselines and tracking and controlling changes.

Refer to the Project Monitoring and Control process area for more information about monitoring the project against the plan and managing corrective action to closure.

Refer to the Project Planning process area for more information about establishing and maintaining plans that define project activities.

Refer to the Risk Management process area for more information about identifying and analyzing risks.

Specific Goal and Practice Summary

SG 1   Manage Requirements
  SP 1.1   Understand Requirements
  SP 1.2   Obtain Commitment to Requirements
  SP 1.3   Manage Requirements Changes
  SP 1.4   Maintain Bidirectional Traceability of Requirements
  SP 1.5   Ensure Alignment Between Project Work and Requirements

Specific Practices by Goal

SG 1   MANAGE REQUIREMENTS

Requirements are managed and inconsistencies with project plans and work products are identified.

The project maintains a current and approved set of requirements over the life of the project by doing the following:

- Managing all changes to requirements
- Maintaining relationships among requirements, project plans, and work products
- Ensuring alignment among requirements, project plans, and work products
- Taking corrective action

Refer to the Requirements Development process area for more information about analyzing and validating requirements.

Refer to the Develop Alternative Solutions and Selection Criteria specific practice in the Technical Solution process area for more information about determining the feasibility of the requirements.

Refer to the Project Monitoring and Control process area for more information about managing corrective action to closure.

TIP

Requirements communicate expectations for the final product. These expectations evolve as the project progresses.

REQM

SP 1.1 UNDERSTAND REQUIREMENTS

Develop an understanding with the requirements providers on the meaning of the requirements.

TIP

"Requirements creep" is the tendency for requirements to continually flow into a project (often from multiple sources) and expand the project's scope beyond what was planned.

As the project matures and requirements are derived, all activities or disciplines will receive requirements. To avoid requirements creep, criteria are established to designate appropriate channels or official sources from which to receive requirements. Those who receive requirements conduct analyses of them with the provider to ensure that a compatible, shared understanding is reached on the meaning of requirements. The result of these analyses and dialogs is a set of approved requirements.

Example Work Products

1. Lists of criteria for distinguishing appropriate requirements providers
2. Criteria for evaluation and acceptance of requirements
3. Results of analyses against criteria
4. A set of approved requirements

TIP

Official sources of requirements are the people you select to get requirements from. Unofficial discussions that result in additional requirements can cause trouble.

Subpractices

1. Establish criteria for distinguishing appropriate requirements providers.
2. Establish objective criteria for the evaluation and acceptance of requirements.

   Lack of evaluation and acceptance criteria often results in inadequate verification, costly rework, or customer rejection.

X-REF

Refer to GP 2.7 for examples of requirements providers (and other relevant stakeholders) that may be involved with the REQM process.

Examples of evaluation and acceptance criteria include the following:
- Clearly and properly stated
- Complete
- Consistent with one another
- Uniquely identified
- Consistent with architectural approach and quality attribute priorities
- Appropriate to implement
- Verifiable (i.e., testable)
- Traceable
- Achievable
- Tied to business value
- Identified as a priority for the customer

3. Analyze requirements to ensure that established criteria are met.
4. Reach an understanding of requirements with requirements providers so that project participants can commit to them.

SP 1.2 OBTAIN COMMITMENT TO REQUIREMENTS

Obtain commitment to requirements from project participants.

Refer to the Project Monitoring and Control process area for more information about monitoring commitments.

The previous specific practice dealt with reaching an understanding with requirements providers. This specific practice deals with agreements and commitments among those who carry out activities necessary to implement requirements. Requirements evolve throughout the project. As requirements evolve, this specific practice ensures that project participants commit to the current and approved requirements and the resulting changes in project plans, activities, and work products.

Example Work Products

1. Requirements impact assessments
2. Documented commitments to requirements and requirements changes

Subpractices

1. Assess the impact of requirements on existing commitments.

    The impact on the project participants should be evaluated when the requirements change or at the start of a new requirement.
2. Negotiate and record commitments.

    Changes to existing commitments should be negotiated before project participants commit to a new requirement or requirement change.

SP 1.3 MANAGE REQUIREMENTS CHANGES

Manage changes to requirements as they evolve during the project.

Refer to the Configuration Management process area for more information about tracking and controlling changes.

Requirements change for a variety of reasons. As needs change and as work proceeds, changes may have to be made to existing requirements. It is essential to manage these additions and changes efficiently and effectively. To effectively analyze the impact of changes, it is necessary that the source of each requirement is known and the

---

TIP

Two-way communication is critical to ensuring that a shared understanding of requirements exists between the project and the requirements providers.

TIP

Typically, at the beginning of a project, only about 50% of the requirements are known.

TIP

Project members who make commitments must continually evaluate whether they can meet their commitments, communicate immediately when they realize they cannot meet a commitment, and mitigate the impacts of not being able to meet a commitment.

TIP

Commitments are a recurring theme in CMMI. They are also documented and reconciled in PP, monitored in PMC, and addressed more thoroughly in IPM.

TIP

Documented commitments can be in the form of meeting minutes, signed-off documents, or email.

TIP

Commitments comprise both the resources involved and the schedule for completion.

TIP

Controlling changes ensures that project members and customers have a clear and shared understanding of the requirements.

REQM

rationale for the change is documented. The project may want to track appropriate measures of requirements volatility to judge whether new or revised approach to change control is necessary.

Example Work Products

1. Requirements change requests
2. Requirements change impact reports
3. Requirements status
4. Requirements database

Subpractices

1. Document all requirements and requirements changes that are given to or generated by the project.
2. Maintain a requirements change history, including the rationale for changes.

    Maintaining the change history helps to track requirements volatility.
3. Evaluate the impact of requirement changes from the standpoint of relevant stakeholders.

    Requirements changes that affect the product architecture can affect many stakeholders.
4. Make requirements and change data available to the project.

SP 1.4 MAINTAIN BIDIRECTIONAL TRACEABILITY OF REQUIREMENTS

Maintain bidirectional traceability among requirements and work products.

The intent of this specific practice is to maintain the bidirectional traceability of requirements. (See the definition of "bidirectional traceability" in the glossary.) When requirements are managed well, traceability can be established from a source requirement to its lower level requirements and from those lower level requirements back to their source requirements. Such bidirectional traceability helps to determine whether all source requirements have been completely addressed and whether all lower level requirements can be traced to a valid source.

Requirements traceability also covers relationships to other entities such as intermediate and final work products, changes in design documentation, and test plans. Traceability can cover horizontal relationships, such as across interfaces, as well as vertical relationships. Traceability is particularly needed when assessing the impact of requirements changes on project activities and work products.

> Examples of what aspects of traceability to consider include the following:
> • Scope of traceability: The boundaries within which traceability is needed
> • Definition of traceability: The elements that need logical relationships
> • Type of traceability: When horizontal and vertical traceability is needed

Such bidirectional traceability is not always automated. It can be done manually using spreadsheets, databases, and other common tools.

Example Work Products

1. Requirements traceability matrix
2. Requirements tracking system

Subpractices

1. Maintain requirements traceability to ensure that the source of lower level (i.e., derived) requirements is documented.
2. Maintain requirements traceability from a requirement to its derived requirements and allocation to work products.

   Work products for which traceability may be maintained include the architecture, product components, development iterations (or increments), functions, interfaces, objects, people, processes, and other work products.

3. Generate a requirements traceability matrix.

SP 1.5 *ENSURE ALIGNMENT BETWEEN PROJECT WORK AND REQUIREMENTS*

Ensure that project plans and work products remain aligned with requirements.

This specific practice finds inconsistencies between requirements and project plans and work products and initiates corrective actions to resolve them.

Example Work Products

1. Documentation of inconsistencies between requirements and project plans and work products, including sources and conditions
2. Corrective actions

Subpractices

1. Review project plans, activities, and work products for consistency with requirements and changes made to them.
2. Identify the source of the inconsistency (if any).

TIP

Maintaining traceability across horizontal relationships can greatly reduce problems encountered in product integration.

TIP

A traceability matrix can take many forms: a spreadsheet, a database, and so on.

HINT

When a requirement changes, update the traceability matrix to retain insight into the requirements-to-work product relationships mentioned earlier.

TIP

Especially for larger projects, product components are developed in parallel and it is challenging to keep all work products fully consistent with changes to the requirements.

TIP

A traceability matrix can help with this review of project plans, activities, and work products.

REQM

3. Identify any changes that should be made to plans and work products resulting from changes to the requirements baseline.

4. Initiate any necessary corrective actions.

RISK MANAGEMENT
A Project Management Process Area at Maturity Level 3

Purpose

The purpose of Risk Management (RSKM) is to identify potential problems before they occur so that risk handling activities can be planned and invoked as needed across the life of the product or project to mitigate adverse impacts on achieving objectives.

Introductory Notes

Risk management is a continuous, forward-looking process that is an important part of project management. Risk management should address issues that could endanger achievement of critical objectives. A continuous risk management approach effectively anticipates and mitigates risks that can have a critical impact on a project.

Effective risk management includes early and aggressive risk identification through collaboration and the involvement of relevant stakeholders as described in the stakeholder involvement plan addressed in the Project Planning process area. Strong leadership among all relevant stakeholders is needed to establish an environment for free and open disclosure and discussion of risk.

Risk management should consider both internal and external, as well as both technical and non-technical, sources of cost, schedule, performance, and other risks. Early and aggressive detection of risk is important because it is typically easier, less costly, and less disruptive to make changes and correct work efforts during the earlier, rather than the later, phases of the project.

For example, decisions related to product architecture are often made early before their impacts can be fully understood, and thus the risk implications of such choices should be carefully considered.

Industry standards can help when determining how to prevent or mitigate specific risks commonly found in a particular industry. Certain risks can be proactively managed or mitigated by reviewing industry best practices and lessons learned.

TIP

In any project, problems impact the achievement of objectives. Resolving problems after they occur can be disruptive and expensive. RSKM is a systematic approach to identifying potential problems before they occur to provide time to determine how best to address them.

TIP

RSKM also can apply to identifying, evaluating, and maximizing (or realizing) *opportunities*.

TIP

In a dynamic environment, risk management must be a continuous process of identifying, analyzing, and mitigating risks.

TIP

Without a free and open environment, many risks remain undisclosed until they surface as problems.

HINT

Relevant stakeholders external to the project bring perspectives and insight into identifying and evaluating risks. They also may control the resources needed by the project, so it is important to maintain a dialog on related risks.

TIP

Sources of risks are not just technical, but can be programmatic (e.g., cost, schedule, supplier risks) or business related (e.g., competitor getting to market first).

TIP

A precondition to efficient risk management is having shared and consistent project objectives. Project objectives provide focus to risk management and help guide its activities.

X-REF

PP and PMC have risk-management-related practices: See PP, SP 2.2 Identify Project Risks, and PMC, SP 1.3 Monitor Project Risks.

X-REF

For more information, see B. Boehm, "Software Risk Management: Principles and Practices," *IEEE Software*, 1990; Project Management Institute, *A Guide to the Project Management Body of Knowledge (PMBOK Guide) Fourth Edition,* 2008 (Chapter 11 deals with risk management); and www.sei.cmu.edu/risk/index.cfm.

Risk management can be divided into the following parts:

- Defining a risk management strategy
- Identifying and analyzing risks
- Handling identified risks, including the implementation of risk mitigation plans as needed

As represented in the Project Planning and Project Monitoring and Control process areas, organizations initially may focus on risk identification for awareness and react to the realization of these risks as they occur. The Risk Management process area describes an evolution of these specific practices to systematically plan, anticipate, and mitigate risks to proactively minimize their impact on the project.

Although the primary emphasis of the Risk Management process area is on the project, these concepts can also be applied to manage organizational risks.

In Agile environments, some risk management activities are inherently embedded in the Agile method used. For example, some technical risks can be addressed by encouraging experimentation (early "failures") or by executing a "spike" outside of the routine iteration. However, the Risk Management process area encourages a more systematic approach to managing risks, both technical and non-technical. Such an approach can be integrated into Agile's typical iteration and meeting rhythms; more specifically, during iteration planning, task estimating, and acceptance of tasks. (See "Interpreting CMMI When Using Agile Approaches" in Part I.)

Related Process Areas

Refer to the Decision Analysis and Resolution process area for more information about analyzing possible decisions using a formal evaluation process that evaluates identified alternatives against established criteria.

Refer to the Project Monitoring and Control process area for more information about monitoring project risks.

Refer to the Project Planning process area for more information about identifying project risks and planning stakeholder involvement.

Specific Goal and Practice Summary

SG 1 Prepare for Risk Management
    SP 1.1   Determine Risk Sources and Categories
    SP 1.2   Define Risk Parameters
    SP 1.3   Establish a Risk Management Strategy

SG 2 Identify and Analyze Risks
    SP 2.1   Identify Risks
    SP 2.2   Evaluate, Categorize, and Prioritize Risks
SG 3 Mitigate Risks
    SP 3.1   Develop Risk Mitigation Plans
    SP 3.2   Implement Risk Mitigation Plans

Specific Practices by Goal

SG 1 PREPARE FOR RISK MANAGEMENT

Preparation for risk management is conducted.

Prepare for risk management by establishing and maintaining a strategy for identifying, analyzing, and mitigating risks. Typically, this strategy is documented in a risk management plan. The risk management strategy addresses specific actions and the management approach used to apply and control the risk management program. The strategy typically includes identifying sources of risk, the scheme used to categorize risks, and parameters used to evaluate, bound, and control risks for effective handling.

SP 1.1 DETERMINE RISK SOURCES AND CATEGORIES

Determine risk sources and categories.

Identifying risk sources provides a basis for systematically examining changing situations over time to uncover circumstances that affect the ability of the project to meet its objectives. Risk sources are both internal and external to the project. As the project progresses, additional sources of risk can be identified. Establishing categories for risks provides a mechanism for collecting and organizing risks as well as ensuring appropriate scrutiny and management attention to risks that can have serious consequences on meeting project objectives.

Example Work Products

1. Risk source lists (external and internal)
2. Risk categories list

Subpractices

1. Determine risk sources.

    Risk sources are fundamental drivers that cause risks in a project or organization. There are many sources of risks, both internal and external to a project. Risk sources identify where risks can originate.

TIP

Without a risk management strategy, projects fail to identify critical risks, inconsistently evaluate them, and ineffectively and inefficiently handle them.

TIP

When there is a lot of homogeneity in an organization's projects, SG 1 may be cost-effectively implemented at the organizational level (especially if the projects are small and short in duration). Such an approach helps senior managers evaluate risk exposure across multiple projects.

HINT

If a project uses safety and security analysis methods, you should incorporate these methods as part of the risk management strategy.

TIP

Under stress, people lose perspective when it comes to risks. Some risks (e.g., those external to the team) may be given too much emphasis and others too little. Having a list of risk sources, both internal and external, helps bring objectivity to the identification of risks.

TIP

In a typical project, risks and their status change. A standard list of risk sources enables a project to be thorough in its identification of risks at each point in the project.

TIP

Disruptions to the continuity of operations is a risk source (generally) that is often neglected. It may have huge consequences, but also has cost-effective mitigation techniques. Refer to the Service Continuity PA of CMMI for Serices for more information.

TIP

A taxonomy of risk sources can provide a project with a reasonably thorough checklist for identifying new risks, even as situations change.

TIP

Categories are used to group related risks that can often be addressed by the same mitigation activities, thereby increasing risk management efficiency.

TIP

Risks are often grouped by lifecycle phase.

Typical internal and external risk sources include the following:
- Uncertain requirements
- Unprecedented efforts (i.e., estimates unavailable)
- Infeasible design
- Competing quality attribute requirements that affect solution selection and design
- Unavailable technology
- Unrealistic schedule estimates or allocation
- Inadequate staffing and skills
- Cost or funding issues
- Uncertain or inadequate subcontractor capability
- Uncertain or inadequate supplier capability
- Inadequate communication with actual or potential customers or with their representatives
- Disruptions to the continuity of operations
- Regulatory constraints (e.g., security, safety, environment)

Many of these sources of risk are accepted without adequately planning for them. Early identification of both internal and external sources of risk can lead to early identification of risks. Risk mitigation plans can then be implemented early in the project to preclude occurrence of risks or reduce consequences of their occurrence.

2. Determine risk categories.

Risk categories are "bins" used for collecting and organizing risks. Identifying risk categories aids the future consolidation of activities in risk mitigation plans.

The following factors can be considered when determining risk categories:
- Phases of the project's lifecycle model (e.g., requirements, design, manufacturing, test and evaluation, delivery, disposal)
- Types of processes used
- Types of products used
- Project management risks (e.g., contract risks, budget risks, schedule risks, resource risks)
- Technical performance risks (e.g., quality attribute related risks, supportability risks)

A risk taxonomy can be used to provide a framework for determining risk sources and categories.

SP 1.2 DEFINE RISK PARAMETERS

Define parameters used to analyze and categorize risks and to control the risk management effort.

Parameters for evaluating, categorizing, and prioritizing risks include the following:

- Risk likelihood (i.e., probability of risk occurrence)
- Risk consequence (i.e., impact and severity of risk occurrence)
- Thresholds to trigger management activities

Risk parameters are used to provide common and consistent criteria for comparing risks to be managed. Without these parameters, it is difficult to gauge the severity of an unwanted change caused by a risk and to prioritize the actions required for risk mitigation planning.

Projects should document the parameters used to analyze and categorize risks so that they are available for reference throughout the life of the project because circumstances change over time. Using these parameters, risks can easily be re-categorized and analyzed when changes occur.

The project can use techniques such as failure mode and effects analysis (FMEA) to examine risks of potential failures in the product or in selected product development processes. Such techniques can help to provide discipline in working with risk parameters.

Example Work Products

1. Risk evaluation, categorization, and prioritization criteria
2. Risk management requirements (e.g., control and approval levels, reassessment intervals)

Subpractices

1. Define consistent criteria for evaluating and quantifying risk likelihood and severity levels.

   Consistently used criteria (e.g., bounds on likelihood, severity levels) allow impacts of different risks to be commonly understood, to receive the appropriate level of scrutiny, and to obtain the management attention warranted. In managing dissimilar risks (e.g., staff safety versus environmental pollution), it is important to ensure consistency in the end result. (For example, a high-impact risk of environmental pollution is as important as a high-impact risk to staff safety.) One way of providing a common basis for comparing dissimilar risks is assigning dollar values to risks (e.g., through a process of risk monetization).

TIP

These requirements include the thresholds associated with each risk category.

TIP

To be effective, risk management must be objective and quantitative. Therefore, treat risks consistently with respect to key parameters. Defining criteria for evaluating risks helps to ensure consistency (e.g., helping to decide which risks get escalated, mitigated, and so on, based only on the values of their parameters).

TIP

In the middle of a project, you often lose perspective. Defining thresholds in advance enables a more objective treatment of risks.

2. Define thresholds for each risk category.

> For each risk category, thresholds can be established to determine acceptability or unacceptability of risks, prioritization of risks, or triggers for management action.

TIP

These thresholds may need to be refined later as part of risk mitigation planning.

Examples of thresholds include the following:
- Project-wide thresholds could be established to involve senior management when product costs exceed 10 percent of the target cost or when cost performance indices (CPIs) fall below 0.95.
- Schedule thresholds could be established to involve senior management when schedule performance indices (SPIs) fall below 0.95.
- Performance thresholds could be established to involve senior management when specified key items (e.g., processor utilization, average response times) exceed 125 percent of the intended design.

TIP

Bounds are intended to scope the risk management effort in sensible ways that help conserve project resources.

3. Define bounds on the extent to which thresholds are applied against or within a category.

> There are few limits to which risks can be assessed in either a quantitative or qualitative fashion. Definition of bounds (or boundary conditions) can be used to help define the extent of the risk management effort and avoid excessive resource expenditures. Bounds can include the exclusion of a risk source from a category. These bounds can also exclude conditions that occur below a given frequency.

SP 1.3 ESTABLISH A RISK MANAGEMENT STRATEGY

Establish and maintain the strategy to be used for risk management.

TIP

The risk management strategy documents the results of the first two specific practices.

A comprehensive risk management strategy addresses items such as the following:

- The scope of the risk management effort
- Methods and tools to be used for risk identification, risk analysis, risk mitigation, risk monitoring, and communication
- Project specific sources of risks
- How risks are to be organized, categorized, compared, and consolidated
- Parameters used for taking action on identified risks, including likelihood, consequence, and thresholds
- Risk mitigation techniques to be used, such as prototyping, piloting, simulation, alternative designs, or evolutionary development
- The definition of risk measures used to monitor the status of risks
- Time intervals for risk monitoring or reassessment

TIP

An important part of the strategy is to determine the frequency of monitoring activities and of reassessing risks for changes in status.

The risk management strategy should be guided by a common vision of success that describes desired future project outcomes in terms of the product delivered, its cost, and its fitness for the task. The risk management strategy is often documented in a risk management plan for the organization or project. This strategy is reviewed with relevant stakeholders to promote commitment and understanding.

A risk management strategy should be developed early in the project, so that relevant risks are identified and managed proactively. Early identification and assessment of critical risks allows the project to formulate risk handling approaches and adjust project definition and allocation of resources based on critical risks.

Example Work Products

1. Project risk management strategy

SG 2   IDENTIFY AND ANALYZE RISKS

Risks are identified and analyzed to determine their relative importance.

The degree of risk affects the resources assigned to handle the risk and the timing of when appropriate management attention is required.

Risk analysis entails identifying risks from identified internal and external sources and evaluating each identified risk to determine its likelihood and consequences. Risk categorization, based on an evaluation against established risk categories and criteria developed for the risk management strategy, provides information needed for risk handling. Related risks can be grouped to enable efficient handling and effective use of risk management resources.

SP 2.1   IDENTIFY RISKS

Identify and document risks.

Identifying potential issues, hazards, threats, and vulnerabilities that could negatively affect work efforts or plans is the basis for sound and successful risk management. Risks should be identified and described understandably before they can be analyzed and managed properly. Risks are documented in a concise statement that includes the context, conditions, and consequences of risk occurrence.

Risk identification should be an organized, thorough approach to seek out probable or realistic risks in achieving objectives. To be effective, risk identification should not attempt to address every possible event. Using categories and parameters developed in the risk

RSKM

TIP
All relevant stakeholders must understand the risk management strategy fully.

TIP
Some organizations develop a standard risk management strategy template that is tailored to meet the needs of individual projects.

TIP
The risk management strategy is often documented as part of a risk management plan, or as a section in the project plan.

TIP
Risk identification and analysis is a continuing activity for the duration of the project.

TIP
Describing context, conditions, and consequences of a risk in a risk statement provide much of the information that is needed later to understand and evaluate the risk.

TIP
In OPD, process assets can include risk taxonomies, templates for describing risks, lessons learned, and exemplar risk management strategies that can benefit a new project.

HINT

Establish a work environment in which risks can be disclosed and discussed openly, without fear of repercussions. (Don't shoot the messenger!)

TIP

Many of the methods used for identifying risks use organizational process assets such as a risk taxonomy, risk repository, and lessons learned from past projects. Subject-matter experts may also be utilized. Other methods involve reviewing project artifacts such as the project shared vision, WBS, designs, project interfaces, and contractual requirements.

HINT

Sometimes, customers are short-sighted about their requirements. Explain to customers the implications of their requirements and associated risks. However, the result may be a decision to not mitigate the associated risks (unless required or desired for other reasons).

TIP

One approach to identifying risks is to consider the cost, schedule, and performance issues associated with each lifecycle phase. As each phase typically has a clear set of objectives and a completion milestone, a phase is a suitable context for identifying the risks associated with that phase.

management strategy and identified sources of risk can provide the discipline and streamlining appropriate for risk identification. Identified risks form a baseline for initiating risk management activities. Risks should be reviewed periodically to reexamine possible sources of risk and changing conditions to uncover sources and risks previously overlooked or nonexistent when the risk management strategy was last updated.

Risk identification focuses on the identification of risks, not the placement of blame. The results of risk identification activities should never be used by management to evaluate the performance of individuals.

Many methods are used for identifying risks. Typical identification methods include the following:

- Examine each element of the project work breakdown structure.
- Conduct a risk assessment using a risk taxonomy.
- Interview subject matter experts.
- Review risk management efforts from similar products.
- Examine lessons learned documents or databases.
- Examine design specifications and agreement requirements.

Example Work Products

1. List of identified risks, including the context, conditions, and consequences of risk occurrence

Subpractices

1. Identify the risks associated with cost, schedule, and performance.

   Risks associated with cost, schedule, performance, and other business objectives should be examined to understand their effect on project objectives. Risk candidates can be discovered that are outside the scope of project objectives but vital to customer interests. For example, risks in development costs, product acquisition costs, cost of spare (or replacement) products, and product disposition (or disposal) costs have design implications.

   The customer may not have considered the full cost of supporting a fielded product or using a delivered service. The customer should be informed of such risks, but actively managing those risks may not be necessary. Mechanisms for making such decisions should be examined at project and organization levels and put in place if deemed appropriate, especially for risks that affect the project's ability to verify and validate the product.

In addition to the cost risks identified above, other cost risks can include the ones associated with funding levels, funding estimates, and distributed budgets.

Schedule risks can include risks associated with planned activities, key events, and milestones.

TIP

"Can a project have no risks?" "Can multiple projects have the same risk lists?" If these questions are asked, someone does not understand risks. Some risks may be product specific, contract specific, or staff specific.

Performance risks can include risks associated with the following:

- Requirements
- Analysis and design
- Application of new technology
- Physical size
- Shape
- Weight
- Manufacturing and fabrication
- Product behavior and operation with respect to functionality or quality attributes
- Verification
- Validation
- Performance maintenance attributes

TIP

Performance risks may be associated with lifecycle phases, new technology, or desired quality attributes of the product.

Performance maintenance attributes are those characteristics that enable an in-use product or service to provide required performance, such as maintaining safety and security performance.

There are risks that do not fall into cost, schedule, or performance categories, but can be associated with other aspects of the organization's operation.

Examples of these other risks include risks related to the following:

- Strikes
- Diminishing sources of supply
- Technology cycle time
- Competition

TIP

Not all risks fall into the cost, schedule, and performance subcategories.

2. Review environmental elements that can affect the project.

Risks to a project that frequently are missed include risks supposedly outside the scope of the project (i.e., the project does not control whether they occur but can mitigate their impact). These risks can include weather or natural disasters, political changes, and telecommunications failures.

3. Review all elements of the work breakdown structure as part of identifying risks to help ensure that all aspects of the work effort have been considered.

TIP

Environmental risks are often ignored, even though some cost-effective mitigation activities are available.

RSKM

4. Review all elements of the project plan as part of identifying risks to help ensure that all aspects of the project have been considered.

> Refer to the Project Planning process area for more information about identifying project risks.

5. Document the context, conditions, and potential consequences of each risk.

> Risk statements are typically documented in a standard format that contains the risk context, conditions, and consequences of occurrence. The risk context provides additional information about the risk such as the relative time frame of the risk, the circumstances or conditions surrounding the risk that has brought about the concern, and any doubt or uncertainty.

6. Identify the relevant stakeholders associated with each risk.

SP 2.2 EVALUATE, CATEGORIZE, AND PRIORITIZE RISKS

Evaluate and categorize each identified risk using defined risk categories and parameters, and determine its relative priority.

The evaluation of risks is needed to assign a relative importance to each identified risk and is used in determining when appropriate management attention is required. Often it is useful to aggregate risks based on their interrelationships and develop options at an aggregate level. When an aggregate risk is formed by a roll up of lower level risks, care should be taken to ensure that important lower level risks are not ignored.

Collectively, the activities of risk evaluation, categorization, and prioritization are sometimes called a "risk assessment" or "risk analysis."

Example Work Products

1. List of risks and their assigned priority

Subpractices

1. Evaluate identified risks using defined risk parameters.

> Each risk is evaluated and assigned values according to defined risk parameters, which can include likelihood, consequence (i.e., severity, impact), and thresholds. The assigned risk parameter values can be integrated to produce additional measures, such as risk exposure (i.e., the combination of likelihood and consequence), which can be used to prioritize risks for handling.

> Often, a scale with three to five values is used to evaluate both likelihood and consequence.

> Likelihood, for example, can be categorized as remote, unlikely, likely, highly likely, or nearly certain.

> Example categories for consequence include the following:
> - Low
> - Medium
> - High
> - Negligible
> - Marginal
> - Significant
> - Critical
> - Catastrophic

Probability values are frequently used to quantify likelihood. Consequences are generally related to cost, schedule, environmental impact, or human measures (e.g., labor hours lost, severity of injury).

Risk evaluation is often a difficult and time consuming task. Specific expertise or group techniques may be needed to assess risks and gain confidence in the prioritization. In addition, priorities can require reevaluation as time progresses. To provide a basis for comparing the impact of the realization of identified risks, consequences of the risks can be monetized.

2. Categorize and group risks according to defined risk categories.

Risks are categorized into defined risk categories, providing a means to review them according to their source, taxonomy, or project component. Related or equivalent risks can be grouped for efficient handling. The cause-and-effect relationships between related risks are documented.

3. Prioritize risks for mitigation.

A relative priority is determined for each risk based on assigned risk parameters. Clear criteria should be used to determine risk priority. Risk prioritization helps to determine the most effective areas to which resources for risks mitigation can be applied with the greatest positive impact on the project.

> **TIP**
>
> Determining values for risk likelihood and consequence is easier and more repeatable if there are clear statements of objectives, criteria exist for assigning values, there is appropriate representation of relevant stakeholders, and staff has been trained.

> **TIP**
>
> Priority assignment can likewise be a repeatable process.

SG 3 *MITIGATE RISKS*

Risks are handled and mitigated as appropriate to reduce adverse impacts on achieving objectives.

The steps in handling risks include developing risk handling options, monitoring risks, and performing risk handling activities when

SUPPLIER AGREEMENT MANAGEMENT
A Project Management Process Area at Maturity Level 2

Purpose

The purpose of Supplier Agreement Management (SAM) is to manage the acquisition of products and services from suppliers.

Introductory Notes

The scope of this process area addresses the acquisition of products, services, and product and service components that can be delivered to the project's customer or included in a product or service system. This process area's practices can also be used for other purposes that benefit the project (e.g., purchasing consumables).

This process area does not apply in all contexts in which commercial off-the-shelf (COTS) components are acquired but does apply in cases where there are modifications to COTS components, government off-the-shelf components, or freeware, that are of significant value to the project or that represent significant project risk.

Throughout the process areas, where the terms "product" and "product component" are used, their intended meanings also encompass services, service systems, and their components.

The Supplier Agreement Management process area involves the following activities:

- Determining the type of acquisition
- Selecting suppliers
- Establishing and maintaining agreements with suppliers
- Executing supplier agreements
- Accepting delivery of acquired products
- Ensuring successful transition of acquired products

This process area primarily addresses the acquisition of products and product components that are delivered to the project's customer.

> **X-REF**
>
> If you are using SAM to understand best practices for purchasing, outsourcing, and acquiring products and services to deliver or assemble and deliver to your customer, you may want to refer to the CMMI for Acquisition model for more detailed guidance on improving your acquisition processes.

> **TIP**
>
> SAM helps prevent problems such as suppliers who can't meet requirements, supplier agreements that prevent a proactive approach to supplier management, poor visibility into supplier activities, and failing to address risks associated with the use of in-house vendors and COTS.

> **TIP**
>
> Although SAM primarily addresses the acquisition of products and product components that are delivered to your customer, SAM can be of benefit in other acquisitions critical to the success of the business such as training.

HINT

Take a broad view when applying SAM to reduce business-critical risks in obtaining products from suppliers. However, also be aware that not all practices apply equally to all situations.

> Examples of products and product components that can be acquired by the project include the following:
> • Subsystems (e.g., navigational system on an airplane)
> • Software
> • Hardware
> • Documentation (e.g., installation, operator's, and user's manuals)
> • Parts and materials (e.g., gauges, switches, wheels, steel, raw materials)

HINT

If you need to acquire a product, the *earlier* you prepare, the more likely you are to provide the right product of the right quality at the right time for project success.

HINT

When a supplier is integrated into the project team, pick the best process for the situation and then determine whether it maps to SAM, teaming practices (in OPD and IPM), or both.

TIP

Acquisitions from in-house vendors often proceed without well-defined requirements, a supplier agreement, and agreed-to acceptance tests. Is it any wonder that relationships with in-house vendors can be problematic?

To minimize risks to the project, this process area can also address the acquisition of significant products and product components not delivered to the project's customer but used to develop and maintain the product or service (for example, development tools and test environments).

Typically, the products to be acquired by the project are determined during the early stages of planning and development.

The Technical Solution process area provides practices for determining the products and product components that can be acquired from suppliers.

This process area does not directly address arrangements in which the supplier is integrated into the project team and uses the same processes and reports to the same management as the project team members (e.g., integrated teams). Typically, these situations are handled by other processes or functions (e.g., project management processes, processes or functions external to the project) though some of the specific practices of this process area can be useful in managing the supplier agreement.

This process area typically is not implemented to address arrangements in which the project's customer is also a supplier. These situations are usually handled by either informal agreements with the customer or by specification of the customer furnished items in the overall agreement that the project has with the customer. In the latter case, some of the specific practices of this process area can be useful in managing the agreement, although others may not, due to the fundamentally different relationship that exists with a customer as opposed to an ordinary supplier. See the CMMI-ACQ model for more information about other types of agreements.

Suppliers can take many forms depending on business needs, including in-house suppliers (i.e., suppliers that are in the same organization but are external to the project), fabrication departments, suppliers of reuse libraries, and commercial suppliers. (See the definition of "supplier" in the glossary.)

A supplier agreement is established to manage the relationship between the organization and the supplier. A supplier agreement is any written agreement between the organization (representing the project) and the supplier. This agreement can be a contract, license, service level agreement, or memorandum of agreement. The acquired product is delivered to the project from the supplier according to the supplier agreement. (See the definition of "supplier agreement" in the glossary.)

Related Process Areas

Refer to the Technical Solution process area for more information about performing make, buy, or reuse analysis.

Refer to the Requirements Development process area for more information about eliciting, analyzing, and establishing customer, product, and product component requirements.

Refer to the Project Monitoring and Control process area for more information about monitoring the project against the plan and managing corrective action to closure.

Refer to the Requirements Management process area for more information about maintaining bidirectional traceability of requirements.

Specific Goal and Practice Summary

SG 1 Establish Supplier Agreements
    SP 1.1   Determine Acquisition Type
    SP 1.2   Select Suppliers
    SP 1.3   Establish Supplier Agreements
SG 2 Satisfy Supplier Agreements
    SP 2.1   Execute the Supplier Agreement
    SP 2.2   Accept the Acquired Product
    SP 2.3   Ensure Transition of Products

Specific Practices by Goal

SG 1   ESTABLISH SUPPLIER AGREEMENTS

Agreements with the suppliers are established and maintained.

SP 1.1   DETERMINE ACQUISITION TYPE

Determine the type of acquisition for each product or product component to be acquired.

Refer to the Technical Solution process area for more information about performing make, buy, or reuse analyses.

X-REF

The entry point for SAM is normally TS SP 2.4, when the decision is made to buy rather than build a product component.

TIP

The type of acquisition varies according to the nature of products that are available to satisfy the project's needs and requirements (including COTS).

Many different types of acquisitions can be used to acquire products and product components that can be used by the project.

Examples of types of acquisitions include the following:
- Purchasing modified COTS products of significant value to the project
- Obtaining products through a supplier agreement
- Obtaining products from an in-house supplier
- Obtaining products from the customer
- Obtaining products from a preferred supplier
- Combining some of the above (e.g., contracting for a modification to a COTS product, having another part of the business enterprise co-develop products with an external supplier)

X-REF

The use of COTS involves additional considerations. See TS, SAM SP 1.2 Subpractice 5, and SAM SP 1.3 Subpractice 3. Also, see www.sei.cmu.edu/acquisition/tools/methods/cotshome.cfm.

If acquiring modified COTS products of significant value to the project or that represent significant project risk, care in evaluating and selecting these products and the supplier can be critical to the project. Aspects to consider in the selection decision include proprietary issues and the availability of the products.

Example Work Products

1. List of the acquisition types that will be used for all products and product components to be acquired

SP 1.2 SELECT SUPPLIERS

Select suppliers based on an evaluation of their ability to meet the specified requirements and established criteria.

Refer to the Decision Analysis and Resolution process area for more information about analyzing possible decisions using a formal evaluation process that evaluates identified alternatives against established criteria.

Refer to the Requirements Management process area for more information about obtaining commitment to requirements.

TIP

The criteria used to select a supplier depend on the project, its requirements, and other factors. If you enter "supplier selection criteria" into your favorite search engine, you will be amazed by both the commonality and the variety of supplier selection criteria used in different industries.

Criteria should be established to address factors that are important to the project.

Examples of factors that can be important to the project include the following:
- Geographical location of the supplier
- Supplier's performance records on similar work

Continues

Continued

- Engineering capabilities
- Staff and facilities available to perform the work
- Prior experience in similar situations
- Customer satisfaction with similar products delivered by the supplier

Example Work Products

1. Market studies
2. List of candidate suppliers
3. Preferred supplier list
4. Trade study or other record of evaluation criteria, advantages and disadvantages of candidate suppliers, and rationale for selection of suppliers
5. Solicitation materials and requirements

Subpractices

1. Establish and document criteria for evaluating potential suppliers.
2. Identify potential suppliers and distribute solicitation material and requirements to them.

   A proactive manner of performing this activity is to conduct market research to identify potential sources of candidate products to be acquired, including candidates from suppliers of custom made products and suppliers of COTS products.

   Refer to the Organizational Performance Management process area for more information about selecting improvements and validating improvements.

3. Evaluate proposals according to evaluation criteria.
4. Evaluate risks associated with each proposed supplier.

   Refer to the Risk Management process area for more information about identifying and analyzing risks.

5. Evaluate proposed suppliers' abilities to perform the work.

Examples of methods used to evaluate the proposed supplier's abilities to perform the work include the following:

- Evaluation of prior experience in similar applications
- Evaluation of customer satisfaction with similar products provided
- Evaluation of prior performance on similar work
- Evaluation of management capabilities
- Capability evaluations

Continues

HINT

Consider using DAR when evaluating potential suppliers. These subpractices describe some of what is involved in such an evaluation.

TIP

A proactive approach provides benefits such as addressing a capability gap of the organization uniformly, reducing time that projects take to select suppliers, establishing a more efficient umbrella agreement with a preferred supplier, and protecting core competencies.

TIP

Risks are typically included as criteria in a formal evaluation.

X-REF

Capability evaluation methods associated with CMMI include the SCAMPI A and B appraisal methods. See http://www.sei.cmu.edu/cmmi/tools/appraisals/index.cfm.

Continued

- Evaluation of staff available to perform the work
- Evaluation of available facilities and resources
- Evaluation of the project's ability to work with the proposed supplier
- Evaluation of the impact of candidate COTS products on the project's plan and commitments

When modified COTS products are being evaluated, consider the following:
- Cost of the modified COTS products
- Cost and effort to incorporate the modified COTS products into the project
- Security requirements
- Benefits and impacts that can result from future product releases

Future releases of the modified COTS product can provide additional features that support planned or anticipated enhancements for the project, but can result in the supplier discontinuing support of its current release.

6. Select the supplier.

SP 1.3 ESTABLISH SUPPLIER AGREEMENTS

Establish and maintain supplier agreements.

A supplier agreement is any written agreement between the organization (representing the project) and the supplier. This agreement can be a contract, license, service level agreement, or memorandum of agreement.

The content of the supplier agreement should specify the arrangement for selecting supplier processes and work products to be monitored, analyzed, and evaluated, if the arrangement is appropriate to the acquisition or product being acquired. The supplier agreement should also specify the reviews, monitoring, evaluations, and acceptance testing to be performed.

Supplier processes that are critical to the success of the project (e.g., due to complexity, due to importance) should be monitored.

Supplier agreements between independent legal entities are typically reviewed by legal or contract advisors prior to approval.

Example Work Products

1. Statements of work
2. Contracts
3. Memoranda of agreement
4. Licensing agreement

HINT

If it's not documented in the supplier agreement, don't count on it happening! Renegotiating an agreement can be expensive, so make sure it covers everything that is important to you for managing the supplier and receiving the product that you are expecting.

HINT

Create a supplier agreement in the form suitable to the nature of the business transaction. The agreement does not need to be lengthy but usually has a section with signatures.

TIP

The project must engage the supplier in reviews, monitoring, and evaluations to a depth and breadth appropriate to the circumstances and risks. The supplier agreement must cover details of these reviews.

Subpractices

1. Revise the requirements (e.g., product requirements, service level requirements) to be fulfilled by the supplier to reflect negotiations with the supplier when necessary.

    Refer to the Requirements Development process area for more information about developing product requirements.

    Refer to the Requirements Management process area for more information about managing requirements of the project's products and product components and to ensure alignment between those requirements and the project's plans and work products.

2. Document what the project will provide to the supplier.

    Include the following:
    - Project furnished facilities
    - Documentation
    - Services

3. Document the supplier agreement.

    The supplier agreement should include a statement of work, a specification, terms and conditions, a list of deliverables, a schedule, a budget, and a defined acceptance process.

    This subpractice typically includes the following tasks:
    - Identifying the type and depth of project oversight of the supplier, procedures, and evaluation criteria to be used in monitoring supplier performance including selection of processes to be monitored and work products to be evaluated
    - Establishing the statement of work, specification, terms and conditions, list of deliverables, schedule, budget, and acceptance process
    - Identifying who from the project and supplier are responsible and authorized to make changes to the supplier agreement
    - Identifying how requirements changes and changes to the supplier agreement are to be determined, communicated, and addressed
    - Identifying standards and procedures that will be followed
    - Identifying critical dependencies between the project and the supplier
    - Identifying the types of reviews that will be conducted with the supplier
    - Identifying the supplier's responsibilities for ongoing maintenance and support of the acquired products
    - Identifying warranty, ownership, and rights of use for the acquired products
    - Identifying acceptance criteria

TIP

Establishing (and revising) an agreement often requires *negotiation skills.* See *Getting to Yes: Negotiating Agreement Without Giving In,* Revised 2nd Edition by William Ury, Roger Fisher, and Bruce Patton (Penguin USA, 1991).

SAM

HINT

The supplier agreement is the basis for monitoring your supplier and accepting the product. Make sure it covers all critical information.

TIP

Often, projects overlook a supplier's responsibilities for ongoing maintenance and support. Some companies have tied staff compensation, in part, to maintenance and support costs incurred following product delivery, thus motivating the staff to consider longer-term support needs when establishing an agreement with a supplier.

> In some cases, selection of modified COTS products can require a supplier agreement in addition to the agreements in the product's license. Examples of what could be covered in an agreement with a COTS supplier include the following:
>
> - Discounts for large quantity purchases
> - Coverage of relevant stakeholders under the licensing agreement, including project suppliers, team members, and the project's customer
> - Plans for future enhancements
> - On-site support, such as responses to queries and problem reports
> - Additional capabilities that are not in the product
> - Maintenance support, including support after the product is withdrawn from general availability

4. Periodically review the supplier agreement to ensure it accurately reflects the project's relationship with the supplier and current risks and market conditions.
5. Ensure that all parties to the supplier agreement understand and agree to all requirements before implementing the agreement or any changes.
6. Revise the supplier agreement as necessary to reflect changes to the supplier's processes or work products.
7. Revise the project's plans and commitments, including changes to the project's processes or work products, as necessary to reflect the supplier agreement.

> *Refer to the Project Monitoring and Control process area for more information about monitoring commitments.*

TIP

Especially with long-term agreements (more than one year), technical and nontechnical requirements may change. It is necessary to address how such changes will be handled in the supplier agreement because this is often the legal document that will make these significant changes binding.

SG 2 SATISFY SUPPLIER AGREEMENTS

Agreements with suppliers are satisfied by both the project and the supplier.

SP 2.1 EXECUTE THE SUPPLIER AGREEMENT

Perform activities with the supplier as specified in the supplier agreement.

Refer to the Project Monitoring and Control process area for more information about providing an understanding of the project's progress so that appropriate corrective actions can be taken when the project's performance deviates significantly from the plan.

Example Work Products

1. Supplier progress reports and performance measures
2. Supplier review materials and reports

3. Action items tracked to closure
4. Product and documentation deliveries

Subpractices

1. Monitor supplier progress and performance (e.g., schedule, effort, cost, technical performance) as defined in the supplier agreement.
2. Select, monitor, and analyze processes used by the supplier as defined in the supplier agreement.

   Supplier processes that are critical to the success of the project (e.g., due to complexity, due to importance) should be monitored. The selection of processes to monitor should consider the impact of the selection on the supplier.
3. Select and evaluate work products from the supplier as defined in the supplier agreement.

   The work products selected for evaluation should include critical products, product components, and work products that provide insight into quality issues as early as possible. In situations of low risk, it may not be necessary to select any work products for evaluation.
4. Conduct reviews with the supplier as specified in the supplier agreement.

   Refer to the Project Monitoring and Control process area for more information about conducting milestone reviews and conducting progress reviews.

   Reviews cover both formal and informal reviews and include the following steps:
   - Preparing for the review
   - Ensuring that relevant stakeholders participate
   - Conducting the review
   - Identifying, documenting, and tracking all action items to closure
   - Preparing and distributing to the relevant stakeholders a summary report of the review
5. Conduct technical reviews with the supplier as defined in the supplier agreement.

Technical reviews typically include the following:
- Providing the supplier with visibility into the needs and desires of the project's customers and end users as appropriate
- Reviewing the supplier's technical activities and verifying that the supplier's interpretation and implementation of the requirements are consistent with the project's interpretation

Continues

SAM

TIP

In V1.2, subpractices 2 and 3 were SP 2.2 and 2.3.

HINT

Select appropriate processes for monitoring and evaluating work products to obtain visibility into supplier progress and performance and to identify and mitigate risks.

TIP

Monitoring is a cost to both parties, so which processes to select for monitoring depends on which ones provide the most insight into supplier activities, pose the most risk, and provide an early indication of problems. In cases of low risk, no processes are monitored.

HINT

There is often more risk with a custom-made product. The requirements may not be defined fully or the supplier may not address all the requirements fully. Evaluate selected work products to uncover issues early in the lifecycle.

X-REF

Including suppliers in the project's progress and milestone reviews is covered in PMC SP 1.6 and 1.7.

TIP

The purpose of a *technical review* is to review the supplier's technical progress and identify and resolve issues if they arise.

Continued

> • Ensuring that technical commitments are being met and that technical issues are communicated and resolved in a timely manner
> • Obtaining technical information about the supplier's products
> • Providing appropriate technical information and support to the supplier

6. Conduct management reviews with the supplier as defined in the supplier agreement.

> Management reviews typically include the following:
> • Reviewing critical dependencies
> • Reviewing project risks involving the supplier
> • Reviewing schedule and budget
> • Reviewing the supplier's compliance with legal and regulatory requirements

Technical and management reviews can be coordinated and held jointly.

7. Use the results of reviews to improve the supplier's performance and to establish and nurture long-term relationships with preferred suppliers.

8. Monitor risks involving the supplier and take corrective action as necessary.

> *Refer to the Project Monitoring and Control process area for more information about monitoring project risks.*

SP 2.2 ACCEPT THE ACQUIRED PRODUCT

Ensure that the supplier agreement is satisfied before accepting the acquired product.

Acceptance reviews, tests, and configuration audits should be completed before accepting the product as defined in the supplier agreement.

Example Work Products

1. Acceptance procedures
2. Acceptance reviews or test results
3. Discrepancy reports or corrective action plans

Subpractices

1. Define the acceptance procedures.
2. Review and obtain agreement from relevant stakeholders on the acceptance procedures before the acceptance review or test.
3. Verify that the acquired products satisfy their requirements.

   Refer to the Verification process area for more information about verifying selected work products.

4. Confirm that the nontechnical commitments associated with the acquired work product are satisfied.

   This confirmation can include confirming that the appropriate license, warranty, ownership, use, and support or maintenance agreements are in place and that all supporting materials are received.

5. Document the results of the acceptance review or test.
6. Establish an action plan and obtain supplier agreement to take action to correct acquired work products that do not pass their acceptance review or test.
7. Identify, document, and track action items to closure.

   Refer to the Project Monitoring and Control process area for more information about managing corrective action to closure.

SP 2.3 ENSURE TRANSITION OF PRODUCTS

Ensure the transition of products acquired from the supplier.

Before the acquired product is transferred to the project, customer, or end user, appropriate preparation and evaluation should occur to ensure a smooth transition.

Refer to the Product Integration process area for more information about assembling product components.

Example Work Products

1. Transition plans
2. Training reports
3. Support and maintenance reports

Subpractices

1. Ensure that facilities exist to receive, store, integrate, and maintain the acquired products as appropriate.
2. Ensure that appropriate training is provided for those who are involved in receiving, storing, integrating, and maintaining acquired products.

X-REF

Acceptance procedures, reviews, and tests are also covered in PI, VER, and VAL, so consult their practices for more information about establishing the appropriate environment, procedures, and criteria for verification and validation (and thus for accepting the acquired product).

SAM

HINT

Share pertinent parts of the schedule and criteria for assembly with suppliers of work products to reduce the occurrence of delays and component failure (PI SP 3.1).

HINT

Be sure to address proprietary issues related to the acquired product before the project accepts the product.

TIP

A successful transition involves planning for the appropriate facilities, training, use, maintenance, and support.

TIP

In some cases, the supplier may deliver the product directly to the customer or end user.

3. Ensure that acquired products are stored, distributed, and integrated according to the terms and conditions specified in the supplier agreement or license.

TECHNICAL SOLUTION

An Engineering Process Area at Maturity Level 3

Purpose

The purpose of Technical Solution (TS) is to select, design, and implement solutions to requirements. Solutions, designs, and implementations encompass products, product components, and product related lifecycle processes either singly or in combination as appropriate.

Introductory Notes

The Technical Solution process area is applicable at any level of the product architecture and to every product, product component, and product related lifecycle process. Throughout the process areas, where the terms "product" and "product component" are used, their intended meanings also encompass services, service systems, and their components.

This process area focuses on the following:

- Evaluating and selecting solutions (sometimes referred to as "design approaches," "design concepts," or "preliminary designs") that potentially satisfy an appropriate set of allocated functional and quality attribute requirements
- Developing detailed designs for the selected solutions (detailed in the context of containing all the information needed to manufacture, code, or otherwise implement the design as a product or product component)
- Implementing the designs as a product or product component

Typically, these activities interactively support each other. Some level of design, at times fairly detailed, can be needed to select solutions. Prototypes or pilots can be used as a means of gaining sufficient knowledge to develop a technical data package or a complete set of requirements. Quality attribute models, simulations, prototypes

HINT

It is not enough to consider product behavior in the intended operational environment when developing a solution. Also ask questions about other phases in the life of the product, including whether the solution can be manufactured; whether it is easy to test, install, repair, migrate to new versions or platforms, and support; and what the costs and legal implications will be.

X-REF

TS is driven by the requirements established by RD, which are managed by REQM. The processes associated with these PAs interact significantly to accomplish their purposes.

TIP

TS applies not only to developing a product, but also to maintaining a product (i.e., corrective, adaptive, and perfective maintenance).

X-REF

See the definition of "product line" in the glossary.

or pilots can be used to provide additional information about the properties of the potential design solutions to aid in the selection of solutions. Simulations can be particularly useful for projects developing systems-of-systems.

Technical Solution specific practices apply not only to the product and product components but also to product related lifecycle processes. The product related lifecycle processes are developed in concert with the product or product component. Such development can include selecting and adapting existing processes (including standard processes) for use as well as developing new processes.

Processes associated with the Technical Solution process area receive the product and product component requirements from the requirements management processes. The requirements management processes place the requirements, which originate in requirements development processes, under appropriate configuration management and maintain their traceability to previous requirements.

For a maintenance or sustainment project, the requirements in need of maintenance actions or redesign can be driven by user needs, technology maturation and obsolescence, or latent defects in the product components. New requirements can arise from changes in the operating environment. Such requirements can be uncovered during verification of the product(s) where its actual performance can be compared against its specified performance and unacceptable degradation can be identified. Processes associated with the Technical Solution process area should be used to perform the maintenance or sustainment design efforts.

For product lines, these practices apply to both core asset development (i.e., building for reuse) and product development (i.e., building with reuse). Core asset development additionally requires product line variation management (the selection and implementation of product line variation mechanisms) and product line production planning (the development of processes and other work products that define how products will be built to make best use of these core assets).

In Agile environments, the focus is on early solution exploration. By making the selection and tradeoff decisions more explicit, the Technical Solution process area helps improve the quality of those decisions, both individually and over time. Solutions can be defined in terms of functions, feature sets, releases, or any other components that facilitate product development. When someone other than the team will be working on the product in the future, release information, maintenance logs, and other

Continues

Continued

data are typically included with the installed product. To support future product updates, rationale (for trade-offs, interfaces, and purchased parts) is captured so that why the product exists can be better understood. If there is low risk in the selected solution, the need to formally capture decisions is significantly reduced. (See "Interpreting CMMI When Using Agile Approaches" in Part I.)

Related Process Areas

Refer to the Requirements Development process area for more information about allocating product component requirements, establishing operational concepts and scenarios, and identifying interface requirements.

Refer to the Verification process area for more information about performing peer reviews and verifying selected work products.

Refer to the Decision Analysis and Resolution process area for more information about analyzing possible decisions using a formal evaluation process that evaluates identified alternatives against established criteria.

Refer to the Organizational Performance Management process area for more information about selecting improvements and deploying improvements.

Refer to the Requirements Management process area for more information about managing requirements of the project's products and product components and ensuring alignment between those requirements and the project's plans and work products.

Specific Goal and Practice Summary

SG 1 Select Product Component Solutions
    SP 1.1   Develop Alternative Solutions and Selection Criteria
    SP 1.2   Select Product Component Solutions
SG 2 Develop the Design
    SP 2.1   Design the Product or Product Component
    SP 2.2   Establish a Technical Data Package
    SP 2.3   Design Interfaces Using Criteria
    SP 2.4   Perform Make, Buy, or Reuse Analyses
SG 3 Implement the Product Design
    SP 3.1   Implement the Design
    SP 3.2   Develop Product Support Documentation

X-REF

See *Software Architecture in Practice, Second Edition* by L. Bass, P. Clements, and R. Kazman (Addison-Wesley).

X-REF

See *Evaluating Software Architectures: Methods and Case Studies* by P. Clements, R. Kazman, and M. Klein (Addison-Wesley).

X-REF

See *Documenting Software Architectures: Views and Beyond* by P. Clements, F. Bachmann, L. Bass, D. Garlan, J. Ivers, R. Little, R. Nord, and J. Stafford (Addison-Wesley).

X-REF

See *Software Product Lines: Practices and Patterns* by P. Clements and L. Northrop (Addison-Wesley).

X-REF

See *Handbook of Software Architecture* by G. Booch (found at http://www.hand-bookofsoftwarearchitecture.com/).

X-REF

See *Software Architecture Essential Bookshelf* (found at http://www.sei.cmu.edu/architecture/start/publications/bookshelf.cfm).

TS

HINT

When you consider the successful products or services you use, ask what makes them successful. Is it features, usability, cost, customer support, response time, reliability, etc.? These characteristics were achieved through careful identification and evaluation of alternative design approaches.

TIP

Sometimes, an insignificant requirements change can greatly improve the merits of a COTS-based solution, especially with regard to cost and schedule risks. However, the use of COTS may constrain the overall solution's performance and the support that can be offered later in the product's life. A relationship with a vendor may need to be maintained.

X-REF

See www.sei.cmu.edu/ acquisition/tools/methods/ cotshome.cfm for more information about using COTS.

TIP

The iteration in these practices eventually results in a product component solution and design that are either implemented (TS SG 3), acquired (SAM), or reused (TS SP 2.4).

HINT

Whether you are defining or evaluating an alternative solution, treat its components together, not individually. For example, do not rush to select a promising COTS component or new technology without considering the other components it will need to work with, as well as their impacts and risks.

Specific Practices by Goal

SG 1   SELECT PRODUCT COMPONENT SOLUTIONS

Product or product component solutions are selected from alternative solutions.

Alternative solutions and their relative merits are considered in advance of selecting a solution. Key requirements, design issues, and constraints are established for use in alternative solution analysis. Architectural choices and patterns that support achievement of quality attribute requirements are considered. Also, the use of commercial off-the-shelf (COTS) product components are considered relative to cost, schedule, performance, and risk. COTS alternatives can be used with or without modification. Sometimes such items can require modifications to aspects such as interfaces or a customization of some of the features to correct a mismatch with functional or quality attribute requirements, or with architectural designs.

One indicator of a good design process is that the design was chosen after comparing and evaluating it against alternative solutions. Decisions about architecture, custom development versus off the shelf, and product component modularization are typical of the design choices that are addressed. Some of these decisions can require the use of a formal evaluation process.

Refer to the Decision Analysis and Resolution process area for more information about analyzing possible decisions using a formal evaluation process that evaluates identified alternatives against established criteria.

Sometimes the search for solutions examines alternative instances of the same requirements with no allocations needed for lower level product components. Such is the case at the bottom of the product architecture. There are also cases where one or more of the solutions are fixed (e.g., a specific solution is directed or available product components, such as COTS, are investigated for use).

In the general case, solutions are defined as a set. That is, when defining the next layer of product components, the solution for each of the product components in the set is established. The alternative solutions are not only different ways of addressing the same requirements, but they also reflect a different allocation of requirements among the product components comprising the solution set. The objective is to optimize the set as a whole and not the individual pieces. There will be significant interaction with processes associated with the Requirements Development process area to support the provisional allocations to product components until a solution set is selected and final allocations are established.

Product related lifecycle processes are among the product component solutions that are selected from alternative solutions.

Examples of these product related lifecycle processes are the manufacturing, delivery, and support processes.

SP 1.1 DEVELOP ALTERNATIVE SOLUTIONS AND SELECTION CRITERIA

Develop alternative solutions and selection criteria.

Refer to the Allocate Product Component Requirements specific practice in the Requirements Development process area for more information about obtaining allocations of requirements to solution alternatives for the product components.

Refer to the Decision Analysis and Resolution process area for more information about establishing evaluation criteria.

Alternative solutions should be identified and analyzed to enable the selection of a balanced solution across the life of the product in terms of cost, schedule, performance, and risk. These solutions are based on proposed product architectures that address critical product quality attribute requirements and span a design space of feasible solutions. Specific practices associated with the Develop the Design specific goal provide more information on developing potential product architectures that can be incorporated into alternative solutions for the product.

Alternative solutions frequently encompass alternative requirement allocations to different product components. These alternative solutions can also include the use of COTS solutions in the product architecture. Processes associated with the Requirements Development process area would then be employed to provide a more complete and robust provisional allocation of requirements to the alternative solutions.

Alternative solutions span the acceptable range of cost, schedule, and performance. The product component requirements are received and used along with design issues, constraints, and criteria to develop the alternative solutions. Selection criteria would typically address costs (e.g., time, people, money), benefits (e.g., product performance, capability, effectiveness), and risks (e.g., technical, cost, schedule). Considerations for alternative solutions and selection criteria include the following:

- Cost of development, manufacturing, procurement, maintenance, and support
- Achievement of key quality attribute requirements, such as product timeliness, safety, reliability, and maintainability

X-REF

RD SP 2.2 describes allocating requirements after a solution has been selected. However, it can also be applied prior to selection (a "provisional allocation") to gain insight into the relative merits of an alternative solution.

HINT

It is important to involve relevant stakeholders in establishing selection criteria and alternative solutions.

TIP

Selection criteria typically include cost, schedule, performance, and risk. How these criteria are defined in detail, however, depends on the requirements.

HINT

Consider the entire life of the product when selecting, designing, and implementing a solution to ensure that it will have the desired versatility and market endurance.

HINT

Consider a range of alternative solutions. Input from stakeholders with diverse skills and backgrounds can help teams identify and address assumptions, constraints, and biases. Brainstorming sessions may stimulate innovative alternatives. Also, consider which quality attributes are critical to product success.

- Complexity of the product component and product related lifecycle processes
- Robustness to product operating and use conditions, operating modes, environments, and variations in product related lifecycle processes
- Product expansion and growth
- Technology limitations
- Sensitivity to construction methods and materials
- Risk
- Evolution of requirements and technology
- Disposal
- Capabilities and limitations of end users and operators
- Characteristics of COTS products

The considerations listed here are a basic set; organizations should develop screening criteria to narrow down the list of alternatives that are consistent with their business objectives. Product lifecycle cost, while being a desirable parameter to minimize, can be outside the control of development organizations. A customer may not be willing to pay for features that cost more in the short term but ultimately decrease cost over the life of the product. In such cases, customers should at least be advised of any potential for reducing lifecycle costs. The criteria used to select final solutions should provide a balanced approach to costs, benefits, and risks.

Example Work Products

1. Alternative solution screening criteria
2. Evaluation reports of new technologies
3. Alternative solutions
4. Selection criteria for final selection
5. Evaluation reports of COTS products

Subpractices

1. Identify screening criteria to select a set of alternative solutions for consideration.
2. Identify technologies currently in use and new product technologies for competitive advantage.

    Refer to the Organizational Performance Management process area for more information about selecting improvements and deploying improvements.

The project should identify technologies applied to current products and processes and monitor the progress of currently used technologies throughout the life of the project. The project should identify, select, evaluate, and invest in new technologies to achieve competitive advantage. Alternative solutions could include newly developed technologies, but could also include applying mature technologies in different applications or to maintain current methods.

3. Identify candidate COTS products that satisfy the requirements.

   Refer to the Supplier Agreement Management process area for more information about selecting suppliers.

   The supplier of the COTS product will need to meet requirements that include the following:

   • Product functionality and quality attributes
   • Terms and conditions of warranties for the products
   • Expectations (e.g., for review activities), constraints, or checkpoints to help mitigate suppliers' responsibilities for ongoing maintenance and support of the products

4. Identify re-usable solution components or applicable architecture patterns.

   For product lines, the organization's core assets can be used as a basis for a solution.

5. Generate alternative solutions.

6. Obtain a complete requirements allocation for each alternative.

7. Develop the criteria for selecting the best alternative solution.

   Criteria should be included that address design issues for the life of the product, such as provisions for more easily inserting new technologies or the ability to better exploit commercial products. Examples include criteria related to open design or open architecture concepts for the alternatives being evaluated.

SP 1.2 SELECT PRODUCT COMPONENT SOLUTIONS

Select the product component solutions based on selection criteria.

Refer to the Allocate Product Component Requirements and Identify Interface Requirements specific practices of the Requirements Development process area for more information about establishing the allocated requirements for product components and interface requirements among product components.

Selecting product components that best satisfy the criteria establishes the requirement allocations to product components. Lower level requirements are generated from the selected alternative and used to develop product component designs. Interfaces among product components

---

HINT

Explore the use of COTS (or open source or new technology) early in product development because to use COTS effectively, you may need to consider changes to requirements. Fully understand such requirements-and-design tradeoffs early, before committing to (and putting under contract) a particular development approach.

TIP

Because a solution has yet to be selected, this requirements allocation is referred to as a "provisional allocation of requirements." Such allocation provides better insight into the solutions' pros and cons.

HINT

You can incorporate in subsequent releases new technologies, COTS, or open source components that were too immature to incorporate into a product's first release.

TIP

DAR supports the selection of product component solutions from among alternative solutions, especially in novel situations.

TIP

Selecting product component solutions from alternative solutions positions us for further requirements development and design.

TS

HINT

You may want to examine the rationale for a particular selection when you later learn that a promising technology or COTS component is now available. It may be unnecessary to interrupt product development to explore the implications if they were already explored earlier and records were maintained.

HINT

To gain the insight needed to fully evaluate alternative solutions, you may need to refine operational concepts and scenarios to understand the implications of each alternative solution.

X-REF

You may also consider different user roles and types. See RD SP 3.1 for more information.

HINT

Following the evaluation, you may conclude that the selection criteria were not complete or detailed enough to adequately differentiate alternative solutions. If so, you may need to iterate through SP 1.1 and 1.2.

TIP

Documentation assists product maintenance and support later in the life of the product.

are described. Physical interface descriptions are included in the documentation for interfaces to items and activities external to the product.

The description of the solutions and the rationale for selection are documented. The documentation evolves throughout development as solutions and detailed designs are developed and those designs are implemented. Maintaining a record of rationale is critical to downstream decision making. Such records keep downstream stakeholders from redoing work and provide insights to apply technology as it becomes available in applicable circumstances.

Example Work Products

1. Product component selection decisions and rationale
2. Documented relationships between requirements and product components
3. Documented solutions, evaluations, and rationale

Subpractices

1. Evaluate each alternative solution/set of solutions against the selection criteria established in the context of the operational concepts and scenarios.

    Develop timeline scenarios for product operation and user interaction for each alternative solution.

2. Based on the evaluation of alternatives, assess the adequacy of the selection criteria and update these criteria as necessary.

3. Identify and resolve issues with the alternative solutions and requirements.

4. Select the best set of alternative solutions that satisfy the established selection criteria.

5. Establish the functional and quality attribute requirements associated with the selected set of alternatives as the set of allocated requirements to those product components.

6. Identify the product component solutions that will be reused or acquired.

    Refer to the Supplier Agreement Management process area for more information about managing the acquisition of products and services from suppliers.

7. Establish and maintain the documentation of the solutions, evaluations, and rationale.

SG 2 DEVELOP THE DESIGN

Product or product component designs are developed.

Product or product component designs should provide the appropriate content not only for implementation, but also for other phases of the product lifecycle such as modification, reprocurement, maintenance, sustainment, and installation. The design documentation provides a reference to support mutual understanding of the design by relevant stakeholders and supports future changes to the design both during development and in subsequent phases of the product lifecycle. A complete design description is documented in a technical data package that includes a full range of features and parameters including form, fit, function, interface, manufacturing process characteristics, and other parameters. Established organizational or project design standards (e.g., checklists, templates, object frameworks) form the basis for achieving a high degree of definition and completeness in design documentation.

SP 2.1 DESIGN THE PRODUCT OR PRODUCT COMPONENT

Develop a design for the product or product component.

Product design consists of two broad phases that can overlap in execution: preliminary and detailed design. Preliminary design establishes product capabilities and the product architecture, including architectural styles and patterns, product partitions, product component identifications, system states and modes, major intercomponent interfaces, and external product interfaces. Detailed design fully defines the structure and capabilities of the product components.

Refer to the Establish a Definition of Required Functionality and Quality Attributes specific practice in the Requirements Development process area for more information about developing architectural requirements.

Architecture definition is driven from a set of architectural requirements developed during the requirements development processes. These requirements identify the quality attributes that are critical to the success of the product. The architecture defines structural elements and coordination mechanisms that either directly satisfy requirements or support the achievement of the requirements as the details of the product design are established. Architectures can include standards and design rules governing development of product components and their interfaces as well as guidance to aid product developers. Specific practices in the Select Product Component

TIP

A design describes a product's components' behavior and their interconnections. It guides the activities of a broad range of stakeholders, including implementers, testers, installers, and maintainers. Thus, stakeholders will use a design over the life of the product.

TIP

Organizational standards can help achieve consistency and completeness in design.

TIP

A good design does more than identify functionality. In the words of Steve Jobs, "Design is not just what it looks like and feels like. Design is how it works. . . . Design is the fundamental soul of a human-made creation that ends up expressing itself in successive outer layers of the product or service."

TIP

The design activity is often divided into two phases: preliminary design and detailed design. In preliminary design, the product architecture is established.

TS

X-REF

Architecture requirements express the qualities and performance points (i.e., thresholds) critical to the success of the product. They are developed in RD SP 2.1.

TIP

An architecture includes structural elements (e.g., product partitions and components), coordination mechanisms (e.g., interfaces), design rules and principles, standards, and guidance. An architecture may also include views that support reasoning about particular quality attributes or other features, issues, or perspectives.

HINT

Scenarios can be used to help refine the architecture and evaluate it against the architecture requirements.

TIP

In detailed design, we fully define the structure and capabilities of the product components. Product component designs may be optimized relative to particular quality attributes (e.g., response time).

Solutions specific goal contain more information about using product architectures as a basis for alternative solutions.

Architects postulate and develop a model of the product, making judgments about allocation of functional and quality attribute requirements to product components including hardware and software. Multiple architectures, supporting alternative solutions, can be developed and analyzed to determine the advantages and disadvantages in the context of the architectural requirements.

Operational concepts and operational, sustainment, and development scenarios are used to generate use cases and quality attribute related scenarios that are used to refine the architecture. They are also used as a means to evaluate the suitability of the architecture for its intended purpose during architecture evaluations, which are conducted periodically throughout product design.

Refer to the Establish Operational Concepts and Scenarios specific practice in the Requirements Development process area for more information about developing operational concepts and scenarios used in architecture evaluation.

Examples of architecture definition tasks include the following:
- Establishing the structural relations of partitions and rules regarding interfaces between elements within partitions, and between partitions
- Selecting architectural patterns that support the functional and quality attribute requirements, and instantiating or composing those patterns to create the product architecture
- Identifying major internal interfaces and all external interfaces
- Identifying product components and interfaces between them
- Formally defining component behavior and interaction using an architecture description language
- Defining coordination mechanisms (e.g., for software, hardware)
- Establishing infrastructure capabilities and services
- Developing product component templates or classes and frameworks
- Establishing design rules and authority for making decisions
- Defining a process/thread model
- Defining physical deployment of software to hardware
- Identifying major reuse approaches and sources

During detailed design, the product architecture details are finalized, product components are completely defined, and interfaces are fully characterized. Product component designs can be optimized for certain quality attributes. Designers can evaluate the use of legacy or COTS products for the product components. As the design matures, the requirements assigned to lower level product components are tracked to ensure that those requirements are satisfied.

Refer to the Requirements Management process area for more information about ensuring alignment between project work and requirements.

For software engineering, detailed design is focused on software product component development. The internal structure of product components is defined, data schemas are generated, algorithms are developed, and heuristics are established to provide product component capabilities that satisfy allocated requirements.

For hardware engineering, detailed design is focused on product development of electronic, mechanical, electro-optical, and other hardware products and their components. Electrical schematics and interconnection diagrams are developed, mechanical and optical assembly models are generated, and fabrication and assembly processes are developed.

Example Work Products

1. Product architecture
2. Product component design

Subpractices

1. Establish and maintain criteria against which the design can be evaluated.

Examples of quality attributes, in addition to expected product performance, for which design criteria can be established, include the following:
- Modular
- Clear
- Simple
- Maintainable
- Verifiable
- Portable
- Reliable
- Accurate
- Secure
- Scalable
- Usable

---

2. Identify, develop, or acquire the design methods appropriate for the product.

Effective design methods can embody a wide range of activities, tools, and descriptive techniques. Whether a given method is effective or not depends on the situation. Two companies may have effective design methods for products in which they specialize, but these

HINT

A design is a document used by stakeholders over the life of the product, and thus must communicate clearly and accommodate change. Consider this when selecting criteria to be used in evaluating a design.

TIP

An effective design method (and design language and tool) enables a designer to describe the entities that comprise a design and its connections, analyze attributes of interest (e.g., design cohesiveness, presence of race conditions), test the design against use cases or scenarios, and revise the design to reflect decisions made.

methods may not be effective in cooperative ventures. Highly sophisticated methods are not necessarily effective in the hands of designers who have not been trained in the use of the methods.

Whether a method is effective also depends on how much assistance it provides the designer, and the cost effectiveness of that assistance. For example, a multiyear prototyping effort may not be appropriate for a simple product component but might be the right thing to do for an unprecedented, expensive, and complex product development. Rapid prototyping techniques, however, can be highly effective for many product components. Methods that use tools to ensure that a design will encompass all the necessary attributes needed to implement the product component design can be effective. For example, a design tool that "knows" the capabilities of the manufacturing processes can allow the variability of the manufacturing process to be accounted for in the design tolerances.

Examples of techniques and methods that facilitate effective design include the following:
- Prototypes
- Structural models
- Object oriented design
- Essential systems analysis
- Entity relationship models
- Design reuse
- Design patterns

3. Ensure that the design adheres to applicable design standards and criteria.

Examples of design standards include the following (some or all of these standards may be design criteria, particularly in circumstances where the standards have not been established):
- Operator interface standards
- Test scenarios
- Safety standards
- Design constraints (e.g., electromagnetic compatibility, signal integrity, environmental)
- Production constraints
- Design tolerances
- Parts standards (e.g., production scrap, waste)

4. Ensure that the design adheres to allocated requirements.

> Identified COTS product components should be taken into account. For example, putting existing product components into the product architecture might modify the requirements and the requirements allocation.

5. Document the design.

SP 2.2 ESTABLISH A TECHNICAL DATA PACKAGE

Establish and maintain a technical data package.

A technical data package provides the developer with a comprehensive description of the product or product component as it is developed. Such a package also provides procurement flexibility in a variety of circumstances such as performance based contracting or build-to-print. (See the definition of "technical data package" in the glossary.)

The design is recorded in a technical data package that is created during preliminary design to document the architecture definition. This technical data package is maintained throughout the life of the product to record essential details of the product design. The technical data package provides the description of a product or product component (including product related lifecycle processes if not handled as separate product components) that supports an acquisition strategy, or the implementation, production, engineering, and logistics support phases of the product lifecycle. The description includes the definition of the required design configuration and procedures to ensure adequacy of product or product component performance. It includes all applicable technical data such as drawings, associated lists, specifications, design descriptions, design databases, standards, quality attribute requirements, quality assurance provisions, and packaging details. The technical data package includes a description of the selected alternative solution that was chosen for implementation.

Because design descriptions can involve a large amount of data and can be crucial to successful product component development, it is advisable to establish criteria for organizing the data and for selecting the data content. It is particularly useful to use the product architecture as a means of organizing this data and abstracting views that are clear and relevant to an issue or feature of interest. These views include the following:

- Customers
- Requirements
- The environment

TIP

Verification methods that help ensure that a design adheres to allocated requirements are identified in the previous tip. (See VER for more information.)

TIP

A technical data package is the complete design documentation for a product or product component and the additional information needed to support its effective use.

TIP

A technical data package is maintained throughout the life of the product. It is an essential input to the acquisition of the product (if it is to be "bought") as well as to implementation, production, maintenance, and support (if it is to be "built").

- Functional
- Logical
- Security
- Data
- States/modes
- Construction
- Management

These views are documented in the technical data package.

Example Work Products

1. Technical data package

Subpractices

1. Determine the number of levels of design and the appropriate level of documentation for each design level.

   Determining the number of levels of product components (e.g., subsystem, hardware configuration item, circuit board, computer software configuration item [CSCI], computer software product component, computer software unit) that require documentation and requirements traceability is important to manage documentation costs and to support integration and verification plans.

2. Determine the views to be used to document the architecture.

   Views are selected to document the structures inherent in the product and to address particular stakeholder concerns.

3. Base detailed design descriptions on the allocated product component requirements, architecture, and higher level designs.

4. Document the design in the technical data package.

5. Document the key (i.e., significant effect on cost, schedule, or technical performance) decisions made or defined, including their rationale.

6. Revise the technical data package as necessary.

SP 2.3 DESIGN INTERFACES USING CRITERIA

Design product component interfaces using established criteria.

Interface designs include the following:

- Origination
- Destination
- Stimulus and data characteristics for software, including sequencing constraints or protocols

- Resources consumed processing a particular stimulus
- Exception or error handling behavior for stimuli that are erroneous or out of specified limits
- Electrical, mechanical, and functional characteristics for hardware
- Services lines of communication

The criteria for interfaces frequently reflect critical parameters that should be defined, or at least investigated, to ascertain their applicability. These parameters are often peculiar to a given type of product (e.g., software, mechanical, electrical, service) and are often associated with safety, security, durability, and mission critical characteristics.

Refer to the Identify Interface Requirements specific practice in the Requirements Development process area for more information about identifying product and product component interface requirements.

Example Work Products

1. Interface design specifications
2. Interface control documents
3. Interface specification criteria
4. Rationale for selected interface design

Subpractices

1. Define interface criteria.

    These criteria can be a part of the organizational process assets.

    Refer to the Organizational Process Definition process area for more information about establishing and maintaining a usable set of organizational process assets and work environment standards.

2. Identify interfaces associated with other product components.
3. Identify interfaces associated with external items.
4. Identify interfaces between product components and the product related lifecycle processes.

    For example, such interfaces could include the ones between a product component to be fabricated and the jigs and fixtures used to enable that fabrication during the manufacturing process.

5. Apply the criteria to the interface design alternatives.

    Refer to the Decision Analysis and Resolution process area for more information about analyzing possible decisions using a formal evaluation process that evaluates identified alternatives against established criteria.

6. Document the selected interface designs and the rationale for the selection.

TIP

Interface design may sometimes follow a formal evaluation (DAR) process: Establish criteria for desired attributes (e.g., correctness) of an interface (based in part on interface requirements), identify design alternatives, and so on.

TIP

Because of the importance of interfaces to effective product development, interfaces are addressed in multiple places: Interface requirements is covered in RD SP 2.3, design of interfaces is covered in TS SP 2.3, and ensuring interface compatibility is covered in PI SG 2.

TIP

Interface control documents define interfaces in terms of data items passed, protocols used for interaction, and so on. These documents are particularly useful in controlling product components being built by different teams.

X-REF

For examples of interfaces, see PI SP 2.1.

HINT

Interface designs should be documented in the technical data package.

TS

SG 3 IMPLEMENT THE PRODUCT DESIGN

Product components, and associated support documentation, are implemented from their designs.

Product components are implemented from the designs established by the specific practices in the Develop the Design specific goal. The implementation usually includes unit testing of the product components before sending them to product integration and development of end-user documentation.

SP 3.1 IMPLEMENT THE DESIGN

Implement the designs of the product components.

Once the design has been completed, it is implemented as a product component. The characteristics of that implementation depend on the type of product component.

Design implementation at the top level of the product hierarchy involves the specification of each of the product components at the next level of the product hierarchy. This activity includes the allocation, refinement, and verification of each product component. It also involves the coordination between the various product component development efforts.

Refer to the Product Integration process area for more information about managing interfaces and assembling product components.

Refer to the Requirements Development process area for more information about the allocating product component requirements and analyzing requirements.

> **TIP**
>
> At an upper level of the product hierarchy, implementing the design implies recursion (i.e., repeating RD SG 2-3 and TS SG 1-2) to establish the next level of product components. At the lowest level of the product hierarchy, there is no more decomposition or recursion; the design is directly implemented.

Example characteristics of this implementation are as follows:
- Software is coded.
- Data are documented.
- Services are documented.
- Electrical and mechanical parts are fabricated.
- Product-unique manufacturing processes are put into operation.
- Processes are documented.
- Facilities are constructed.
- Materials are produced (e.g., a product-unique material could be petroleum, oil, a lubricant, a new alloy).

Example Work Products

1. Implemented design

Subpractices

1. Use effective methods to implement the product components.

TIP

Which implementation method to use depends on the type of product component being implemented. An organization may establish its own implementation methods.

> Examples of software coding methods include the following:
> - Structured programming
> - Object oriented programming
> - Aspect oriented programming
> - Automatic code generation
> - Software code reuse
> - Use of applicable design patterns

> Examples of hardware implementation methods include the following:
> - Gate level synthesis
> - Circuit board layout (place and route)
> - Computer aided design drawing
> - Post layout simulation
> - Fabrication methods

2. Adhere to applicable standards and criteria.

TIP

The implementation standards and criteria used depend on the type of product component being implemented. An organization may establish its own implementation standards and criteria.

> Examples of implementation standards include the following:
> - Language standards (e.g., standards for software programming languages, hardware description languages)
> - Drawing requirements
> - Standard parts lists
> - Manufactured parts
> - Structure and hierarchy of software product components
> - Process and quality standards

> Examples of criteria include the following:
> - Modularity
> - Clarity
> - Simplicity
> - Reliability
> - Safety
> - Maintainability

TS

X-REF

In VER SP 1.1, you select work products to be verified and the verification method to use for each. In particular, you select which product components to be verified through peer review (e.g., software code).

3. Conduct peer reviews of the selected product components.

> *Refer to the Verification process area for more information about performing peer reviews.*

4. Perform unit testing of the product component as appropriate.

> Note that unit testing is not limited to software. Unit testing involves the testing of individual hardware or software units or groups of related items prior to integration of those items.

> *Refer to the Verification process area for more information about verifying selected work products.*

> Examples of unit testing methods (manual or automated) include the following:
> * Statement coverage testing
> * Branch coverage testing
> * Predicate coverage testing
> * Path coverage testing
> * Boundary value testing
> * Special value testing

> Examples of unit testing methods include the following:
> * Functional testing
> * Radiation inspection testing
> * Environmental testing

TIP

The product component may now be ready for product integration (see PI).

TIP

Another reason to revise the product component is to remove defects discovered through peer reviews or unit testing.

5. Revise the product component as necessary.

> An example of when the product component may need to be revised is when problems surface during implementation that could not be foreseen during design.

TIP

Documentation can be treated as a type of product component for which a solution may be selected, designed, and implemented. There are design and implementation methods and standards for documentation.

SP 3.2 DEVELOP PRODUCT SUPPORT DOCUMENTATION

Develop and maintain the end-use documentation.

This specific practice develops and maintains the documentation that will be used to install, operate, and maintain the product.

Example Work Products

1. End-user training materials

2. User's manual
3. Operator's manual
4. Maintenance manual
5. Online help

Subpractices

1. Review the requirements, design, product, and test results to ensure that issues affecting the installation, operation, and maintenance documentation are identified and resolved.
2. Use effective methods to develop the installation, operation, and maintenance documentation.
3. Adhere to the applicable documentation standards.

> Examples of documentation standards include the following:
> - Compatibility with designated word processors
> - Acceptable fonts
> - Numbering of pages, sections, and paragraphs
> - Consistency with a designated style manual
> - Use of abbreviations
> - Security classification markings
> - Internationalization requirements

4. Develop preliminary versions of the installation, operation, and maintenance documentation in early phases of the project lifecycle for review by the relevant stakeholders.
5. Conduct peer reviews of the installation, operation, and maintenance documentation.

   Refer to the Verification process area for more information about performing peer reviews.

6. Revise the installation, operation, and maintenance documentation as necessary.

> Examples of when documentation may need to be revised include when the following events occur:
> - Requirements changes are made
> - Design changes are made
> - Product changes are made
> - Documentation errors are identified
> - Workaround fixes are identified

TIP

Installers, operators, end users, and maintainers may have different documentation needs that may be addressed in different documents.

TIP

Relevant stakeholders (product installers, field support staff, trainers, technical writers, and so on) can reduce the number of serious issues that must be resolved through documentation by participating in reviews of intermediate work products. In these reviews, issues impacting installation, operation, and so on are identified and resolved.

TIP

A preliminary version of a document produced for review by relevant stakeholders can be considered a prototype of the final document.

VALIDATION
An Engineering Process Area at Maturity Level 3

Purpose

The purpose of Validation (VAL) is to demonstrate that a product or product component fulfills its intended use when placed in its intended environment.

Introductory Notes

Validation activities can be applied to all aspects of the product in any of its intended environments, such as operation, training, manufacturing, maintenance, and support services. The methods employed to accomplish validation can be applied to work products as well as to the product and product components. (Throughout the process areas, where the terms "product" and "product component" are used, their intended meanings also encompass services, service systems, and their components.) The work products (e.g., requirements, designs, prototypes) should be selected on the basis of which are the best predictors of how well the product and product component will satisfy end user needs and thus validation is performed early (concept/exploration phases) and incrementally throughout the product lifecycle (including transition to operations and sustainment).

The validation environment should represent the intended environment for the product and product components as well as represent the intended environment suitable for validation activities with work products.

Validation demonstrates that the product, as provided, will fulfill its intended use; whereas, verification addresses whether the work product properly reflects the specified requirements. In other words, verification ensures that "you built it right"; whereas, validation ensures that "you built the right thing." Validation activities use approaches similar to verification (e.g., test, analysis, inspection, demonstration, simulation). Often, the end users and other relevant

VAL

stakeholders are involved in the validation activities. Both validation and verification activities often run concurrently and can use portions of the same environment.

Refer to the Verification process area for more information about ensuring that selected work products meet their specified requirements.

Whenever possible, validation should be accomplished using the product or product component operating in its intended environment. The entire environment can be used or only part of it. However, validation issues can be discovered early in the life of the project using work products by involving relevant stakeholders. Validation activities for services can be applied to work products such as proposals, service catalogs, statements of work, and service records.

When validation issues are identified, they are referred to processes associated with the Requirements Development, Technical Solution, or Project Monitoring and Control process areas for resolution.

The specific practices of this process area build on each other in the following way:

- The Select Products for Validation specific practice enables the identification of the product or product component to be validated and methods to be used to perform the validation.
- The Establish the Validation Environment specific practice enables the determination of the environment to be used to carry out the validation.
- The Establish Validation Procedures and Criteria specific practice enables the development of validation procedures and criteria that are aligned with the characteristics of selected products, customer constraints on validation, methods, and the validation environment.
- The Perform Validation specific practice enables the performance of validation according to methods, procedures, and criteria.

Related Process Areas

Refer to the Requirements Development process area for more information about eliciting, analyzing, and establishing customer, product, and product component requirements.

Refer to the Technical Solution process area for more information about selecting, designing, and implementing solutions to requirements.

Refer to the Verification process area for more information about ensuring that selected work products meet their specified requirements.

Specific Goal and Practice Summary

SG 1 Prepare for Validation
    SP 1.1   Select Products for Validation
    SP 1.2   Establish the Validation Environment
    SP 1.3   Establish Validation Procedures and Criteria

SG 2 Validate Product or Product Components
    SP 2.1   Perform Validation
    SP 2.2   Analyze Validation Results

Specific Practices by Goal

SG 1   PREPARE FOR VALIDATION

Preparation for validation is conducted.

Preparation activities include selecting products and product components for validation and establishing and maintaining the validation environment, procedures, and criteria. Items selected for validation can include only the product or it can include appropriate levels of product components used to build the product. Any product or product component can be subject to validation, including replacement, maintenance, and training products, to name a few.

The environment required to validate the product or product component is prepared. The environment can be purchased or can be specified, designed, and built. Environments used for product integration and verification can be considered in collaboration with the validation environment to reduce cost and improve efficiency or productivity.

SP 1.1 SELECT PRODUCTS FOR VALIDATION

Select products and product components to be validated and validation methods to be used.

Products and product components are selected for validation based on their relationship to end user needs. For each product component, the scope of the validation (e.g., operational behavior, maintenance, training, user interface) should be determined.

> Examples of products and product components that can be validated include the following:
> - Product and product component requirements and designs
> - Product and product components (e.g., system, hardware units, software, service documentation)
>
> *Continues*

HINT

Any product or product component can benefit from validation. What you select to validate should depend on the issues relating to user needs that pose the highest risk to project success and on available resources.

TIP

Integration tests can address validation-type activities (with an end user present to evaluate the integrated product under different scenarios). Thus, for some product components, product integration, verification, and validation activities may be addressed together.

TIP

Validation can be an expensive activity. It takes good judgment to select (and limit) what needs to be validated.

VAL

Continued

- User interfaces
- User manuals
- Training materials
- Process documentation
- Access protocols
- Data interchange reporting formats

The requirements and constraints for performing validation are collected. Then, validation methods are selected based on their ability to demonstrate that end user needs are satisfied. The validation methods not only define the approach to product validation, but also drive the needs for the facilities, equipment, and environments. The validation approach and needs can result in the generation of lower level product component requirements that are handled by the requirements development processes. Derived requirements, such as interface requirements to test sets and test equipment, can be generated. These requirements are also passed to the requirements development processes to ensure that the product or product components can be validated in an environment that supports the methods.

Validation methods should be selected early in the life of the project so they are clearly understood and agreed to by relevant stakeholders.

Validation methods address the development, maintenance, support, and training for the product or product component as appropriate.

Examples of validation methods include the following:
- Discussions with end users, perhaps in the context of a formal review
- Prototype demonstrations
- Functional demonstrations (e.g., system, hardware units, software, service documentation, user interfaces)
- Pilots of training materials
- Tests of products and product components by end users and other relevant stakeholders
- Incremental delivery of working and potentially acceptable product
- Analyses of product and product components (e.g., simulations, modeling, user analyses)

Hardware validation activities include modeling to validate form, fit, and function of mechanical designs; thermal modeling; maintainability and reliability analysis; timeline demonstrations; and electrical design simulations of electronic or mechanical product components.

Example Work Products

1. Lists of products and product components selected for validation
2. Validation methods for each product or product component
3. Requirements for performing validation for each product or product component
4. Validation constraints for each product or product component

Subpractices

1. Identify the key principles, features, and phases for product or product component validation throughout the life of the project.
2. Determine which categories of end user needs (operational, maintenance, training, or support) are to be validated.

   The product or product component should be maintainable and supportable in its intended operational environment. This specific practice also addresses the actual maintenance, training, and support services that can be delivered with the product.

An example of evaluation of maintenance concepts in the operational environment is a demonstration that maintenance tools are operating with the actual product.

---

3. Select the product and product components to be validated.
4. Select the evaluation methods for product or product component validation.
5. Review the validation selection, constraints, and methods with relevant stakeholders.

SP 1.2 ESTABLISH THE VALIDATION ENVIRONMENT

Establish and maintain the environment needed to support validation.

The requirements for the validation environment are driven by the product or product components selected, by the type of the work products (e.g., design, prototype, final version), and by the methods of validation. These selections can yield requirements for the purchase or development of equipment, software, or other resources. These requirements are provided to the requirements development processes for development. The validation environment can include the reuse of existing resources. In this case, arrangements for the use of these resources should be made.

HINT

Items selected for validation might be shown as *a table* with columns identifying items to be validated, issues to be investigated, related requirements and constraints, and validation methods. The table might also list the work products to be verified and the verification methods to be used. Using one table to address both may lead you to discover opportunities to combine verification and validation.

TIP

Validation is not only applied to discover missing functionality; nor limited to only the end-user operational environment. Quality attributes, other environments, and other phases of the product lifecycle should be considered.

VAL

HINT

Preparing for and conducting validation requires coordination with many external groups. Obtain commitment from these groups to support the planned validation efforts.

> Example types of elements in a validation environment include the following:
> - Test tools interfaced with the product being validated (e.g., scope, electronic devices, probes)
> - Temporary embedded test software
> - Recording tools for dump or further analysis and replay
> - Simulated subsystems or components (e.g., software, electronics, mechanics)
> - Simulated interfaced systems (e.g., a dummy warship for testing a naval radar)
> - Real interfaced systems (e.g., aircraft for testing a radar with trajectory tracking facilities)
> - Facilities and customer supplied products
> - Skilled people to operate or use all the preceding elements
> - Dedicated computing or network test environment (e.g., pseudo-operational telecommunications network test bed or facility with actual trunks, switches, and systems established for realistic integration and validation trials)

TIP

Validation, verification, and product integration environments can sometimes be one and the same, or at a minimum, can share some of the same resources.

Early selection of products or product components to be validated, work products to be used in validation, and validation methods is needed to ensure that the validation environment will be available when necessary.

The validation environment should be carefully controlled to provide for replication, results analysis, and revalidation of problem areas.

Example Work Products

1. Validation environment

Subpractices

TIP

Because validation resembles a controlled experiment and because of the need for fidelity with the operational environment, many tools, simulations, computers, networks, and skilled people may need to be involved. Thus, validation planning may itself be challenging.

1. Identify requirements for the validation environment.
2. Identify customer supplied products.
3. Identify test equipment and tools.
4. Identify validation resources that are available for reuse and modification.
5. Plan the availability of resources in detail.

SP 1.3 ESTABLISH VALIDATION PROCEDURES AND CRITERIA

Establish and maintain procedures and criteria for validation.

Validation procedures and criteria are defined to ensure the product or product component will fulfill its intended use when placed in its intended environment. Test cases and procedures for acceptance testing can be used for validation procedures.

The validation procedures and criteria include test and evaluation of maintenance, training, and support services.

TIP

This practice helps answer questions such as how you will exercise the product prototype to better understand a particular issue (validation procedures) and how you will know whether the behavior is acceptable (validation criteria).

TIP

Validation procedures and criteria should address operations, but can address other product lifecycle phases as well such as transition and sustainment.

> Examples of sources for validation criteria include the following:
> - Product and product component requirements
> - Standards
> - Customer acceptance criteria
> - Environmental performance
> - Thresholds of performance deviation

Example Work Products

1. Validation procedures
2. Validation criteria
3. Test and evaluation procedures for maintenance, training, and support

Subpractices

1. Review the product requirements to ensure that issues affecting validation of the product or product component are identified and resolved.
2. Document the environment, operational scenario, procedures, inputs, outputs, and criteria for the validation of the selected product or product component.
3. Assess the design as it matures in the context of the validation environment to identify validation issues.

SG 2 VALIDATE PRODUCT OR PRODUCT COMPONENTS

The product or product components are validated to ensure they are suitable for use in their intended operating environment.

The validation methods, procedures, and criteria are used to validate the selected products and product components and any associated maintenance, training, and support services using the appropriate

VAL

validation environment. Validation activities are performed throughout the product lifecycle.

SP 2.1 *PERFORM VALIDATION*

Perform validation on selected products and product components.

To be acceptable to stakeholders, a product or product component should perform as expected in its intended operational environment.

Validation activities are performed and the resulting data are collected according to established methods, procedures, and criteria.

The as-run validation procedures should be documented and the deviations occurring during the execution should be noted as appropriate.

Example Work Products

1. Validation reports
2. Validation results
3. Validation cross reference matrix
4. As-run procedures log
5. Operational demonstrations

SP 2.2 *ANALYZE VALIDATION RESULTS*

Analyze results of validation activities.

The data resulting from validation tests, inspections, demonstrations, or evaluations are analyzed against defined validation criteria. Analysis reports indicate whether needs were met. In the case of deficiencies, these reports document the degree of success or failure and categorize probable causes of failure. The collected test, inspection, or review results are compared with established evaluation criteria to determine whether to proceed or to address requirements or design issues in the requirements development or technical solution processes.

Analysis reports or as-run validation documentation can also indicate that bad test results are due to a validation procedure problem or a validation environment problem.

Example Work Products

1. Validation deficiency reports
2. Validation issues
3. Procedure change request

Subpractices

1. Compare actual results to expected results.
2. Based on the established validation criteria, identify products and product components that do not perform suitably in their intended operating environments, or identify problems with methods, criteria, or the environment.
3. Analyze validation data for defects.
4. Record results of the analysis and identify issues.
5. Use validation results to compare actual measurements and performance to the intended use or operational need.
6. Provide information on how defects can be resolved (including validation methods, criteria, and validation environment) and initiate corrective action.

   Refer to the Project Monitoring and Control process area for more information about managing corrective actions.

HINT

If requirements are missing, you need to revisit your engineering processes. If there are problems with the validation methods, environment, procedures, or criteria, you need to revisit project activities that correspond to the specific practices of SG 1.

VAL

VERIFICATION
An Engineering Process Area at Maturity Level 3

Purpose

The purpose of Verification (VER) is to ensure that selected work products meet their specified requirements.

TIP

Testing and peer reviews are verification methods covered in this process area.

Introductory Notes

The Verification process area involves the following: verification preparation, verification performance, and identification of corrective action.

X-REF

Managing corrective action to closure is addressed in PMC SG 2.

Verification includes verification of the product and intermediate work products against all selected requirements, including customer, product, and product component requirements. For product lines, core assets and their associated product line variation mechanisms should also be verified. Throughout the process areas, where the terms "product" and "product component" are used, their intended meanings also encompass services, service systems, and their components.

Verification is inherently an incremental process because it occurs throughout the development of the product and work products, beginning with verification of requirements, progressing through the verification of evolving work products, and culminating in the verification of the completed product.

The specific practices of this process area build on each other in the following way:

- The Select Work Products for Verification specific practice enables the identification of work products to be verified, methods to be used to perform the verification, and the requirements to be satisfied by each selected work product.
- The Establish the Verification Environment specific practice enables the determination of the environment to be used to carry out the verification.

VER

541

- The Establish Verification Procedures and Criteria specific practice enables the development of verification procedures and criteria that are aligned with selected work products, requirements, methods, and characteristics of the verification environment.
- The Perform Verification specific practice conducts the verification according to available methods, procedures, and criteria.

Verification of work products substantially increases the likelihood that the product will meet the customer, product, and product component requirements.

The Verification and Validation process areas are similar, but they address different issues. Validation demonstrates that the product, as provided (or as it will be provided), will fulfill its intended use, whereas verification addresses whether the work product properly reflects the specified requirements. In other words, verification ensures that "you built it right"; whereas, validation ensures that "you built the right thing."

Peer reviews are an important part of verification and are a proven mechanism for effective defect removal. An important corollary is to develop a better understanding of the work products and the processes that produced them so that defects can be prevented and process improvement opportunities can be identified.

Peer reviews involve a methodical examination of work products by the producers' peers to identify defects and other changes that are needed.

TIP

Peer reviews also focus on obtaining the data necessary to prevent defects and improve the process.

TIP

"Inspections" and "structured walkthroughs" are peer review methods that have been widely used for decades and have many variants. "Deliberate refactoring" and "pair programming" are techniques characteristic of some Agile methods.

Examples of peer review methods include the following:
- Inspections
- Structured walkthroughs
- Deliberate refactoring
- Pair programming

In Agile environments, because of customer involvement and frequent releases, verification and validation mutually support each other. For example, a defect can cause a prototype or early release to fail validation prematurely. Conversely, early and continuous validation helps ensure verification is applied to the right product. The Verification and Validation process areas help ensure a systematic approach to selecting the work products to be reviewed and tested, the methods and environments to be used, and the interfaces to be managed, which help ensure that defects are identified and addressed early. The more complex the product, the more systematic the approach needs to be to ensure compatibility among requirements and solutions, and consistency with how the product will be used. (See "Interpreting CMMI When Using Agile Approaches" in Part I.)

Related Process Areas

Refer to the Requirements Development process area for more information about eliciting, analyzing, and establishing customer, product, and product component requirements.

Refer to the Validation process area for more information about demonstrating that a product or product component fulfills its intended use when placed in its intended environment.

Refer to the Requirements Management process area for more information about ensuring alignment between project work and requirements.

X-REF

Many books and other sources describe testing and peer reviews (sometimes known as inspections). For a summary of software testing principles and terminology, see the entry for "Software Testing" on the Wikipedia site, www.wikipedia.org. Also, many other forums exist that may be of benefit, e.g., http://spac.wordpress.com.

Specific Goal and Practice Summary

SG 1 Prepare for Verification
    SP 1.1   Select Work Products for Verification
    SP 1.2   Establish the Verification Environment
    SP 1.3   Establish Verification Procedures and Criteria
SG 2 Perform Peer Reviews
    SP 2.1   Prepare for Peer Reviews
    SP 2.2   Conduct Peer Reviews
    SP 2.3   Analyze Peer Review Data
SG 3 Verify Selected Work Products
    SP 3.1   Perform Verification
    SP 3.2   Analyze Verification Results

Specific Practices by Goal

SG 1 PREPARE FOR VERIFICATION

Preparation for verification is conducted.

Up-front preparation is necessary to ensure that verification provisions are embedded in product and product component requirements, designs, developmental plans, and schedules. Verification includes the selection, inspection, testing, analysis, and demonstration of work products.

Methods of verification include, but are not limited to, inspections, peer reviews, audits, walkthroughs, analyses, architecture evaluations, simulations, testing, and demonstrations. Practices related to peer reviews as a specific verification method are included in specific goal 2.

Preparation also entails the definition of support tools, test equipment and software, simulations, prototypes, and facilities.

HINT

Identify which work products put the project (or product) at the highest risk.

HINT

Don't forget to verify work products important to other phases of the product lifecycle, such as maintenance documentation, installation services, and operator training.

TIP

When a work product cannot be executed (e.g., designs), testing is not an option. It may be possible to develop prototypes and models, and "execute" these to gain insight into product characteristics. Peer reviews may be another option.

X-REF

One source of information on software architecture evaluations is Clements, P., Kazman, R., Klein, M. *Evaluating Software Architectures: Methods and Case Studies*, Addison-Wesley, 2001.

TIP

Reverification is not called out separately in this process area, because reverification is actually an iteration of the verification process. However, reverification should be considered when planning verification activities.

HINT

Work products that have been "reworked" need to be reverified.

SP 1.1 SELECT WORK PRODUCTS FOR VERIFICATION

Select work products to be verified and verification methods to be used.

Work products are selected based on their contribution to meeting project objectives and requirements, and to addressing project risks.

The work products to be verified can include the ones associated with maintenance, training, and support services. The work product requirements for verification are included with the verification methods. The verification methods address the approach to work product verification and the specific approaches that will be used to verify that specific work products meet their requirements.

Examples of verification methods include the following:
- Software architecture evaluation and implementation conformance evaluation
- Path coverage testing
- Load, stress, and performance testing
- Decision table based testing
- Functional decomposition based testing
- Test case reuse
- Acceptance testing
- Continuous integration (i.e., Agile approach that identifies integration issues early)

Verification for systems engineering typically includes prototyping, modeling, and simulation to verify adequacy of system design (and allocation).

Verification for hardware engineering typically requires a parametric approach that considers various environmental conditions (e.g., pressure, temperature, vibration, humidity), various input ranges (e.g., input power could be rated at 20V to 32V for a planned nominal of 28V), variations induced from part to part tolerance issues, and many other variables. Hardware verification normally tests most variables separately except when problematic interactions are suspected.

Selection of verification methods typically begins with the definition of product and product component requirements to ensure that the requirements are verifiable. Re-verification should be addressed by verification methods to ensure that rework performed on work products does not cause unintended defects. Suppliers should be involved in this selection to ensure that the project's methods are appropriate for the supplier's environment.

Example Work Products

1. Lists of work products selected for verification
2. Verification methods for each selected work product

Subpractices

1. Identify work products for verification.
2. Identify requirements to be satisfied by each selected work product.

   Refer to the Maintain Bidirectional Traceability of Requirements specific practice in the Requirements Management process area for more information about tracing requirements to work products.

3. Identify verification methods available for use.
4. Define verification methods to be used for each selected work product.
5. Submit for integration with the project plan the identification of work products to be verified, the requirements to be satisfied, and the methods to be used.

   Refer to the Project Planning process area for more information about developing the project plan.

SP 1.2 ESTABLISH THE VERIFICATION ENVIRONMENT

Establish and maintain the environment needed to support verification.

An environment should be established to enable verification to take place. The verification environment can be acquired, developed, reused, modified, or obtained using a combination of these activities, depending on the needs of the project.

The type of environment required depends on the work products selected for verification and the verification methods used. A peer review can require little more than a package of materials, reviewers, and a room. A product test can require simulators, emulators, scenario generators, data reduction tools, environmental controls, and interfaces with other systems.

Example Work Products

1. Verification environment

Subpractices

1. Identify verification environment requirements.
2. Identify verification resources that are available for reuse or modification.

TIP

Methods used for each work product may be shown in a *table* with columns identifying the work product to be verified, requirements to be satisfied, and verification methods to be used.

TIP

By incorporating such a table into the project plan (perhaps by reference), resources can be provided and commitments made to perform the appropriate verification activities.

TIP

Some work products and verification methods may require special facilities and tools. These should be identified and obtained in advance.

TIP

In the case of peer reviews, a co-located team might meet in a room where the document being peer reviewed can be displayed. Remote team members might participate through teleconferencing and use of a web-based collaboration tool that allows them to see the document and engage in the discussion.

VER

TIP

The organization's IT or Facilities Group, or perhaps other projects, might have some of the verification resources that a project might need. In some cases, special facilities such as environmental labs or antenna ranges used by multiple projects must be reserved well in advance for use.

HINT

The bottom line is to determine verification methods, environments, and procedures early to allow time for preparation and coordination.

TIP

In the case of engineering artifacts (e.g., architectures, designs, and implementations), the primary source for verification criteria is likely to be the requirements assigned to the work product being verified.

HINT

Remember to establish comprehensive verification procedures and criteria for nondevelopmental items (such as off-the-shelf products) that subject the project to moderate or high risk.

HINT

Often, there isn't a single right result but a range of results that might be acceptable. In such instances, specify how much variability from the expected answer is still acceptable.

3. Identify verification equipment and tools.
4. Acquire verification support equipment and an environment (e.g., test equipment, software).

SP 1.3 ESTABLISH VERIFICATION PROCEDURES AND CRITERIA

Establish and maintain verification procedures and criteria for the selected work products.

Verification criteria are defined to ensure that work products meet their requirements.

Examples of sources for verification criteria include the following:
- Product and product component requirements
- Standards
- Organizational policies
- Test type
- Test parameters
- Parameters for tradeoff between quality and cost of testing
- Type of work products
- Suppliers
- Proposals and agreements
- Customers reviewing work products collaboratively with developers

---

Example Work Products

1. Verification procedures
2. Verification criteria

Subpractices

1. Generate a set of comprehensive, integrated verification procedures for work products and commercial off-the-shelf products, as necessary.
2. Develop and refine verification criteria as necessary.
3. Identify the expected results, tolerances allowed, and other criteria for satisfying the requirements.
4. Identify equipment and environmental components needed to support verification.

SG 2 PERFORM PEER REVIEWS

Peer reviews are performed on selected work products.

Peer reviews involve a methodical examination of work products by the producers' peers to identify defects for removal and to recommend other changes that are needed.

The peer review is an important and effective verification method implemented via inspections, structured walkthroughs, or a number of other collegial review methods.

Peer reviews are primarily applied to work products developed by the projects, but they can also be applied to other work products such as documentation and training work products that are typically developed by support groups.

SP 2.1 PREPARE FOR PEER REVIEWS

Prepare for peer reviews of selected work products.

Preparation activities for peer reviews typically include identifying the staff to be invited to participate in the peer review of each work product; identifying key reviewers who should participate in the peer review; preparing and updating materials to be used during peer reviews, such as checklists and review criteria and scheduling peer reviews.

Example Work Products

1. Peer review schedule
2. Peer review checklist
3. Entry and exit criteria for work products
4. Criteria for requiring another peer review
5. Peer review training material
6. Selected work products to be reviewed

Subpractices

1. Determine the type of peer review to be conducted.

Examples of types of peer reviews include the following:
- Inspections
- Structured walkthroughs
- Active reviews
- Architecture implementation conformance evaluation

TIP

Peers are generally coworkers from your project that have interest in the item under peer review. Peer review participants should generally not include your management because that could restrain open and beneficial dialog.

TIP

Peer reviews provide opportunities to learn and share information across the team.

HINT

Use peer reviews not just for development artifacts, but also for project management artifacts (e.g., plans), process management artifacts (e.g., process descriptions), and support artifacts (e.g., measure definitions).

TIP

Easily overlooked, training improves the effectiveness of peer reviews.

TIP

Although many different types of reviews might be considered "peer reviews" (e.g., informal walkthroughs), these specific practices focus on those having some formality and discipline in their performance.

VER

X-REF

For a summary of peer review principles and terminology, see the entry for "Software Inspections" on the Wikipedia site, www.wikipedia.org.

2. Define requirements for collecting data during the peer review.

   Refer to the Measurement and Analysis process area for more information about obtaining measurement data.

3. Establish and maintain entry and exit criteria for the peer review.

4. Establish and maintain criteria for requiring another peer review.

5. Establish and maintain checklists to ensure that work products are reviewed consistently.

> **Examples of items addressed by the checklists include the following:**
> • Rules of construction
> • Design guidelines
> • Completeness
> • Correctness
> • Maintainability
> • Common defect types

The checklists are modified as necessary to address the specific type of work product and peer review. The peers of the checklist developers and potential end-users review the checklists.

6. Develop a detailed peer review schedule, including the dates for peer review training and for when materials for peer reviews will be available.

7. Ensure that the work product satisfies the peer review entry criteria prior to distribution.

8. Distribute the work product to be reviewed and related information to participants early enough to enable them to adequately prepare for the peer review.

9. Assign roles for the peer review as appropriate.

> **Examples of roles include the following:**
> • Leader
> • Reader
> • Recorder
> • Author

10. Prepare for the peer review by reviewing the work product prior to conducting the peer review.

SP 2.2 *Conduct Peer Reviews*

Conduct peer reviews of selected work products and identify issues resulting from these reviews.

One of the purposes of conducting a peer review is to find and remove defects early. Peer reviews are performed incrementally as work products are being developed. These reviews are structured and are not management reviews.

Peer reviews can be performed on key work products of specification, design, test, and implementation activities and specific planning work products.

The focus of the peer review should be on the work product in review, not on the person who produced it.

When issues arise during the peer review, they should be communicated to the primary developer of the work product for correction.

Refer to the Project Monitoring and Control process area for more information about monitoring the project against the plan.

Peer reviews should address the following guidelines: there should be sufficient preparation, the conduct should be managed and controlled, consistent and sufficient data should be recorded (an example is conducting a formal inspection), and action items should be recorded.

Example Work Products

1. Peer review results
2. Peer review issues
3. Peer review data

Subpractices

1. Perform the assigned roles in the peer review.
2. Identify and document defects and other issues in the work product.
3. Record results of the peer review, including action items.
4. Collect peer review data.

    Refer to the Measurement and Analysis process area for more information about obtaining measurement data.

5. Identify action items and communicate issues to relevant stakeholders.
6. Conduct an additional peer review if needed.
7. Ensure that the exit criteria for the peer review are satisfied.

TIP

The ratios often reported that compare the cost to find a defect late in the project to the cost to find a defect early in the project range from 5:1 to 100:1.

HINT

Provide a nonthreatening environment so that open discussions can occur.

HINT

During peer review training, train the staff in all of the roles necessary to conduct the peer reviews. These roles can vary from one peer review to the next.

TIP

Defects and issues are often recorded in a *table* with columns for such things as location of defect, defect description (including type and origin), discussion, and action items.

VER

TIP

The analysis can help answer questions such as what types of defects you are encountering, their severity, in which phases they are being injected and detected, the peer review "yield" (percent of defects detected), the review rate (pages per hour), and the cost (or hours expended) per defect found.

SP 2.3 ANALYZE PEER REVIEW DATA

Analyze data about the preparation, conduct, and results of the peer reviews.

Refer to the Measurement and Analysis process area for more information about obtaining measurement data and analyzing measurement data.

Example Work Products

1. Peer review data
2. Peer review action items

Subpractices

1. Record data related to the preparation, conduct, and results of the peer reviews.

   Typical data are product name, product size, composition of the peer review team, type of peer review, preparation time per reviewer, length of the review meeting, number of defects found, type and origin of defect, and so on. Additional information on the work product being peer reviewed can be collected, such as size, development stage, operating modes examined, and requirements being evaluated.

2. Store the data for future reference and analysis.

3. Protect the data to ensure that peer review data are not used inappropriately.

> Examples of the inappropriate use of peer review data include using data to evaluate the performance of people and using data for attribution.

4. Analyze the peer review data.

> Examples of peer review data that can be analyzed include the following:
> - Phase defect was injected
> - Preparation time or rate versus expected time or rate
> - Number of defects versus number expected
> - Types of defects detected
> - Causes of defects
> - Defect resolution impact
> - User stories or case studies associated with a defect
> - The end users and customers who are associated with defects

SG 3 *VERIFY SELECTED WORK PRODUCTS*

Selected work products are verified against their specified requirements.

Verification methods, procedures, and criteria are used to verify selected work products and associated maintenance, training, and support services using the appropriate verification environment. Verification activities should be performed throughout the product lifecycle. Practices related to peer reviews as a specific verification method are included in specific goal 2.

SP 3.1 *PERFORM VERIFICATION*

Perform verification on selected work products.

Verifying products and work products incrementally promotes early detection of problems and can result in the early removal of defects. The results of verification save the considerable cost of fault isolation and rework associated with troubleshooting problems.

Example Work Products

1. Verification results
2. Verification reports
3. Demonstrations
4. As-run procedures log

Subpractices

1. Perform the verification of selected work products against their requirements.
2. Record the results of verification activities.
3. Identify action items resulting from the verification of work products.
4. Document the "as-run" verification method and deviations from available methods and procedures discovered during its performance.

SP 3.2 *ANALYZE VERIFICATION RESULTS*

Analyze results of all verification activities.

Actual results should be compared to established verification criteria to determine acceptability.

TIP

This goal should align with the planning and preparation activities addressed in SG 1.

TIP

Performing peer reviews is addressed in SG 2; this specific practice addresses all other forms of verification.

TIP

Verification often means "testing." However, verification methods may also include analyses, simulations, demonstrations, and formal methods.

X-REF

For more information, see the entries for "Software Testing," "Computer Simulation," and "Formal Methods" on the Wikipedia site, www.wikipedia.org.

TIP

When requirements change, it is necessary to determine the work products affected (REQM), rework them (RD, TS, and PI), and reverify them against the changed requirements. Thus, requirements volatility can significantly increase the cost of verification activities and can lead to schedule slips.

HINT

Sometimes, the verification procedure cannot be run as defined (e.g., incorrect assumptions were made as to the nature of the work product or verification environment). If so, record any deviations.

VER

The results of the analysis are recorded as evidence that verification was conducted.

For each work product, all available verification results are incrementally analyzed to ensure that requirements have been met. Since a peer review is one of several verification methods, peer review data should be included in this analysis activity to ensure that verification results are analyzed sufficiently.

Analysis reports or "as-run" method documentation can also indicate that bad verification results are due to method problems, criteria problems, or a verification environment problem.

Example Work Products

1. Analysis report (e.g., statistics on performance, causal analysis of nonconformances, comparison of the behavior between the real product and models, trends)
2. Trouble reports
3. Change requests for verification methods, criteria, and the environment

Subpractices

1. Compare actual results to expected results.
2. Based on the established verification criteria, identify products that do not meet their requirements or identify problems with methods, procedures, criteria, and the verification environment.
3. Analyze defect data.
4. Record all results of the analysis in a report.
5. Use verification results to compare actual measurements and performance to technical performance parameters.
6. Provide information on how defects can be resolved (including verification methods, criteria, and verification environment) and initiate corrective action.

   Refer to the Project Monitoring and Control process area for more information about taking corrective action.

PART THREE

The Appendices

APPENDIX A

REFERENCES

Ahern 2005 Ahern, Dennis M.; Armstrong, Jim; Clouse, Aaron; Ferguson, Jack R.; Hayes, Will; & Nidiffer, Kenneth E. *CMMI SCAMPI Distilled: Appraisals for Process Improvement*. Boston: Addison-Wesley, 2005.

Ahern 2008 Ahern, Dennis M.; Clouse, Aaron; & Turner, Richard. *CMMI Distilled: A Practical Introduction to Integrated Process Improvement, Third Edition*. Boston: Addison-Wesley, 2008.

Beck 2001 Beck, Kent et al. *Manifesto for Agile Software Development*. 2001.
agilemanifesto.org/.

Chrissis 2011 Chrissis, Mary Beth; Konrad, Mike; & Shrum, Sandy. *CMMI: Guidelines for Process Integration and Product Improvement, Third Edition*. Boston: Addison-Wesley, 2011.

Crosby 1979 Crosby, Philip B. *Quality Is Free: The Art of Making Quality Certain*. New York: McGraw-Hill, 1979.

Curtis 2009 Curtis, Bill; Hefley, William E.; & Miller, Sally A. *The People CMM: A Framework for Human Capital Management, Second Edition*. Boston: Addison-Wesley, 2009.

Deming 1986 Deming, W. Edwards. *Out of the Crisis*. Cambridge, MA: MIT Center for Advanced Engineering, 1986.

DoD 1996 Department of Defense. *DoD Guide to Integrated Product and Process Development (Version 1.0)*. Washington, DC: Office of the Under Secretary of Defense (Acquisition and Technology), February 5, 1996.
https://www.acquisition.gov/sevensteps/library/dod-guide-to-integrated.pdf.

Dymond 2005   Dymond, Kenneth M. *A Guide to the CMMI: Interpreting the Capability Maturity Model Integration, Second Edition.* Annapolis, MD: Process Transition International Inc., 2005.

EIA 2002a   Electronic Industries Alliance. *Systems Engineering Capability Model (EIA/IS-731.1).* Washington, DC, 2002.

EIA 2002b   Government Electronics and Information Technology Alliance. *Earned Value Management Systems (ANSI/EIA-748).* New York, NY, 2002. webstore.ansi.org/RecordDetail.aspx?sku=ANSI%2FEIA-748-B.

EIA 2003   Electronic Industries Alliance. *EIA Interim Standard: Systems Engineering (EIA/IS-632).* Washington, DC, 2003.

Forrester 2011   Forrester, Eileen; Buteau, Brandon; & Shrum, Sandy. *CMMI for Services: Guidelines for Superior Service, 2nd Edition.* Boston: Addison-Wesley, 2011.

Gallagher 2011   Gallagher, Brian; Phillips, Mike; Richter, Karen; & Shrum, Sandy. *CMMI-ACQ: Guidelines for Improving the Acquisition of Products and Services, 2nd Edition.* Boston: Addison-Wesley, 2011.

GEIA 2004   Government Electronic Industries Alliance. *Data Management (GEIA-859).* Washington, DC, 2004. webstore.ansi.org/RecordDetail.aspx?sku=ANSI%2FGEIA+859-2009.

Gibson 2006   Gibson, Diane L.; Goldenson, Dennis R. & Kost, Keith. *Performance Results of CMMI-Based Process Improvement.* (CMU/SEI-2006-TR-004, ESC-TR-2006-004). Pittsburgh: Software Engineering Institute, Carnegie Mellon University, August 2006. www.sei.cmu.edu/library/abstracts/reports/06tr004.cfm.

Glazer 2008   Glazer, Hillel; Dalton, Jeff; Anderson, David; Konrad, Mike; & Shrum, Sandy. *CMMI or Agile: Why Not Embrace Both!* (CMU/SEI-2008-TN-003). Pittsburgh: Software Engineering Institute, Carnegie Mellon University, November 2008. www.sei.cmu.edu/library/abstracts/reports/08tn003.cfm.

Humphrey 1989   Humphrey, Watts S. *Managing the Software Process.* Reading, MA: Addison-Wesley, 1989.

IEEE 1991   Institute of Electrical and Electronics Engineers. *IEEE Standard Computer Dictionary: A Compilation of IEEE Standard Computer Glossaries.* New York, NY: IEEE, 1991.

ISO 2005a   International Organization for Standardization. *ISO 9000: International Standard.* 2005. www.iso.org/iso/iso_catalogue/catalogue_tc/catalogue_detail.htm? csnumber=42180.

ISO 2005b   International Organization for Standardization and International Electrotechnical Commission. *ISO/IEC 20000-1 Information Technology – Service Management, Part 1: Specification; ISO/IEC 20000-2 Information Technology – Service Management, Part 2: Code of Practice,* 2005. www.iso.org/iso/iso_catalogue/catalogue_tc/catalogue_tc_ browse.htm?commid=45086.

ISO 2006a   International Organization for Standardization and International Electrotechnical Commission. *ISO/IEC 15504 Information Technology—Process Assessment Part 1: Concepts and Vocabulary, Part 2: Performing an Assessment, Part 3: Guidance on Performing an Assessment, Part 4: Guidance on Use for Process Improvement and Process Capability Determination, Part 5: An Exemplar Process Assessment Model,* 2003–2006. www.iso.org/iso/iso_catalogue/catalogue_tc/catalogue_tc_ browse.htm?commid=45086.

ISO 2006b   International Organization for Standardization and International Electrotechnical Commission. *ISO/IEC 14764 Software Engineering – Software Life Cycle Processes – Maintenance,* 2006. www.iso.org/iso/iso_catalogue/catalogue_tc/catalogue_tc_ browse.htm?commid=45086.

ISO 2007   International Organization for Standardization and International Electrotechnical Commission. *ISO/IEC 15939 Systems and Software Engineering—Measurement Process,* 2007. www.iso.org/iso/iso_catalogue/catalogue_tc/catalogue_tc_ browse.htm?commid=45086.

ISO 2008a   International Organization for Standardization and International Electrotechnical Commission. *ISO/IEC 12207 Systems and Software Engineering—Software Life Cycle Processes,* 2008. www.iso.org/iso/iso_catalogue/catalogue_tc/catalogue_ tc_browse.htm?commid=45086.

ISO 2008b   International Organization for Standardization and International Electrotechnical Commission. *ISO/IEC 15288 Systems and Software Engineering—System Life Cycle Processes,* 2008.

www.iso.org/iso/iso_catalogue/catalogue_tc/catalogue_tc_browse.htm?commid=45086.

ISO 2008c   International Organization for Standardization. *ISO 9001, Quality Management Systems—Requirements*, 2008. www.iso.org/iso/iso_catalogue/catalogue_tc/catalogue_tc_browse.htm?commid=53896.

IT Governance 2005   IT Governance Institute. *CobiT 4.0*. Rolling Meadows, IL: IT Governance Institute, 2005. www.isaca.org/Content/NavigationMenu/Members_and_Leaders/COBIT6/Obtain_COBIT/Obtain_COBIT.htm.

Juran 1988   Juran, Joseph M. *Juran on Planning for Quality*. New York: Macmillan, 1988.

McFeeley 1996   McFeeley, Robert. *IDEAL: A User's Guide for Software Process Improvement* (CMU/SEI-96-HB-001, ADA305472). Pittsburgh: Software Engineering Institute, Carnegie Mellon University, February 1996. www.sei.cmu.edu/library/abstracts/reports/96hb001.cfm.

McGarry 2001   McGarry, John; Card, David; Jones, Cheryl; Layman, Beth; Clark, Elizabeth; Dean, Joseph; & Hall, Fred. *Practical Software Measurement: Objective Information for Decision Makers*. Boston: Addison-Wesley, 2001.

Office of Government Commerce 2007a   Office of Government Commerce. *ITIL: Continual Service Improvement*. London: Office of Government Commerce, 2007.

Office of Government Commerce 2007b   Office of Government Commerce. *ITIL: Service Design*. London: Office of Government Commerce, 2007.

Office of Government Commerce 2007c   Office of Government Commerce. *ITIL: Service Operation*. London: Office of Government Commerce, 2007.

Office of Government Commerce 2007d   Office of Government Commerce. *ITIL: Service Strategy*. London: Office of Government Commerce, 2007.

Office of Government Commerce 2007e   Office of Government Commerce. *ITIL: Service Transition*. London: Office of Government Commerce, 2007.

SEI 1995   Software Engineering Institute. *The Capability Maturity Model: Guidelines for Improving the Software Process*. Reading, MA: Addison-Wesley, 1995.

SEI 2002   Software Engineering Institute. *Software Acquisition Capability Maturity Model (SA-CMM) Version 1.03* (CMU/SEI-2002-TR-010, ADA399794). Pittsburgh: Software Engineering Institute, Carnegie Mellon University, March 2002. www.sei.cmu.edu/publications/documents/02.reports/02tr010.html.

SEI 2006   CMMI Product Team. *CMMI for Development, Version 1.2* (CMU/SEI-2006-TR-008, ADA455858). Pittsburgh: Software Engineering Institute, Carnegie Mellon University, August 2006. www.sei.cmu.edu/library/abstracts/reports/06tr008.cfm.

SEI 2010a   CMMI Product Team. *CMMI for Services, Version 1.3* (CMU/SEI-2010-TR-034). Pittsburgh: Software Engineering Institute, Carnegie Mellon University, November 2010. www.sei.cmu.edu/library/abstracts/reports/10tr034.cfm.

SEI 2010b   CMMI Product Team. *CMMI for Acquisition, Version 1.3* (CMU/SEI-2010-TR-032). Pittsburgh: Software Engineering Institute, Carnegie Mellon University, November 2010. www.sei.cmu.edu/library/abstracts/reports/10tr032.cfm.

SEI 2010c   CMMI Product Team. *CMMI for Development, Version 1.3* (CMU/SEI-2010-TR-033). Pittsburgh: Software Engineering Institute, Carnegie Mellon University, November 2010. www.sei.cmu.edu/library/abstracts/reports/10tr033.cfm.

SEI 2010d   Caralli, Richard; Allen, Julia; Curtis, Pamela; White, David; and Young, Lisa. *CERT Resilience Management Model, Version 1.0* (CMU/SEI-2010-TR-012). Pittsburgh: Software Engineering Institute, Carnegie Mellon University, May 2010. www.sei.cmu.edu/library/abstracts/reports/10tr012.cfm.

SEI 2011a   SCAMPI Upgrade Team. *Standard CMMI Appraisal Method for Process Improvement (SCAMPI) A, Version 1.3: Method Definition Document* (CMU/SEI-2011-HB-001). Pittsburgh: Software Engineering Institute, Carnegie Mellon University, expected January 2011. www.sei.cmu.edu/library/abstracts/reports/11hb001.cfm.

SEI 2011b   SCAMPI Upgrade Team. *Appraisal Requirements for CMMI, Version 1.2 (ARC, V1.3)* (CMU/SEI-2011-TR-001). Pittsburgh: Software Engineering Institute, Carnegie Mellon University, expected January 2011. www.sei.cmu.edu/library/abstracts/reports/11tr001.cfm.

Shewhart 1931   Shewhart, Walter A. *Economic Control of Quality of Manufactured Product.* New York: Van Nostrand, 1931.

Information Assurance/Information Security Related Sources

DHS 2009   Department of Homeland Security. *Assurance Focus for CMMI (Summary of Assurance for CMMI Efforts)*, 2009. https://buildsecurityin.us-cert.gov/swa/proself_assm.html.

DoD and DHS 2008   Department of Defense and Department of Homeland Security. *Software Assurance in Acquisition: Mitigating Risks to the Enterprise, 2008.* https://buildsecurityin.us-cert.gov/swa/downloads/SwA_in_ Acquisition_102208.pdf.

ISO/IEC 2005   International Organization for Standardization and International Electrotechnical Commission. *ISO/IEC 27001 Information Technology – Security Techniques – Information Security Management Systems – Requirements, 2005.* www.iso.org/iso/iso_catalogue/catalogue_tc/catalogue_ detail.htm?csnumber= 42103.

NDIA 2008   NDIA System Assurance Committee. *Engineering for System Assurance.* Arlington, VA: NDIA, 2008. www.ndia.org/Divisions/Divisions/SystemsEngineering/ Documents/Studies/SA-Guidebook-v1-Oct2008-REV.pdf.

APPENDIX B

ACRONYMS

ANSI   American National Standards Institute
API   application program interface
ARC   Appraisal Requirements for CMMI
CAD   computer-aided design
CAR   Causal Analysis and Resolution (process area)
CCB   configuration control board
CL   capability level
CM   Configuration Management (process area)
CMU   Carnegie Mellon University
CMF   CMMI Model Foundation
CMM   Capability Maturity Model
CMMI   Capability Maturity Model Integration
CMMI-ACQ   CMMI for Acquisition
CMMI-DEV   CMMI for Development
CMMI-SVC   CMMI for Services
CobiT   Control Objectives for Information and related Technology
COTS   commercial off-the-shelf
CPI   cost performance index
CPM   critical path method
CSCI   computer software configuration item
DAR   Decision Analysis and Resolution (process area)
DHS   Department of Homeland Security
DoD   Department of Defense
EIA   Electronic Industries Alliance
EIA/IS   Electronic Industries Alliance/Interim Standard
FCA   functional configuration audit
FMEA   failure mode and effects analysis
GG   generic goal
GP   generic practice

IBM   International Business Machines

IDEAL   Initiating, Diagnosing, Establishing, Acting, Learning

IEEE   Institute of Electrical and Electronics Engineers

INCOSE   International Council on Systems Engineering

IPD-CMM   Integrated Product Development Capability Maturity Model

IPM   Integrated Project Management (process area)

ISO   International Organization for Standardization

ISO/IEC   International Organization for Standardization and International Electrotechnical Commission

ITIL   Information Technology Infrastructure Library

MA   Measurement and Analysis (process area)

MDD   Method Definition Document

ML   maturity level

NDIA   National Defense Industrial Association

OID   Organizational Innovation and Deployment (former process area)

OPD   Organizational Process Definition (process area)

OPF   Organizational Process Focus (process area)

OPM   Organizational Performance Management (process area)

OPP   Organizational Process Performance (process area)

OT   Organizational Training (process area)

P-CMM   People Capability Maturity Model

PCA   physical configuration audit

PERT   Program Evaluation and Review Technique

PI   Product Integration (process area)

PMC   Project Monitoring and Control (process area)

PP   Project Planning (process area)

PPQA   Process and Product Quality Assurance (process area)

QFD   Quality Function Deployment

QPM   Quantitative Project Management (process area)

RD   Requirements Development (process area)

REQM   Requirements Management (process area)

RSKM   Risk Management (process area)

SA-CMM   Software Acquisition Capability Maturity Model

SAM   Supplier Agreement Management (process area)

SCAMPI   Standard CMMI Appraisal Method for Process Improvement

SECAM   Systems Engineering Capability Assessment Model

SECM   Systems Engineering Capability Model

SEI   Software Engineering Institute

SG   specific goal

SP   specific practice

SPI   schedule performance index

SSD   Service System Development (process area in CMMI-SVC)

SSE-CMM   Systems Security Engineering Capability Maturity
Model

SW-CMM   Capability Maturity Model for Software or Software
Capability Maturity Model

TS   Technical Solution (process area)

VAL   Validation (process area)

VER   Verification (process area)

WBS   work breakdown structure

CMMI VERSION 1.3 PROJECT PARTICIPANTS

Many talented people were part of the product team that developed CMMI Version 1.3 models. Listed here are those who participated in one or more of the following teams during the development of CMMI Version 1.3. The organizations listed by members' names are those they represented at the time of their team membership.

The following are the primary groups involved in the development of this model:

- CMMI Steering Group
- CMMI for Services Advisory Group
- CMMI V1.3 Coordination Team
- CMMI V1.3 Configuration Control Board
- CMMI V1.3 Core Model Team
- CMMI V1.3 Translation Team
- CMMI V1.3 High Maturity Team
- CMMI V1.3 Acquisition Mini Team
- CMMI V1.3 Services Mini Team
- CMMI V1.3 SCAMPI Upgrade Team
- CMMI V1.3 Training Teams
- CMMI V1.3 Quality Team

CMMI Steering Group

The CMMI Steering Group guides and approves the plans of the CMMI Product Team, provides consultation on significant CMMI project issues, ensures involvement from a variety of interested communities, and approves the final release of the model.

Steering Group Members

Alan Bemish, U.S. Air Force
Anita Carleton, Software Engineering Institute
Clyde Chittister, Software Engineering Institute
James Gill, Boeing Integrated Defense Systems
John C. Kelly, NASA
Kathryn Lundeen, Defense Contract Management Agency
Larry McCarthy, Motorola
Lawrence Osiecki, U.S. Army
Robert Rassa, Raytheon Space and Airborne Systems (lead)
Karen Richter, Institute for Defense Analyses
Joan Weszka, Lockheed Martin Corporation
Harold Wilson, Northrop Grumman Corporation
Brenda Zettervall, U.S. Navy

Ex-Officio Steering Group Members

Mike Konrad, Software Engineering Institute
Susan LaFortune, National Security Agency
David (Mike) Phillips, Software Engineering Institute

Steering Group Support

Mary Beth Chrissis, Software Engineering Institute (CCB)
Eric Hayes, Software Engineering Institute (secretary)
Rawdon Young, Software Engineering Institute (Appraisal program)

CMMI for Services Advisory Group

The Services Advisory Group provides advice to the product development team about service industries.

Brandon Buteau, Northrop Grumman Corporation
Christian Carmody, University of Pittsburgh Medical Center
Sandra Cepeda, Cepeda Systems & Software Analysis/RDECOM SED
Annie Combelles, DNV IT Global Services
Jeff Dutton, Jacobs Technology, Inc.
Eileen Forrester, Software Engineering Institute
Craig Hollenbach, Northrop Grumman Corporation (lead)
Bradley Nelson, Department of Defense

Lawrence Osiecki, U.S. Army ARDEC
David (Mike) Phillips, Software Engineering Institute
Timothy Salerno, Lockheed Martin Corporation
Sandy Shrum, Software Engineering Institute
Nidhi Srivastava, Tata Consultancy Services
Elizabeth Sumpter, NSA
David Swidorsky, Bank of America

CMMI V1.3 Coordination Team

The Coordination Team brings together members of other product development teams to ensure coordination across the project.

Rhonda Brown, Software Engineering Institute
Mary Beth Chrissis, Software Engineering Institute
Eileen Forrester, Software Engineering Institute
Will Hayes, Software Engineering Institute
Mike Konrad, Software Engineering Institute
So Norimatsu, Norimatsu Process Engineering Lab, Inc.
Mary Lynn Penn, Lockheed Martin Corporation
David (Mike) Phillips, Software Engineering Institute (lead)
Mary Lynn Russo, Software Engineering Institute (nonvoting member)
Sandy Shrum, Software Engineering Institute
Kathy Smith, Hewlett-Packard
Barbara Tyson, Software Engineering Institute
Rawdon Young, Software Engineering Institute

CMMI V1.3 Configuration Control Board

The Configuration Control Board approves all changes to CMMI materials, including the models, the SCAMPI MDD, and introductory model training.

Rhonda Brown, Software Engineering Institute (nonvoting member)
Michael Campo, Raytheon
Mary Beth Chrissis, Software Engineering Institute (chair)
Kirsten Dauplaise, NAVAIR
Mike Evanoo, Systems and Software Consortium, Inc.
Rich Frost, General Motors

Brian Gallagher, Northrop Grumman Corporation

Sally Godfrey, NASA

Stephen Gristock, JP Morgan Chase and Co.

Eric Hayes, Software Engineering Institute (nonvoting member)

Nils Jacobsen, Motorola

Steve Kapurch, NASA

Mike Konrad, Software Engineering Institute

Chris Moore, U.S. Air Force

Wendell Mullison, General Dynamics Land Systems

David (Mike) Phillips, Software Engineering Institute

Robert Rassa, Raytheon Space and Airborne Systems

Karen Richter, Institute for Defense Analyses

Mary Lou Russo, Software Engineering Institute (nonvoting member)

Warren Schwomeyer, Lockheed Martin Corporation

John Scibilia, U.S. Army

Dave Swidorsky, Bank of America

Barbara Tyson, Software Engineering Institute

Mary Van Tyne, Software Engineering Institute (nonvoting member)

Rawdon Young, Software Engineering Institute

CMMI V1.3 Core Model Team

The Core Model Team develops the model material for all three constellations.

Jim Armstrong, Stevens Institute of Technology

Rhonda Brown, Software Engineering Institute (co-lead)

Brandon Buteau, Northrop Grumman Corporation

Michael Campo, Raytheon

Sandra Cepeda, Cepeda Systems & Software Analysis/RDECOM SED

Mary Beth Chrissis, Software Engineering Institute

Mike D'Ambrosa, Process Performance Professionals

Eileen Forrester, Software Engineering Institute

Will Hayes, Software Engineering Institute

Mike Konrad, Software Engineering Institute (co-lead)

So Norimatsu, Norimatsu Process Engineering Lab, Inc.

Mary Lynn Penn, Lockheed Martin Corporation

David (Mike) Phillips, Software Engineering Institute

Karen Richter, Institute for Defense Analyses

Mary Lynn Russo, Software Engineering Institute (nonvoting member)

John Scibilia, U.S. Army

Sandy Shrum, Software Engineering Institute (co-lead)

Kathy Smith, Hewlett-Packard

Katie Smith-McGarty, U.S. Navy

CMMI V1.3 Translation Team

The Translation Team coordinates translation work on CMMI materials.

Richard Basque, Alcyonix

Jose Antonio Calvo-Manzano, Universidad Politecnica de Madrid

Carlos Caram, Integrated Systems Diagnostics Brazil

Gonzalo Cuevas, Universidad Politecnica de Madrid

Mike Konrad, Software Engineering Institute

Antoine Nardeze, Alcyonix

So Norimatsu, Norimatsu Process Engineering Lab, Inc. (lead)

Steven Ou, Institute for Information Industry

Ricardo Panero Lamothe, Accenture

Mary Lynn Russo, Software Engineering Institute (nonvoting member)

Winfried Russwurm, Siemens AG

Tomas San Feliu, Universidad Politecnica de Madrid

CMMI V1.3 High Maturity Team

The High Maturity Team develops high maturity model material.

Dan Bennett, U.S. Air Force

Will Hayes, Software Engineering Institute

Rick Hefner, Northrop Grumman Corporation

Jim Kubeck, Lockheed Martin Corporation

Alice Parry, Raytheon

Mary Lynn Penn, Lockheed Martin Corporation (lead)

Kathy Smith, Hewlett-Packard

Rawdon Young, Software Engineering Institute

Suzanne Miller, Software Engineering Institute
Judah Mogilensky, PEP
Heather Oppenheimer, Oppenheimer Partners
Pat O'Toole, PACT
Agapi Svolou, Alexanna
Jeff Welch, Software Engineering Institute

CMMI V1.3 Quality Team

The Quality Team conducts various quality assurance checks on the model material to ensure its accuracy, readability, and consistency.

Rhonda Brown, Software Engineering Institute (co-lead)
Erin Harper, Software Engineering Institute
Mike Konrad, Software Engineering Institute
Mary Lou Russo, Software Engineering Institute
Mary Lynn Russo, Software Engineering Institute
Sandy Shrum, Software Engineering Institute (co-lead)

GLOSSARY

The glossary defines the basic terms used in CMMI models. Glossary entries are typically multiple-word terms consisting of a noun and one or more restrictive modifiers. (There are some exceptions to this rule that account for one-word terms in the glossary.)

The CMMI glossary of terms is not a required, expected, or informative component of CMMI models. Interpret the terms in the glossary in the context of the model component in which they appear.

To formulate definitions appropriate for CMMI, we consulted multiple sources. We first consulted the *Merriam-Webster Online* dictionary (www.merriam-webster.com/). We also consulted other standards as needed, including the following:

- ISO 9000 [ISO 2005a]
- ISO/IEC 12207 [ISO 2008a]
- ISO/IEC 15504 [ISO 2006a]
- ISO/IEC 15288 [ISO 2008b]
- ISO/IEC 15939 [ISO 2007]
- ISO 20000-1 [ISO 2005b]
- IEEE [IEEE 1991]
- CMM for Software (SW-CMM) V1.1
- EIA 632 [EIA 2003]
- SA-CMM [SEI 2002]
- People CMM (P-CMM) [Curtis 2009]
- CobiT v. 4.0 [IT Governance 2005]
- ITIL v3 (Service Improvement, Service Design, Service Operation, Service Strategy, and Service Transition) [Office of Government Commerce 2007]

We developed the glossary recognizing the importance of using terminology that all model users can understand. We also recognized that words and terms can have different meanings in different contexts and environments. The glossary in CMMI models is designed to document the meanings of words and terms that should have the widest use and understanding by users of CMMI products.

Even though the term "product" includes services as well as products and the term "service" is defined as a type of product, many of the terms in the glossary contain both the words "product" and "service" to emphasize that CMMI applies to both products and services.

Every glossary entry has two to three components. There is always a term and always a definition. Sometimes additional notes are provided.

The term defined is listed on the left side of the page. The definition appears first in a type size similar to the term listed. Glossary notes follow the definition and are in a smaller type size.

acceptance criteria   The criteria that a deliverable must satisfy to be accepted by a user, customer, or other authorized entity. (See also "deliverable.")

Refer to the Decision Analysis and Resolution process area for more information about analyzing possible decisions using a formal evaluation process that evaluates identified alternatives against established criteria.

acceptance testing   Formal testing conducted to enable a user, customer, or other authorized entity to determine whether to accept a deliverable. (See also "unit testing.")

achievement profile   A list of process areas and their corresponding capability levels that represent the organization's progress for each process area while advancing through the capability levels. (See also "capability level profile," "target profile," and "target staging.")

acquirer   The stakeholder that acquires or procures a product or service from a supplier. (See also "stakeholder.")

acquisition   The process of obtaining products or services through supplier agreements. (See also "supplier agreement.")

acquisition strategy   The specific approach to acquiring products and services that is based on considerations of supply sources, acquisition methods, requirements specification types, agreement types, and related acquisition risks.

addition   A clearly marked model component that contains information of interest to particular users.

In a CMMI model, all additions bearing the same name can be optionally selected as a group for use. In CMMI for Services, the Service System Development (SSD) process area is an addition.

allocated requirement   Requirement that results from levying all or part of a higher level requirement on a lower level architectural element or design component.

More generally, requirements can be allocated to other logical or physical components including people, consumables, delivery increments, or the architecture as a whole, depending on what best enables the product or service to achieve the requirements.

appraisal   An examination of one or more processes by a trained team of professionals using an appraisal reference model as the basis for determining, at a minimum, strengths and weaknesses.

This term has a special meaning in the CMMI Product Suite besides its common standard English meaning.

appraisal findings   The results of an appraisal that identify the most important issues, problems, or opportunities for process improvement within the appraisal scope.

Appraisal findings are inferences drawn from corroborated objective evidence.

appraisal participants   Members of the organizational unit who participate in providing information during an appraisal.

appraisal rating   The value assigned by an appraisal team to (a) a CMMI goal or process area, (b) the capability level of a process area, or (c) the maturity level of an organizational unit.

This term is used in CMMI appraisal materials such as the SCAMPI MDD. A rating is determined by enacting the defined rating process for the appraisal method being employed.

appraisal reference model   The CMMI model to which an appraisal team correlates implemented process activities.

This term is used in CMMI appraisal materials such as the SCAMPI MDD.

appraisal scope   The definition of the boundaries of an appraisal encompassing the organizational limits and CMMI model limits within which the processes to be investigated operate.

This term is used in CMMI appraisal materials such as the SCAMPI MDD.

architecture   The set of structures needed to reason about a product. These structures are comprised of elements, relations among them, and properties of both.

In a service context, the architecture is often applied to the service system.

Note that functionality is only one aspect of the product. Quality attributes, such as responsiveness, reliability, and security, are also important to reason about. Structures provide the means for highlighting different portions of the architecture. (See also "functional architecture.")

audit An objective examination of a work product or set of work products against specific criteria (e.g., requirements). (See also "objectively evaluate.")

This is a term used in several ways in CMMI, including configuration audits and process compliance audits.

baseline A set of specifications or work products that has been formally reviewed and agreed on, which thereafter serves as the basis for further development, and which can be changed only through change control procedures. (See also "configuration baseline" and "product baseline.")

base measure Measure defined in terms of an attribute and the method for quantifying it. (See also "derived measure.")

A base measure is functionally independent of other measures.

bidirectional traceability An association among two or more logical entities that is discernable in either direction (i.e., to and from an entity). (See also "requirements traceability" and "traceability.")

business objectives (See "organization's business objectives.")

capability level Achievement of process improvement within an individual process area. (See also "generic goal," "specific goal," "maturity level," and "process area.")

A capability level is defined by appropriate specific and generic goals for a process area.

capability level profile A list of process areas and their corresponding capability levels. (See also "achievement profile," "target profile," and "target staging.")

A capability level profile can be an "achievement profile" when it represents the organization's progress for each process area while advancing through the capability levels. Or, it can be a "target profile" when it represents an objective for process improvement.

capability maturity model A model that contains the essential elements of effective processes for one or more areas of interest and describes an evolutionary improvement path from ad hoc, immature processes to disciplined, mature processes with improved quality and effectiveness.

capable process A process that can satisfy its specified product quality, service quality, and process performance objectives. (See also "stable process" and "standard process.")

causal analysis   The analysis of outcomes to determine their causes.

change management   Judicious use of means to effect a change, or a proposed change, to a product or service. (See also "configuration management.")

CMMI Framework   The basic structure that organizes CMMI components, including elements of current CMMI models as well as rules and methods for generating models, appraisal methods (including associated artifacts), and training materials. (See also "CMMI model" and "CMMI Product Suite.")

The framework enables new areas of interest to be added to CMMI so that they will integrate with the existing ones.

CMMI model   A model generated from the CMMI Framework. (See also "CMMI Framework" and "CMMI Product Suite.")

CMMI model component   Any of the main architectural elements that compose a CMMI model.

Some of the main elements of a CMMI model include specific practices, generic practices, specific goals, generic goals, process areas, capability levels, and maturity levels.

CMMI Product Suite   The complete set of products developed around the CMMI concept. (See also "CMMI Framework" and "CMMI model.")

These products include the framework itself, models, appraisal methods, appraisal materials, and training materials.

commercial off-the-shelf   Items that can be purchased from a commercial supplier.

common cause of variation   The variation of a process that exists because of normal and expected interactions among components of a process. (See also "special cause of variation.")

configuration audit   An audit conducted to verify that a configuration item or a collection of configuration items that make up a baseline conforms to a specified standard or requirement. (See also "audit" and "configuration item.")

configuration baseline   The configuration information formally designated at a specific time during a product's or product component's life. (See also "product lifecycle.")

Configuration baselines plus approved changes from those baselines constitute the current configuration information.

configuration control   An element of configuration management consisting of the evaluation, coordination, approval or disapproval, and implementation of changes to configuration items after formal establishment of their configuration identification. (See also "configuration identification," "configuration item," and "configuration management.")

configuration control board A group of people responsible for evaluating and approving or disapproving proposed changes to configuration items and for ensuring implementation of approved changes. (See also "configuration item.")

Configuration control boards are also known as "change control boards."

configuration identification An element of configuration management consisting of selecting the configuration items for a product, assigning unique identifiers to them, and recording their functional and physical characteristics in technical documentation. (See also "configuration item," "configuration management," and "product.")

configuration item An aggregation of work products that is designated for configuration management and treated as a single entity in the configuration management process. (See also "configuration management.")

configuration management A discipline applying technical and administrative direction and surveillance to (1) identify and document the functional and physical characteristics of a configuration item, (2) control changes to those characteristics, (3) record and report change processing and implementation status, and (4) verify compliance with specified requirements. (See also "configuration audit," "configuration control," "configuration identification," and "configuration status accounting.")

configuration status accounting An element of configuration management consisting of the recording and reporting of information needed to manage a configuration effectively. (See also "configuration identification" and "configuration management.")

This information includes a list of the approved configuration, the status of proposed changes to the configuration, and the implementation status of approved changes.

constellation A collection of CMMI components that are used to construct models, training materials, and appraisal related documents for an area of interest (e.g., acquisition, development, services).

continuous representation A capability maturity model structure wherein capability levels provide a recommended order for approaching process improvement within each specified process area. (See also "capability level," "process area," and "staged representation.")

contractor   (See "supplier.")

contractual requirements   The result of the analysis and refinement of customer requirements into a set of requirements suitable to be included in one or more solicitation packages, or supplier agreements. (See also "acquirer," "customer requirement," "supplier agreement," and "solicitation package.")

Contractual requirements include both technical and nontechnical requirements necessary for the acquisition of a product or service.

corrective action   Acts or deeds used to remedy a situation or remove an error.

customer   The party responsible for accepting the product or for authorizing payment.

The customer is external to the project or work group (except possibly in certain project structures in which the customer effectively is on the project team or in the work group) but not necessarily external to the organization. The customer can be a higher level project or work group. Customers are a subset of stakeholders. (See also "stakeholder.")

In most cases where this term is used, the preceding definition is intended; however, in some contexts, the term "customer" is intended to include other relevant stakeholders. (See also "customer requirement.")

End users can be distinguished from customers if the parties that directly receive the value of products and services are not the same as the parties that arrange for, pay for, or negotiate agreements. In contexts where customers and end users are essentially the same parties, the term "customer" can encompass both types. (See also "end user.")

customer requirement   The result of eliciting, consolidating, and resolving conflicts among the needs, expectations, constraints, and interfaces of the product's relevant stakeholders in a way that is acceptable to the customer. (See also "customer.")

data   Recorded information.

Recorded information can include technical data, computer software documents, financial information, management information, representation of facts, numbers, or datum of any nature that can be communicated, stored, and processed.

data management   The disciplined processes and systems that plan for, acquire, and provide stewardship for business and technical data, consistent with data requirements, throughout the data lifecycle.

defect density   Number of defects per unit of product size.

An example is the number of problem reports per thousand lines of code.

defined process   A managed process that is tailored from the organization's set of standard processes according to the organization's tailoring guidelines; has a maintained process description; and contributes process related experiences to the organizational process assets. (See also "managed process.")

definition of required functionality and quality attributes   A characterization of required functionality and quality attributes obtained through "chunking," organizing, annotating, structuring, or formalizing the requirements (functional and non-functional) to facilitate further refinement and reasoning about the requirements as well as (possibly, initial) solution exploration, definition, and evaluation. (See also "architecture," "functional architecture," and "quality attribute.")

As technical solution processes progress, this characterization can be further evolved into a description of the architecture versus simply helping scope and guide its development, depending on the engineering processes used; requirements specification and architectural languages used; and the tools and the environment used for product or service system development.

deliverable   An item to be provided to an acquirer or other designated recipient as specified in an agreement. (See also "acquirer.")

This item can be a document, hardware item, software item, service, or any type of work product.

delivery environment   The complete set of circumstances and conditions under which services are delivered in accordance with service agreements. (See also "service" and "service agreement.")

The delivery environment encompasses everything that has or can have a significant effect on service delivery, including but not limited to service system operation, natural phenomena, and the behavior of all parties, whether or not they intend to have such an effect. For example, consider the effect of weather or traffic patterns on a transportation service. (See also "service system.")

The delivery environment is uniquely distinguished from other environments (e.g., simulation environments, testing environments). The delivery environment is the one in which services are actually delivered and count as satisfying a service agreement.

derived measure   Measure that is defined as a function of two or more values of base measures. (See also "base measure.")

derived requirements   Requirements that are not explicitly stated in customer requirements but are inferred (1) from contextual requirements (e.g., applicable standards, laws, policies, common practices, management decisions) or (2) from requirements needed to specify a product or service component.

Derived requirements can also arise during analysis and design of components of the product or service. (See also "product requirements.")

design review   A formal, documented, comprehensive, and systematic examination of a design to determine if the design meets the applicable requirements, to identify problems, and to propose solutions.

development   To create a product or service system by deliberate effort.

In some contexts, development can include the maintenance of the developed product.

document   A collection of data, regardless of the medium on which it is recorded, that generally has permanence and can be read by humans or machines.

Documents include both paper and electronic documents.

end user   A party that ultimately uses a delivered product or that receives the benefit of a delivered service. (See also "customer.")

End users may or may not also be customers (who can establish and accept agreements or authorize payments).

In contexts where a single service agreement covers multiple service deliveries, any party that initiates a service request can be considered an end user. (See also "service agreement" and "service request.")

enterprise   The full composition of a company. (See also "organization.")

A company can consist of many organizations in many locations with different customers.

entry criteria   States of being that must be present before an effort can begin successfully.

equivalent staging   A target staging, created using the continuous representation that is defined so that the results of using the target staging can be compared to maturity levels of the staged representation. (See also "capability level profile," "maturity level," "target profile," and "target staging.")

Such staging permits benchmarking of progress among organizations, enterprises, projects, and work groups, regardless of the CMMI representation used. The organization can implement components of CMMI models beyond the ones reported as part of equivalent staging. Equivalent staging relates how the organization compares to other organizations in terms of maturity levels.

establish and maintain   Create, document, use, and revise work products as necessary to ensure they remain useful.

The phrase "establish and maintain" plays a special role in communicating a deeper principle in CMMI: work products that have a central or key role in work group, project, and organizational performance should be given attention to ensure they are used and useful in that role.

This phrase has particular significance in CMMI because it often appears in goal and practice statements (though in the former as "established and maintained") and should be taken as shorthand for applying the principle to whatever work product is the object of the phrase.

example work product   An informative model component that provides sample outputs from a specific practice.

executive   (See "senior manager.")

exit criteria   States of being that must be present before an effort can end successfully.

expected CMMI components   CMMI components that describe the activities that are important in achieving a required CMMI component.

Model users can implement the expected components explicitly or implement equivalent practices to these components. Specific and generic practices are expected model components.

findings   (See "appraisal findings.")

formal evaluation process   A structured approach to evaluating alternative solutions against established criteria to determine a recommended solution to address an issue.

framework   (See "CMMI Framework.")

functional analysis   Examination of a defined function to identify all the subfunctions necessary to accomplish that function; identification of functional relationships and interfaces (internal and external) and capturing these relationships and interfaces in a functional architecture; and flow down of upper level requirements and assignment of these requirements to lower level subfunctions. (See also "functional architecture.")

functional architecture   The hierarchical arrangement of functions, their internal and external (external to the aggregation itself) functional interfaces and external physical interfaces, their respective requirements, and their design constraints. (See also "architecture," "functional analysis," and "definition of required functionality and quality attributes.")

generic goal   A required model component that describes characteristics that must be present to institutionalize processes that implement a process area. (See also "institutionalization.")

generic practice   An expected model component that is considered important in achieving the associated generic goal.

The generic practices associated with a generic goal describe the activities that are expected to result in achievement of the generic goal and contribute to the institutionalization of the processes associated with a process area.

generic practice elaboration   An informative model component that appears after a generic practice to provide guidance on how the generic practice could be applied uniquely to a process area. (This model component is not present in all CMMI models.)

hardware engineering   The application of a systematic, disciplined, and quantifiable approach to transforming a set of requirements that represent the collection of stakeholder needs, expectations, and constraints, using documented techniques and technology to design, implement, and maintain a tangible product. (See also "software engineering" and "systems engineering.")

In CMMI, hardware engineering represents all technical fields (e.g., electrical, mechanical) that transform requirements and ideas into tangible products.

higher level management   The person or persons who provide the policy and overall guidance for the process but do not provide the direct day-to-day monitoring and controlling of the process. (See also "senior manager.")

Such persons belong to a level of management in the organization above the immediate level responsible for the process and can be (but are not necessarily) senior managers.

incomplete process   A process that is not performed or is performed only partially; one or more of the specific goals of the process area are not satisfied.

An incomplete process is also known as capability level 0.

informative CMMI components   CMMI components that help model users understand the required and expected components of a model.

These components can be examples, detailed explanations, or other helpful information. Subpractices, notes, references, goal titles, practice titles, sources, example work products, and generic practice elaborations are informative model components.

institutionalization   The ingrained way of doing business that an organization follows routinely as part of its corporate culture.

interface control   In configuration management, the process of (1) identifying all functional and physical characteristics relevant to the interfacing of two or more configuration items provided by one or more organizations and (2) ensuring that proposed changes to these characteristics are evaluated and approved prior to implementation. (See also "configuration item" and "configuration management.")

lifecycle model   A partitioning of the life of a product, service, project, work group, or set of work activities into phases.

managed process   A performed process that is planned and executed in accordance with policy; employs skilled people having adequate resources to produce controlled outputs; involves relevant stakeholders; is monitored, controlled, and reviewed; and is evaluated for adherence to its process description. (See also "performed process.")

manager   A person who provides technical and administrative direction and control to those who perform tasks or activities within the manager's area of responsibility.

This term has a special meaning in the CMMI Product Suite besides its common standard English meaning. The traditional functions of a manager include planning, organizing, directing, and controlling work within an area of responsibility.

maturity level   Degree of process improvement across a predefined set of process areas in which all goals in the set are attained. (See also "capability level" and "process area.")

measure (noun)   Variable to which a value is assigned as a result of measurement. (See also "base measure," "derived measure," and "measurement.")

The definition of this term in CMMI is consistent with the definition of this term in ISO 15939.

measurement   A set of operations to determine the value of a measure. (See also "measure.")

The definition of this term in CMMI is consistent with the definition of this term in ISO 15939.

measurement result   A value determined by performing a measurement. (See also "measurement.")

memorandum of agreement   Binding document of understanding or agreement between two or more parties.

A memorandum of agreement is also known as a "memorandum of understanding."

natural bounds   The inherent range of variation in a process, as determined by process performance measures.

Natural bounds are sometimes referred to as "voice of the process."

Techniques such as control charts, confidence intervals, and prediction intervals are used to determine whether the variation is due to common causes (i.e., the process is predictable or stable) or is due to some special cause that can and should be identified and removed. (See also "measure" and "process performance.")

nondevelopmental item   An item that was developed prior to its current use in an acquisition or development process.

Such an item can require minor modifications to meet the requirements of its current intended use.

nontechnical requirements   Requirements affecting product and service acquisition or development that are not properties of the product or service.

Examples include numbers of products or services to be delivered, data rights for delivered COTS and nondevelopmental items, delivery dates, and milestones with exit criteria. Other nontechnical requirements include work constraints associated with training, site provisions, and deployment schedules.

objectively evaluate   To review activities and work products against criteria that minimize subjectivity and bias by the reviewer. (See also "audit.")

An example of an objective evaluation is an audit against requirements, standards, or procedures by an independent quality assurance function.

operational concept   A general description of the way in which an entity is used or operates.

An operational concept is also known as "concept of operations."

operational scenario   A description of an imagined sequence of events that includes the interaction of the product or service with its environment and users, as well as interaction among its product or service components.

Operational scenarios are used to evaluate the requirements and design of the system and to verify and validate the system.

organization   An administrative structure in which people collectively manage one or more projects or work groups as a whole, share a senior manager, and operate under the same policies.

However, the word "organization" as used throughout CMMI models can also apply to one person who performs a function in a small organization that might be performed by a group of people in a large organization. (See also "enterprise.")

organizational maturity   The extent to which an organization has explicitly and consistently deployed processes that are documented, managed, measured, controlled, and continually improved.

Organizational maturity can be measured via appraisals.

organizational policy   A guiding principle typically established by senior management that is adopted by an organization to influence and determine decisions.

organizational process assets   Artifacts that relate to describing, implementing, and improving processes.

Examples of these artifacts include policies, measurement descriptions, process descriptions, process implementation support tools.

The term "process assets" is used to indicate that these artifacts are developed or acquired to meet the business objectives of the organization and that they represent investments by the organization that are expected to provide current and future business value. (See also "process asset library.")

organization's business objectives   Senior-management-developed objectives designed to ensure an organization's continued existence and enhance its profitability, market share, and other factors influencing the organization's success. (See also "quality and process performance objectives" and "quantitative objective.")

organization's measurement repository   A repository used to collect and make measurement results available on processes and work products, particularly as they relate to the organization's set of standard processes.

This repository contains or references actual measurement results and related information needed to understand and analyze measurement results.

organization's process asset library   A library of information used to store and make process assets available that are useful to those who are defining, implementing, and managing processes in the organization.

This library contains process assets that include process related documentation such as policies, defined processes, checklists, lessons learned documents, templates, standards, procedures, plans, and training materials.

organization's set of standard processes   A collection of definitions of the processes that guide activities in an organization.

These process descriptions cover the fundamental process elements (and their relationships to each other such as ordering and interfaces) that should be incorporated into the defined processes that are implemented in projects, work groups, and work across the organization. A standard process enables consistent development and maintenance activities across the organization and is essential for long-term stability and improvement. (See also "defined process" and "process element.")

outsourcing   (See "acquisition.")

peer review   The review of work products performed by peers during the development of work products to identify defects for removal. (See also "work product.")

The term "peer review" is used in the CMMI Product Suite instead of the term "work product inspection."

performance parameters   The measures of effectiveness and other key measures used to guide and control progressive development.

performed process   A process that accomplishes the needed work to produce work products; the specific goals of the process area are satisfied.

planned process   A process that is documented by both a description and a plan.

The description and plan should be coordinated and the plan should include standards, requirements, objectives, resources, and assignments.

policy   (See "organizational policy.")

process   A set of interrelated activities, which transform inputs into outputs, to achieve a given purpose. (See also "process area," "subprocess," and "process element.")

There is a special use of the phrase "the process" in the statements and descriptions of the generic goals and generic practices. "The process," as used in Part Two, is the process or processes that implement the process area.

The terms "process," "subprocess" and "process element" form a hierarchy with "process" as the highest, most general term, "subprocesses" below it, and "process element" as the most specific. A particular process can be called a subprocess if it is part of another larger process. It can also be called a process element if it is not decomposed into subprocesses.

This definition of process is consistent with the definition of process in ISO 9000, ISO 12207, ISO 15504, and EIA 731.

process action plan   A plan, usually resulting from appraisals, that documents how specific improvements targeting the weaknesses uncovered by an appraisal will be implemented.

process action team   A team that has the responsibility to develop and implement process improvement activities for an organization as documented in a process action plan.

process and technology improvements   Incremental and innovative improvements to processes and to process, product, or service technologies.

process architecture   (1) The ordering, interfaces, interdependencies, and other relationships among the process elements in a standard process, or (2) the interfaces, interdependencies, and other relationships between process elements and external processes.

process area   A cluster of related practices in an area that, when implemented collectively, satisfies a set of goals considered important for making improvement in that area.

process asset   Anything the organization considers useful in attaining the goals of a process area. (See also "organizational process assets.")

process asset library   A collection of process asset holdings that can be used by an organization, project, or work group. (See also "organization's process asset library.")

process attribute   A measurable characteristic of process capability applicable to any process.

process capability   The range of expected results that can be achieved by following a process.

process definition   The act of defining and describing a process.

The result of process definition is a process description. (See also "process description.")

process description   A documented expression of a set of activities performed to achieve a given purpose.

A process description provides an operational definition of the major components of a process. The description specifies, in a complete, precise, and verifiable manner, the requirements, design, behavior, or other characteristics of a process. It also can include procedures for determining whether these provisions have been satisfied. Process descriptions can be found at the activity, project, work group, or organizational level.

process element   The fundamental unit of a process.

A process can be defined in terms of subprocesses or process elements. A subprocess is a process element when it is not further decomposed into subprocesses or process elements. (See also "process" and "subprocess.")

Each process element covers a closely related set of activities (e.g., estimating element, peer review element). Process elements can be portrayed using templates to be completed, abstractions to be refined, or descriptions to be modified or used. A process element can be an activity or task.

The terms "process," "subprocess," and "process element" form a hierarchy with "process" as the highest, most general term, "subprocesses" below it, and "process element" as the most specific.

process group   A collection of specialists who facilitate the definition, maintenance, and improvement of processes used by the organization.

process improvement   A program of activities designed to improve the process performance and maturity of the organization's processes, and the results of such a program.

process improvement objectives   A set of target characteristics established to guide the effort to improve an existing process in a specific, measurable way either in terms of resultant product or service characteristics (e.g., quality, product performance, conformance to standards) or in the way in which the process is executed (e.g., elimination of redundant process steps, combination of process steps, improvement of cycle time). (See also "organization's business objectives" and "quantitative objective.")

process improvement plan   A plan for achieving organizational process improvement objectives based on a thorough understanding of current strengths and weaknesses of the organization's processes and process assets.

process measurement   A set of operations used to determine values of measures of a process and its resulting products or services for the purpose of characterizing and understanding the process. (See also "measurement.")

process owner   The person (or team) responsible for defining and maintaining a process.

At the organizational level, the process owner is the person (or team) responsible for the description of a standard process; at the project or work group level, the process owner is the person (or team) responsible for the description of the defined process. A process can therefore have multiple owners at different levels of responsibility. (See also "defined process" and "standard process.")

process performance   A measure of results achieved by following a process. (See also "measure.")

Process performance is characterized by both process measures (e.g., effort, cycle time, defect removal efficiency) and product or service measures (e.g., reliability, defect density, response time).

process performance baseline   A documented characterization of process performance, which can include central tendency and variation. (See also "process performance.")

A process performance baseline can be used as a benchmark for comparing actual process performance against expected process performance.

process performance model   A description of relationships among the measurable attributes of one or more processes or work products that is developed from historical process performance data and is used to predict future performance. (See also "measure.")

One or more of the measurable attributes represent controllable inputs tied to a subprocess to enable performance of "what-if" analyses for planning, dynamic re-planning, and problem resolution. Process performance models include statistical, probabilistic and simulation based models that predict interim or final results by connecting past performance with future outcomes. They model the variation of the factors, and provide insight into the expected range and variation of predicted results. A process performance model can be a collection of models that (when combined) meet the criteria of a process performance model.

process tailoring   Making, altering, or adapting a process description for a particular end.

For example, a project or work group tailors its defined process from the organization's set of standard processes to meet objectives, constraints, and the environment of the project or work group. (See also "defined process," "organization's set of standard processes," and "process description.")

product   A work product that is intended for delivery to a customer or end user.

This term has a special meaning in the CMMI Product Suite besides its common standard English meaning. The form of a product can vary in different contexts. (See also "customer," "product component," "service," and "work product.")

product baseline   The initial approved technical data package defining a configuration item during the production, operation, maintenance, and logistic support of its lifecycle. (See also "configuration item," "configuration management," and "technical data package.")

This term is related to configuration management.

product component   A work product that is a lower level component of the product. (See also "product" and "work product.")

Product components are integrated to produce the product. There can be multiple levels of product components.

Throughout the process areas, where the terms "product" and "product component" are used, their intended meanings also encompass services, service systems, and their components.

This term has a special meaning in the CMMI Product Suite besides its common standard English meaning.

product component requirements   A complete specification of a product or service component, including fit, form, function, performance, and any other requirement.

product lifecycle   The period of time, consisting of phases, that begins when a product or service is conceived and ends when the product or service is no longer available for use.

Since an organization can be producing multiple products or services for multiple customers, one description of a product lifecycle may not be adequate. Therefore, the organization can define a set of approved product lifecycle models. These models are typically found in published literature and are likely to be tailored for use in an organization.

A product lifecycle could consist of the following phases: (1) concept and vision, (2) feasibility, (3) design/development, (4) production, and (5) phase out.

product line   A group of products sharing a common, managed set of features that satisfy specific needs of a selected market or mission and that are developed from a common set of core assets in a prescribed way. (See also "service line.")

The development or acquisition of products for the product line is based on exploiting commonality and bounding variation (i.e., restricting unnecessary product variation) across the group of products. The managed set of core assets (e.g., requirements, architectures, components, tools, testing artifacts, operating procedures, software) includes prescriptive guidance for their use in product development. Product line operations involve interlocking execution of the broad activities of core asset development, product development, and management.

Many people use "product line" just to mean the set of products produced by a particular business unit, whether they are built with shared assets or not. We call that collection a "portfolio," and reserve "product line" to have the technical meaning given here.

product related lifecycle processes   Processes associated with a product or service throughout one or more phases of its life (e.g., from conception through disposal), such as manufacturing and support processes.

product requirements   A refinement of customer requirements into the developers' language, making implicit requirements into explicit derived requirements. (See also "derived requirements" and "product component requirements.")

The developer uses product requirements to guide the design and building of the product or service.

product suite   (See "CMMI Product Suite.")

project   A managed set of interrelated activities and resources, including people, that delivers one or more products or services to a customer or end user.

A project has an intended beginning (i.e., project startup) and end. Projects typically operate according to a plan. Such a plan is frequently documented and specifies what is to be delivered or implemented, the resources and funds to be used, the work to be done, and a schedule for doing the work. A project can be composed of projects. (See also "project startup.")

In some contexts, the term "program" is used to refer to a project.

project plan   A plan that provides the basis for performing and controlling the project's activities, which addresses the commitments to the project's customer.

Project planning includes estimating the attributes of work products and tasks, determining the resources needed, negotiating commitments, producing a schedule, and identifying and analyzing project risks. Iterating through these activities may be necessary to establish the project plan.

project progress and performance   What a project achieves with respect to implementing project plans, including effort, cost, schedule, and technical performance. (See also "technical performance.")

project startup   When a set of interrelated resources for a project are directed to develop or deliver one or more products or services for a customer or end user. (See also "project.")

prototype   A preliminary type, form, or instance of a product, service, product component, or service component that serves as a model for later stages or for the final, complete version of the product or service.

This model of the product or service (e.g., physical, electronic, digital, analytical) can be used for the following (and other) purposes:

- *Assessing the feasibility of a new or unfamiliar technology*
- *Assessing or mitigating technical risk*
- *Validating requirements*
- *Demonstrating critical features*
- *Qualifying a product or service*
- *Qualifying a process*
- *Characterizing performance or features of the product or service*
- *Elucidating physical principles*

quality   The degree to which a set of inherent characteristics fulfills requirements.

quality and process performance objectives   Quantitative objectives and requirements for product quality, service quality, and process performance.

Quantitative process performance objectives include quality; however, to emphasize the importance of quality in the CMMI Product Suite, the phrase "quality and process performance objectives" is used. "Process performance objectives" are referenced in maturity level 3; the term "quality and process performance objectives" implies the use of quantitative data and is only used in maturity levels 4 and 5.

quality assurance A planned and systematic means for assuring management that the defined standards, practices, procedures, and methods of the process are applied.

quality attribute A property of a product or service by which its quality will be judged by relevant stakeholders. Quality attributes are characterizable by some appropriate measure.

Quality attributes are non-functional, such as timeliness, throughput, responsiveness, security, modifiability, reliability, and usability. They have a significant influence on the architecture.

quality control The operational techniques and activities that are used to fulfill requirements for quality. (See also "quality assurance.")

quantitative management Managing a project or work group using statistical and other quantitative techniques to build an understanding of the performance or predicted performance of processes in comparison to the project's or work group's quality and process performance objectives, and identifying corrective action that may need to be taken. (See also "statistical techniques.")

Statistical techniques used in quantitative management include analysis, creation, or use of process performance models; analysis, creation, or use of process performance baselines; use of control charts; analysis of variance, regression analysis; and use of confidence intervals or prediction intervals, sensitivity analysis, simulations, and tests of hypotheses.

quantitative objective Desired target value expressed using quantitative measures. (See also "measure," "process improvement objectives," and "quality and process performance objectives.")

quantitatively managed (See "quantitative management.")

reference model A model that is used as a benchmark for measuring an attribute.

relevant stakeholder A stakeholder that is identified for involvement in specified activities and is included in a plan. (See also "stakeholder.")

representation The organization, use, and presentation of a CMM's components.

Overall, two types of approaches to presenting best practices are evident: the staged representation and the continuous representation.

required CMMI components   CMMI components that are essential to achieving process improvement in a given process area.

Specific goals and generic goals are required model components. Goal satisfaction is used in appraisals as the basis for deciding whether a process area has been satisfied.

requirement   (1) A condition or capability needed by a user to solve a problem or achieve an objective. (2) A condition or capability that must be met or possessed by a product, service, product component, or service component to satisfy a supplier agreement, standard, specification, or other formally imposed documents. (3) A documented representation of a condition or capability as in (1) or (2). (See also "supplier agreement.")

requirements analysis   The determination of product or service specific functional and quality attribute characteristics based on analyses of customer needs, expectations, and constraints; operational concept; projected utilization environments for people, products, services, and processes; and measures of effectiveness. (See also "operational concept.")

requirements elicitation   Using systematic techniques such as prototypes and structured surveys to proactively identify and document customer and end-user needs.

requirements management   The management of all requirements received by or generated by the project or work group, including both technical and nontechnical requirements as well as those requirements levied on the project or work group by the organization. (See also "nontechnical requirements.")

requirements traceability   A discernable association between requirements and related requirements, implementations, and verifications. (See also "bidirectional traceability" and "traceability.")

return on investment   The ratio of revenue from output (product or service) to production costs, which determines whether an organization benefits from performing an action to produce something.

risk analysis   The evaluation, classification, and prioritization of risks.

risk identification   An organized, thorough approach used to seek out probable or realistic risks in achieving objectives.

risk management   An organized, analytic process used to identify what might cause harm or loss (identify risks); to assess and quantify the identified risks; and to develop and, if needed, implement an appropriate approach to prevent or handle causes of risk that could result in significant harm or loss.

Typically, risk management is performed for the activities of a project, a work group, an organization, or other organizational units that are developing or delivering products or services.

senior manager A management role at a high enough level in an organization that the primary focus of the person filling the role is the long-term vitality of the organization rather than short-term concerns and pressures. (See also "higher level management.")

A senior manager has authority to direct the allocation or reallocation of resources in support of organizational process improvement effectiveness.

A senior manager can be any manager who satisfies this description, including the head of the organization. Synonyms for senior manager include "executive" and "top-level manager." However, to ensure consistency and usability, these synonyms are not used in CMMI models.

This term has a special meaning in the CMMI Product Suite besides its common standard English meaning.

service A product that is intangible and non-storable. (See also "product," "customer," and "work product.")

Services are delivered through the use of service systems that have been designed to satisfy service requirements. (See also "service system.")

Many service providers deliver combinations of services and goods. A single service system can deliver both types of products. For example, a training organization can deliver training materials along with its training services.

Services may be delivered through combinations of manual and automated processes.

This term has a special meaning in the CMMI Product Suite besides its common standard English meaning.

service agreement A binding, written record of a promised exchange of value between a service provider and a customer. (See also "customer.")

Service agreements can be fully negotiable, partially negotiable, or non-negotiable, and they can be drafted either by the service provider, the customer, or both, depending on the situation.

A "promised exchange of value" means a joint recognition and acceptance of what each party will provide to the other to satisfy the agreement. Typically, the customer provides payment in return for delivered services, but other arrangements are possible.

A "written" record need not be contained in a single document or other artifact. Alternatively, it may be extremely brief for some types of services (e.g., a receipt that identifies a service, its price, its recipient).

service catalog   A list or repository of standardized service definitions.

Service catalogs can include varying degrees of detail about available service levels, quality, prices, negotiable/tailorable items, and terms and conditions.

A service catalog need not be contained in a single document or other artifact, and can be a combination of items that provide equivalent information (such as web pages linked to a database.) Alternatively, for some services an effective catalog can be a simple printed menu of available services and their prices.

Service catalog information can be partitioned into distinct subsets to support different types of stakeholders (e.g., customers, end users, provider staff, suppliers).

service incident   An indication of an actual or potential interference with a service.

Service incidents can occur in any service domain because customer and end-user complaints are types of incidents and even the simplest of services can generate complaints.

The word "incident" can be used in place of "service incident" for brevity when the context makes the meaning clear.

service level   A defined magnitude, degree, or quality of service delivery performance. (See also "service" and "service level measure.")

service level agreement   A service agreement that specifies delivered services; service measures; levels of acceptable and unacceptable services; and expected responsibilities, liabilities, and actions of both the provider and customer in anticipated situations. (See also "measure," "service," and "service agreement.")

A service level agreement is a kind of service agreement that documents the details indicated in the definition.

The use of the term "service agreement" always includes "service level agreement" as a subcategory and the former may be used in place of the latter for brevity. However, "service level agreement" is the preferred term when it is desired to emphasize situations in which distinct levels of acceptable services exist, or other details of a service level agreement are likely to be important to the discussion.

service level measure   A measure of service delivery performance associated with a service level. (See also "measure" and "service level.")

service line   A consolidated and standardized set of services and service levels that satisfy specific needs of a selected market or mission area. (See also "product line" and "service level.")

service request   A communication from a customer or end user that one or more specific instances of service delivery are desired. (See also "service agreement.")

These requests are made within the context of a service agreement.

In cases where services are to be delivered continuously or periodically, some service requests may be explicitly identified in the service agreement itself.

In other cases, service requests that fall within the scope of a previously established service agreement are generated over time by customers or end users as their needs develop.

service requirements   The complete set of requirements that affect service delivery and service system development. (See also "service system.")

Service requirements include both technical and nontechnical requirements. Technical requirements are properties of the service to be delivered and the service system needed to enable delivery. Nontechnical requirements may include additional conditions, provisions, commitments, and terms identified by agreements, and regulations, as well as needed capabilities and conditions derived from business objectives.

service system   An integrated and interdependent combination of component resources that satisfies service requirements. (See also "service system component" and "service requirements.")

A service system encompasses everything required for service delivery, including work products, processes, facilities, tools, consumables, and human resources.

Note that a service system includes the people necessary to perform the service system's processes. In contexts where end users perform some processes for service delivery to be accomplished, those end users are also part of the service system (at least for the duration of those interactions).

A complex service system may be divisible into multiple distinct delivery and support systems or subsystems. While these divisions and distinctions may be significant to the service provider organization, they may not be as meaningful to other stakeholders.

service system component   A resource required for a service system to successfully deliver services.

Some components can remain owned by a customer, end user, or third party before service delivery begins and after service delivery ends. (See also "customer" and "end user.")

Some components can be transient resources that are part of the service system for a limited time (e.g., items that are under repair in a maintenance shop).

Components can include processes and people.

The word "component" can be used in place of "service system component" for brevity when the context makes the meaning clear.

The word "infrastructure" can be used to refer collectively to service system components that are tangible and essentially permanent. Depending on the context and type of service, infrastructure can include human resources.

service system consumable   A service system component that ceases to be available or becomes permanently changed by its use during the delivery of a service.

Fuel, office supplies, and disposable containers are examples of commonly used consumables. Particular types of services can have their own specialized consumables (e.g., a health care service may require medications or blood supplies).

People are not consumables, but their labor time is a consumable.

shared vision   A common understanding of guiding principles, including mission, objectives, expected behavior, values, and final outcomes, which are developed and used by a project or work group.

software engineering   (1) The application of a systematic, disciplined, quantifiable approach to the development, operation, and maintenance of software. (2) The study of approaches as in (1). (See also "hardware engineering" and "systems engineering.")

solicitation   The process of preparing a package to be used in selecting a supplier. (See also "solicitation package.")

solicitation package   A collection of formal documents that includes a description of the desired form of response from a potential supplier, the relevant statement of work for the supplier, and required provisions in the supplier agreement.

special cause of variation   A cause of a defect that is specific to some transient circumstance and is not an inherent part of a process. (See also "common cause of variation.")

specific goal   A required model component that describes the unique characteristics that must be present to satisfy the process area. (See also "capability level," "generic goal," "organization's business objectives," and "process area.")

specific practice   An expected model component that is considered important in achieving the associated specific goal. (See also "process area" and "specific goal.")

The specific practices describe the activities expected to result in achievement of the specific goals of a process area.

stable process The state in which special causes of process variation have been removed and prevented from recurring so that only common causes of process variation of the process remain. (See also "capable process," "common cause of variation," "special cause of variation," and "standard process.")

staged representation A model structure wherein attaining the goals of a set of process areas establishes a maturity level; each level builds a foundation for subsequent levels. (See also "maturity level" and "process area.")

stakeholder A group or individual that is affected by or is in some way accountable for the outcome of an undertaking. (See also "customer" and "relevant stakeholder.")

Stakeholders may include project or work group members, suppliers, customers, end users, and others.

This term has a special meaning in the CMMI Product Suite besides its common standard English meaning.

standard (noun) Formal requirements developed and used to prescribe consistent approaches to acquisition, development, or service.

Examples of standards include ISO/IEC standards, IEEE standards, and organizational standards.

standard process An operational definition of the basic process that guides the establishment of a common process in an organization.

A standard process describes the fundamental process elements that are expected to be incorporated into any defined process. It also describes relationships (e.g., ordering, interfaces) among these process elements. (See also "defined process.")

statement of work A description of work to be performed.

statistical and other quantitative techniques Analytic techniques that enable accomplishing an activity by quantifying parameters of the task (e.g., inputs, size, effort, and performance). (See also "statistical techniques" and "quantitative management.")

This term is used in the high maturity process areas where the use of statistical and other quantitative techniques to improve understanding of project, work, and organizational processes is described.

Examples of non-statistical quantitative techniques include trend analysis, run charts, Pareto analysis, bar charts, radar charts, and data averaging.

The reason for using the compound term "statistical and other quantitative techniques" in CMMI is to acknowledge that while statistical techniques are expected, other quantitative techniques can also be used effectively.

statistical process control   Statistically based analysis of a process and measures of process performance, which identify common and special causes of variation in process performance and maintain process performance within limits. (See also "common cause of variation," "special cause of variation," and "statistical techniques.")

statistical techniques   Techniques adapted from the field of mathematical statistics used for activities such as characterizing process performance, understanding process variation, and predicting outcomes.

Examples of statistical techniques include sampling techniques, analysis of variance, chi-squared tests, and process control charts.

subpractice   An informative model component that provides guidance for interpreting and implementing specific or generic practices.

Subpractices may be worded as if prescriptive, but they are actually meant only to provide ideas that can be useful for process improvement.

subprocess   A process that is part of a larger process. (See also "process," "process description," and "process element.")

A subprocess may or may not be further decomposed into more granular subprocesses or process elements. The terms "process," "subprocess," and "process element" form a hierarchy with "process" as the highest, most general term, "subprocesses" below it, and "process element" as the most specific. A subprocess can also be called a process element if it is not decomposed into further subprocesses.

supplier   (1) An entity delivering products or performing services being acquired. (2) An individual, partnership, company, corporation, association, or other entity having an agreement with an acquirer for the design, development, manufacture, maintenance, modification, or supply of items under the terms of an agreement. (See also "acquirer.")

supplier agreement   A documented agreement between the acquirer and supplier. (See also "supplier.")

Supplier agreements are also known as contracts, licenses, and memoranda of agreement.

sustainment   The processes used to ensure that a product or service remains operational.

system of systems   A set or arrangement of systems that results when independent and useful systems are integrated into a large system that delivers unique capabilities.

systems engineering The interdisciplinary approach governing the total technical and managerial effort required to transform a set of customer needs, expectations, and constraints into a solution and to support that solution throughout its life. (See also "hardware engineering" and "software engineering.")

This approach includes the definition of technical performance measures, the integration of engineering specialties toward the establishment of an architecture, and the definition of supporting lifecycle processes that balance cost, schedule, and performance objectives.

tailoring The act of making, altering, or adapting something for a particular end.

For example, a project or work group establishes its defined process by tailoring from the organization's set of standard processes to meet its objectives, constraints, and environment. Likewise, a service provider tailors standard services for a particular service agreement.

tailoring guidelines Organizational guidelines that enable projects, work groups, and organizational functions to appropriately adapt standard processes for their use.

The organization's set of standard processes is described at a general level that may not be directly usable to perform a process.

Tailoring guidelines aid those who establish the defined processes for project or work groups. Tailoring guidelines cover (1) selecting a standard process, (2) selecting an approved lifecycle model, and (3) tailoring the selected standard process and lifecycle model to fit project or work group needs. Tailoring guidelines describe what can and cannot be modified and identify process components that are candidates for modification.

target profile A list of process areas and their corresponding capability levels that represent an objective for process improvement. (See also "achievement profile" and "capability level profile.")

Target profiles are only available when using the continuous representation.

target staging A sequence of target profiles that describes the path of process improvement to be followed by the organization. (See also "achievement profile," "capability level profile," and "target profile.")

Target staging is only available when using the continuous representation.

team A group of people with complementary skills and expertise who work together to accomplish specified objectives.

A team establishes and maintains a process that identifies roles, responsibilities, and interfaces; is sufficiently precise to enable the team to measure, manage, and improve their work performance; and enables the team to make and defend their commitments.

Collectively, team members provide skills and advocacy appropriate to all aspects of their work (e.g., for the different phases of a work product's life) and are responsible for accomplishing the specified objectives.

Not every project or work group member must belong to a team (e.g., a person staffed to accomplish a task that is largely self-contained). Thus, a large project or work group can consist of many teams as well as project staff not belonging to any team. A smaller project or work group can consist of only a single team (or a single individual).

technical data package   A collection of items that can include the following if such information is appropriate to the type of product and product component (e.g., material and manufacturing requirements may not be useful for product components associated with software services or processes):

- Product architecture description
- Allocated requirements
- Product component descriptions
- Product related lifecycle process descriptions if not described as separate product components
- Key product characteristics
- Required physical characteristics and constraints
- Interface requirements
- Materials requirements (bills of material and material characteristics)
- Fabrication and manufacturing requirements (for both the original equipment manufacturer and field support)
- Verification criteria used to ensure requirements have been achieved
- Conditions of use (environments) and operating/usage scenarios, modes and states for operations, support, training, manufacturing, disposal, and verifications throughout the life of the product
- Rationale for decisions and characteristics (e.g., requirements, requirement allocations, design choices)

technical performance   Characteristic of a process, product, or service, generally defined by a functional or technical requirement.

Examples of technical performance types include estimating accuracy, end-user functions, security functions, response time, component accuracy, maximum weight, minimum throughput, allowable range.

technical performance measure   Precisely defined technical measure of a requirement, capability, or some combination of requirements and capabilities. (See also "measure.")

technical requirements   Properties (i.e., attributes) of products or services to be acquired or developed.

traceability A discernable association among two or more logical entities such as requirements, system elements, verifications, or tasks. (See also "bidirectional traceability" and "requirements traceability.")

trade study An evaluation of alternatives, based on criteria and systematic analysis, to select the best alternative for attaining determined objectives.

training Formal and informal learning options.

These learning options can include classroom training, informal mentoring, web-based training, guided self study, and formalized on-the-job training programs.

The learning options selected for each situation are based on an assessment of the need for training and the performance gap to be addressed.

unit testing Testing of individual hardware or software units or groups of related units. (See also "acceptance testing.")

validation Confirmation that the product or service, as provided (or as it will be provided), will fulfill its intended use.

In other words, validation ensures that "you built the right thing." (See also "verification.")

verification Confirmation that work products properly reflect the requirements specified for them.

In other words, verification ensures that "you built it right." (See also "validation.")

version control The establishment and maintenance of baselines and the identification of changes to baselines that make it possible to return to the previous baseline.

In some contexts, an individual work product may have its own baseline and a level of control less than formal configuration control may be sufficient.

work breakdown structure (WBS) An arrangement of work elements and their relationship to each other and to the end product or service.

work group A managed set of people and other assigned resources that delivers one or more products or services to a customer or end user. (See also "project.")

A work group can be any organizational entity with a defined purpose, whether or not that entity appears on an organization chart. Work groups can appear at any level of an organization, can contain other work groups, and can span organizational boundaries.

A work group together with its work can be considered the same as a project if it has an intentionally limited lifetime.

work plan A plan of activities and related resource allocations for a work group.

Work planning includes estimating the attributes of work products and tasks, determining the resources needed, negotiating commitments, producing a schedule, and identifying and analyzing risks. Iterating through these activities can be necessary to establish the work plan.

work product A useful result of a process.

This result can include files, documents, products, parts of a product, services, process descriptions, specifications, and invoices. A key distinction between a work product and a product component is that a work product is not necessarily part of the end product. (See also "product" and "product component.")

In CMMI models, the definition of "work product" includes services, however, the phrase "work products and services" is sometimes used to emphasize the inclusion of services in the discussion.

work product and task attributes Characteristics of products, services, and tasks used to help in estimating work. These characteristics include items such as size, complexity, weight, form, fit, and function. They are typically used as one input to deriving other resource estimates (e.g., effort, cost, schedule).

work startup When a set of interrelated resources for a work group is directed to develop or deliver one or more products or services for a customer or end user. (See also "work group.")

Book Contributors

BOOK AUTHORS

Sandy Shrum, Mary Beth Chrissis, Mike Konrad (l. to r.)

Mary Beth Chrissis
Senior Member of the Technical Staff
CMMI Initiative
Software Engineering Institute

Mary Beth Chrissis is a senior member of the technical staff at the Software Engineering Institute (SEI). Since joining the SEI in 1988, Chrissis has been a coauthor of the Capability Maturity Model Integration for Development (CMMI-DEV) and Capability Maturity Model for Software (SW-CMM) models. Currently, Chrissis chairs the CMMI Configuration Control Board (CCB), is a member of the IEEE Software and Systems Engineering Standards Executive Committee, and is an instructor of various CMMI model-related courses at the SEI. Prior to joining the SEI, Chrissis worked at GTE Government Systems in Rockville, MD; Dravo Automation Sciences in Pittsburgh, PA; and Sperry Corporation in Great Neck, NY. Before coming to the SEI, Mary Beth was pursuing her masters in Computer

Science from Johns Hopkins University and in 1983 she received a B.S. from Carnegie Mellon University.

Mike Konrad
Senior Member of the Technical Staff
CMMI Initiative
Software Engineering Institute

Mike Konrad has been with the Software Engineering Institute (SEI) at Carnegie Mellon University since 1988. Dr. Konrad is the Chief Architect of CMMI and Manager of SEI's CMMI Modeling Team. Previously, he was Chair of the CMMI Configuration Control Board (2001–2006) and a member of the International Process Research Consortium (2004–2006). Also, he was a member of the teams that developed the original Software CMM Version 1.0 (1988–1991) and ISO 15504 (1993–1997). Prior to the SEI, Mike worked with several companies in computer science-related positions, including ISSI, SAIC, and Honeywell and briefly with George Mason University and the University of Maryland. Mike obtained his Ph.D. in Mathematics in 1978 from Ohio University, Athens, Ohio.

Sandy Shrum
Senior Writer/Editor
Communications
Software Engineering Institute

Sandy Shrum is a senior writer/editor and communications point of contact for the Software Engineering Process Management program at the Software Engineering Institute. In addition to this book, she has coauthored two other CMMI books: *CMMI-ACQ: Guidelines for Improving the Acquisition of Products and Services* and *CMM for Services: Guidelines for Superior Service*. She has been with the SEI since 1995 and has been a member of the CMMI Development Team since the CMMI project's inception in 1998. Her roles on the project have included model author, small review team member, reviewer, editor, model development process coordinator, and quality assurance process owner. Before joining the SEI, Sandy worked for eight years with Legent Corporation, a Virginia-based software company. Her experience as a technical communicator dates back to 1988, when she earned her M.A. in Professional Writing from Carnegie Mellon University. Her undergraduate degree, a B.S. in Business Administration, was earned at Gannon University, Erie, Pennsylvania.

CONTRIBUTING AUTHORS

Steve Baldassano
Manager of Business Process Improvement
KNORR Brake Corporation

Steve Baldassano is the Manager of Business Process  Improvement at KNORR Brake Corporation. Steve has experience and training in Quality Practices for Process Improvements; and is a Certified Quality Manager from ASQ and a student of TQM Deming/Duran. He has more than 25 years of experience with Program Management and Facilitation with Process Improvement Teams, managing both projects and processes. Since January 2009, he has been assigned full time to facilitate the improvement efforts for the Software Development Group using the CMMI DEV 1.2 model as a guide. Steve held positions at KNORR as Quality Manager for five years and Program Manager for six years prior to his current assignment.

Victor R. Basili
Professor Emeritus of Computer Science
University of Maryland
Senior Research Fellow
Fraunhofer Center

Dr. Victor R. Basili is Professor Emeritus of Computer Science at the University of Maryland, College Park, and Senior Research Fellow at the Fraunhofer Center–Maryland. He was one of the founders and principals in the Software Engineering Laboratory (SEL). He works on measuring, evaluating, and improving the software development process and product via mechanisms for observing and evolving knowledge through empirical research (e.g., the Goal/Question/Metric Approach, the Quality Improvement Paradigm, the Experience Factory, GQM+Strategies).

Kathleen C. Dangle and Michele Shaw
Applied Technology Engineer
Fraunhofer Center for Experimental
Software Engineering

Kathleen C. Dangle and Michele A. Shaw are Applied Technology Engineers at the Fraunhofer Center for Experimental Software Engineering, Maryland, a not-for-profit affiliate of the Computer Science Department of the University of Maryland, College Park. They are responsible for helping organizations improve their software business through process improvement initiatives. They work closely with Dr. Basili to apply empirical thinking in real-world software contexts.

Roger Bate
Late CMMI Chief Architect
Software Engineering Institute

Roger Bate was a visiting scientist at the Software Engineering Institute (SEI) at Carnegie Mellon University. He was the visionary behind CMMI and the chief architect of the CMMI Framework. Before that, Roger was chief computer scientist for Texas Instruments and a TI fellow, chief of the Reactor Theory Branch of the Oak Ridge National Laboratory, and a professor at the U.S. Air Force Academy. He was a fellow of the ACM, a fellow of the Society for Design and Process Science, and a recipient of the SEI Leadership Award. Roger passed away in March 2009.

Michael Campo
Principal Engineering Fellow
Raytheon Company

Michael Campo is a Principal Engineering Fellow at Raytheon Company. As process group leader for Raytheon Integrated Defense Systems (IDS), Mike developed and deployed processes that led to the achievement of CMMI Maturity Level 3 in 2003, Maturity Level 4 in 2005, and Maturity Level 5 in 2008. Mike's present position is IDS Process Technical Director. Mike is a certified CMMI instructor, and a member of the CMMI V1.3 Core Model Team, the CMMI V1.3 Training Team, the CMMI Configuration Control Board, and the National Defense Industrial Association CMMI Working Group.

David N. Card
Fellow
Q-Labs
Editor-in-Chief
Journal of Systems and Software

David N. Card is a fellow of Q-Labs. He is the author of *Measuring Software Design Quality* (Prentice Hall, 1990), coauthor of *Practical Software Measurement* (Addison-Wesley, 2002), coeditor of *ISO/IEC Standard 15939: Software Measurement Process* (International Organization for Standardization, 2002), and Editor-in-Chief of the *Journal of Systems and Software*.

Bill Curtis
Senior Vice President and Chief Scientist
CAST Software
Founding Director
Consortium for IT Software Quality

Bill Curtis is Senior Vice President and Chief Scientist at CAST Software and the Founding Director of the Consortium for IT Software Quality. He coauthored the Capability Maturity Model (CMM), the People CMM, and the Business Process MM. Until its acquisition by Borland, he was Cofounder and Chief Scientist of TeraQuest, the global leader in providing CMM-based services. He is a former Director of the Software Process Program in the Software Engineering Institute at Carnegie Mellon University. Prior to joining the SEI, Dr. Curtis worked for MCC, ITT's Programming Technology Center, GE Space Division, and taught statistics at the University of Washington. He has published five books, more than 150 articles, and was elected a Fellow of the IEEE for his contributions to software process improvement and measurement.

Aldo Dagnino
System Architectures and Technology Group Lead
US Corporate Research Center
ABB, Inc.

Dr. Aldo Dagnino has more than 20 years of experience in the software industry and close to 10 years of experience using the CMMI model. He is currently leading the System Architectures and Technologies Group at the US Corporate Research Center of ABB Inc. Dr. Dagnino is also an Adjunct Assistant Professor in the Department of Computer Science at North Carolina State University. He has given several presentations at software engineering conferences such as IEEE, NDIA, and SEPG, among others. Dr. Dagnino was honored to receive the 2008 SEI Member Award Winner for most Outstanding Technical Contributor at the 2008 SEPG Conference in Tampa, FL. His primary areas of interest include CMMI models, process improvement, Empirical Software Engineering, system architectures, data mining, and knowledge-intensive systems.

Khaled El Emam
Associate Professor
Canada Research Chair in Electronic Health Information
University of Ottawa
Senior Investigator
Children's Hospital of Eastern Ontario Research Institute

Dr. Khaled El Emam is an Associate Professor at the University of Ottawa, Faculty of Medicine, and the School of Information Technology and Engineering, a senior investigator at the Children's Hospital of Eastern Ontario Research Institute, and a Canada Research Chair in Electronic Health Information at the University of Ottawa. His main area of research is developing techniques for health data anonymization. Previously, Khaled was a Senior Research Officer at the National Research Council of Canada; and prior to that, he was head of the Quantitative Methods Group at the Fraunhofer Institute in Kaiserslautern, Germany. He has (co)founded two companies to commercialize the results of his research work. In 2003 and 2004, he was ranked as the top systems and software engineering scholar worldwide by the *Journal of Systems and Software* based on his research on measurement and quality evaluation and improvement, and ranked second in 2002 and 2005. He holds a Ph.D. from the Department of Electrical and Electronics, King's College, at the University of London (UK). His lab's website is www.ehealthinformation.ca/.

Hillel Glazer
Principal and CEO
Entinex, Inc.

Hillel has been working in process improvement since his first job out of college. He is a CMMI High Maturity Lead Appraiser and CMMI Instructor working with Agile teams as well as an SEI Visiting Scientist. Hillel is the lead author on the SEI's first-ever official publication addressing Agile development. His diverse experience base, which includes aerospace/defense and systems engineering, large and small consulting practices, federal agencies, dot-com operations, and financial systems support, is probably what gave him the necessary perspective to pioneer how to bring CMMI and Agile together as far back as his 2001 CrossTalk article highlighting the compatibilities of (then) CMM and XP.

Kileen Harrison
Lead Associate
Booz Allen Hamilton

Kileen Harrison is a Lead Associate with Booz Allen Hamilton, specializing in Process Improvement. She has a Masters of Business Administration from Johns Hopkins University and more than 15 years of experience in the industry. Throughout her career, Kileen has played key leadership roles in the development, documentation, maintenance, and implementation of process, to enable projects and organizations to achieve their process improvement goals. Her experience includes working with external clients as well as helping to ensure Booz Allen Hamilton maintains its CMMI-DEV +IPPD, Maturity Level 3 rating. She is an authorized SCAMPI B&C Team Lead for CMMI-DEV, CMMI-ACQ, and CMMI-SVC; and a certified instructor for Introduction to CMMI, Acquisition Supplement, and Services Supplement. She is a trained Lean Six Sigma Green Belt and ITIL Foundation Certified.

Will Hayes
SCAMPI Upgrade Team Leader
Software Engineering Institute

Will Hayes has served in a variety of roles at the Software Engineering Institute for nearly twenty years. His present focus is on leading the team updating the Standard CMMI Appraisal Method for Process Improvement (SCAMPI) for Version 1.3 of the CMMI product suite. He recently served on the team updating the High Maturity Process Areas of CMMI. Prior to these assignments, Will was the leader of the SEI Appraisal Program's Quality Management Team and initiated the process for auditing SCAMPI Appraisals. He has been a frequent presenter at conferences throughout the world on topics relating to Process Improvement, Measurement, and High Maturity Practices.

Watts Humphrey
Founder of Software Process Program
Software Engineering Institute

Watts S. Humphrey founded the Software Process Program of the Software Engineering Institute at Carnegie Mellon University, led the initial development of the Capability Maturity Model (CMM), and was a Fellow of the Institute. From 1959 to 1986, he was at IBM where he was director of programming and VP of Technical Development. His publications include many technical papers and thirteen books, including *Winning With Software: An Executive Strategy* (2002), *PSP: A Self-Improvement Process for Software Engineers* (2005), and *TSP: Coaching Development Teams* (2006). He held five U.S. patents and served on the Malcolm Baldridge National Quality Award Board of Examiners. He held degrees in physics, a master's degree in Business Administration, and an honorary Ph.D. degree in Software Engineering. The Watts Humphrey Software Quality Institute in Chennai, India was named in his honor; and, in 2005, the President of the United States awarded Mr. Humphrey the National Medal of Technology. Watts passed away in October 2010.

Gargi Keeni
Vice President
Tata Consultancy Services, Ltd.

Gargi Keeni, Vice President at Tata Consultancy Services Ltd., serves on the Industry Advisory Board (IAB) of IEEE Computer Society, the business planning group (SWG1) of ISO/IEC JTC1 SC7, and is the cochair of the advisory panel of NASSCOM Quality forum. An SEI authorized lead appraiser and instructor for CMMI and an examiner for JRD-QV (in lines of MBNQA), she was also a lead appraiser for People CMM. Dr Keeni's research interests include process improvement, quality management systems, and business excellence. For more information, see Gargi Keeni, "The Evolution of Quality Processes at Tata Consultancy Services" *IEEE Software* (July/August 2000).

Peter Kraus
Engineering Fellow
Raytheon Integrated Defense Systems

Dr. Peter Kraus is an Engineering Fellow focusing on statistical engineering training and consulting efforts within Raytheon Integrated Defense Systems. Peter is responsible for implementing Design for Six Sigma techniques across Engineering and Operations to achieve Mission Assurance. Peter earned a master's degree in Mathematics from Northeastern University and a Ph.D. in Operations Research from the University of Massachusetts in Amherst.

Hans-Jürgen Kugler
Principal and Chief Scientist
KUGLER MAAG CIE, GmbH
Industry Advisory
Lero

Hans-Jürgen Kugler is Principal and Chief Scientist of KUGLER MAAG CIE GmbH. In addition, he is industry advisor to Lero, the Irish Software Engineering Research Centre. Mr. Kugler was previously a lecturer at Trinity College Dublin, a director of software product and services companies, and Technical Director of the European Software Institute. He was involved in the design industry competence development in the automotive sector, and conducted the first independent CMM assessment in the automotive industry in Germany.

Neal Mackertich
Engineering Fellow and Founder
Raytheon Six Sigma Institute

Dr. Neal Mackertich is an Engineering Fellow and founder of the Raytheon Six Sigma Institute. A Six Sigma Master Black Belt versatile in technical background and application experience, Neal is presently responsible for the Systems Engineering enablement of Mission Assurance through product and process optimization strategies within Raytheon's Integrated Defense Systems business. Dr. Mackertich holds a B.S. in Chemical Engineering, an M.S. in Engineering Management, and a Ph.D. in Engineering Operations Research from the University of Massachusetts-Amherst.

Tomoo Matsubara
Independent Consultant
Software Technology, Management,
and Business

Tomoo Matsubara is an independent consultant of software technology, management, and business. Currently, he is an Editorial Board member of the Cutter IT Journal and an Advisory Board member of IEEE Software. For six years, he served as an editor of the "Soapbox" column. He started his career at the Hitachi's machine factory. When Hitachi initiated its computer business, he was conscripted from its computer department. For a period of time, he was involved in almost any kind of software development projects. He left Hitachi Software Engineering at the end of 1991 and initiated a consulting business. He became actively involved in many international activities, wrote a score of English papers, and made presentations at international conferences. Two of his papers were chosen for a book of influential papers "Software State-of-the-Art: Selected Papers," (Dorset House) compiled by Tom DeMarco and Timothy Lister. He has published a dozen books, including translation of software engineering books.

Judah Mogilensky
Owner/Partner
Process Enhancement Partners, Inc.

Judah Mogilensky, an Owner/Partner of Process Enhancement Partners, Inc., is a leader in the process improvement field. He is a

Certified High Maturity Lead Appraiser for the SCAMPI method (DEV, SVC, and People CMM) and a trainer for Introduction to CMMI-DEV, Introduction to CMMI-SVC, and Introduction to the People CMM courses. Judah is a cofounder of the first SPIN, in the Washington, D.C. area. He is a qualified user of the MBTI and a graduate of Satir System Training. He is also a Visiting Scientist at the SEI.

James W. Moore
Software Engineer
MITRE Corporation
Vice President for Professional Activities
Member of Board of Governors
IEEE Computer Society

James W. Moore is a 40-year veteran of software engineering in IBM and now the MITRE Corporation. He serves as the IEEE Computer Society's Vice President for Professional Activities and as a member of its Board of Governors. He was an Executive Editor of the Society's 2004 "Guide to the Software Engineering Body of Knowledge" and a member of the Editorial Board of the recent revision of the "Encyclopedia of Software Engineering." He performs software and systems engineering standardization for the IEEE, serving as its liaison to ISO/IEC JTC1/SC7 and as a member of the Executive Committee of the IEEE Software and Systems Engineering Standards Committee. The IEEE Computer Society has recognized him as a Charter Member of their Golden Core, and the IEEE has named him a Fellow of the IEEE. His work on software engineering standards has been recognized by the International Committee on Information Technology Standards (INCITS) with their International Award, by the Computer Society with the Hans Karlsson Award, and by the IEEE with the Charles Proteus Steinmetz Award. His latest book on software engineering standards was published in 2006 by John Wiley and Sons. He holds two U.S. patents and, dating to times when software was not regarded as patentable, two "defensive publications." He graduated from the University of North Carolina with a B.S. in Mathematics and Syracuse University with an M.S. in Systems and Information Science.

Joseph Morin
Principal and CEO
Integrated System Diagnostics, Inc.

Joseph Morin is principal and CEO of Integrated System Diagnostics, Inc., one of the original SEI Partners. He has more than 35 years of experience in systems and software engineering, management, and process improvement. He is a Certified High Maturity Lead Appraiser and Instructor for CMMI. Since leaving the SEI in 1994 to found ISD, Mr. Morin has continued to contribute to SEI initiatives including participation as a member of the core author team for the SCAMPI V1.1 method and serving as Chairman of the SEI Partner Advisory Board.

Heather Oppenheimer
Senior Partner
Oppenheimer Partners, LLC

Heather Oppenheimer is a Senior Partner in Oppenheimer Partners, LLC, a process improvement consulting company. She is a certified CMMI instructor and SCAMPI Lead Appraiser, with more than 20 years of experience in all areas of product development, service delivery, and software engineering. She has cochaired workshops for the International Conference on Systems Engineering, reviews software engineering journals, and referees grants for the Natural Sciences and Engineering Research Council of Canada. She is a member of the team that developed the SEI-authorized 3-day Introduction to CMMI-SVC course. Although she is known for her work with large, globally distributed development projects, she is currently focusing on coaching very small service delivery and embedded software development organizations in how to apply Agile methodologies along with the CMMI model for lightweight, but robust, processes.

Pat O'Toole
Principal Consultant
PACT

As Principal Consultant, Pat O'Toole is PACT's only, and certainly most highly regarded, employee. He is a certified high maturity SCAMPI Lead Appraiser as well as a certified instructor for a variety of CMMI-related courses. Pat has published more than 50 articles related to process and performance improvement and, on behalf of the SEI-certified community, facilitates the ATLAS forum (ATLAS = Ask The Lead AppraiserS). Pat is also a Visiting Scientist at the SEI and coteaches a course in the University of Minnesota's Master of Science in Software Engineering degree program.

Mike Phillips
Program Manager
CMMI Initiative
Software Engineering Institute

Mike Phillips is the Program Manager for CMMI at the Software Engineering Institute (SEI), a position created to lead the Capability Maturity Model Integration [CMMI] product suite evolution. He has led the team, which spans government, industry, and the SEI, through three significant upgrades to the original version of the integrated model, which now covers engineering, acquisition, and services. He was previously responsible for Transition Enabling activities at the SEI. He has authored Technical Reports, Technical Notes, CMMI Columns, and various articles in addition to presenting CMMI material at conferences around the world. He is a coauthor of the first edition of the Addison-Wesley book on CMMI for Acquisition.

Prior to his retirement as a colonel from the U.S. Air Force, he was the program manager of the $36B development program for the B-2 stealth bomber in the B-2 System Program Office at Wright-Patterson AFB, Ohio. In addition to more than five years of B-2 experience, he has four years of experience guiding acquisition programs in the Pentagon for both the Air Force and the Office of the Secretary of Defense. His bachelor's degree in Astronautical Engineering is from the Air Force Academy, and his masters' degrees are in Nuclear Engineering from Georgia Tech, Systems Management from the University of Southern California, and International Affairs from Salve Regina College and the Naval War College. He is a graduate of the Program Management Course at the Defense Systems Management College and of the Air Force Test Pilot School.

Anne Prem
Process Improvement Associate
Booz Allen Hamilton

Anne Prem is an Associate at Booz Allen Hamilton specializing in process improvement. She has more than eight years of experience supporting the Department of Defense (DoD) in systems/software design and development, leveraging various process improvement disciplines. Anne's current focus is process definition and deployment using CMMI-DEV, CMMI-ACQ, and CMMI-SVC, while capitalizing on the benefits of an integrated CMMI and Lean Six Sigma (LSS) approach. She has a Bachelor of Arts in Psychology and a Certificate in Markets & Management from Duke University. Anne is also certified by the Project Management Institute (PMI) as a Project Management Professional (PMP) and is LSS Green Belt trained.

Bob Rassa
Director of Engineering Programs
Space and Airborne Systems
Raytheon
Founder and Chairman
National Defense Industry Association (NDIA)

Bob Rassa is Director of Engineering Programs at Raytheon's Space and Airborne Systems (formerly Hughes Aircraft), in El Segundo, California. He is founder and Chairman of the National Defense Industry Association (NDIA) Systems Engineering Division (SE Div), as well as a founding member of their Automatic Test Committee. Mr. Rassa is the Industry Sponsor of CMMI (Capability Maturity Model Integration, the worldwide-adopted model for process improvement for systems engineering, software, project management, and hardware design), and serves as the Chair of the CMMI Steering Group. He is an elected Fellow of IEEE and has served IEEE as Past President & Founder, IEEE Systems Council, Past President, IEEE Aerospace & Electronic Systems Society, and Past President, IEEE Instrumentation & Measurement Society. He holds a BSEE from the University of California–Berkeley, and has numerous published papers and delivered presentations. He holds the U.S. patent for a satellite-based Advanced Maintenance System for Aircraft & Military Weapons, issued in August 1999. He is recipient of the Westinghouse Order of Merit, the IEEE Third Millennium Medal, the Man of The Year Award from IEEE-AUTOTESTCON, the Lt. General Thomas Ferguson Award for Systems Engineering Excellence from NDIA, and the Raytheon Award for Excellence in Engineering Process Improvement.

Kevin Schaaff
Senior Member of the Technical Staff
Software Engineering Institute

Kevin Schaaff is a senior member of the technical staff at the Software Engineering Institute. He is a certified High Maturity Lead Appraiser and Instructor, with more than 30 years of experience in systems engineering and project management. His previous experience includes managing a variety of programs ranging from large Navy R&D efforts to implementing small to medium IT systems. Before joining the SEI, Kevin led other organizations' quality programs to SW-CMM and CMMI Maturity Level 3 and CMMI Maturity Level 5, and he was responsible for numerous sites being both ISO and AS9100 registered. He currently serves as a process improvement consultant to several commercial and government organizations implementing a variety of models and standards.

Alexander Stall
Senior Member of the Technical Staff
Software Engineering Institute

Alexander Stall is a senior member of the technical staff at the Software Engineering Institute. He is a certified High Maturity Lead Appraiser and Instructor, and a member of the SCAMPI Quality Management Team. He has more than 20 years of experience as a software engineer, manager, and consultant across the systems development life cycle, and has worked in both the public and private sectors. As a Process Improvement specialist, he has worked in and led efforts for process development, deployment, implementation, and appraisal. He currently works with several commercial and government organizations to implement a variety of models and standards.

Rawdon Young
Appraisal Manager
Software Engineering Institute

Mr. Young has worked in systems and software development for more than 35 years and has extensive experience in systems and software development at all levels from entry level programmer/analyst through senior manager. Additionally, he has both provided and managed engineering and management consulting services. He has worked in small organizations, large organizations, government, and private industry. In 2006, he joined the SEI and has concentrated on appraisal quality, high maturity, Lead Appraiser certification and training. He is a SCAMPI High Maturity Lead Appraiser and an Instructor for the Introduction to CMMI and is an expert in high maturity development and management. He is currently the SEI Appraisal Manager.

INDEX

The SEI Partner Network:
Helping hands with a global reach

Do you need help getting started with adoption of SEI tools and methods in your organization? Or are you an experienced professional in the field who wants to join a global network of SEI service providers?

The SEI Partner Network is a world-wide group of licensed organizations with individuals qualified by the SEI to deliver SEI services. SEI Partners can provide you with the training courses, adoption assistance, appraisal methods, and teamwork and management processes that you need to succeed.

To find an SEI Partner near you, or to learn more about this global network of professionals, please visit the SEI Partner Network website at *http://www.sei.cmu.edu/partners*

ESSENTIAL GUIDES TO CMMI®

**CMMI® for Development:
Guidelines for Process Integration
and Product Improvement,
Third Edition**

Mary Beth Chrissis, Mike Konrad,
and Sandy Shrum

ISBN-13: 978-0-321-71150-2

The definitive guide to CMMI—now
updated for CMMI v1.3. Whether you are
new to CMMI or already familiar with
some version of it, this book is the essential resource for managers, practitioners,
and process improvement team members
who to need to understand, evaluate,
and/or implement a CMMI model.

**CMMI® for Services:
Guidelines for Superior Service,
Second Edition**

Eileen C. Forrester, Brandon L. Buteau,
and Sandy Shrum

ISBN-13: 978-0-321-71152-6

The authoritative guide to CMMI for
Services v1.3, a model designed to help
service-provider organizations improve
their processes and thereby gain business
advantage. This book, which contains
the complete model, also includes helpful commentary by the authors and case
studies to illustrate how the model is
being used.

**CMMI® for Acquisition:
Guidelines for Improving the
Acquisition of Products and
Services, Second Edition**

Brian P. Gallagher, Mike Phillips,
Karen J. Richter, and Sandy Shrum

ISBN-13: 978-0-321-71151-9

The official guide to CMMI-ACQ—an
extended CMMI framework for improving product and service acquisition
processes. In addition to the complete
CMMI-ACQ itself, the book includes tips,
hints, and case studies to enhance your
understanding and to provide valuable,
practical advice.

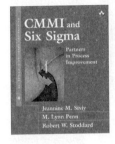

**CMMI® and Six Sigma:
Partners in Process Improvement**

Jeannine M. Siviy, M. Lynn Penn, and
Robert W. Stoddard

ISBN-13: 978-0-321-51608-4

Focuses on the synergistic, rather than
competitive, implementation of CMMI
and Six Sigma—with synergy translating
to "faster, better, cheaper" achievement
of mission success.

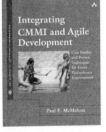

**Integrating CMMI® and Agile
Development: Case Studies and
Proven Techniques for Faster
Performance Improvement**

Paul E. McMahon

ISBN-13: 978-0-321-71410-7

Explains how combining an Agile
approach with the CMMI process
improvement framework is the fastest,
most effective way to achieve your
business objectives.

**CMMI® Distilled: A Practical
Introduction to Integrated Process
Improvement, Third Edition**

Dennis M. Ahern, Aaron Clouse,
and Richard Turner

ISBN-13: 978-0-321-46108-7

Updated for CMMI version 1.2, this
third edition again provides a concise
and readable introduction to the model,
as well as straightforward, no-nonsense
information on integrated, continuous
process improvement.

**For more information on these and other CMMI-related books, as well as on all
titles in The SEI Series in Software Engineering, please visit informit.com/seiseries.**

The SEI Series in Software Engineering

ISBN 0-321-46108-8

ISBN 0-321-22876-6

ISBN 0-321-11886-3

ISBN 0-201-73723-X

ISBN 0-321-50917-X

ISBN 0-321-15495-9

ISBN 0-321-17935-8

ISBN 0-321-27967-0

ISBN 0-201-70372-6

ISBN 0-201-70482-X

ISBN 0-201-70332-7

ISBN 0-201-60445-0

ISBN 0-201-60444-2

ISBN 0-321-42277-5

ISBN 0-201-52577-1

ISBN 0-201-25592-8

ISBN 0-321-47717-0

ISBN 0-201-54597-7

ISBN 0-201-54809-7

ISBN 0-321-30549-3

ISBN 0-201-18095-2

ISBN 0-201-54610-8

ISBN 0-201-47719-X

ISBN 0-321-34962-8

ISBN 0-201-77639-1

ISBN 0-201-73-1134

ISBN 0-201-61626-2

ISBN 0-201-70454-4

ISBN 0-201-73409-5

ISBN 0-201-85-4805

ISBN 0-321-11884-7

ISBN 0-321-33572-4

ISBN 0-321-51608-7

ISBN 0-201-70312-2

ISBN 0-201-70-0646

ISBN 0-201-17782-X

Please see our web site at informit.com/seiseries for more information on these titles.

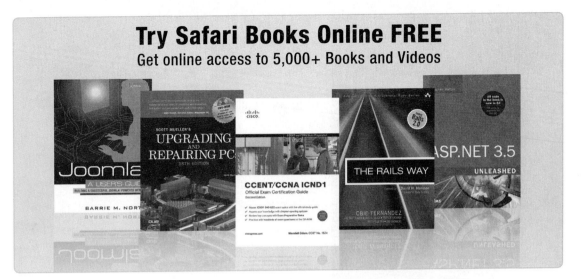

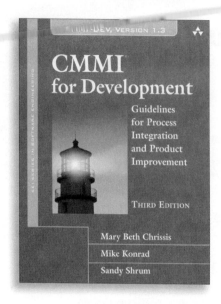

FREE Online Edition

Your purchase of **CMMI® for Development, Third Edition,** includes access to a free online edition for 45 days through the Safari Books Online subscription service. Nearly every Addison-Wesley Professional book is available online through Safari Books Online, along with more than 5,000 other technical books and videos from publishers such as, Cisco Press, Exam Cram, IBM Press, O'Reilly, Prentice Hall, Que, and Sams.

SAFARI BOOKS ONLINE allows you to search for a specific answer, cut and paste code, download chapters, and stay current with emerging technologies.

Activate your FREE Online Edition at www.informit.com/safarifree

> **STEP 1:** Enter the coupon code: IDQIZAA.

> **STEP 2:** New Safari users, complete the brief registration form. Safari subscribers, just log in.

If you have difficulty registering on Safari or accessing the online edition, please e-mail customer-service@safaribooksonline.com

Safari Books Online

Process Areas by Maturity Level

Maturity Level 2

CM   Configuration Management
MA   Measurement and Analysis
PPQA   Process and Product Quality Assurance
PMC   Project Monitoring and Control
PP   Project Planning
REQM   Requirements Management
SAM   Supplier Agreement Management

Maturity Level 3

DAR   Decision Analysis and Resolution
IPM   Integrated Project Management
OPD   Organizational Process Definition
OPF   Organizational Process Focus
OT   Organizational Training
PI   Product Integration
RD   Requirements Development
RSKM   Risk Management
TS   Technical Solution
VAL   Validation
VER   Verification

Maturity Level 4

OPP   Organizational Process Performance
QPM   Quantitative Project Management

Maturity Level 5

CAR   Causal Analysis and Resolution
OPM   Organizational Performance Management